The Question of
Discrimination

EDITED BY STEVEN SHULMAN
AND WILLIAM DARITY, JR.

The Question of Discrimination

Racial Inequality in the U.S. Labor Market

Essays by

ROBERT HIGGS

JOHN BOUND

RICHARD B. FREEMAN

JAMES J. HECKMAN

SAMUEL L. MYERS, JR.

STEVEN SHULMAN

JAMES P. SMITH

FINIS WELCH

HERBERT HILL

GLENN C. LOURY

SHERRIE A. KOSSOUDJI

ZENA SMITH BLAU

WILLIAM DARITY, JR.

 Wesleyan University Press
Middletown, Connecticut

Chapter 9 originally appeared in *Social Philosophy & Policy*, volume 5, number 1, Autumn 1987.

All inquiries and permissions requests should be addressed to the Publisher, Wesleyan University Press, 110 Mt. Vernon Street, Middletown, Connecticut 06457

Library of Congress Cataloging-in-Publication Data

The Question of discrimination : racial inequality in the U.S. labor market/Zena Smith Blau . . . [et al.].—1st ed.
    p. cm.
  Includes bibliographies and index.
  ISBN 0-8195-5214-3
    1. Discrimination in employment—United States. 2. Affirmative action programs—United States. 3. Race discrimination—United States. 4. United States—Race relations. I. Blau, Zena Smith, 1922–   .
  HD4903.5.U58Q47   1989   89-5481
  331.13'3'0973—dc19   CIP

MANUFACTURED IN THE UNITED STATES OF AMERICA

FIRST EDITION, 1989

CONTENTS

v

TABLES

FIGURES

The Question of
Discrimination

STEVEN SHULMAN

WILLIAM DARITY, JR.

Introduction

ALTHOUGH RACIAL DISCRIMINATION may appear to be a self-evident fact of life to many people—and an equally self-evident rationale for preferential treatment to others—it is a notoriously contentious concept among social scientists. The social condemnation of overt bigotry and the legal sanctions against discrimination have made the mechanisms of racial subordination more covert and therefore difficult to identify. Economic inequality may be due to causes aside from discrimination, such as differences in cultural or educational backgrounds. Furthermore, trends in racial inequality vary among regions, time periods, age-sex cohorts, and labor market outcomes, so that a comprehensive interpretation has been difficult to develop. Finally, and perhaps most critically, we lack a consensus on the definition and theory of discrimination, reducing our ability to agree upon appropriate policy initiatives.

As a result of these factors, social scientists have developed diverse and often conflicting interpretations of modern race relations. Some believe that racial discrimination is a dead issue while others hold that discrimination continues to depress the standard of living of blacks relative to whites. Some are greatly heartened by trends toward economic equality while others believe that black progress has been slow, limited, reversible, and restricted to a subset of the population. In between the extremes of optimism and pessimism lies the bulk of more cautious and uncertain opinion. Social scientists have been unable to reach any agreement about how discrimination works, whether it persists, how it is influenced by macroeconomic and microeconomic processes, who benefits from it, and whether governmental policies make it worse or better.

To the layperson this may sound like a cacophony of academic argument. But to the participant it is a vigorous and healthy representation of the underlying tensions that motivate the field of study. Social scientists experience nothing like the consensus of belief that binds together physical scientists. Economists in particular fall into several

1

schools of thought, disagreeing on the most basic questions and unable
to achieve a coherent intellectual synthesis. Yet it is exactly this diversity of approaches that makes economics creative, infuriating, and
above all, interesting. And what holds true for the discipline as a whole
holds true for the analysis of discrimination in particular.

Various models of discrimination explain the phenomenon in terms
of subjective preferences, informational uncertainties, class conflict,
competitive dynamics, adaptive organizational behavior, and still other
factors. Each of these explanations rests on a particular methodology
with implications concerning the relation of discrimination to more
fundamental economic processes. Consequently, the debates about the
importance of discrimination in understanding racial inequality represent but one front in a larger dispute over how to characterize our
economic system as a whole.

Most Americans cherish the ideals of freedom, equality, and opportunity. The genocide of Native Americans, the enslavement of Africans, and the long and bitter history of racial exclusion and subordination stand in uneasy contrast to the American self-image as a
democracy, forcing us to question the concordance of ideals and
institutions. Is racism the exception or the rule for U.S. capitalism?

The majority of economists hold that competitive market mechanisms work against the perpetuation of discrimination. In this view,
the motivation of self-interest conflicts with the propensity to discriminate. Nondiscriminatory employers win out against their discriminatory competition because they take better advantage of their
human resources and so face lower costs of production. The basic
mechanisms of supply and demand (possibly bolstered by governmental policies designed to raise even higher the costs of satisfying discriminatory preferences) ensure that our economy and our ideals co-
exist in fundamental harmony. Racism thus represents a temporary
diversion from the underlying teleological development of the market
system.

This analytical stance may be characterized as methodological individualism because it presumes that economic institutions are structured such that society-wide outcomes result from an aggregation of
individual behaviors. If individuals act on the basis of pecuniary self-
interest (entrepreneurs have no choice in this regard), then labor market dynamics dictate equal treatment for equal individuals regardless
of ascriptive characteristics such as race. Consequently, observed racial
inequality must be due to familial, educational, or other background
differences among individuals who are unevenly distributed between
blacks and whites as groups. Individual variation will always result in

differences in labor market outcomes, but if differing individuals are evenly distributed between groups, then aggregate outcomes will be evenly distributed as well. The causes of a dissimilar distribution of individuals between races may be genetic, cultural, historical, or some combination thereof. While the first cause has been employed by some psychologists and criminologists, it is not popular among most social scientists. The second stresses the value families and neighborhoods place on education, attitudes, and work habits. The third refers primarily to the impact of past discrimination on current inequality.

Economists who subscribe to some version of methodological individualism take the observed decline in wage and occupational differentials over the 1960s and 1970s to constitute evidence of a decline in discrimination. As overt bigotry and discriminatory governmental policies recede further into the past, blacks and whites would be expected to become more similar in the distribution of background characteristics and hence should experience increasingly similar labor market outcomes. In contrast, economists who may be classified as methodological structuralists accept neither the evidence nor the interpretation. Structuralism as an analytical method holds that aggregate outcomes are not the result of a simple summation of individual behaviors, but rather arise from the constraints and incentives imposed by organizational and social hierarchies. In this view, individual behavior achieves its importance within the context of group formation, cooperation, and conflict. These groups are variously described in terms of technological or managerial elites, large-scale organizational behavior, and property rights; but they all express the determinations and consequences of individual behaviors in terms of the distribution of resources and the exercise of power between groups. Economic and political outcomes are thus a function of the hegemony exercised by dominant groups, the resistance offered by subordinate groups, and the institutions that mediate their relationship.

Racial discrimination, in this view, is an inherent feature of our economic system. Competition is either not powerful enough to offset the group dynamics of identity and interest, or it actually operates so as to sustain discriminatory behaviors. The perpetrator may be the white working class trying to insulate itself from competition by black workers, the owners of capital whose bargaining position is strengthened by racial divisions in the working class, the industrial relations system that perpetuates a racial division of labor so as to sustain an alliance between management and white workers, or the organization that incorporates and thereby reproduces its social environment. Discrimination is due to the dynamics of group identification, competition, and conflict rather than irrational, individual attitudes. Despite the changes in law and attitude that result from popular movements, the institutional structure of society makes real (as opposed to nominal) change costly, risky, and time-consuming. Consequently, the continuing underemployment and low incomes of the majority of the black population would be an expected outcome of an economic system that satisfies human needs only as an incidental by-product of profit maximization. Market mechanisms, far from being relied upon to eliminate discrimination of their own accord, must be scrutinized and pressured to further the goal of equality of opportunity.

It would be natural to try to synthesize these two perspectives, and efforts to do so are not unknown. However, the methodological rupture runs deep. Each school of thought's vision of the economic process is at odds with the other, one stressing the essentially neutral character of that process (and consequently its determination by self-interested individual behaviors) and the other stressing its essentially skewed character (and consequently its determination by concentrations of wealth and power). Fortunately, this knocking of heads has stimulated a great deal of creativity. The chapters in this book implicitly reflect both the incompatibility of these views and the stimulus provided by their clash. Sometimes overtly and other times in a more subtle fashion, each chapter asks how important discrimination is in the explanation of racial inequality or, phrased more ambitiously, if capitalism tends to sustain or erode racism. To the degree to which discrimination is perceived to be powerful and symbiotically connected to the socioeconomic dynamics of the marketplace, the structuralist critique of capitalism will be supported. To the degree to which discrimination is seen to be economically irrational and unimportant in the explanation of inequality, the affirmation of capitalism provided by methodological individualism will be supported.

This distinction identifies the basic poles of the debate even if it does not neatly classify every analyst. In some cases elements of both positions may be intermingled. For example, if it is believed that market mechanisms work against discrimination, but only very slowly, then regulatory policies can be rationalized without condemning capitalism as such. Nonetheless, the key interpretive issue still concerns the impact of underlying economic processes on racial discrimination and inequality. Although the methodological categorization of some authors cannot be unambiguous, the implicit or explicit tension between these alternative perspectives lies at the heart of the most provocative work in the field.

As will be clear from our contributions to this volume, the editors are active participants in the debates about labor market discrimination. Both of us fall into the structuralist camp. However, we believe that the book presents a balanced view, with some of the best-known authors on each side represented. We subscribe to a perhaps romantic belief that controversy can be productive and can push us closer to a better understanding of the dynamics of race relations.

The book is divided into three sections that reflect the areas of greatest debate. Part I focuses on the measurement and interpretation of trends in racial economic inequality. The controversy over whether discrimination has declined is directly based on this question, since inequality is taken to constitute necessary (but not sufficient) proof of discrimination. The evidence is complicated and open to conflicting interpretations. For example, wage differentials have declined while employment differentials have widened. The former is frequently cited as proof that market mechanisms erode discrimination (methodological individualism), while the latter is often used to illustrate the tenacity of inequality in the face of growing similarities in the background characteristics of blacks and whites (methodological structuralism). As would be expected, each approach can "explain" the other's evidence, so that the decline in wage differentials is seen by structuralism to be due to political pressures, while the increase in employment differentials is seen by methodological individualism to be caused by changes in family structure and occupational aspirations. The picture is further confused by the failure of wage differentials to continue to fall after 1980, as well as by the sensitivity of racial differences in unemployment to overall labor market conditions. What would appear to be a straightforward question about inequality is thus confounded by contradictory trends, changes in historical context, and the ability of alternative perspectives to assimilate each other's evidence.

Part II confronts the most contentious of policy options: affirmative action. Along with bussing, the legislation of employment opportunity has become the new flash point for racial hostility and divisiveness. To justify affirmative action as a remedial policy, we must presuppose that the degree to which discrimination causes imbalances in employment can be measured, that affirmative action's impact on covered firms is not offset by reactions in the uncovered sector, that imbalances would continue in the absence of the policy, and that the economic and social costs of affirmative action do not exceed its benefits. Ethical issues abound on both sides. Is equality of opportunity being confused with equality of result? Is the hostility of white workers toward affirmative action a reaction "against" the policy or "for" employment privileges? Does the history of white racism mean that blacks deserve compensation akin to Germany's reparations to Israel? Thus, Part II is concerned with one potential solution (or nonsolution) to the problem (or nonproblem) treated in Part I.

Part III concludes the book with discussions of the social basis of inequality. Socialization patterns among whites may result in racist attitudes that reinforce inequality, while socialization patterns among blacks may result in behaviors counterproductive to economic success that can be used to rationalize inequality. Again, the importance of discrimination is the crucial issue dividing individualism and structuralism as methodologies for the analysis of racial inequality. If negative white attitudes toward blacks—whether irrational or self-interested—are governed solely by color, then formal equality as citizens may not be sufficient to eliminate substantive inequities in the economic arena. Discrimination in this case may continue in the absence of affirmative policies. On the other hand, if inequality reflects differences in socialization patterns, then the problem is more one of black behaviors than of white attitudes. Discrimination is then an inappropriate target in the struggle for racial equality. The history of different ethnic groups may shed light on these questions, since the black experience may be too unique to be captured by the traditional melting pot model wherein behavioral adjustments are the key to immigrant success. If blacks are prevented from assimilating in the same manner as other ethnic groups, then changes in black behaviors will not result in equal treatment, and "color-blind" policies will be ineffective remedies for discrimination. The issue of racial inequality necessarily conjoins social and economic dynamics, so it is fitting that the book ends on this note.

All of the chapters in this volume represent new and original research, and most are published here for the first time. Each implicitly reflects its methodological orientation in terms of its motivating question, its analytical stance, and its interpretation of results. The strengths of each perspective can therefore be assessed in terms of the puzzles posed and solved. Different approaches—for example, statistical, historical, and theoretical—are deliberately mixed to present and contrast the full range of applications each paradigm has produced. This book therefore offers not only new information and speculation on an issue of pressing human concern, but also an opportunity to evaluate alternative analytical perspectives in terms of their ability to produce creative and useful insights. It is our hope that the research and perspectives presented here will move the debate forward and contribute in some small way to the practical amelioration of the continuing "problem" of American race relations.

PART ONE

Trends in Racial Inequality: Measurement and Interpretation

Chapter 1. Black Progress and the Persistence of Racial Economic Inequalities, 1865-1940

THE ERA from the Civil War to the Second World War is in many respects the least known and most controversial in the socio-economic history of black Americans. The paucity of crucial evidence and also the unsettled interpretations of events and trends during this period are both unfortunate—and not just for historians—since no one can understand contemporary race relations or current socio-economic differences between blacks and whites without knowing what happened during the first seventy-five years after emancipation of the slaves. Yet some of the common assumptions of analysts of the era can be shown to be false. Consider, for example, the widely held belief that the typical white employer discriminated by paying a lower wage to a black worker than to a white who did the same work. Employers were free of legal constraints on this form of discrimination, but the evidence (documented below) indicates that they usually did not practice it. Therefore, Gary Becker's model of labor market discrimination—like many others that adopt a similar formulation of the problem—rests on a foundation that is empirically unwarranted. If only to avoid embedding such misapprehensions in our theories, we need to know more about how blacks fared in the economy during the years between 1865 and 1940.

Slavery was obviously a poor preparation for freedom; at emancipation black people suffered from many deficiencies and disadvantages, among them illiteracy, destitution, illness, and a lack of highly valued skills. Ninety percent lived in the South, where the war had brought death, destruction, and social disorganization on a wide scale. Predominantly rural, agricultural, and southern, blacks could hardly have occupied a more inauspicious position in a society where economic prog-

I am grateful to Lee J. Alston and Price Fishback for comments on a preliminary draft. For sending me reprints and unpublished materials, thanks to Alston, Fishback, Robert Margo, Sam Preston, Jennifer Roback, and Ralph Shlomowitz.

ress was bound up with the sort of urban-industrial transformation that characterized the North and West.[1]

The manner in which slavery had been abolished only worsened the plight of the newly freed men and women. They were separated forcibly from their owners, who received no compensation. After the long and bloody war, southern whites, defeated, impoverished, and embittered, displaced much of their anger and frustration onto blacks. Although the former rebels acknowledged their defeat, they had not accepted the legitimacy of the new race relations. Slavery as a legal institution might be dead, but the ideology of racism that had sustained it remained as vital as ever. One contemporary observer declared that southern whites were "unable to conceive of the negro as possessing any rights at all." They retained "an ingrained feeling that the blacks at large belong to the whites at large."[2]

Southern whites insisted that blacks continue to behave in the manner prescribed by the established racial etiquette. Unwritten but universally understood rules included: don't knock at a white's front door; don't interrupt a white's conversation for any reason; don't dispute a white's word even if he or she speaks wrongly; do appear cheerful, agreeable, and subservient; do address all whites, even children, with respect; do stand aside for whites to pass on the street or sidewalk; do obey all white commands without hesitation or complaint. In short, blacks must never appear "uppity"; they must stay at all times "in their place."[3]

Constrained by so many geographical, socio-economic, and cultural barriers, could the freed persons substantially improve their economic condition? The answer is that they could and they did. Those who insist, as many still do, upon viewing them and their descendants as chronic victims do a disservice to the truth and to the memory of people who, by persistent struggle and with notable courage, discovered and traveled along various avenues of progress.

In 1865, probably 95 percent of adult blacks were illiterate. They understood how vulnerable this deficiency made them and strove eagerly to acquire education, if not for themselves then for their children. In 1870 more than 80 percent of those 10 or older were reported as illiterate, probably an understatement. But by 1940 the ratio of illiteracy had shrunk to 12 percent; that is, the proportions literate and illiterate had been approximately reversed from what they had been seven decades earlier.[4] Even allowing for substantial misreporting on the eve of the Second World War, blacks in 1940 were enormously more literate than their ancestors had been in 1865.

One consequence of the increasing literacy was a changing pattern of sectoral and occupational composition of the black labor force. Immediately after the Civil War the majority of blacks were occupied in unskilled labor, principally as farm workers, casual laborers, and domestic servants. A few artisans, most of them plantation blacksmiths or building craftsmen, continued to practice trades for which they had been trained as slaves. It has been alleged, and most historians have accepted the allegation, that the artisans were progressively driven out of their jobs during the late nineteenth century. Although the evidence is too fragmentary to resolve the matter, there are good reasons to doubt both that the average artisan was highly skilled and that many of the truly skilled were actually driven out.[5] In any event blacks progressively occupied other skilled jobs that virtually no blacks had held during slavery: teachers, lawyers, doctors, dentists, farm and business managers, and skilled operatives of various sorts in industries like coal mining, iron and steel, automobile manufacturing, and meat packing.[6] In 1940 more than 119,000 blacks (2.7 percent of those employed) reported employment in professional and semiprofessional jobs. Included were some 64,000 school teachers, 2,300 professors, 5,000 doctors and dentists, and more than 1,000 lawyers. Many workers were affected by the shift out of agricultural employment; by 1940, farm jobs were only 32 percent of total black employment. Included among the nonfarm workers were some 3,500 blacksmiths, 26,000 carpenters, 5,000 machinists, 9,000 masons, 30,000 mechanics, 6,000 metal molders, 17,000 painters, 10,000 plasterers, 4,000 plumbers, and 4,500 tailors.[7] It is unjustifiable to describe the period before the Second World War as "an era of more than half a century during which there had been no fundamental change."[8] In fact, black people made tremendous sectoral and occupational adjustments to enhance their position in the labor market.

Finding out how rapidly black incomes advanced is more difficult than tracking black occupational progress. The information needed to construct a precise time series of black income over the period 1865–1940 simply does not exist. The indexes of relative income presented by Becker (1957), Vickery (1969), and Smith (1984) are not what they claim to be; each is an incomplete (more or less) measure of relative occupational standing, although Smith's index, which is the most comprehensive, can be used, in combination with other information, to construct an estimate of relative black income circa 1940. This estimate can be compared with my own previous estimates for circa 1867–1868 and circa 1900 to gain a rough impression of long-term trends.

I have derived the following formula as an approximation of total black income per capita relative to total white income per capita.[9] (The approximation requires that black property income per capita be very small relative to white total income per capita, which it was, and that labor's share of all income—that is, all income of both races combined—be approximately equal to labor's share of white income alone, which was so because white income amounted to more than 95 percent of all income.)

$$y(b)/y(w) \approx E \cdot P \cdot L$$

where $y(b)/y(w)$ = total black income per capita divided by total white income per capita; E = the earnings ratio = labor earnings per black worker divided by labor earnings per white worker; P = the participation ratio = black labor force per capita of black population divided by white labor force per capita of white population; and L = labor's share of all income.

Using available data and the formula, one can approximate relative black income circa 1940.[10] The numbers are

$$y(b)/y(w) \approx (0.42)(1.03)(0.79) = 0.34.$$

Thus, according to a rough estimate, total black income per capita in 1940 equaled about a third of the corresponding white income.

My previous estimates place relative black income per capita at about 24 percent circa 1867–1868 and about 35 percent circa 1900.[11] Ransom and Sutch consider my estimate for circa 1867–1868 probably too low; Shlomowitz considers it probably too high; I continue to regard it as imprecise but probably biased upward. Unless one makes large upward revisions to it, however, the following conclusion holds: between the late 1860s and the turn of the century, black income per capita grew at a faster percentage rate than did white income per capita. Comparing my present estimate for circa 1940 (0.34) with my previous estimate for circa 1900 (0.35), one can further conclude that black income per capita grew at about the same percentage rate as did white income per capita during the first four decades of the twentieth century.[12]

What happened to relative black income *within* the periods 1865–1900 and 1900–1940 remains open to speculation. One can base a conjecture about its course on annual time-series measures of black property accumulation, assuming an association between relatively high rates of property accumulation and relatively high rates of income growth. Recent studies have found that blacks accumulated property at a faster percentage rate than did whites in several southern states during the half-century after the Civil War.[13] In Georgia, for example, the state for which the evidence is most reliable, black real wealth grew by almost 9 percent per year during 1875–1892; it did not grow

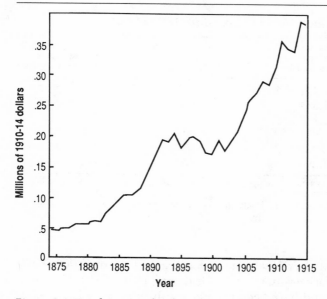

Figure 1.1. Total Assessed Value of Property Owned by Blacks, Georgia, 1874–1915

for about a decade during and after the severe depression of the nineties; then it grew by more than 6 percent per year during 1902–1915 (see Figure 1.1). As blacks began a massive migration out of Georgia in 1916, black property holdings in the state dropped. Between 1920 and 1937, Georgia blacks did not increase their share of the state's total wealth.[14] (Out-migrants might have continued to accumulate wealth, of course, but it would no longer have shown up in Georgia records. No comparable national data exist.)

Estimates of relative occupational standing for black males also show no gains between 1920 and 1940; some show slight losses in the 1930s.[15] Although the indices do not take into account income gains by blacks who moved from the South to the North (except when they also moved into higher-ranking job classifications), the general stagnation of the indices during the interwar period is consistent with other evidence. Consider, for example, the figures on home ownership in Table 1.1. Between 1890 and 1930 the proportion of black families owning their own homes rose steadily, but the decline during the 1930s brought the proportion in 1940 back approximately to its level of twenty years earlier.

My own conjecture, based on evidence too extensive and fragmentary to catalog here, is that black income per capita grew faster than white income per capita from the late 1860s to the early 1890s, slower

TABLE 1.1. *Black Home Ownership, 1890–1940*

Year	Total units occupied (thousands)	Owner-occupied units (thousands)	Percentage of total units owner-occupied
1890	1,411	264	18.7
1900	1,834	373	20.3
1910	2,173	489	22.5
1920	2,526	603	23.9
1930	2,922	737	25.2
1940	3,293	778	23.6

Sources: For 1890–1910, U.S. Bureau of the Census, 1918, pp. 466, 470; for 1920–1940, U.S. Bureau of the Census, 1984, p. 735.
    Note: Figures for 1890–1910 are for blacks; figures for 1920–1940 are for blacks and other non-whites.

for about a decade after 1892, and at least as fast during 1902–1920. Apparently no relative gains were made during 1920–1940. The inter-war stagnation could have been the net result of small relative gains in the 1920s, most likely associated with migration to the North, and relative losses in the 1930s, when the Great Depression reduced employment and occupational standing more for blacks than for whites.

Demographic evidence sheds additional light on long-term changes in black socio-economic conditions. Perhaps the most important single change can be summarized in the following contrast: in 1870 more than 80 percent of all blacks lived in the rural South; in 1940 only about 50 percent did. As Table 1.2 shows, by 1940 almost half the black population lived in urban areas, and almost a quarter lived outside the South. Although the greatest interregional migration of the pre–World War II era occurred between 1915 and 1930, there was also substantial migration earlier. The earlier movement had a negligible effect on the broad regional distribution before 1910, partly because much of it took place *within* the South and partly because in the North, where blacks were concentrated in large cities, their fertility was much lower and their mortality much higher.[16] Only substantial in-migration would have kept the northern proportion constant. After 1915, as out-migration from the South rose severalfold and the urban–rural mortality differential diminished, the proportion of blacks living outside the South increased markedly. Even during the economically depressed 1930s the northern percentage increased.

Changes in mortality are especially pertinent for an assessment of long-term changes in black economic well-being because, during the period 1865–1940, the level of living, particularly the quality of diet

TABLE 1.2. *Population and Its Distribution, by Race,*
          1870–1940

Year	Total population (millions)		Percentage in south		Percent urban of southern population		Percent urban of total population	
	White	Black	White	Black	White	Black	White	Black
1870	33.6	5.4	23	90	10	9	28	13
1880	43.4	6.6	24	90	10	9	28	14
1890	55.1	7.8	24	90	13	14	38	20
1900	66.9	8.8	25	90	19	16	43	23
1910	82.1	9.8	25	89	23	20	49	27
1920	95.5	10.5	25	85	29	24	53	34
1930	110.6	11.9	25	79	35	30	58	44
1940	118.6	12.9	27	77	37	34	58	49

Sources: U.S. Bureau of the Census, 1918, pp. 29, 88; U.S. Bureau of the Census, 1975, pp. 9, 14, 16–17, 22–23; Eldridge and Thomas, 1964, p. 204.

and housing, was probably the primary determinant of mortality rates. Various estimates of black mortality in the 1850s agree that the expectation of life at birth was around thirty to thirty-two years.[17] Black health certainly deteriorated during the mid-1860s, as the socio-economic disruptions associated with emancipation facilitated the spread of infectious diseases and diminished the blacks' resistance, but evidently these abysmal conditions did not persist for more than a few years.[18] The course of black mortality during the last third of the nineteenth century remains in doubt. Demographic historians' estimates of mortality changes between 1870 and 1900 disagree widely, some indicating virtually no change, others showing major improvement. Urbanization worked against favorable changes, with urban mortality rates exceeding rural rates by a considerable margin during the late nineteenth and early twentieth centuries. From recent estimates by Preston and Haines one can infer that black life expectancy at birth had reached about forty to forty-two years by the mid-1890s, although these demographers caution that the estimate may not be reliable.[19] After 1900, mortality data improved steadily, as did black health conditions. By 1940, when comprehensive national registration data permitted a precise measure, black life expectancy at birth had reached about fifty-four years, that is, perhaps twice its level during the mid-1860s and almost certainly two-thirds greater than its level under slavery in the 1850s.[20] It is extremely unlikely that such gains in life expectancy could have been achieved in the absence of substantial improvements in the level of living. Hence the mortality declines corroborate the long-term trend that is estimated above for real income per capita.

Between the Civil War and the Second World War, therefore, blacks realized large gains in real income, wealth, level of living, and life expectancy. By 1940, blacks had accumulated a nontrivial amount of wealth, acquired a high level of literacy and many new job-specific skills, doubled their life expectancy, and migrated in enormous numbers from the rural South into cities both in the South and in the North, where they found higher-paying employment, greater personal security, and wider opportunities for education and occupational upgrading. Great economic progress had been achieved, and the achievement deserves more recognition than scholars have generally given it.

Still, black income per capita in 1940 equaled only about a third of the corresponding white income. Although blacks had made major absolute gains, raising their real income per capita probably fourfold, they had not closed the socio-economic gap between the average black and the average white. Why had *relative* progress been so limited?

Part of the answer, an important and neglected part, is that complete elimination of racial difference in income per capita would have required a long time even under the best conditions. By a long time I mean several generations at least. More rapid elimination of the enormous racial economic differences that existed in 1865 simply was not feasible. For example, to catch up with whites before the First World War, given the rate at which white income was growing, blacks would have needed to increase their income per capita almost elevenfold, that is, to maintain an average annual rate of growth of almost 5 percent over a fifty-year period. Alternatively, to close the gap before the Second World War, black income per capita would have had to grow about twice as fast as white income per capita, which was itself growing rapidly on average over this seventy-five-year span.[21]

Another part of the answer, equally important and even more neglected, concerns income from property, that is, rents, interest, and profits. In the late nineteenth century about a third of the national income took the form of returns to property owners. During the interwar period the property share was smaller but still more than a quarter of total income.[22] Before the Civil War whites owned almost all of the blacks and the entire tangible capital stock. After the war blacks owned themselves, but the whites still owned virtually all the tangible wealth. So long as the whites continued to own almost all the income-generating property—and they have done so right up to the present day, notwithstanding blacks' modest accumulations—blacks had no chance to achieve complete racial income equality.[23] From the formula employed above it is apparent that (given the assumptions required for the approximation to hold) even if blacks had achieved complete equality of earnings per worker and participated in the labor force at the same rate as whites, their relative income per capita would have been only as large as the labor share of all income. In 1940, for example, even under these extremely favorable hypothetical conditions, black income per capita would have equaled only about 79 percent of the corresponding white income. DeCanio, one of the few economists to consider this issue seriously, concluded from his simulation study:

Even if all markets had operated perfectly and no discrimination had been practiced against the freedmen either in wage payments or in their access to occupations, this initial gap in tangible capital would have produced by itself most of the gap in income between blacks and whites throughout the late 19th and early 20th centuries.[24]

Whether or not one accepts the arguable claim that lack of property explains *most* of the income gap, it clearly explains a large part of it.

Of course, the assumption of no discrimination, employed to evaluate the importance of property ownership, is counterfactual. In reality blacks encountered many kinds of racial discrimination that adversely affected their economic progress. The important and controversial issues here have to do with how the market system and the political–governmental system operated in the context of racial prejudice and hostility. Many of the pertinent questions can be reduced to inquiries about the degree to which competitive processes ameliorated the plight of blacks.

The evidence is overwhelming that active market competition for the labor services of freed slaves and their descendants did occur,[25] although debate continues over the degree to which competitive pressures on employers resulted in equalization of the wages paid for black and for white labor services. Theory alone cannot resolve this question. It is essential that empirical inquiries into the matter be conducted. Unfortunately, most reported studies have been slipshod. Studies of relative black earnings typically have made a logically flawed leap: observing that black workers *received* lower earnings on the average, analysts have concluded that the average (presumably white) employer *paid* black workers a lower wage than he paid white workers for the same work. To answer the question properly requires firm-specific, occupation-specific wage data for employers who actually hired both blacks and whites.

Studies of such data have found that wage discrimination by employers was the exception rather than the rule. In my study of Virginia wages in 1900 and 1909, the unit of analysis is the "contract," which means the daily wage rates paid by a specific firm to workers of each race employed in a particular occupation (for instance, the observation that a firm hired 12 white carpenters at $2.00 per day and 3 black carpenters at $1.75 per day is a single contract). The study examined 290 firms that made 490 contracts in 1900 and 636 firms that made 1,595 contracts in 1909. The contracts involved 5,292 workers (2,247 whites) in 1900 and 13,995 (6,937 whites) in 1909. The data show that in 1900, 36 percent of the contracts paid whites more, 61 percent paid both races the same, and 3 percent paid blacks more; in 1909 the percentages were 38, 57, and 5. Separation of the occupations according to presumed skill levels shows that in firms with integrated work forces, contracts paying whites a higher wage occurred relatively more frequently in skilled than in unskilled occupations. In 1900, whites received an apparent premium in 20 of 33 contracts for skilled jobs but in only 20 of 77 contracts for unskilled jobs; in 1909 the breakdowns were 41 of 63 for skilled jobs, 59 of 198 for unskilled jobs. These differences are consistent with the hypothesis that white workers were better trained and more productive, on the average, as much auxiliary evidence confirms. In unskilled jobs, where little scope existed for such productivity differences, the most common practice was to pay the same wage to workers of both races. Work-force segregation was much more common in this sample than racial wage differentials within integrated work forces, but workers got about the same wage within a given occupation whether they worked in integrated or segregated occupational work forces.[26]

In 1938 the U.S. Bureau of Labor Statistics reported results of a study of racial differences in employment and earnings in the iron and steel industry, a major employer of blacks; it found that although blacks earned less than whites, on the average, the difference did not result from racial wage discrimination by employers: "A very careful examination of the reports for plants employing both whites and Negroes revealed that whenever whites and Negroes were found in the same occupations in any given plant, both were receiving the same basic rates." The bureau ascribed the difference in average earnings to the blacks' lower occupational standing in the industry.[27]

Various studies have shown that during the late nineteenth and early twentieth centuries employers generally paid blacks and whites the same rate for unskilled labor services—the closest thing in reality to the homogeneous labor services assumed in many models of discrimination. Equality of real wage rates, or at least a close approximation to it, is well documented for wage workers in southern agriculture.[28] Blacks and whites who entered into farm tenancy arrangements adopted similar mixes of contracts (share versus fixed rent) under similar eco-

TABLE 1.3.   *Distribution of Plants with Integrated Work Forces, by Racial Difference of Wages Paid to Entry-Level Common Laborers, Twenty Industries, 1936 and 1937*

	North		South		United States	
	Number	Percent	Number	Percent	Number	Percent
1936						
Plants paying whites more	86	9.4	142	28.2	228	16.1
Plants paying both same	772	84.6	341	67.6	1,113	78.5
Plants paying blacks more	55	6.0	21	4.2	76	5.4
Total plants	913	100.0	504	100.0	1,417	100.0
1937						
Plants paying whites more	60	6.8	151	28.3	211	14.9
Plants paying both same	782	88.7	370	69.3	1,152	81.4
Plants paying blacks more	40	4.5	13	2.4	53	3.7
Total plants	882	100.0	534	100.0	1,416	100.0

Sources: Billips, 1937, pp. 944–945; Perlman and Frazier, 1937, p. 1499.

nomic conditions.[29] Almost all piece-rate wage contracts, like those for cotton picking or coal mining, set the same rate regardless of the workers' race, again indicating that when the work done for a given employer was the same, the pay was usually the same.[30] (The equality of piece-rate wages deserves more attention than it has received, as it is especially telling evidence. If lower black time-rate wages were the result of discrimination, one wonders why employers discriminated when paying time rates but not when paying piece rates.) Massive studies of common laborers' wages in 1936 and 1937 surveyed some 220,000 workers, about one-sixth of them black, in twenty industries across the United States. It was found that 80 percent of the more than 1,400 integrated plants surveyed paid the same wage rate to black and white entry-level common laborers. Even in the South, where a premium was more frequently paid to white workers, about 68–69 percent of the employers paid both races the same rate (see Table 1.3). A 1935 U.S. Labor Department survey of cities hiring common laborers for street and sewer work found that almost 98 percent of the 700 cities that hired workers of both races paid the same rate to each. Even in the South, 100 of the 109 cities surveyed paid the same rate to blacks and whites.[31]

The evidence is overwhelming: relatively low earnings sprang not so much from racial wage discrimination by employers as from disproportionate black occupancy of the lower regions of the occupational hierarchy and from disproportionate black occupancy of geographic locations where earnings were relatively low for all workers, white as well as black. Blacks were disproportionately southern, which implied relatively low earnings in almost any occupation, and disproportionately unskilled, which implied relatively low earnings in any region. Moreover, their locational and industrial distributions placed them at a disadvantage even *within* the South. A U.S. Labor Department study of entry-level common laborers in July 1935, for example, reported that in the South the black workers were "employed in practically all industries, but they [were] found particularly in the lumber industry, which reported the lowest average hourly entrance rate in the South," while the white workers were "employed especially in large numbers in petroleum refining and in the iron and steel industry which showed the highest average entrance rates per hour in the South."[32] The so-called black belt—a crescent stretching from southeastern Virginia through central Georgia and on to eastern Texas—long the home of most blacks, was the worst location for any worker, black or white, skilled or unskilled.

With respect to the persistence of relatively low black earnings, the critical question has to do with the persistence of an apparent "disequilibrium" among labor markets: why did blacks not leave the disadvantaged geographic and occupational positions they occupied? The short answer is that many did, but the important qualification is that too few did to eliminate the racial earnings gap. The question then becomes: what kept the geographic and occupational migration rates so low? The question can be broken down into inquiries about knowledge, coercion, and adverse feedback effects.

Obviously, many blacks had little or no reliable information about distant opportunities. As late as 1900, 45 percent of all blacks over nine years of age reported themselves illiterate, and of the others, many had such limited schooling that reading a newspaper was difficult, even when they had a newspaper to read, as few poor people did. Blacks living on isolated plantations, especially in the rural South, knew virtually nothing about events in the wider world. They got most of their information by word of mouth from friends and relatives. It is hardly surprising that "local labor markets . . . had some links with the outside, but they were poorly integrated with each other. . . . regional 'southern backwardness' and 'black poverty' [had] a basic common element: the isolation of southern labor markets from national labor markets."[33]

After 1915 the isolation of blacks began to dissolve as massive black migration set in motion a process of self-reinforcing mobility at once physical, informational, and psychological. With the decline of immigration and the combination of northern prosperity and southern adversity during the 1920s, black workers continued the movements begun during the war, arbitraging the regional labor markets on an unprecedented scale. The process shifted into a lower gear when the depression sharply curtailed interregional movements during the 1930s.[34]

Black mobility among labor markets would have been greater had not public school authorities discriminated against blacks in allocating educational resources, thereby retarding literacy and a consequent awareness of distant opportunities. The racial gap in the provision of schooling widened considerably when blacks effectively lost political rights in one southern state after another from 1890 to 1910. That the school boards provided any resources at all reflected the blacks' ability to "vote with their feet." To prevent a mass exodus of black workers and farm tenants, local governments did maintain black schools, but the separate and unequal education ensured that many blacks would remain unaware of economic opportunities in the wider world.[35]

Discrimination by school boards was one aspect of a larger reality: across-the-board discrimination by state and local governmental authorities. The most important feature of such discrimination was the denial of equal protection of life and property. Southern governments ignored, condoned, encouraged, or participated in unspeakable crimes against blacks. It has been estimated that in Texas, for example, "approximately *one percent* of the black population between 15 and 49 years old was killed in the early years of Reconstruction." The number and variety of beatings, rapes, cuttings, hangings, shootings, drownings, burnings, tortures, assaults, and lynchings of every kind defy comprehension. Whites committed these crimes with impunity. "Local officials, by allowing those who committed attacks on blacks to go free or to receive a ridiculously small fine, did nothing to discourage these crimes. This made other whites aware that if they did use violence as a tool of control, they would not be punished." Thus the South became and remained, as W. E. B. Du Bois said, "an armed camp for intimidating black folk."[36]

According to the standard enumeration, no doubt incomplete, some 70 blacks per year were lynched in the 1880s. The number rose to a peak of 161 in 1892 and averaged about 111 per year during the 1890s— that is, a black was publicly murdered about every third day, on the average, for an entire decade. In the twentieth century lynchings declined; by the 1930s the average had fallen to "only" a dozen blacks per year.[37] Various trends have been credited for the decline, including urbanization, growing legal opposition, reduction in the social backwardness of rural whites, the slow advance of more civilized public opinion, and the threat of federal intervention. Whatever the cause, the number of lynchings declined by some 90 percent during the half-century before the Second World War. Other forms of brutal and lawless treatment of southern blacks seem to have followed the same downward trend, although only the impressions of contemporaries exist as evidence.[38]

Enforcement of southern states' laws and ordinances, apparently designed to immobilize black laborers and farm tenants or lock them into peonage, varied across times and places; in most places, most such laws were always effectively nullified by competition in the labor markets. Nor were they ever the binding constraint. What Roback has said of so-called peonage laws can also be said of many other legal impediments: "A system that can force people to work can do so whether or not they are indebted"—so, too, whether or not they are legally adjudged vagrants, misdemeanants, breachers of contract, enticers of laborers under contract, and so forth. Roback also notes that such laws commonly only "provided a veneer of legality for brutal activities that were actually illegal."[39] Most well-documented cases of genuine peonage, for example, appear actually to have been kidnapping or enslavement abetted by local legal authorities.

The fundamental problem was not so much that the southern governments enacted discriminatory laws as that they failed to protect the basic personal and property rights of blacks, formally in effect, against a pervasive reign of "private" lawlessness. Gunnar Myrdal observed that

in the South the Negro's person and property are practically subject to the whim of any white person who wishes to take advantage of him or to punish him for any real or fancied wrongdoing or "insult." A white man can steal from or maltreat a Negro in almost any way without fear of reprisal, because the Negro cannot claim the protection of the police or courts, and personal vengeance on the part of the offended Negro usually results in organized retaliation in the form of bodily injury (including lynching), home burning or banishment.[40]

Myrdal noted that not all white people took advantage of the blacks, that actual physical violence and threats of violence occurred episodically, and that many blacks got through life experiencing few such incidents; but he added that "violence *may* occur at any time, and it is the fear of it as much as violence itself which creates the injustice and the insecurity." In this risky environment "inequality of justice [was] undoubtedly responsible for no small part of the Negro's difficulties in rising economically and socially."[41]

Blacks could often minimize the hazards of life in the South only by attaching themselves to and performing appropriate services for a white patron, preferably a powerful landlord or employer with enough influence in the community to protect "his people." Such paternalistic relationships brought some blacks a modicum of security, but even so, they exacted a cost in the perpetuation of dependency and subservience.[42]

The northern state governments, for their part, typically obstructed black economic progress indirectly, not by law but by the labor union practices they condoned. Labor unions kept blacks out of a wide range of skilled jobs—including some, such as craft jobs in the building trades, that blacks routinely entered in the largely nonunionized South. "They hang the negro in the south but they are not so bad in the north," said a Kansas newspaper in 1899; "they just simply starve him to death by labor's union." Black leaders like Booker T. Washington and Du Bois condemned unions as extremely harmful to black workers. The "Chinese wall erected by the trades unions," as one black editor called it, was a barrier only a few northern blacks could surmount. Not every union excluded blacks—coal miners and longshoremen, for example, hardly discriminated—but most did. Of some, like the railroad operating brotherhoods, exclusion of blacks was a given. Other unions accepted black members but organized them into segregated locals. From time to time, blacks gained employment by entering an occupation as strikebreakers, but the practice was dangerous.[43]

Besides having to cope with all the discriminatory actions of governments, unions, and even some parties in the market—after all, the market itself was never *completely* free of discrimination, especially job discrimination—many blacks found themselves caught in a web of adverse feedback relations. These consisted of incentives for personal behaviors by individual blacks that, in the aggregate, helped to perpetuate the poverty of blacks as a group. A black disadvantage arose from the conjunction of two elements: (1) the concentration of black population in the rural South at the time of emancipation and (2) the fact that the rural South, though hardly "stagnant," was to be the least dynamic part of a rapidly developing national economy for the next seventy-five years.[44]

Consider the situation of the typical young black man throughout this period. Living in the rural South, barely literate if he had any schooling at all, knowing little or nothing about alternatives beyond his local community, lacking skills except as a farm worker, he was likely to consider his best available course of action to be, first, to get married and produce as soon as possible a large number of children; second, to enter into a sharecropping arrangement with a local landlord, hoping in time to accumulate enough money to buy a mule and the necessary equipment to become a true tenant (share*croppers* were only quasi-tenants) and eventually to acquire his own land. For share-croppers and tenants, large families were an important asset; their high fertility rates reflected this fact.[45] Because children had greater value when they worked on the family's plot than when they were in school, education had a low priority. As Margo has shown, "black children attended poorer quality schools and far fewer days per year than the national average. Black school performance was further handicapped by low family incomes and high rates of adult illiteracy."[46] Education-related "voting with the feet" was too limited to offset the effects of these adverse incentives.

Thus did rural southern blacks find it personally advantageous to behave in a way that tended to reproduce the socio-economic conditions that had prompted the behavior in the first place. A large, rapidly growing black population in the rural South kept the entire region relatively poor by heaping up labor in low-productivity agriculture.[47] Progressively more out-migration was necessary to keep real earnings in the rural South from declining. Participation in entrepreneurial undertakings was discouraged by the blacks' limited degree of urbanization.[48] Illiteracy slowed the accumulation of tangible property as well as the acquisition of knowledge needed to acquire many job-specific skills and to respond to alternative opportunities in the cities of the South and the North.[49] Finally, blacks, concentrated in the rural South, were especially vulnerable to white crimes against their persons and their property. A consequence was prolonged paternalistic dependence on white landlords and bosses, giving few blacks experience in managing their own affairs. Circumstances militated against escape from such adverse relationships and raised the costs of adjustment to changing economic conditions. The apparent "disequilibrium," which entailed relatively low black incomes as one of its consequences, persisted.

During the first seventy-five years after the Civil War, black economic history exhibited progress in absolute increases of income, wealth, and life expectancy, but even by 1940 the income per capita of blacks was only about a third as large as that of whites. Desperate initial conditions made a rapid convergence with whites impossible. At emancipation freed blacks received no lands or other compensation for their years in slavery. Destitution, illiteracy, and poor health virtually condemned them and their descendants in the rural South to a position in the socio-economic order that would have been grossly inferior even had the society suddenly become color-blind, which it had not. White American society remained racist to its core. Discriminatory barriers obstructed black progress at almost every turn, least frequently in the payment of wages, the setting of terms for farm tenants' contracts, and other market transactions where black mobility could impose a cost on individual discriminators; more frequently in job discrimination, often because of labor union pressures but sometimes simply in response to employee or employer hostility in settings where few blacks possessed the requisite qualifications for skilled positions and where employers bore little or no cost by denying them an opportunity to learn on the job.[50] The most pervasive aspect of job discrimination was the refusal to employ blacks in positions where they would give orders or advice to whites. Racial discrimination by whites concentrated *not* on avoiding personal contact with blacks, as most economic models assume, but rather on confining blacks to positions of subservience to and dependence on whites.[51]

Most damaging of all was the discriminatory behavior of the southern state and local governments. By providing only scant resources for black education, public school boards helped to perpetuate illiteracy and ignorance, and they thereby set in motion a variety of adverse effects. By denying blacks equal protection of personal and property rights, governments discouraged black investment in human or tangible capital and risk-taking endeavors of many kinds. As noted above, the lawlessness of the South, especially the rural South, drove blacks into the arms of powerful white patrons, prolonging black dependency and subservience. Competitive pressures in the political–governmental system, unlike those in the markets, worked in support of discrimination rather than in opposition to it.[52] Had the governments of the era been more actively involved in economic affairs, blacks would have suffered even more.

Notes

1. Higgs, 1971, Chap. 2; Higgs, 1977a, pp. 4, 14–15; Ransom and Sutch, 1977, pp. 14–19, 54; Litwack, 1979; Jaynes 1986.
2. As quoted in Higgs, 1977a, p. 9. See also Ransom and Sutch, 1977, pp. 22–23; Litwack, 1979, pp. 186, 219, 364, 397; Jaynes, 1986, pp. 101–137.
3. Doyle, 1971; Higgs, 1977a, pp. 10, 125. The whites did not seek to distance themselves physically from the blacks. The assumption that they did, which forms the basis of Becker's model and many others adopting his formulation, misses the point completely. The whites did not object at all to having blacks around them so long as the blacks always behaved deferentially and occupied subordinate positions.
4. Smith, 1984, p. 691.
5. Higgs, 1977a, pp. 80–83; Ransom and Sutch, 1977, pp. 31–39, 220–231; Goldin, 1977, pp. 96–97; Foner and Lewis, 1979, pp. 350–351, citing Atlanta University study of 1901; Jaynes, 1986, pp. 261–262.

6. U.S. Bureau of the Census, 1918, pp. 508–511.
7. U.S. Bureau of the Census, 1943, pp. 88–90.
8. Myrdal, 1962, p. xxiii.
9. Let y = total income per capita, e = labor earnings per capita, r = property income per capita. Parenthetical indexes (b) and (w) denote black and white. By definition,

$$y(b) = e(b) + r(b)$$

Divide through by $e(w)$:

$$y(b)/e(w) = e(b)/e(w) + r(b)/e(w)$$

Rearrange terms:

$$y(b)/e(w) = EP + r(b)/e(w)$$

where E = the earnings ratio = (earnings/black worker)/(earnings/white worker); P = the participation ratio = (black labor force participation rate)/(white labor force participation rate), participation being relative to the total population of each racial group.
   Multiply through by $e(w)$ to get black income per capita:

$$y(b) = EP\, e(w) + r(b)$$

Divide through by $y(w)$ to get an exact expression for the total per capita income ratio:

$$y(b)/y(w) = EPL(w) + r(b)/y(w)$$

where $L(w)$ = labor's share of white income.
   Empirically, for the United States in the period 1865–1940, a good approximation is

$$y(b)/y(w) \approx EPL$$

because $L(w) \approx L$, and $r(b)/y(w)$ is very small relative to the other term on the right-hand side of the exact expression.
10. The earnings ratio of 0.42 is calculated as a weighted average (weights are 2/3 for males, 1/3 for females, their actual shares in the black labor force) of the male earnings ratio (0.45) computed from data in Smith, 1984, p. 697, and the female earnings ratio (0.36) given in Gwartney, 1970, p. 881. The participation ratio is calculated from data in U.S. Bureau of the Census, 1943, p. 25. Labor's share of national income is for 1937, as estimated by Kendrick, 1961, p. 121.
11. Higgs, 1977a, pp. 95–102, 145–146.
12. Ransom and Sutch, 1979, pp. 227–228; Shlomowitz, 1983, p. 274. See also DeCanio, 1979, p. 190. Incidentally, the present calculations resolve the apparent discrepancies noted in Higgs, 1978a, p. 99, p. 154, fn. 5.
13. DeCanio, 1979; Higgs, 1982; Margo, 1984b; Higgs, 1984.
14. DeCanio, 1979, p. 200, fn. 19.
15. Smith, 1984, p. 695; Reich, 1981, p. 26, citing indexes constructed by Hiestand and Freeman. For region-specific indexes, see Becker, 1957, and Vickery, 1969.
16. Eldridge and Thomas, 1964, pp. 90, 99; Higgs, 1973a; Higgs, 1976a; Higgs, 1977a, pp. 24–36; Graves, Sexton, and Vedder, 1983; Meeker, 1977; Tolnay, 1981; Preston and Haines, 1984, p. 278.
17. Meeker, 1976, p. 20.
18. Higgs, 1977a, pp. 20–24; Ransom and Sutch, 1977, pp. 53–54, 329; Litwack, 1979, pp. 98, 133.
19. Preston and Haines, 1984, pp. 275, 278–279. See also Suliman, 1983, pp. 149–180.
20. U.S. Bureau of the Census, 1975, p. 56, Series B116-117.
21. Higgs, 1977a, p. 126.
22. Budd, 1960, p. 387; Kendrick, 1961, p. 121.

23. von Furstenberg, 1974, p. 152; Levitan, Johnson, and Taggart, 1975, p. 172.
24. DeCanio, 1979, p. 184. See also Higgs, 1977a, pp. 77–80, 125–126; Wright, 1982, p. 177.
25. Higgs, 1977a, esp. Chaps. 3, 4; Litwack, 1979, pp. 435–437 and passim; Shlomowitz, 1979; Shlomowitz, 1984; DeCanio, 1974, pp. 51–76; Wright, 1982, p. 172; Jaynes, 1986, pp. 84, 118, 257, 301–302.
26. Higgs, 1977b. See also Fishback, 1984, pp. 766–769; and the data from a Labor Department study conducted during the First World War, as reproduced in Whatley, 1986, Table 1.
27. Baril, 1940, p. 1143.
28. Higgs, 1972a; Higgs, 1975; Higgs, 1977a, pp. 63–66; Higgs, 1978b; Jaynes, 1986, pp. 259–262.
29. Higgs, 1973b, pp. 157–159; Higgs, 1974, pp. 477–479.
30. Fishback, 1983, pp. 160–166. See also Fishback, 1985, pp. 653, 668; Litwack, 1979, pp. 313, 353.
31. Billips, 1936, pp. 1240–1241.
32. Moncure, 1936, p. 702. See also Frazier and Perlman, 1939, pp. 1454–1455; Myrdal, 1962, p. 1094.
33. Wright, 1982, p. 173. See also Wright 1986, 1987.
34. Higgs, 1976a; Higgs, 1978a.
35. Margo, 1982; Margo, 1984a; Margo, 1984c; Margo, 1985; Margo, 1986a; Margo, 1986b. Fishback, 1986, analyzes the apparently aberrant case of West Virginia, where coal mining companies used their influence to promote equalization of the per capita resources devoted to black and white schooling.
36. Crouch, 1984, pp. 219, 227. See also Higgs, 1977a, pp. 9–11, 39, 123–125 (Du Bois quotation on p. 125); Litwack, 1979, pp. 282–288; Jaynes, 1986, pp. 144, 256–257, 297–298.
37. U.S. Bureau of the Census, 1975, p. 422, Series H1170.
38. Higgs, 1978a, pp. 113–114; Raper, 1970; White, 1969.
39. Roback, 1984, pp. 1168, 1175. See also Higgs, 1977a, pp. 74–76, 124–125.
40. Myrdal, 1962, p. 530.
41. Ibid., pp. 530, 534. See also pp. 523–569, and Litwack, 1979, pp. 282–288.
42. Higgs and Alston, 1981; Alston, 1985a, Chap. 4; Alston, 1986; Alston and Ferrie, 1985a; Alston and Ferrie, 1985b, pp. 98–104.
43. Quotations from documents in Foner and Lewis, 1979, pp. 292–293. See also pp. 72, 250, and Higgs, 1977a, pp. 85–86.
44. Higgs, 1978a, pp. 108–109, emphasizes the disproportionate burden of adjustment borne by blacks.
45. Higgs, 1972b; Tolnay, 1984.
46. Margo, 1986b, p. 195. See also Margo, 1984a, p. 320; Margo, 1985, p. 3; Margo, 1986a.
47. Higgs, 1980, pp. 9–11.
48. Higgs, 1976b, p. 157.
49. Higgs, 1982, p. 735; Margo, 1984b, p. 772; Higgs, 1984, p. 777.
50. Wright, 1981.
51. Higgs, 1977b, pp. 243–244; Higgs, 1978a, pp. 100–102, 109–111; Fishback, 1984, pp. 772–774.
52. For a recent, revealing case study, see Roback, 1986.

References

Alston, Lee J., 1986. "Race Etiquette in the South: The Role of Tenancy." *Research in Economic History* 10 (January): 193–205.

————, 1985. *Costs of Contracting and the Decline of Tenancy in the South, 1930–1960.* New York: Garland.

Alston, Lee J., and Joseph P. Ferrie, 1985a. "The Use of In-Kind Benefits in Agriculture: A Synthesis and Test." Unpublished discussion paper, Williams College (July).

————, 1985b. "Labor Costs, Paternalism, and Loyalty in Southern Agriculture: A Constraint on the Growth of the Welfare State." *Journal of Economic History* 45 (March): 95–117.

Baril, Victor S., 1940. "Earnings of Negro Workers in the Iron and Steel Industry, April 1938." *Monthly Labor Review* 51 (November): 1139–1149.

Becker, Gary S., 1957. *The Economics of Discrimination.* Chicago: University of Chicago Press.

Billips, Robert S., 1937. "Hourly Entrance Rates of Common Laborers in 20 Industries, July 1936." *Monthly Labor Review* 44 (April): 938–952.

————, 1936. "Entrance Rates and Full-Time Hours of Common Laborers in Cities, September 1935." *Monthly Labor Review* 43 (November): 1228–1242.

Budd, Edward C., 1960. "Factor Shares, 1850–1910." In *Trends in the American Economy in the Nineteenth Century*, 365–398. National Bureau of Economic Research, Conference on Research in Income and Wealth. Princeton: Princeton University Press.

Crouch, Barry A., 1984. "A Spirit of Lawlessness: White Violence; Texas Blacks, 1865–1868." *Journal of Social History* 18 (Winter): 217–232.

DeCanio, Stephen J., 1979. "Accumulation and Discrimination in the Postbellum South." *Explorations in Economic History* 16 (April): 182–206.

————, 1974. *Agriculture in the Postbellum South: The Economics of Production and Supply.* Cambridge: M.I.T. Press.

Doyle, Bertram Wilbur, 1971. *The Etiquette of Race Relations in the South: A Study in Social Control.* New York: Schocken.

Eldridge, Hope T., and Dorothy Swaine Thomas, 1964. *Population Redistribution and Economic Growth, United States, 1870–1950. III. Demographic Analyses and Interrelations.* Philadelphia: American Philosophical Society.

Fishback, Price, 1986. "Separate But Equal? Coal Companies and Segregated Schools in West Virginia in the Early 1900s." Unpublished paper presented to the International Economic History Congress, Bern, Switzerland. (August).

————, 1985. "Discrimination on Nonwage Margins: Safety in the West Virginia Coal Industry, 1906–1925." *Economic Inquiry* 23 (October): 651–669.

————, 1984. "Segregation in Job Hierarchies: West Virginia Coal Mining, 1906–1932." *Journal of Economic History* 44 (September): 755–774.

————, 1983. "Employment Conditions of Blacks in the Coal Industry, 1900–1930." Ph.D. diss., University of Washington.

Foner, Philip S., and Ronald L. Lewis, eds., 1979. *The Black Worker: A Documentary History from Colonial Times to the Present. IV. The Black Worker During the Era of the American Federation of Labor and the Railroad Brotherhoods.* Philadelphia: Temple University Press.

Frazier, Edward K., and Jacob Perlman, 1939. "Entrance Rates of Common Laborers, July 1939." *Monthly Labor Review* 49 (December): 1450–1465.

von Furstenberg, George M., 1974. "The Interrelation between Labor and Capital Components of Racial Income Differences." *Journal of Political Economy* 82 (January/February): 152–162.

Goldin, Claudia, 1977. "Female Labor Force Participation: The Origin of Black and White Differences, 1870 and 1880." *Journal of Economic History* 37 (March): 87–108.

Graves, Philip E., Robert L. Sexton, and Richard K. Vedder, 1983. "Slavery, Amenities, and Factor Price Equalization: A Note on Migration and Freedom." *Explorations in Economic History* 20 (April): 156–162.

Gwartney, James, 1970. "Changes in the Nonwhite/White Income Ratio—1939–67." *American Economic Review* 60 (December): 872–883.

Higgs, Robert, 1984. "Accumulation of Property by Southern Blacks before World War I: Reply." *American Economic Review* 74 (September): 777–781.

———, 1982. "Accumulation of Property by Southern Blacks before World War I." *American Economic Review* 72 (September): 725–737.

———, 1980. "Urbanization and Invention in the Process of Economic Growth: Simultaneous-Equations Estimates for the United States, 1880–1920." *Research in Population Economics* 2: 3–20.

———, 1978a. "Race and Economy in the South, 1890–1950." In *The Age of Segregation: Race Relations in the South, 1890–1945,* ed. Robert Haws. Jackson: University Press of Mississippi.

———, 1978b. "Racial Wage Differentials in Agriculture: Evidence from North Carolina in 1887." *Agricultural History* 52 (April): 308–311.

———, 1977a. *Competition and Coercion: Blacks in the American Economy, 1865–1914.* New York: Cambridge University Press.

———, 1977b. "Firm-Specific Evidence on Racial Wage Differentials and Workforce Segregation." *American Economic Review* 67 (March): 236–245.

———, 1976a. "The Boll Weevil, the Cotton Economy, and Black Migration, 1910–1930." *Agricultural History* 50 (April): 325–350.

———, 1976b. "Participation of Blacks and Immigrants in the American Merchant Class, 1890–1910: Some Demographic Relations." *Explorations in Economic History* 13 (April): 153–164.

———, 1975. "Did Southern Farmers Discriminate?—Interpretive Problems and Further Evidence." *Agricultural History* 49 (April): 445–447.

———, 1974. "Patterns of Farm Rental in the Georgia Cotton Belt, 1880–1900." *Journal of Economic History* 34 (June): 468–482.

———, 1973a. "Mortality in Rural America, 1870–1920: Estimates and Conjectures." *Explorations in Economic History* 10 (Winter): 177–195.

———, 1973b. "Race, Tenure, and Resource Allocation in Southern Agriculture, 1910." *Journal of Economic History* 33 (March): 149–169.

———, 1972a. "Did Southern Farmers Discriminate?" *Agricultural History* 46 (April): 325–328.

———, 1972b. "Property Rights and Resource Allocation Under Alternative Land Tenure Forms: A Comment." *Oxford Economic Papers* 24 (November): 428–431.

———, 1971. *The Transformation of the American Economy, 1865–1914: An Essay in Interpretation.* New York: Wiley.

Higgs, Robert, and Lee J. Alston, 1981. "An Economist's Perspective on Southern Paternalism, 1865–1965." Unpublished paper presented to the Second Sewanee Economics Symposium, University of the South (April).

Jaynes, Gerald David, 1986. *Branches Without Roots: Genesis of the Black Working Class in the American South.* New York: Oxford University Press.

Kendrick, John W., 1961. *Productivity Trends in the United States.* Princeton: Princeton University Press.

Levitan, Sar A., William B. Johnson, and Robert Taggart, 1975. *Still a Dream: The Changing Status of Blacks since 1960.* Cambridge: Harvard University Press.

Litwack, Leon F., 1979. *Been in the Storm So Long: The Aftermath of Slavery.* New York: Vintage.

Margo, Robert A., 1986a. "Educational Achievement in Segregated School Systems: The Effects of 'Separate-but-Equal.' " *American Economic Review* 76 (September): 794–801.

———, 1986b. "Race, Educational Attainment, and the 1940 Census." *Journal of Economic History* 46 (March): 189–198.

———, 1985. "Educational Achievement in Segregated School Systems: The Effects of 'Separate-But-Equal.' " National Bureau of Economic Research Working Paper no. 1620 (May).

———, 1984a. " 'Teacher Salaries in Black and White': The South in 1910." *Explorations in Economic History* 21 (July): 306–326.

———, 1984b. "Accumulation of Property by Southern Blacks before World War I:

Comment and Further Evidence." *American Economic Review* 74 (September): 768–776.

———, 1984c. "Segregated Schools and the Tiebout Hypothesis." Unpublished discussion paper, University of Pennsylvania (October).

———, 1982. "Race Differences in Public School Expenditures: Disfranchisement and School Finance in Louisiana, 1890–1910." *Social Science History* 6 (Winter): 9–33.

Meeker, Edward, 1977. "Freedom, Economic Opportunity, and Fertility: Black Americans, 1860–1910." *Economic Inquiry* 15 (July): 397–412.

———, 1976. "Mortality Trends of Southern Blacks, 1850–1910: Some Preliminary Findings." *Explorations in Economic History* 13 (January): 13–42.

Moncure, Paul H., 1936. "Entrance Rates Paid to Common Labor, July 1935." *Monthly Labor Review* 42 (March): 698–706.

Myrdal, Gunnar, 1944. *An American Dilemma: The Negro Problem and Modern Democracy.* New York: Harper & Row.

Perlman, Jacob, and Edward K. Frazier, 1937. "Entrance Rates of Common Laborers in 20 Industries, July 1937." *Monthly Labor Review* 45 (December): 1491–1510.

Preston, Samuel H., and Michael R. Haines, 1984. "New Estimates of Child Mortality in the United States at the Turn of the Century." *Journal of the American Statistical Association* 79 (June): 272–281.

Ransom, Roger L., and Richard Sutch, 1979. "Growth and Welfare in the American South of the Nineteenth Century." *Explorations in Economic History* 16 (April): 207–236.

———, 1977. *One Kind of Freedom: The Economic Consequences of Emancipation.* New York: Cambridge University Press.

Raper, Arthur F., 1933. *The Tragedy of Lynching.* New York: Dover.

Reich, Michael, 1981. *Racial Inequality: A Political-Economic Analysis.* Princeton: Princeton University Press.

Roback, Jennifer, 1986. "The Political Economy of Segregation: The Case of Segregated Streetcars." *Journal of Economic History* 46 (December): 893–917.

———, 1984. "Southern Labor Law in the Jim Crow Era: Exploitative or Competitive?" *University of Chicago Law Review* 51 (Fall): 1161–1192.

Shlomowitz, Ralph, 1984. " 'Bound' or 'Free'? Black Labor in Cotton and Sugarcane Farming, 1865–1880." *Journal of Southern History* 50 (November): 569–596.

———, 1983. "New and Old Views on the Rural Economy of the Postbellum South: A Review Article." *Australian Economic History Review* 23 (September): 258–275.

———, 1979. "The Origins of Southern Sharecropping." *Agricultural History* 53 (July): 557–575.

Smith, James P., 1984. "Race and Human Capital." *American Economic Review* 74 (September): 685–698.

Suliman, Sirag Eldin Hassan, 1983. "Estimation of Levels and Trends of the U.S. Adult Black Mortality During the Period 1870–1900." Ph.D. diss., University of Pennsylvania.

Tolnay, Stewart E., 1984. "Black Family Formation and Tenancy in the Farm South, 1900." *American Journal of Sociology* 90 (September): 305–325.

———, 1981. "Trends in Total and Marital Fertility for Black Americans, 1886–1899." *Demography* 18 (November): 443–463.

U.S. Bureau of the Census, 1984. *Statistical Abstract: 1985.* Washington D.C.

———, 1975. *Historical Statistics of the United States, Colonial Times to 1970.* Washington D.C.

———, 1943. *Sixteenth Census: 1940. Population. III. The Labor Force: Occupation, Industry, Employment, and Income. Pt. I: United States Summary.* Washington D.C.

———, 1918. *Negro Population, 1790–1915.* Washington D.C.

Vickery, William Edward, 1969. "The Economics of Negro Migration, 1900–1960." Ph.D. diss., University of Chicago.

Whatley, Warren C., 1986. "Tapping the Reserve: The Demand for Black Labor During World War I." Unpublished discussion paper, University of Michigan (March).

White, Walter, 1969. *Rope and Faggot: A Biography of Judge Lynch.* New York: Arno.

Wright, Gavin, 1987. "The Economic Revolution in the American South." *Journal of Economic Perspectives* 1 (Summer): 161–178.

———, 1986. *Old South, New South: Revolutions in the Southern Economy Since the Civil War.* New York: Basic Books.

———, 1982. "The Strange Career of the New Southern Economic History." *Reviews in American History* (December): 164–180.

———, 1981. "Black and White Labor in the Old New South." In *Business in the New South: A Historical Perspective,* ed. Fred Bateman, 35–50. Sewanee, Tenn.: University Press of the University of the South.

JOHN BOUND

RICHARD B. FREEMAN

Chapter 2. Black Economic Progress: Erosion of the Post-1965 Gains in the 1980s?

B EGINNING in the mid-1960s, following the passage of the Civil Rights Act of 1964, the relative income of black workers began to rise sharply. Spurred in part by antibias pressure from the federal government, demand for black and other minority workers increased. The Equal Employment Opportunity (EEO) provisions of the Civil Rights Act made employment discrimination illegal and established the Equal Employment Opportunity Commission (EEOC) to monitor employment provisions (state and local governments were not covered by the federal law until the 1972 amendments). Court interpretations of the law forced employers to eliminate many long-standing employ-ment practices, including various types of employment tests, that had limited opportunities for minorities. Revised Order No. 4 to Execu-tive Order 11246, issued by President Lyndon Johnson, brought pres-sure on government contractors to take "affirmative action" to in-crease employment of blacks, other minorities, and women. While attribution of causality is difficult, there is general agreement that such pressures helped account for the improvement in the incomes of blacks, and particularly for the movement of young educated blacks into the mainstream of the American economy that characterized the period from 1965 to the mid-1970s.[2]

In the 1970s and 1980s the economic and political environments changed markedly. The rate of growth of GNP per capita slowed from 1973 to the mid-1980s. Unemployment rose in 1983 to the highest levels since the Great Depression, and despite a U.S. employment re-covery that was faster than Europe's, real wages advanced only mod-estly, and poverty worsened. On the policy front, the Reagan admin-

We thank Sanders Korenman for his research assistance.

istration took office in 1981 with an approach toward affirmative action that differed markedly from that of previous administrations; it viewed the goal-setting process as bordering on a quota system. The administration went before the U.S. Supreme Court to oppose affirmative action remedies and, in 1985, debated amending Executive Order 11246 to eliminate mandatory requirements, timetables, and statistical measures of compliance. This stance was opposed not only by civil rights groups and the AFL–CIO but also by major business organizations, such as the National Association of Manufacturers and the Business Roundtable.[3] The public statements of major officials like the attorney general, the assistant attorney general in charge of civil rights, and the heads of the EEOC and U.S. Civil Rights Commission made clear that the period of intense pressure for improving black economic status through affirmative action had come to an end.

What has happened to the economic position of blacks in the new environment of the 1970s and 1980s? Have these years eroded the gains that accrued in the period of intense antibias and affirmative action pressure? To what extent, if at all, can any changes in the economic position of blacks be attributed to slackened governmental pressure to employ black workers?

To answer these questions, we examine published data and computer files on the earnings, employment, and education of black and white men from the March Current Population Survey (CPS).[4] Since 1948 the U.S. Bureau of the Census has conducted this survey each month, interviewing between 21,000 and 65,000 households to collect data on the labor force activity of household members. In addition, supplementary questions are asked each March about the money income and work experience of household members during the previous year. (This file is often referred to as the Annual Demographic Supplement.) Summary information from the file has been reported since 1948 in the P-60 series put out by the census and is available as microdata back to 1964.

We find that the relative economic position of black men worsened from the late 1970s through the mid-1980s and attribute this in part to slackened governmental affirmative action and antibias efforts. As the economic and policy changes under study are relatively moderate (compared, say, to the economic collapse of the Great Depression, which had disastrous effects on black incomes, or to the passage of the 1964 Civil Rights Act) and as CPS measures of economic position are subject to considerable year-to-year random fluctuations, our attribution of some of the erosion in the relative economic position of blacks to changes in government policy should be viewed as highly tentative.

As a starting point for analysis, we present in Table 2.1 measures

TABLE 2.1.   *Aggregate Changes in Various Measures of Relative Black (Nonwhite) Male Economic Status*

Measure	1964	1969	1975	1979	1984	1986
1. Black/white median wage and salary income	.59	.67	.73	.72	.69	.72[a]
2. Black/white median wage and salary income year-round full-time workers	.66	.69	.77	.76	.73	.74[a]
3. Black/white median usual weekly earnings	—	.71	.77	.78	.75	.73
4. Proportion of black men working as professionals or managers/proportion of white men working as professionals or managers	.32	.38	.53	.57	.62	.64
5. Employment to population rate, men 20 and over						
Black	77.7	77.5	77.1	68.8	65.6	66.8
White	82.2	81.4	80.7	77.2	74.5	74.2
6. Unemployment rates, men 20 and over						
Black	7.7	3.7	11.7	8.7	13.0	11.7
White	3.1	2.3	6.2	3.6	5.7	5.3
7. Enrollment ratio, college						
18–19 year old black	16.1	23.0	23.2	23.1	21.3	23.3[a]
18–19 year old white	42.9	47.3	38.4	36.4	40.2	40.0[a]

Sources: 1 and 2, U.S. Bureau of the Census, *Current Population Reports,* Series P-60, various editions. 3, 5 and 6, U.S. Bureau of Labor Statistics, *Employment and Earnings,* various editions. 7, U.S. Bureau of the Census, *Current Population Reports,* Series P-20, various editions. 4, U.S. Bureau of Labor Statistics, *Handbook of Labor Statistics* and *Employment and Earnings,* various editions, with technical workers added with professionals for 1984 and 1986 for consistency with earlier data. Because the published data made two changes in this period—moving from reporting nonwhites to blacks and changing definitions of occupations—the figures in the table are spliced together. Specifically, we took the ratio of nonwhite to white percentages in the old professional and managerial categories for 1982 for males and the ratio of black to white percentages in the new executive and professional and technical support categories for 1983 as linking the series (this ratio was 1.24) and multiplied it by the ratios of black to white percentages in the new categories in later years.
    [a] Data are for 1985.

based on published data of the relative economic position of blacks (or nonwhites) from the mid-1970s to the mid-1980s and, for purposes of background comparison, from 1964 to 1979. While we would prefer to restrict our analyses to blacks, in the early years of the CPS survey the census often published information only on nonwhites, which dictates our use of data on nonwhites in some entries in the table. Since most nonwhites are black, the figures for nonwhites are reasonably representative for blacks. Because numerous social scientists have analyzed the period immediately following the Civil Rights Act, we simply note here that, consistent with the earlier studies, the figures in the table show a sharp upward trend in all of the ratios from the mid-1960s through the mid-1970s.[5] We direct the reader's attention to the figures for 1975, 1979, and 1985 or 1986.

Entries 1 and 2 of the table show that after 1975 (or thereabouts) the upward trend in the ratio of nonwhite to white incomes ended, and then dropped from 1975 through 1986. Entry 3 shows a similar pattern in the ratios of median usual weekly earnings of blacks to whites from the Bureau of Labor Statistics' tabulations of March CPS tapes.[6] While CPS income and earnings data show considerable year-to-year variability, with occasional blips that make one leery of reaching conclusions from changes between any two years, the figures certainly suggest the possibility of erosion in the black male relative economic position post-1975.

Entry 4 turns to a measure of occupational attainment, which tends to be more stable and, arguably, a better indicator of permanent economic position than annual incomes or earnings. It records the ratio of the proportion of black men in professional and managerial jobs to the proportion of white men working in those jobs. Ratios greater than one indicate that employed nonwhites have a higher probability of being in that kind of job than employed whites, while ratios less than one indicate the converse. While changes in the definitions of occupational categories in the published data make any conclusions uncertain, the figures suggest continued improvement in the relative position of nonwhites through 1986—a result inconsistent, as we shall see, with our tabulations on the underlying tapes.

Entries 5 and 6 examine employment/population and unemployment rates, respectively. They show that even during the period of rapid black advancement in relative incomes, neither black employment/population nor unemployment rates converged toward the rates for whites. In the 1970s, in fact, black male employment/population ratios fell relative to white male employment/population ratios, due to a greater decline in black than white male labor participation.

Finally, entry 7 compares college enrollment rates of 18–19-year-olds. A significant increase in black enrollments in college relative to white enrollments was one of the hallmarks of the post-1964 period, when colleges and universities recruited blacks, and young blacks, in response, sought to prepare for the improved job market facing them. Here, too, the data show a leveling off in the relative enrollment rates in the late 1970s, followed by a decline into the 1980s.

Overall, the data in Table 2.1 suggest that something was different in the job market for blacks in the late-1970s and 1980s than in the previous decade of rapid relative improvement.

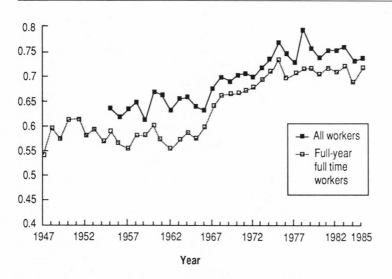

Figure 2.1. Ratio of Nonwhite to White Median Wage and Salary
Incomes, 1947–1985
Source: U.S. Bureau of the Census, *Current Population Reports,* Series P-60, various
editions.

CPS income data of the type recorded in Table 2.1 show considerable
year-to-year jumpiness, sometimes for "technical" reasons owing to
changes in CPS procedures, and sometimes for reasons that remain
unclear.[7] In addition, different CPS series (for instance, those for mean
earnings as opposed to median earnings, or for the income of all workers as opposed to the income of year-round full-time workers) also
sometimes show different patterns of change.

To get a handle on this variability and evaluate the reliability of the
patterns shown in Table 2.1, we have graphed income ratios from the
published data year by year from 1947 to 1985. Figure 2.1 shows the
resultant ratios of nonwhite to white median wage and salary incomes
for all workers and of nonwhite to white median wage and salary
incomes for full-time year-round workers. The former reflect both
relative wages and time worked over the year while the latter are a
better indicator of wage differentials. Both statistics show a similar
pattern over time—one that will be found, with slight variation, in all
of the data examined in this study: a rough stability to modest dip in
the relative position of nonwhites in the late 1970s and 1980s, following the post-1964 rise in income ratios.

We conclude that the picture given in Table 2.1 accurately captures the changes over time in the published data, and we turn next to our more detailed tabulations of the March CPS tapes.

There are three reasons for preferring this analysis to the Table 2.1 analysis of published data. First, the computer tapes allow us to control for the composition of the black and white work forces by holding fixed such factors as age, education, area of residence, and so forth, that can differ between blacks and whites in the published data. Such controls allow us to verify that the observed patterns, magnitude, and timing of changes are not due to changes in the distribution of blacks and whites along these dimensions. Second, the computer files allow us to explore whether alternative measures of income tell a different story of change. From them we can calculate medians, means, and geometric means (which are the subject of concern in log-earnings equations) over exactly the same samples. Third, the tapes allow us to contrast the changes among groups of workers likely to be more or less affected by the economic and policy changes of the period and thus to assess the causality of the changes, at least in part.

Our analysis of the 1964 to 1985 March CPS tapes treats a sample of male workers reporting annual earnings from 1963 to 1984. The sample consists of all black men and a 20 percent sample of white men, giving us from 5,000 to 14,000 individuals depending on the size of the CPS, of whom roughly one-third are black. For each year we estimated log-earnings equations of the standard human capital type, taking the log of annual wage and salary earnings and the log of earnings divided by weeks worked as our dependent variables and various personal demographic factors as controls—education, age, area of residence—in addition to a 0–1 dichotomous variable for race.[8]

Table 2.2 records the resultant estimates for the effect on log earnings of being black. The coefficient estimates in the early years show the decline in racial earnings differences in the period of intense governmental equal opportunity and affirmative action pressure, with differentials of − .23 to − .26 in 1963–1965 dropping to − .02 to − .05 in 1975–1977. The coefficient estimates for the later period show the leveling off and erosion of black economic gains in the 1980s depicted in the published data, with the differentials rising to − .08 to − .10.

To what extent might the patterns in the table be affected by our choice of the log-earnings form and, hence, of the geometric mean as opposed to the arithmetic mean as a measure of differences? To answer this question we have tabulated ratios of black to white median wage and salary incomes, mean wage and salary incomes, and geometric means of the incomes. As can be seen in Figure 2.2, ratios of median, mean, and geometric mean show approximately the same picture of change, with, moreover, the commonly used arithmetic mean evinc-

TABLE 2.2. *Estimated Black–White Differentials in Annual and Weekly Earnings, Males 20–64*

Year	Annual earnings, all workers	Weekly earnings		
			By region	
		All workers	Non-South	South
1963	−.261	−.245	−.111	−.424
1964	−.241	−.234	−.118	−.395
1965	−.231	−.222	−.091	−.385
1966	−.149	−.171	−.039	−.329
1967	−.175	−.179	−.089	−.299
1968	−.143	−.139	−.043	−.268
1969	−.138	−.135	−.047	−.243
1970	−.108	−.111	−.003	−.170
1971	−.084	−.092	−.011	−.188
1972	−.082	−.080	−.024	−.145
1973	−.076	−.081	−.003	−.170
1974	−.074	−.069	.006	−.153
1975	−.021	−.025	.071	−.126
1976	−.045	−.038	.044	−.175
1977	−.049	−.031	.031	−.157
1978	−.051	−.035	.037	−.188
1979	−.057	−.051	.001	−.102
1980	−.059	−.040	−.005	−.075
1981	−.051	−.043	.015	−.131
1982	−.084	−.049	.034	−.127
1983	−.100	−.068	−.006	−.127
1984	−.090	−.074	−.032	−.116

Source: The authors' tabulations are based on CPS Annual March Demographic Files. The dependent variables are ln annual earnings and ln annual earnings/weeks worked. The control variables consist of dummy variables for region, urban status, age, and education. Our region dummy variables were for the four major census regions. Our urban status control was whether or not the person was in a Standard Metropolitan Statistical Area. Our age dummy variables were entered as a single dummy for each year of age. For education we used a spline function with breaks at 8, 12, and 16 years and with separate dummies for 12 and 16 years to allow for "diploma effects."

Note: The standard errors for the "all workers" column are below .015. The standard errors for the columns with region are below .020.

ing the greatest annual variability. This picture suggests to us that the arithmetic mean is, if anything, the least reliable indicator of change in these data, possibly because of the effect of outliers on its value.

Because discrimination has historically been most severe in the South, it is also important to examine black–white income differentials on a regional basis. Accordingly, we divided our sample between the South and the rest of the country and estimated separate regressions for the two areas. Columns 4 and 5 of Table 2.2 present the results of these regressions. Income differentials are shown to have fallen exception-

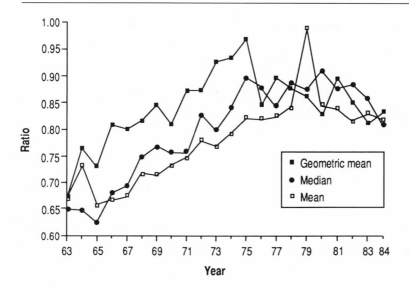

Figure 2.2. Ratio of Black to White Yearly Wage and Salary Income,
1963–1984

ally rapidly from 1965 through the mid-1970s in the South, as one
would expect given greater levels of initial discrimination in that region and the extensive antibias and affirmative action pressure of the
period. Thereafter the ratios for the South leveled off. Outside the South,
income differentials declined from 11 or so log n points until blacks
held a slight advantage in the mid-1970s; then they dropped modestly.

We have also performed a separate analysis for "young workers"—
those aged 20–29. The reason for this is that the economic position of
young workers tends to respond more rapidly to changes in market
conditions than does the position of older workers. Young workers are
more mobile. Their wages are more likely to reflect external than
internal markets and thus are more dependent on general economic
forces than the wages of older workers. If the economic position of
black men eroded in the period under study, we would expect to see
especially marked changes in the relative incomes of younger black
workers. To see if there were such changes, we estimated log earnings
equations for men aged 20–29 using the same education and other
controls used in the Table 2.2 regressions (save, of course, for age). The
results of our calculations are summarized in Figure 2.3, which displays the estimated ratio of black to white earnings for young workers
adjusted for differences in the personal and "human capital" (education, experience) of those workers. As the figure indicates, the break

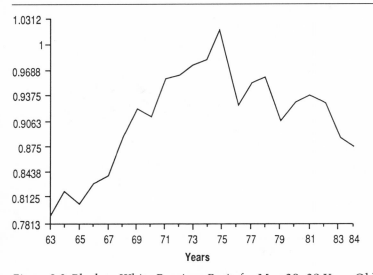

Figure 2.3. Black to White Earnings Ratio for Men 20–29 Years Old,
Adjusted for Personal and "Human Capital" Factors, 1963–1984
Source: Based on regression analysis using the same model as Table 2.2 but limited to
20–29-year-old men. Ratios calculated by taking the exponent of the estimated
regression coefficient for black men.

in the upward trend and ensuing drop in the relative position of black
workers is, indeed, especially marked for the young, with income ratios falling from 1.02 in the peak year 1975 to .82 in 1984.

Figure 2.4 turns from comparisons of incomes to comparisons of
occupational position, as measured by the ratio of the percentage of
blacks to the percentage of whites working in professional and managerial occupations. As suggested earlier, occupational position has
advantages over income as an indicator of economic well-being because a person's occupation is more likely to characterize permanent
economic status than a single year's income. In the human capital
model, in fact, income is a potentially poor measure of economic position because lower incomes may reflect not so much a bad position
in the market as investments in human capital that will pay off with
higher incomes in the future. Such an interpretation cannot be made
for movement into the professional and managerial occupations shown
in Figure 2.4, as it is the entry into those occupations itself that is the
outcome of human capital investments in education. Another advantage is that occupational distributions rarely show the unstable year-
to-year variation often found in income figures.

The figure records both "raw" ratios and ratios "corrected" for differences in schooling via a simple standardization procedure. Specif-

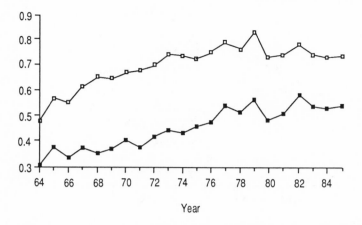

Figure 2.4. Ratio of the Percentage of Blacks Working as Professionals and Managers to the Percentage of Whites Working in Those Occupations, 1964–1985. Legend: ■ Raw ratios, + Ratios adjusted for educational attainment.

ically, we calculated in each year the proportion of blacks who would be in professional and managerial occupations if blacks had the same educational distribution as whites but had the black probability of holding those kinds of jobs for the specified education.[9] The gap between the two lines represents the continued black disadvantage in educational attainment in the United States. Perhaps because education and training are so important in movement into professional and managerial jobs, the line giving the ratios unadjusted for education shows a delayed pattern of change compared to that given by income ratios: gains come mainly in the 1970s and continue into the 1980s. The ratios adjusted for education, in contrast, follow basically the same time pattern as the income ratios, with the rise in the post-1964 period arrested somewhere in the late 1970s to early 1980s. Note, however, that this pattern is not consistent with the pattern of change shown in entry 4 of Table 2.1, which is based on published figures. The published figures show a continued relative increase in the proportion of nonwhites (after 1983, black men) into professional and managerial jobs in the 1980s, rather than the rough stability seen in Figure 2.4. While we put greater faith in Figure 2.4, the changes in categories after 1983 make it impossible to reach an unequivocal conclusion about changes in relative occupational status after that year.

Changes in the relative income of a population of the type shown

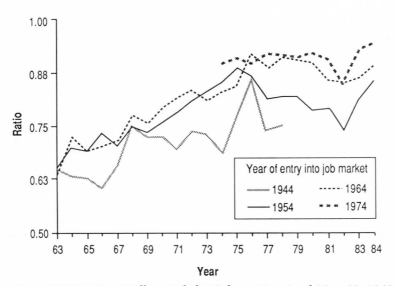

Figure 2.5. Earnings Differentials by Cohort, Men Aged 20 to 29, 1963–1984

in Table 2.2 and Figure 2.3 can occur in several ways. New cohorts can enter the job market at different relative incomes from older retiring cohorts. The relative income of existing cohorts can also change over time, increasing or decreasing as the cohort ages. While the CPS is not a longitudinal survey that follows individuals as they progress in their careers, it is possible to analyze the economic progress or retrogression of "synthetic cohorts"—different persons in the same age group—in the CPS by comparing persons aged n at time t with persons aged $n + d$ at time $t + d$. Such an examination is useful not only for showing the way aggregate income ratios have changed but also for testing competing explanations of those changes. Accordingly, we have analyzed the relative incomes of several cohorts over the decades of the 1960s and 1970s and into the 1980s. For persons aged 20 to 29 when they "entered" the labor market, we have estimated the same regression model as in Table 2.2, year by year as they age, yielding a picture of how initial economic differentials changed over time.

Figure 2.5 summarizes the results of our analysis. Each of the lines records our estimates of black–white income differences for persons in the same synthetic cohort dated by the year in which they were 20 to 29; that is, the 1964 point for the 1964 line shows the income ratio for persons 20 to 29 in that year, and the 1974 point for the same line shows the income ratio for that cohort a decade later (i.e., for persons aged 30 to 39 in 1974), and so on. The figure distinguishes among four cohorts: the 20–29-year-olds who entered the job market in 1944 (and were 40 to 49 in the first year of our graph); those who entered the job market in 1954 (30 to 39 in the first year of our graph); those who entered the job market in 1964; and those who entered the job market in 1974.

By comparing the pattern of change in income ratios as cohorts age with the pattern of change in income ratios for new entrants shown in Figure 2.2, we can assess potential explanations of the observed increase and erosion of black to white income ratios. Consider first the "better schooling" explanation of Smith and Welch (1977): if black economic progress were strictly due to improvements in the quality of schooling, as they suggest, we would anticipate finding higher income ratios for newer cohorts, but no changes in income ratios for a given cohort over time. If, on the other hand, rising income ratios for blacks were due to the youths taking jobs with high initial pay at the expense of on-the-job training, which raises incomes later on, as Lazear (1979) has suggested, one would expect to see synthetic-cohort income ratios falling for the groups enjoying significant gains and rising for the groups that suffered relative erosion of gains when they entered the job market. Finally, if changes in demand for black workers owing to economic and policy developments dominate the market, one would expect income ratios to rise for cohorts when new entrants do better and to fall when new entrants do worse.

It is the latter pattern that stands out in Figure 2.5. During the post-1964 to mid- or late-1970 period when black to white income ratios rose for new entrants, according to Figure 2.2 the relative incomes of even the oldest cohort of black workers rose significantly, whereas during the latter part of the 1970s to the early 1980s, when our data show that new entrants suffered relative economic losses, the relative incomes of older cohorts either leveled off or dipped as they aged.

To illustrate the concordance between changes in the relative incomes for new entrants and for older cohorts as they age, we compare in Table 2.3 the percentage point changes in black to white income ratios for new entrants and cohorts over time. Because of the random variation in the data, we take averages of income ratios for the cohorts for four-year periods, rather than single-year numbers. Thus, the .14 change for new entrants in the table's first entry represents the difference in income ratio for persons aged 20 to 29 in the period 1963–1966 and the income ratio for persons aged 20–29 in 1969–1973. Similarly, the figures for the cohorts represent changes in averages of income ratios over the specified years—for instance, the .13 in the second entry represents the difference in the average income ratio of persons aged 20 to 29 in 1944 (and thus 40 to 49 in 1964) between 1963–1966 and 1969–1972.

As can be seen in the numbers, when the relative incomes of new entrants increased especially rapidly from 1963–1966 to 1969–1972,

TABLE 2.3.   *The Relation Between the Changed Relative Incomes of New Entrants and the Progress of Cohorts, 1974–1984 Compared to 1964–1974*

	1963–66 to 1969–72	1969–72 to 1974–77	1974–77 to 1981–84
Change in relative income of new entrants, 20–29[a] (averaged over period)	.14	.07	− .08
Changes in relative incomes of cohorts, as they age[b]			
20–29 cohort in 1944	.13	.06	—
20–29 cohort in 1954	.11	.10	− .07
20–29 cohort in 1964	.14	.10	.00
20–29 cohort in 1974	—	—	.00

Source: Tabulated from sample taken from CPS March tapes.

[a] Average income ratio 20–29-year-olds in end period minus ratio in earlier period.

[b] Average income ratio of relative cohort in end period minus average ratio in beginning period.

the relative incomes of all cohorts also increased as they aged, whereas when the relative incomes of new entrants fell from 1974–1977 to 1981–1984, the income ratios for older cohorts either stabilized or dropped. The period from 1969–1972 to 1974–1977 shows income ratios rising for both new entrants and cohorts, but less rapidly than in the period immediately following the Civil Rights Act.

This pattern of cohort income change is, we argue, inconsistent with the "improved schooling" and "less on-the-job training" explanations of observed changes. Hence, we reject both of those hypotheses as plausible explanations for observed changes and focus on explanations that concentrate on shifts in demand for black workers.

The first demand-side explanation for the erosion in black to white income ratios of the late 1970s and 1980s is that the worsened state of the economy—the sluggish economic growth, high unemployment, and small real wage increases noted earlier—had a greater negative impact on black workers than on white workers. The second possible explanation is that the demand for black workers fell relative to that for whites because of the weakened affirmative action pressure emanating from the federal government. To examine these two possible explanations we have regressed the log of black to white income ratios on an indicator of the state of the economy, the log of real GNP, and a set of trend variables designed to test whether the timing of erosions and gains is associated with changes in policy. When our data begins in 1950, we include the following trend variables: a general trend term

(1 in 1950, 2 in 1951, and so on) to reflect the influence of trends over the entire post–World War II period; a trend beginning in 1965 (0 in all preceding years, 1 in 1965, 2 in 1966, and so on), to pick up the impact of the Civil Rights Act; a trend beginning in 1969 (1 in 1969, 2 in 1970, and so on) and a trend beginning in 1975, to reflect possible changes in the relative economic position of blacks prior to the weakened antibias pressure of the Reagan administration; and a trend beginning in 1981, to reflect the policies of the administration. When our data begins in 1964 we exclude the general trend term.

The regressions are set up so that the key question is which of the trend terms capture the slackened growth and retrogression of the relative economic position of blacks. If the trend term for 1975 picks up the bulk of the erosion, we would conclude that the observed changes are likely to be the result of factors other than weakened federal affirmative action pressures, as there was no weakening in federal pressures in late seventies. If, in contrast, the 1981 trend is substantially negative, then it is reasonable to look for the cause of the erosion in the weakened affirmative action policies of the Reagan administration. While we do not regard the timing of changes as strong evidence for a change-in-policy explanation of the observed erosion, it is a first step toward assessing causality.

Table 2.4 presents our estimated regression coefficients on log GNP and our time-trend variables, derived from a simple autoregressive time-series regression with various measures of black–white economic differences as our dependent variable.[10] Because the trend variables are entered additively, however, it is incorrect to read the actual trend from the regression coefficient for a given period; to determine the actual trend one must sum trend coefficients, as is done in the bottom entries of the table.

The regressions in Table 2.4 show, first, that GNP has had a poorly estimated and inconsistent impact on the income ratios for all men, with coefficients less than their standard errors. This rules out an explanation of the change in their economic position as resulting from broad economic expansion or contraction. Turning to the estimated trends, those in columns 1–2 for income ratios document the rise in black to white income ratios following 1964 and show the ratios continuing upward, although at decreasing rates, through 1980; those in column 3 for earning ratio of men 20 to 29 show a rise until 1974. The relative occupational attainment regression, in contrast, shows an acceleration in the relative proportion of blacks working in professional and managerial occupations from 1970 through 1980, which we have attributed to the delayed entry of blacks into these areas owing to the need to obtain the relevant education and training. Thereafter there

TABLE 2.4. *Estimates of the Effect of GNP and Time Periods on Relative Black Male Economic Position, 1950–1984*

	Ratio of median income from published source, 1950–84	Log annual earnings differential from regressions, 1964–84	Log annual earnings differential men 20–29 from our regressions, 1964–84	Ratio of proportions working as professionals and managers, 1964–84
Constant	1.51	−.55	−.42	.98
Time	.15	—	—	—
	(.51)			
T64	4.58	3.03	2.03	.96
	(.64)	(1.21)	(1.44)	(1.37)
T69	−3.00	−1.06	.15	.81
	(.88)	(.97)	(1.08)	(.97)
T75	−1.01	1.45	−3.61	−.11
	(.62)	(.62)	(.65)	(.63)
T81	−.80	1.43	.55	−1.87
	(.89)	(.92)	(1.07)	(1.03)
Log GNP	−18.79	2.22	1.73	−8.40
	(16.38)	(25.09)	(30.88)	(28.90)
R-squared	.93	.95	.82	.90
Estimated trends:				
pre-1964	.15	—	—	—
1964–1969	4.73	3.03	2.03	.96
1970–1974	1.73	1.97	2.18	1.77
1975–1980	.72	.52	−1.43	1.66
1981–1984	−.08	−.91	−.88	−.21

Source: Based on regressions with a single period autoregressive error structure [AR(1)], with autoregressive parameters of −.01 (column 1); −.03 (column 2); −.43 (column 3); −.34 (column 4).
  Note: All regression coefficients were multiplied by 100.

is a turnaround, with the ratio of black men to white men working in professional and managerial jobs falling.

How is one to interpret these time patterns? On the one hand, they show that the rate of increase in black to white earnings ratios, but not in black to white occupational penetration ratios, began to fall *before* the 1980s' change in policy. On the other hand, in three of four calculations the decline became markedly worse in the 1980s. As one might suspect from inspecting the earlier graphs, one is left with a mixed picture, which in our view is best interpreted as indicating that the policy changes of the 1980s contributed to the erosions of black to white income gains, but were far from being the sole factor behind it.

To reach a stronger conclusion about the impact of policy on the observed patterns of change requires additional information, such as on employment in companies subject to and not subject to affirmative action. During the period of intense affirmative action pressure, Leonard (1985) found, employment of blacks grew more rapidly in companies with affirmative action plans than in other companies. If the weakened affirmative action policy contributed to the 1980s' erosion of gains, one would expect this pattern to have diminished in the 1980s. While our data do not permit such a conclusion, Leonard's analysis of company data shows that companies covered by affirmative action no longer had exceptionally rapid growth of black employment in the 1980s.

In sum, while our analysis of published CPS data and of the March CPS tapes has not yielded definitive conclusions about the magnitude or causality of the changing pattern of black to white income and occupational penetration ratios, it does demonstrate fairly conclusively that the epoch of rapid black relative economic advance ended sometime in the late 1970s and early 1980s and that some of the earlier gains eroded in the 1980s. The erosion has been, we stress, relatively moderate—several points down—compared to the tremendous improvements in income ratios of the earlier period. Still, the leveling and decline in income ratios is found in a sufficiently wide body of data to merit attention from analysts and policy makers.

Notes

1. A review of court decisions is given in Freeman, 1977, pp. 124–125.
2. For a valuable review of the diverse studies, see Brown, 1982.
3. See Castillo, 1985, for a summary of the debate in the administration.
4. While women are an increasingly important part of the labor force, a careful analysis of their relative economic position would require consideration of too many additional factors, such as childbearing and the changing composition of families, to fit into this analysis.
5. See, for example, Freeman, 1973, 1981; Smith and Welch, 1977; Vroman, 1974; Butler and Heckman, 1977; Fairly, 1984; Burnstein, 1985; Brown, 1984.
6. Note that the 1979–1985 figures cover a period in which the census changed its definitions of occupations (1983), making definitive comparisons difficult.
7. The biggest change in the CPS procedure for estimating earnings occurred in 1975 when the U.S. Bureau of the Census changed the "hot deck" procedure for imputing incomes for those who did not report their incomes. See U.S. Bureau of the Census, 1976. In addition, the census made slight changes in various other years, such as in

the ordering of questions and their exact wording. As can be seen in Table 2.2, there were also changes in sample sizes.

8. Because of our sampling procedure, we are giving greater weight to blacks in estimating the effect of control variables on earnings than one would in a random sample. This will bias slightly our estimates of the coefficients on being black.

9. In particular, we calculated the ratio of black men with a given level of education working as professionals or managers to the number of black men with that level of education and formed a weighted average, using the white educational distribution as weights. The numbers in the figure reflect the ratio of the standardized black rate of employment to the actual white rate of employment.

10. To deal with the change in incomes owing to the change in hot deck procedures in 1975, we experimented with various dummy variables and trend variables beginning in 1975. The regressions with these controls did not differ systematically from those with no such controls.

References

Ashenfelter, Orley, and James Heckman, 1976. "Measuring the Effect of an Antidiscrimination Program." In *Evaluating the Labor Market Effects of Social Programs*, eds. Orley Ashenfelter and James Blum, 46–84. Princeton: Princeton University Press.

Brown, Charles, 1984. "Black/White Earnings Ratios Since the Civil Rights Act of 1964: The Importance of Labor Market Dropouts." *Quarterly Journal of Economics* 99(1): 33–44.

———, 1982. "The Federal Attack on Labor Market Discrimination: The Mouse That Roared?" *Research in Labor Economics* 5: 33–68.

Burnstein, Paul, 1985. *Discrimination, Jobs, and Politics*. Chicago: University of Chicago Press.

Butler, Richard, and James J. Heckman, 1977. "The Government's Impact on the Labor Market Status of Black Americans: A Critical Review." In *Equal Rights and Industrial Relations*, eds. Leonard J. Hausman et al. 235–281. Madison: Industrial Relations Research Association.

Castillo, Alida, 1985. "Should the Executive Order Mandating Affirmative Action be Amended?" Harvard University. Unpublished paper, John F. Kennedy School of Government.

Darity, William, and Samuel L. Myers, 1980. "Changes in Black–White Income Inequality, 1968–78: A Decade of Progress?" *Review of Black Political Economy* 10 (4): 365–379.

Farley, Reynolds, 1984. *Blacks and Whites: Narrowing the Gap?* Cambridge: Harvard University Press.

Freeman, Richard B., 1981. "Black Economic Progress After 1964: Who Has Gained and Why?" In *Studies in Labor Markets*, ed. Sherwin Rosen, 247–294. Chicago: University of Chicago Press/National Bureau of Economic Research.

———, 1977. *Black Elite*. New York: McGraw-Hill.

———, 1973. "Changes in the Labor Market for Black Americans 1948–72." *Brookings Papers on Economic Activity*. Brookings: Washington, D.C. (Summer), 67–131.

Ginsburg, Alan, and Wayne Vroman, 1976. "Black Men's Relative Earnings in Major SMSA's: 1957–72." Unpublished paper presented at the September meeting of the Econometric Society.

Goldstein, Morris, and Robert S. Smith, 1976. "The Estimated Impact of the Antidiscrimination Program Aimed at Federal Contractors." *Industrial and Labor Relations Review* 29 (4): 523–543.

Heckman, James J., and Kenneth I. Wolpin, 1976. "Does the Contract Compliance Program Work? An Analysis of Chicago Data." *Industrial and Labor Relations Review* 29 (4): 544–564.

Johnson, George, and Finis Welch, 1976. "The Labor Market Implications of an Econ-omy-wide Affirmative Action Program." *Industrial and Labor Relations Review* 29 (4): 508–522.

Lazear, Edward, 1979. "The Narrowing of Black–White Wage Differentials is Illusory." *American Economic Review* 69 (4): 553–564.

Leonard, Jonathan, 1985a. "The Effectiveness of Equal Employment Law and Affirma-tive Action Regulation." Unpublished paper prepared for Congressional Oversight Hearings on Affirmative Action, University of California, Berkeley.

———, 1985b. "What Promises Are Worth: The Impact of Affirmative Action Goals." *Journal of Human Resources* 20 (1): 3–20.

———, 1984a. "The Impact of Affirmative Action on Employment." *Journal of Labor Economics* 2 (4): 439–463.

———, 1984b. "Employment and Occupational Advance under Affirmative Action." *Review of Economics and Statistics* 66 (3): 377–385.

Raisian, John, and Elaine Donovan, 1980. "Patterns of Real Wage Growth, 1967–77: Who Has Prospered?" U.S. Bureau of Labor Statistics, Office of Research and Eval-uation Working Paper No. 104 (November).

Smith, James P., and Finis Welch, 1977. "Black–White Wage Ratios: 1960–70." *Amer-ican Economic Review* 67 (3): 323–338.

U.S. Bureau of the Census, various years. *Current Population Reports,* Consumer In-come Series P-60. Washington, D.C.

Vroman, Wayne, 1974. "Changes in Black Workers' Relative Earnings: Evidence from the 1960's." In *Patterns of Racial Discrimination,* vol 2, eds. George M. von Fur-stenberg, Ann R. Horowitz, and Bennet Harrison, 167–196. Lexington: Lexington Books.

JAMES J. HECKMAN

Chapter 3. The Impact of Government on the Economic Status of Black Americans

T HE MODERN history of federal activity aimed at improving the economic status of blacks begins in the optimistic era of the Kennedy–Johnson administration. The War on Poverty, affirmative action programs, and major civil rights legislation were launched during that period. The main features of the civil rights activity were:

1. The 1964 Civil Rights Act and related legislation banned discrimination in employment, housing, and voting. "Equal treatment of equals" became embodied in the law, and voting rights were assured.

2. "Affirmative action" programs, which encouraged firms to employ minority workers, were begun—initially among larger firms and federal contractors. This policy was instituted in recognition of the difficulty blacks would encounter in overcoming historical discrimination patterns.

Coincident with this activity was a commitment to a War on Poverty that had two main thrusts:

1. Efforts were made to improve the skills of poor blacks (and other poor people) through (a) expansion of manpower training programs and (b) direct intervention in ghetto schools via busing, Head Start programs, and the like.

2. Many programs, designed to transfer income to the less fortunate, were introduced or expanded. By virtue of their more lowly position in the distribution of income, blacks were disproportionately represented in these programs. The mix of social spending shifted from

This chapter extends the 28th annual Abbot Memorial Lecture given at Colorado College in Colorado Springs, Colorado, on April 17, 1985. Norman Bradburn, William Darity, Reynolds Farley, Joe Hotz, Jim Smith, Jim Walker, and William Wilson provided useful comments. This research was supported by NSF 84-11242.

training to transfers after initial dissatisfaction with the results of training programs.

Many social scientists proclaimed success for the Kennedy–Johnson policies. At first glance, the evidence seemed clear. Although aggregate parity had not been achieved, the social statistics seemed to indicate that the new programs were off to a good start. Consider, for example, Panel A of Figure 3.1. The three curves placed on the same diagram trace out, respectively, the ratio of the median income of black males, of white females, and of black females, to white male median income for full-time workers. The uppermost curve reveals near stability in the black male income/white male income ratio pre-1965—1965 was the date when much of the civil rights legislation went into effect— and a sharp upward jump after 1965. The lowest curve in that figure— for black females—tells a similar story, as do relative trends in median incomes of all persons, irrespective of their work status. (See Figure 3.2.)

Table 3.1 demonstrates a significant breakthrough in the occupational position of employed blacks. The proportion of the black work force in the professional category expanded greatly. Measures of occupational similarity between blacks and whites show substantial and unprecedented improvement in the period 1960–1970.

Even more dramatic was the breakthrough in black employment in certain traditionally segregated industries. Figure 3.3 displays the share of total employment held by white males, white females, black males, and black females in the South Carolina textile industry over the period 1910–1980. Total employment in the textile industry, the largest industrial employer in the state, continued to expand until the late sixties, and skill requirements are low. There was a large black population in the state throughout this period, both relatively and absolutely, and many blacks were qualified to perform low-skill textile jobs. (See Heckman and Payner, 1989).

The topmost curve or line in Figure 3.3 indicates the share of total employment held by white males in that period. The second line from the top displays the share of total employment held by white females. The bottom line presents the share of black females, and the line just above it shows the share of black males.

The share of white males is roughly constant at 60 percent. Through two world wars, the Korean War, the 1920s boom, and the Great Depression the proportion of blacks in the industry is low and stable. The black female share is virtually zero. For black men the share of employment is less than 10 percent despite the fact that the black share in the total population is closer to 40 percent.

Panel A: Median income as a percentage of the median income of white men

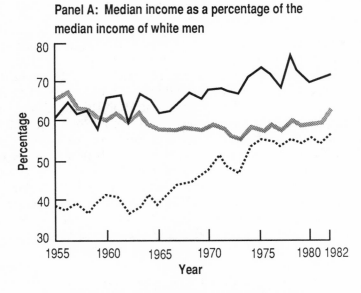

Panel B: Gap in median income separating a group from white men

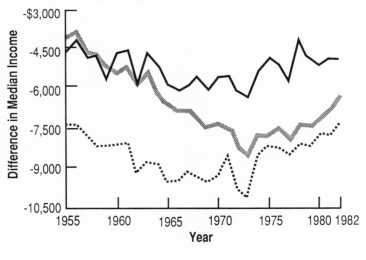

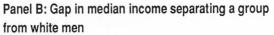

—— Black men　▬▬ White women　······ Black women

Figure 3.1. Median Income of Black Men, Black Women, and White Women as a Percentage of That of White Men, and Gaps in Median Income, for Full-Time, Year-Round Workers, 1955–1982 (Constant 1979 Dollars);

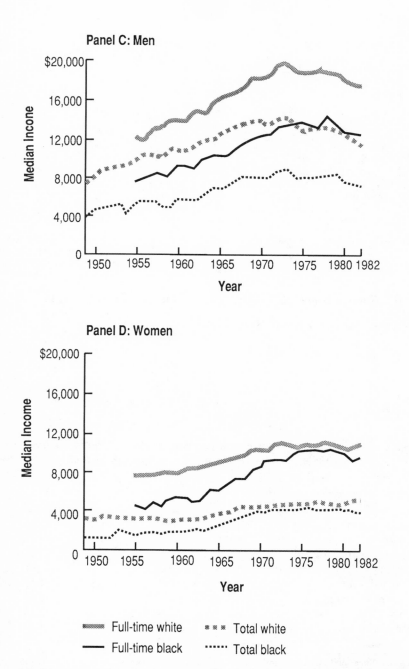

Median Income (Constant 1979 Dollars) of Total Income Recipients, 1949–1982, and of Full-Time, Year-Round Workers, 1955–1982, by Race and Sex
Source: U.S. Bureau of the Census, *Current Population Reports,* Series P-60.

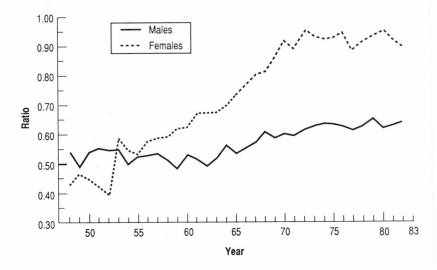

Figure 3.2. Ratio of Nonwhite to White Median Incomes for the United States, 1948–1982
Source: Current Population Reports, Series P-60.

TABLE 3.1. *Percentage of Employed Black Males (Fourteen Years Old and Over) in Major Occupations in 1940, 1950, 1960, and 1970*

Occupation	1940	1950	1960	1970
Professional and technical workers	1.8	2.1	4.6	7.0
Proprietors, managers and officials	1.3	2.2	1.9	3.0
Clerical, sales, etc.	2.0	4.3	6.8	10.2
Craftsmen, foremen, etc.	4.5	7.8	10.7	15.2
Operatives	12.7	21.3	26.6	29.4
Service workers	37.1	38.4	38.1	38.4
Farm workers	41.0	24.0	12.3	4.4

Sources: U.S. Bureau of the Census, Census of the Population: 1940, Characteristics of the Nonwhite Population by Race, Table 8; Census of the Population: 1950, vol. 4, Special Reports, Nonwhite Poulation by Race, Table 9; Census of the Population: 1960, Subject Reports, Nonwhite Population by Race, Final Report PC(2)-1C, Table 32; Census of the Population: 1970, Subject Reports, Final Report PC(2)-1B, Negro Population, Table 7.

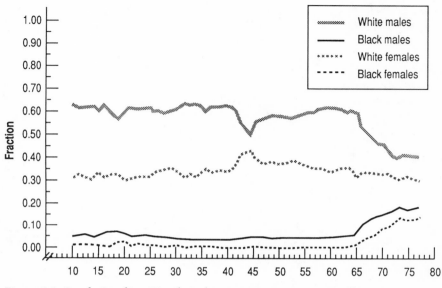

Figure 3.3. South Carolina Textile Industry State Aggregate Employment
Shares, 1910–1977
Source: Heckman and Payner, 1989.

In the post-1965 Vietnam era, textile plants were natural targets of
federal contract compliance programs that instituted affirmative action programs and forbade discriminatory practices by federal contractors. Failure to comply could lead to loss of contracts. Sales to the
federal government in the form of materials for uniforms and the like
were sizable. (The total volume of sales to the government by South
Carolina firms increased from $20 million in 1965 to roughly $120
million in 1966 as the Vietnam build-up began, although the latter
figure was still less than 5 percent of the total sales of the South
Carolina industry.) In many counties of the state, textile firms were
the principal industrial employers and visible targets for federal civil
rights activity. Hearings on discrimination in the textile industry were
instituted by the Equal Employment Opportunity Commission in 1966–
1967. The share of black employment—and the level—increased dramatically after 1965. By 1970, the industry was roughly 30 percent
black; before 1965 it was less than 10 percent black. Penetration rates
for blacks rose in other segregated industries, the apparel industry, for
example.

As black political power rose, measured by voter registration rolls
in the South and elsewhere, so did black employment in government
(see Table 3.2).[1] Such evidence has led many scholars of American race

TABLE 3.2. *Distribution of Labor Force by Sector (percentages)*

	1950	1960	1970	1980
Black Males				
Agriculture	21.0	12.0	5.8	2.8
Private—nonagriculture	70.9	76.1	75.8	74.7
Government	8.1	11.9	18.4	22.5
White Males				
Agriculture	13.5	7.9	5.1	4.3
Private—nonagriculture	77.9	81.6	81.3	82.1
Government	8.6	10.5	13.6	13.5

Source: Census of Population, 1940–1980 as cited in U.S. Civil Rights Clearinghouse Publication, October 1986, pp. 175–176.

relations to declare the success of the Kennedy–Johnson policies. Richard Freeman of Harvard wrote in 1973, "While black–white differences have not disappeared, the convergence in economic position [of blacks] . . . suggests a virtual collapse in traditional discriminatory patterns" (Freeman 1973, 67).

He continues in the same article:

Much of the improvement in black economic position that took place in the late 60's appears to be the result of governmental and related antidiscriminatory activity associated with the 1964 Civil Rights Act. . . . More education for blacks and the general boom of the period cannot account for the sharp increase in relative incomes and occupational position of blacks after 1964. (Freeman 1973, 119)

Writing in *Commentary* magazine in the same year—1973—Benjamin Wattenberg and Richard Scammon described the success of the Kennedy–Johnson social program:

A better deal has been given to the poor and black to the point where many of them are now in the middle class just as the Presidential pledges and legislation promised. . . . To be sure, we cannot say absolutely that the legislation was *totally* responsible for the progress made but we can say absolutely that it was crucial. Liberalism worked. (Wattenberg and Scammon 1973)

From the perspective of 1989 these claims seem exaggerated to some and absurd to others. In an influential book that has been described as the "Bible of the second Reagan administration," conservative author Charles Murray writes in 1984:

As the Sturm und Drang of the 1960's faded and we settled into the 1970's, the realization gradually spread that things were getting worse, not better, for blacks and poor people in this country . . . the inner cities were more violent

and ravaged than ever before . . . it was difficult to take much satisfaction in
the legal edifice of black rights when teenage unemployment was approaching
40 percent. (Murray 1984, 145)

Elsewhere in his monograph he writes

If an impartial observer from another country were shown the statistics on
the black lower class from 1950 to 1980 but given no information about the
contemporaneous changes in society or public policy, the observer would infer
that racial discrimination against the black poor increased dramatically during
the late 1960's and 1970's (Murray 1984, 221). The consequences of [af-
firmative action] were disastrous . . . for poor blacks especially. (Murray 1984,
223)

Summarizing his study, he recommends that "My proposal . . . is to
repeal every bit of legislation and reverse every court decision . . . [so
that] we are back on the track left in 1965" (Murray 1984, 223). In his
work, Murray cites evidence of the failure of schooling and training
programs and warns that there are incentives to fail built into many
social programs because they require a person to be poor in order to
qualify for benefits.

Murray's assessment of the position of poor blacks—if not his policy
conclusions—is shared by such liberal black scholars as William Wilson, who writes that "Since 1970, both poor whites and nonwhites
have evidenced very little progress in their elevation from the ranks of
the underclass" (Wilson 1980, 154). Wilson describes the black community as polarized, with a prospering upper class and an immiserated
lower class.[2]

Considerable evidence supports a less optimistic view of black economic progress over the last twenty years. Panel B of Figure 3.1 reveals
that the *absolute difference* in income for all minority groups taken
with respect to white males and measured in inflation constant dollars
widened in the 1960s. The gap remains sizable as of 1989. Panels C
and D of Figure 3.1 reveal that while black incomes rose, white incomes rose as well and real income differences increased after 1965.

Empirical social scientists have focused on income and wage *ratios*
and not *differences* in real income in making comparisons between
blacks and whites.[3] This focus is partly a consequence of the widespread influence of certain demand-side oriented economic theories
of discrimination (largely empirically discredited) that focus on *relative* wage costs of workers of different race groups as faced by employers. Other theories, such as those that focus on educational and training decisions of workers, note the importance of wage *differences* in
determining such decisions (assuming that some portion of training
costs is not directly proportional to pretraining skill levels).

TABLE 3.3. *Median Income of Black and White Families (in Constant 1979 Dollars), 1959 and 1982*

	White families	Black families	Racial gap in income	Black income as % of white
1959	$14,301	$ 7,587	$6,714	53.1%
1982	$18,502	$10,277	8,275	55.3%
Change in income	$ 4,201	$ 2,640		
Average annual rate of change	+ 1.1%	+ 1.3%		

Sources: U.S. Bureau of the Census, Census of Population: 1960, PC(2)-1C, Table 14; Current Population Reports, Series P-60, no. 140, Tables 2 and A-1.

Panels C and D of Figure 3.1 reveal that sizable gains in black real income occurred in the 1950s when relative black status did not change. They also reveal that sizable gains in relative black status occurred in the mid-1970s when real incomes stagnated for both blacks and whites. In the late 1960s, black income rose relative to white income while the gap in real incomes widened. Whites could buy even more goods than blacks *after* the civil rights "revolution" than they could before it.

Developments since the mid-seventies have tempered the enthusiasm of initially optimistic scholars. Bound and Freeman (1987) note that the relative economic status of blacks has stagnated in the last decade for most groups of black workers. College enrollment rates for blacks—an index of optimism about future labor market prospects—rose dramatically after 1965, peaked out in the mid-seventies, and began to decline thereafter. (The cause of the decline may have as much to do with educational financing problems as with black expectations about their labor market prospects.) Black unemployment rates in the 1980s are at the same ratio to white unemployment rates as they were in the fifties. For black teenage males the ratio *increased* in the eighties.

There are other signs that all is not well in the black community. Table 3.3 shows that the real income gap between black and white families has grown in absolute terms since 1959; the ratio has barely changed. This phenomenon arises in part from the growth of female headship among black families coupled with the near constancy of real incomes in black female households. Although the percentage of blacks living in poverty has greatly decreased since 1959, a substantial portion of this decline is due to increased cash transfers and not to the growth of employment income. As transfer programs began to be cut back in the Carter administration in 1977, the median family income began to decrease (see Figure 3.4).

Figure 3.5 charts the growth over time in the labor force dropout

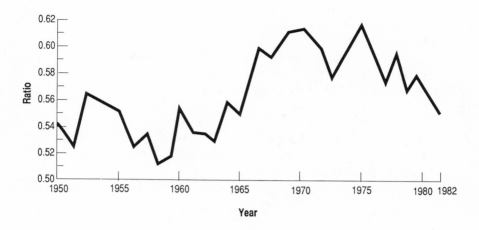

Figure 3.4. Ratio of Black to White Family Median Incomes, 1950–1982
Source: Current Population Reports, Series P-60.

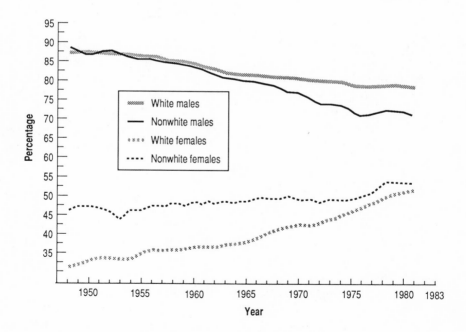

Figure 3.5. U.S. Labor Force Participation Rates, 1948–1982
Source: Current Population Reports, Series P-60.

rate—those not looking for work or at work—among prime-age males 25–54. This age group has traditionally had a virtually 100 percent labor force participation rate. For both race groups, the dropout rate has grown, but the rate of growth has been much more rapid for blacks. By 1982, fully 12 percent of prime-age black males in the civilian population were unattached to the work force. The dropout phenomenon has been much more important for blacks than whites.

A complete accounting of the status of blacks must reckon with this phenomenon. Any recent history of black progress that focuses only on the improvement of demand conditions in the labor market for blacks fails to account for the growth in black dropout rates. Not only is this dropout phenomenon a potential sign of distress in the black community, but it also points out an important problem that may arise in comparing the earnings and occupational positions of blacks and whites. Earnings and occupation data are only collected for labor force participants. More precisely, the published wage and salary data that underlie Figure 3.1 count only those persons employed in one year who were also employed in March of the following year. As the fraction of blacks in the labor force declines and as more blacks enter the unstable marginal worker category and are excluded from the standard statistics, the available evidence on black status becomes increasingly unreliable.

In making comparisons between black and white incomes and black and white occupational status of the sort presented in Figure 3.1 and Tables 3.1 and 3.2, it is important to notice that these are derived for *workers in the labor force.* By 1982, more than 12 percent of prime-age black males are not in the work force and *do not contribute to the earnings statistics used to measure black progress.* The difficulty with the published statistics cited by Freeman and others is that they exclude such individuals.

This exclusion is in addition to the now widely acknowledged undercount of blacks—especially poor blacks—that has attracted considerable attention in the literature and is the basis for the suit by the city of Detroit against the U.S. Census.[4] There is evidence of an undercount of blacks, especially economically marginal blacks, although later censuses are more likely to interview marginal individuals than are earlier ones.

A substantial portion of the measured relative wage growth of black males may be due to their differential rate of omission from the published statistics. The omitted workers may be the low-wage workers, and the growing rate of omission of blacks relative to whites may lead to an artificial acceleration in the measured rate of black progress. In

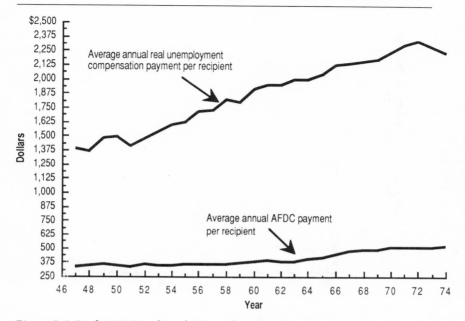

Figure 3.6. Real AFDC and Real Unemployment Compensation Per Capita, 1947–1975
Sources: AFDC Data: Annual Statistical Supplement to the Social Security Bulletin, 1974 and 1975. Unemployment Insurance Data: 1975 Statistical Abstract of the United States and Historical Statistics of the United States, 1970.

short, the evidence of dramatic improvement cited by Freeman and by Wattenberg and Scammon may be flawed.

The decline in black prime-age male labor force activity taken in isolation appears to be anomalous—especially in view of monolithic stories that speak of the decline in the U.S. discriminatory system engineered by Title VII of the Civil Rights Act of 1964. If market opportunities had been expanded for blacks, they surely should have expanded their labor force activity, yet black labor force activity declined, even for prime-age males.

One explanation of this decline that receives strong *a priori* and intuitive support but weak empirical support is that the decline in black male labor force activity is linked to the growth in the benefits from a variety of social transfer programs that made not working a more attractive alternative than working, especially for low-wage individuals.

The War on Poverty stressed job training but it also offered enhanced income transfers. Benefits for all sorts of social programs expanded dramatically in the late sixties and early seventies, as Figures 3.6 and

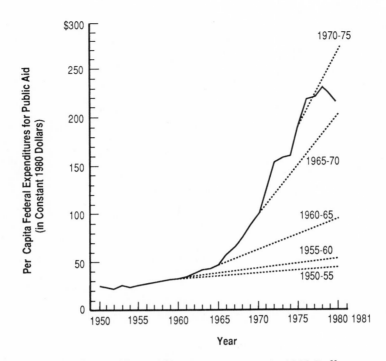

Figure 3.7. Welfare and Unemployment Payments in 1980 Dollars, 1950–1980
Sources: Statistical Abstract of the United States, various years; *Employment and Training Report of the President.*

TABLE 3.4. *Data on the Disability Payment Program*

Year	Number of disability beneficiaries	Change (base 1960)
1960	687,000	
1965	1,739,000	+ 153%
1970	2,665,000	+ 288%
1975	4,352,000	+ 533%

Source: Social Security Bulletin, 44 (November 1981), Table M-3. Figures include dependents.

3.7 and Tables 3.4 and 3.5 reveal. The rate of growth of real transfers per capita increased until the mid-1970s. Some of these programs did discourage labor force activity. Participation in disability payments programs—to individuals who suffer from work-related disabilities—expanded greatly as benefit levels rose and eligibility standards were lowered (see Table 3.4). Participation in these programs was proportionately higher for blacks than whites because of the position of blacks in the income distribution. These programs *probably* have had some effect on discouraging labor market activity, but the precise magnitude of their effect is not known and the evidence is far from clear. (See the

TABLE 3.5. *AFDC Recipients*

Year	No. of families (1,000s)	Total no. of recipients (1,000s)	Number of children (1,000s)	AFDC families as a percentage of all families
1950	651	2,233	1,661	1.66
1951	592	2,041	1,523	1.48
1952	596	1,991	1,495	1.47
1953	547	1,941	1,464	1.34
1954	604	2,173	1,639	1.47
1955	602	2,192	1,661	1.44
1956	615	2,270	1,731	1.43
1957	667	2,497	1,912	1.53
1958	755	2,486	2,181	1.73
1959	776	2,946	2,265	1.75
1960	803	3,073	2,370	1.78
1961	916	3,566	2,753	2.01
1962	932	3,789	2,844	2.01
1963	954	3,930	2,951	2.03
1964	1,012	4,219	3,170	2.13
1965	1,054	4,396	3,316	2.30
1966	1,127	4,666	3,526	2.32
1967	1,297	5,309	3,986	2.64
1968	1,522	6,086	4,555	3.04
1969	1,975	7,313	5,413	3.69
1970	2,552	9,659	7,033	4.95
1971	2,918	10,651	7,707	5.62
1972	3,122	11,064	7,983	5.86
1973	3,156	10,815	7,813	5.80
1974	3,323	11,022	7,901	6.04
1975	3,566	11,401	8,105	6.40
1976	3,585	11,203	7,909	6.37
1977	3,547	10,780	7,572	6.25
1978	3,488	10,349	7,226	6.10
1979	3,560	10,379	7,207	6.16
1980	3,841	11,102	7,600	6.57

Source: For 1950–70, *HSUS* H346-367; for 1971–80, *SAUS-81*, Table 559, and comparable tables in earlier issues.

controversy between Parsons [1980] and Haveman and Wolfe [1984] and the analysis of the U. S. Civil Rights Commission 1986, 56–69.) Moreover, other scholars, such as Brown (1984) and Darity and Myers (1980), do not find that transfer programs caused blacks to leave the labor force at a greater rate than whites.

Conservative scholars such as Becker (1981) and Murray (1984) also claim that government incentives have led to marital instability, greater female family headship, and lower labor force attachment for males

TABLE 3.6. *Welfare, Female Headship, and Unemployment*

Year	Real AFDC plus food stamp guarantee (1)	Percentage of nonaged families with children headed by women (2)	Unemployment rate, civilian workers	
			Nonwhite men, 18–19 years (3)	All men (4)
1960	$6,715	n/a	25.1%	5.4%
1964	6,604	n/a	23.1	4.6
1968	7,129	10.7	19.0	2.9
1972	8,894	13.8	26.3	5.0
1976	8,743	16.7	33.8	7.1
1980	7,486	19.8	32.6	6.9
1984	6,955	20.8[a]	n/a	7.4

Sources: Column (1): Weighted average of states' AFDC and Food Stamp benefit level for a family of four with no income (in 1984 dollars) from *Background Material and Data on Programs Within the Jurisdiction of the Committee on Ways and Means,* February 22, 1985, p. 532. Column (2): March Current Population Survey data. Column (3): *Employment and Training Report of the President, 1982,* p. 196. Column (4): *Economic Report of the President, 1985,* p. 271. See also Danziger and Gottschalk (1985) for related calculations.
  Note: n/a = not available.
  [a] For 1983.

since single men are less likely to work than are married men. Evidence supporting this position is given in Table 3.6. Real Aid to Families with Dependent Children (AFDC) plus food stamp payments rise between 1968 and 1976 (from $7,129 to $8,743), as does the percentage of nonaged families with children headed by women (from 10.7 to 16.7 percent). Such data are consistent with the Becker–Murray view. Reading on in the table, real benefits *decline* between 1976 and 1984 while female headship still continues to rise. (Note that there is also no clear relationship between unemployment and female headship.) The ambiguity of Table 3.6 is typical of that found in the welfare incentive literature.

However achieved, the removal of poor blacks from the social data base leads to an easily misinterpreted narrowing of measured black–white income differences. The remaining working blacks may appear to grow in economic status relative to whites, not because any single black is doing better but because low-wage black males are removed from the statistics. Recent evidence of growing nonreporting of income by higher-income people in the statistics that constitute the base of our knowledge reinforces this story. Only 2 percent of interviewees failed to report income in 1947 compared to the 28 percent who failed to report in 1982. Nonreporting rates are highest in the high-income occupations (see Lillard, Smith, and Welch 1986). Standard imputation procedures have been shown to produce a downward bias in estimated income for imputed observations. Because proportionately more whites are in such occupations, the observed growth in black relative economic status may be partly spurious. In addition, Lillard, Smith, and Welch document the fact that very low incomes are underreported. Imputation tends to overstate the reported incomes of such individuals, leading to further spurious convergence.

How important is the labor force dropout question? Like all important questions in the social sciences, this one can only be resolved by resorting to data. In an earlier paper with Richard Butler (Butler and Heckman 1978), I estimated a sizable role for the dropout phenomenon in affecting measured trends in black–white male earnings. The most recent published study of this problem, by Charles Brown (1984), uses statistical methods to correct the wage data for the effect of undercounting low-wage black dropouts (see especially Table 3.7).

Brown reports both published black–white median earnings ratios for male workers over age 16 and corrected estimates. (His numbers for males appear in columns two and three in Table 3.7.) In 1965, the ratio of black male median earnings to white male median earnings is .576—corrected for selective removal of low-wage blacks, the ratio is .558—little different. In 1975, however, measured black–white median earnings is .734—a growth of .734 − .576 = .158 points—a 25 percent gain. What is the real relative standing of blacks, correcting for labor market dropouts? Turn to column three of Table 3.7. Brown estimates this to be .614. Correcting for labor market dropouts, the growth in black–white median income is only .614 − .558 = .056. *Two-thirds* of the measured gain is due to an undercounting of poor blacks. Brown's research suggests that the evidence of Figure 3.1 may not be due to the decline of discrimination as much as to the elimination of the poor from the statistics of wage earners.[5] In recent work, Vroman (1986) claims to whittle down the contribution of dropouts to measured growth in relative median incomes to 25 percent. However, his work can be subject to severe criticism and seems to offer a definite lower bound estimate of the contribution of dropouts to the elevation of relative black male income.[6] Similar errors mar the analysis of Smith and Welch, who also claim that there is little scope for selection bias in accounting for measured black–white relative wage growth.[7] Estimates by Darity (1983) and Darity and Myers (1980) *assume* that nonworkers make zero earnings (an extreme assumption) and produce estimates even more striking than those of Brown.

Viewing the data in light of this discussion suggests that the polarization hypothesis may explain the lower tail of the black income distribution while the affirmative action hypothesis explains the upper tail, with the primary evidence in support of polarization being the

TABLE 3.7. *Black–White Earnings Ratios*

Year	Males		Females	
	Published	"Corrected"	Published	"Corrected"
1953	.594	.576	.485	.626
1954	.568	.567	.447	.562
1955	.588	.596	.433	.552
1956	.562	.575	.445	.571
1957	.554	.528	.455	.568
1958	.580	.559	.446	.566
1959	.580	.542	.532	.642
1960	.599	.563	.503	.626
1961	.570	.543	.513	.626
1962	.553	.523	.531	.638
1963	.568	.552	.532	.634
1964	.585	.564	.581	.709
1965	.576	.558	.575	.708
1966	.594	.562	.643	.777
1967	.639	.612	.703	.830
1968	.664	.627	.721	.838
1969	.666	.625	.792	.904
1970	.665	.612	.849	.957
1971	.673	.595	.860	.928
1972	.681	.614	.935	1.015
1973	.695	.615	.896	.934
1974	.709	.594	.977	.992
1975	.734	.614	.973	1.011
1976	.700	.591	1.014	1.002
1977	.705	.605	1.009	1.016
1978	.715	.616	1.010	1.010

Source: C. Brown, 1984.

relative growth of zero earners among blacks. Such an account is consistent with the views of scholars such as William Wilson (Wilson 1980).

This discussion has relevance for the recent analysis of black–white status presented by Reynolds Farley (1985). Virtually all of his analysis of black–white differences is conducted for samples of *workers*. Farley tests and rejects Wilson's polarization hypothesis. By neglecting to account for the substantial missing lower tail of the black income distribution, he finds no evidence of any worsening in the status of poor blacks and he overstates the rate of improvement of the economic status of black Americans.

I do not want to exaggerate the importance of the labor market dropout hypothesis by claiming that this phenomenon constitutes the entire explanation for the measured convergence in black–white status. Affirmative action and equal rights legislation might have played an important role. The South Carolina data previously discussed (Figure 3.3) suggest, for example, a positive effect of federal policy on black employment. There are numerous other examples. The study by Richard Freeman on black professionals (Freeman 1976) and the work of Freeman's students document both the prevalence of affirmative action programs and their impact on measured black employment in publicly sensitive large corporations (Leonard 1984a,b). Nonetheless it is easy to overstate the evidence in support of any quantitatively significant impact of affirmative action and equal rights programs on the mass of black Americans. Indeed, many competent scholars—such as Finis Welch and James Smith—claim that there are at best weak measured effects of such programs on black wages although there are documented instances of some firms responding to federal pressure (Smith and Welch 1978, 1986).

The difficulty with interpreting the available evidence on the impact of affirmative action is its inherent ambiguity. Many recent analyses of the impact of federal contract compliance programs have monitored the performance of required affirmative action programs for federal contractors. Analyses of the effect of federal contracting on black status typically consist of a comparison between firms with government contracts and those without. (Government contractor firms are required to implement affirmative action programs.) Small positive effects of firm contract status on minority employment and occupational status have been found, but it is difficult to evaluate this evidence and translate it into measured aggregate wage, occupational, or employment gains. The reasons are these: first, such cross-section comparisons of employment or occupational status might be upward biased because firms are connected through a common labor market. If a contractor firm bids for black labor in an attempt to meet a federally mandated target, its actions may simply reshuffle blacks between contractors and noncontractors. If all the gains in employment or occupational status in contractor firms are at the expense of noncontractor firms, comparisons of differences in employment or occupational status between sectors will overstate true black employment or occupational status gains. In the limit, if no black workers are attracted into the work force or into occupations as a consequence of these programs, a comparison between contractor firms and noncontractor firms may show a big contrast between the employment or occupational patterns of blacks in the two sectors when nothing but a rearrangement of a fixed work force has occurred. This argument suggests that comparisons in employment or occupational status between contractor and noncontractor firms at a point in time or over time may drastically overstate the true effect of such programs. Evidence presented by Leonard (1984a,b) suggesting that contractors hire more blacks than noncontractors cannot, by itself, shed any light on the contribution of affirmative action to the elevation of aggregate black status.

Second, virtually all firms are bidding for government contracts. The receipt of a contract is partly a matter of luck, and there are many opportunities over time to bid on government contracts. Since it is costly to hire and fire workers (see Holt, Modigliani, Muth, and Simon 1960), all firms—contractor or not—should look pretty much alike at any point in time in their employment practices for blacks even though all were hiring and promoting more blacks in response to affirmative action programs. Comparisons across firms would understate true affirmative action effects.

Given the importance of costs of hiring and firing workers, the second story appears to be more plausible than the first. Further, if firms operate in competitive labor markets, evidence of little difference in relative wages between workers in both contractor and noncontractor sectors (of the sort presented in Smith and Welch 1978) is entirely consistent with either strong or weak effects of affirmative action programs. In a competitive market the wages of identical labor must be equal in both sectors. Following the aggregate of firms over time in principle provides a better answer by looking at aggregate movements in black employment, but this is easier said than done. The problem with using aggregate time-series data is that many programs, policies, and economic events occur contemporaneously, and it is difficult to isolate the impacts of a few programs.

Third, there are few good measures of affirmative action. Many time-series studies following firms, states, or the country as a whole over time use a post-1964 time trend to measure affirmative action. The time trend is a possible stand-in for a variety of factors; the evidence on the impact of affirmative action obtained from such studies is necessarily unconvincing. The best summary of our knowledge—despite all of the claims pro and con—is that we still do not know the aggregate effect of these programs.

A recent study of the South Carolina labor market by Heckman and Payner (1989) documents the role of affirmative action programs and equal opportunity legislation in accounting for the breakthrough in black employment in the state that is evident in Figure 3.3. Looking at county time-series data on black employment, these authors note that counties with firms dependent on federal contracts employed more blacks than counties with firms less dependent on federal contracts. They also note that the breakthrough in black employment in the

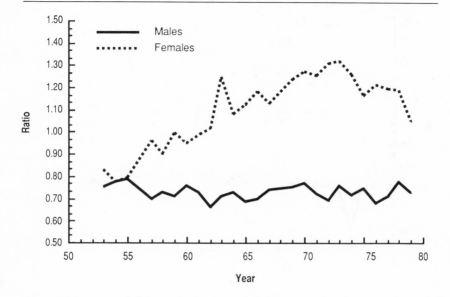

Figure 3.8. Ratio of Nonwhite to White Median Incomes in the
Northeastern Census Region, 1953–1979
Source: Current Population Reports, Series P-60.

state occurred shortly after the implementation of Title VII civil rights
legislation. The highly synchronized breakthrough in black employment that occurred in all counties of the state irrespective of the tight-
ness or slackness of county local labor markets and the available supply of blacks suggests that a common factor was present in all counties:
federal pressure. However, those authors also note that the black breakthrough occurred at a time when the South Carolina and national
economies were generally tight and that federal civil rights activity
may have played primarily a facilitating role for a breakthrough that
underlying economic forces might have produced in any event.

Developments in the South, and in particular in southern educational policy, play an important role in explaining the evolution of
black economic status. There are pronounced regional income patterns
revealed in Figures 3.8–3.11. The pattern of relative income growth
for males that emerges from these figures is as follows:

1. In the Northeast and West regions of the United States as defined
by the census, there is no clear pattern of growth in relative incomes
(Figure 3.8 and Figure 3.9).

2. In the North Central region there is an upward jump in the 1965
period that vanishes by the late seventies (see Figure 3.10).

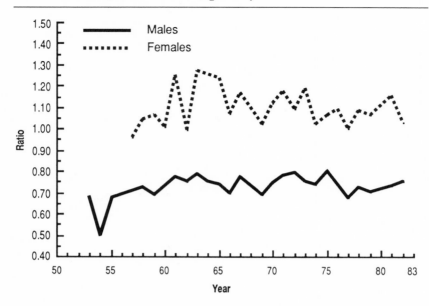

Figure 3.9. Ratio of Nonwhite to White Median Incomes in the Western
Census Region, 1953–1982
Source: Current Population Reports, Series P-60.

3. The only steady upward trend for blacks in any region is in the
South (Figure 3.11).

*The aggregate 1965 jump in black status is a consequence of a North
Central jump superimposed on the southern trend.* The story for the
South is particularly important because more than 50 percent of the
black population lives there; at the turn of the century close to 90
percent of the black population lived in that census region. The regional pattern for women is similar, except that for women the ratios
are above 1—suggesting relative income superiority for black women—
in all regions but the South long before 1964.

The "transparent" post-1965 shift in aggregate earnings so obvious
in Figure 3.1, the focus of so much of the discussion on relative black
status, vanishes in the regional data. The southern growth of black
status begins *before* any Kennedy–Johnson era legislation was passed—
certainly *before* Title VII of the Civil Rights Act.

Recent scholarship stresses the important role of the South in explaining trends in black wage growth. The main contributions are
these:

1. The South has traditionally been a low-wage agricultural region.

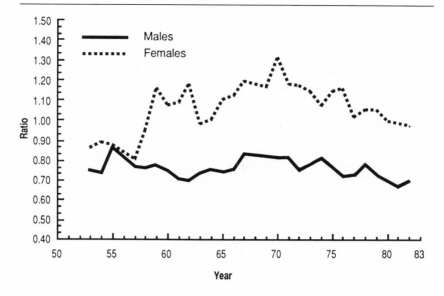

Figure 3.10. Ratio of Nonwhite to White Median Incomes in the North
Central Census Region, 1953–1982
Source: Current Population Reports, Series P-60.

Wage differentials between the South and non-South have historically
been sizable, especially for low-wage, low-educated labor. Migration
from the South has been an avenue of economic improvement for both
racial groups but has been especially important for blacks. Smith and
Welch (1986, 74) estimate that the migration of blacks from the South
to the North as well as from farms to urban areas increased black
relative wage ratios by 11 to 19 percent over the period 1940–1980.
Most of this change occurred before 1970. Since 1970, black out-migration from the South has declined greatly.

The movement of blacks out of agriculture at a faster rate than
whites, documented in Table 3.2, contributed to black measured income growth by the monetization of the nonmarket activity (e.g., people buying eggs rather than raising their own chickens, etc.).

Evidence on selective migration by educational status by Hamilton
(1959) and others indicates that higher-skilled, better-educated blacks
are much more likely to migrate than lower-skilled, less-educated
blacks and that blacks at any education level are more likely to migrate
than whites. This data suggests that the observed growth in black
relative wages in the South is a downward-biased estimate of market-
quality constant relative wage growth.

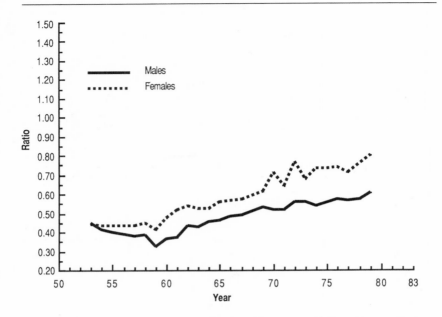

Figure 3.11. Ratio of Nonwhite to White Median Incomes in the Southern Census Region, 1953–1979
Source: Current Population Reports, Series P-60.

2. Industry moved to the South on a large scale after the Second World War. By 1980, North and South Carolina were, respectively, the first and second states ranked by the proportion of their work forces in manufacturing. Smith and Welch (1986) document that the growth in industry raised black and white earnings by the same percentage. Heckman and Payner (1989) show that newer firms and industries entering the South Carolina labor market in the 1950s were color-blind in their hiring practices. They demonstrate that economic development in that state (and presumably in the South as a whole) raised economic opportunities and contributed to the development of a tight labor market in the South. This, in turn, facilitated the black breakthrough in employment in traditionally segregated industries that occurred in the 1960s.

3. The role of governmentally supplied education has received much study (see Smith 1984; Welch 1973). The recent convergence of black–white education ratios is striking, as is apparent from Table 3.8. The left-hand side of the table records the years of birth of various cohorts of individuals and the mean schooling levels of each cohort. For example, white men born between 1906 and 1910 received 9.72 years of

TABLE 3.8. *Mean Schooling Levels by Birth Cohort*
             (Years of Schooling)

Birth cohort	White males	Black males	White females	Black females
1951–54	12.64	11.82	12.70	12.24
1946–50	12.68	11.93	12.45	11.86
1941–45	12.32	11.25	12.14	11.33
1936–40	12.00	10.46	11.81	10.89
1931–35	11.69	9.78	11.52	10.37
1926–30	11.38	9.11	11.33	9.87
1921–25	11.14	8.44	11.12	9.03
1916–20	10.74	7.65	10.79	8.36
1911–15	10.15	6.75	10.36	7.70
1906–10	9.72	6.26	10.02	7.16
1901–05	9.19	5.72	9.45	6.46
1896–1900	8.74	5.42	8.96	6.03
1891–95	8.18	4.96	8.42	5.52
1886–90	7.74	4.72	8.11	5.13
1881–85	7.56	4.38	7.95	4.67
1876–80	7.44	4.11	7.88	4.27
1871–65	7.22	3.56	7.58	3.59
1866–70	7.07	3.06	7.45	2.89
pre-1865	6.76	2.37	7.13	1.99

Source: Smith, 1984.

schooling on average; black men received almost 3.5 years less schooling on average. The differences in years of schooling—white minus
black—are recorded for each sex group in Table 3.9. The narrowing of
these schooling differences is monotone until the period of the enactment of Jim Crow legislation in the South (1886–1915) that excluded
blacks from the polls and the political benefits of participation at the
polls. The difference in years of schooling remains constant until the
cohorts born in the late 1910s or early 1920s.[8] Afterward, convergence
in the black–white educational distributions is rapid.

   The story of the educational disparity between blacks and whites is
fascinating. Beginning in the late 1880s and culminating in the early
1910s, blacks (89 percent of whom lived in the South) were effectively
eliminated from the political system, leading to a reduction in access
to governmental services. In the South at that time these services were
primarily schooling services (see J. M. Kousser 1974). This period of
exclusion was precisely the period in which southern public schooling
was being developed. The *Plessy* v. *Ferguson* decision of 1896 sanctioned "separate but equal" schools, but in reality the schooling was

TABLE 3.9.   *Racial Differences in Mean Schooling Levels
(Additional Years of Schooling of Whites)*

Birth cohort	Men	Women
1951–54	.83	.46
1946–50	.75	.60
1941–45	1.07	.81
1936–40	1.54	.92
1931–35	1.91	1.15
1926–30	2.27	1.47
1921–25	2.71	2.09
1916–20	3.09	2.44
1911–15	3.41	2.69
1906–10	3.46	2.86
1901–05	3.46	3.00
1896–1900	3.32	2.93
1891–95	3.23	2.90
1886–90	3.02	2.98
1881–85	3.18	3.28
1876–80	3.33	3.62
1871–75	3.67	4.00
1865–70	4.01	4.55
pre-1865	4.39	5.13

Source: Smith, 1984.

not equal and ironically only became so around the time of the 1954 *Brown* v. *Topeka Board of Education* decision. Tables 3.10 and 3.11 document this inequality. Black schools met for fewer days per year (panel A, Table 3.10: 97 days for blacks, 143 days for whites in 1929–1930). Classroom size was bigger, teacher salaries were lower, and per pupil expenditures were lower in black schools (Panel C, Table 3.10).

Table 3.11 documents the discrepancy between black and white per pupil schooling expenditure in the school year 1908–1909 in Mississippi. Cohorts born during the peak of the Jim Crow era (1886–1915) may not have experienced any convergence in years of schooling completed. In addition, each year of schooling was less valuable for blacks than for whites because there was less teacher input and fewer schooling days in more crowded schools. Subsequent cohorts of blacks had successively higher quality schooling and more years of schooling.

The cohorts of black workers educated in the Jim Crow era dominate the aggregate statistics on earnings until recently. James Smith (1984) argues that the post-1964 measured improvement in black status is due to the retirement of these cohorts of poorly educated workers from

TABLE 3.10.   *Comparisons of Twentieth-Century Trends in Characteristics Between the Segregated Negro Schools, Southern White Schools, and All U.S. Schools*

A. Days attended and enrollment per teacher. A comparison of segregated Negro schools to other schools, 1900–1954

Year	Average days attended per pupil enrolled		Pupils enrolled per classroom teacher	
	Negro schools	All schools	Negro schools	All schools
1899–1900	57	69[a]	56.7	45.5[a]
1908–1909	71	88[a]	56.4	39.9[a]
1919–1920	80	121	56.0	31.8
1929–1930	97	143	43.7	30.0
1939–1940	126	152	45.3	29.0
1949–1950	148	148	33.6	27.5
1953–1954	151	159	32.9	27.9

B. Enrollment of public school students in the first grade and implicit retention rates for first grade, 1900–1954

Year	% enrolled in first grade		Ratio of enrollment in first to second grade	
	Negro schools	All schools	Negro schools	All schools
1899–1900	31.9	20.6[a]	1.37	1.14[a]
1908–1909	28.7	19.2[a]	1.45	1.49[a]
1919–1920	36.8	22.9	1.96	1.64
1929–1930	34.4	16.2	2.35	1.48
1939–1940	26.0	11.9	2.03	1.29
1949–1950	19.5	12.6	1.62	1.20
1953–1954	16.5	1.27	1.45	1.25

C. Teacher salaries and expenditures per pupil in average daily attendance

Year	Salaries			Annual expenditures per pupil		
	Negro schools	Southern white schools	All schools	Negro schools	Southern white schools	All schools
1899–1900	\$ 25/mo.	\$ 37/mo.	_____	\$ 3	\$ 12	\$_____
1908–1909	\$ 26/mo.	\$ 49/mo.	_____	9	25	_____
1919–1920	\$ 36/mo.	\$ 73/mo.	\$ 871/yr.	10	43	_____
1929–1930	_____	_____	1,420/yr.	15[b]	49[b]	87
1939–1940	601/yr.	1,046/yr.	1,441/yr.	19	59	88
1949–1950	2,143/yr.	_____	3,010/yr.	_____	_____	209
1953–1954	2,861/yr.	3,384/yr.	3,825/yr.	110[c]	181[c]	264

continued on p. 76

TABLE 3.10. *(continued)*

D. Teacher salaries and expenditures: ratios of Negro schools to southern
   white schools (computed from panel C)

Year	Salaries	Annual expenditures per pupil
1899–1900	.68	.25
1908–1909	.53	.36
1919–1920	.52	.23
1929–1930	—	.31[b]
1939–1940	.57	.32
1949–1950	—	—
1953–1954	.85	.61[c]

Sources: U.S. Office of Education, Biennial Survey of Education in the United States, "Statistics of State School Systems," various issues. (Earlier editions are by the Bureau of Education in the Department of the Interior.) State Superintendents of Education, Annual Reports, various states, various years, and David Blose, "Statistics of the Education of Negroes," U.S. Office of Education, Circular 215, June 1943.

Note: See Welch (1973).

[a] Southern white schools only.

[b] Refers to 1931–1932 instead of 1929–1930.

[c] Instructional expenses only.

the labor force. This retirement phenomenon was particularly pronounced in the South and helps explain the southern time-series growth.[9] Part of the southern story of black wage convergence, then, is a story of *governmental* discrimination by states with long-standing consequences.

Smith's analysis documents the importance of education as a source of black secular economic improvement. However, it does not account for the breakthrough in black employment in South Carolina manufacturing (see Heckman and Payner 1989), nor does it explain the sharp change in other series on black economic progress noted previously.

Although the history of exclusion of blacks from schooling is a sorry one, the evidence assembled by Smith is fundamentally optimistic. His data contradict—albeit by a negative example—the claims of Freeman and Murray that government educational policies have had little effect on black status. Over the longer run, they have had an important effect.

In summary, we find:

1. Government has had an impact on the status of blacks. The evidence is that educational policies toward blacks have played an important role in elevating the economic status of blacks over time. Proof of the importance of training and education on determining black economic status is more evident than many would have it.

2. Some governmental policies may have had unintended negative

TABLE 3.11. *Public School Expenditures in Selected Mississippi Counties by Race, 1908–1909*

County	% of Negro pupils in total enrollment	Annual expenditures per pupil enrolled	
		White	Negro
Washington	92	$80.00	$2.50
Noxubee	86	20.00	1.69
Yazoo	73	15.00	1.83
Copiah	61	7.43	2.51
Attala	49	3.42	1.02
Greene	21	9.22	4.59
Itawamba	10	5.65	3.50

Source: W. E. B. Du Bois, *The Common School and the Negro American* (Atlanta: Atlanta University Press, 1910), pp. 72–77, as quoted by H. M. Bond, *The Education of the Negro in the American Social Order* (New York: Octagon Books, 1966), and Welch (1973).

effects. It is possible that some transfer programs may have removed labor force incentives and stimulated the formation of female-headed families, but the evidence on this is far from clear.

3. Very little reliable information is available about the negative or positive effects of affirmative action and equal rights programs on the status of blacks in the aggregate. Evidence from the South Carolina labor market indicates that these programs at the very least facilitated the breakthrough in black employment that occurred in the traditional manufacturing sector of the state. The post-1960 drift in coefficients of earnings equations for blacks indicates some role for government civil rights activity.

4. This chapter demonstrates the importance of looking closely at the data introduced into popular discussions and examining how they have been generated. The aggregate statistics on the time series of black status mask important regional differences and obscure developments in the South that have played and continue to play an important role in elevating the status of blacks. The evidence from the South indicates that naive claims of the importance of the 1964 Civil Rights Act do not receive support in the data since wages began to systematically increase in the region long before passage of this law. We have also seen that the system of social statistics from which we draw our data on black status do not properly account for lower-wage blacks. Part of the measured convergence of black to white status (in relative terms) is simply due to the fact that poor blacks have been eliminated from the social accounting system. This evidence casts a very different light on the recent measured convergence from that obtained in other accounts.

Finally,

5. There exists no satisfactory monolithic overriding explanation of the recent economic history of black Americans. Current claims in the popular literature about the net good or evil of government programs are not based on firm empirical evidence. Government activity has played an important, but not exclusive, role in shaping black economic status. By no means has it always been harmful. And when it has been harmful—as in the case of the exclusion of blacks from southern schooling—the policy lessons to be drawn indicate a real potential for interventions with positive effects.

Notes

1. The movement of blacks into government has been noted by many scholars. Some interpret this movement with alarm, claiming that blacks have not been absorbed into the private sector. Table 3.2 makes clear that blacks have left agriculture for both government and private nonagricultural employment, although much of the growth in black nonagricultural employment in the 1960s was growth in government employment.

2. "Polarization" is an ambiguous concept. Income and wage inequality have increased among blacks *and* whites in the period 1960–1980. A good part of this is due to the dropout phenomenon to be discussed next. Part of the polarization story is one of relative success in which middle-class blacks have escaped inner-city ghettos, leaving behind in the central city the lower tail of the black income distribution. The decline in residential housing segregation has removed middle-class blacks from the inner-city community. The "obvious" decline in the quality of inner-city neighborhoods may well be a consequence of the removal of the black middle class and not the worsening of the position of the urban poor. Moreover, health, consumption, and housing indices do not reveal a decline in inner-city living standards since 1950 (personal communication, Reynolds Farley). There is considerable evidence of income mobility into and out of poverty in both the black and white communities. A static culture of poverty view has proved difficult to document.

3. This also shows up in the widespread use of logarithmic income or wage indices that measure relative status differences.

4. See the discussion in the *Journal of the American Statistical Association* 80, no. 398 (March 1985): 98–132.

5. The main point of Brown's work (1984) is to demonstrate that 100 percent of the black wage growth is not due to the labor force withdrawal of blacks. His estimate of 66 percent seems a bit high but even at half that figure, the effect of black withdrawals on estimated wage growth would be substantial. It is important to note that Brown's methodology is critically dependent on an assumed functional form for the "true" distribution of income and an assumption that all dropouts are from the lower tail of the wage distribution. The latter assumption biases upward his estimate of the dropout effect. His *ad hoc* assumption about the "true" distribution of wages may substantially bias his estimate.

6. Vroman (1986) bases his analysis on CPS and social security data. Biases in the CPS data have previously been discussed. The social security data include earnings for individuals working in the covered sector and plausibly excludes marginal workers not covered. Vroman compares the earnings of transfer recipients and nonworkers in prior years when they worked with current earnings of workers. He finds that dropouts

have higher mean earnings in prior years than do nondropouts in current years. He thus claims to disprove the hypothesis that transfers induced dropouts.

Unfortunately, Vroman's work is not entirely convincing. By lumping together all transfer recipients, he includes those who receive work-conditioned transfers based on previous earnings (i.e., transfers that might be positively affected by high previous earnings, such as unemployment insurance, social security old-age payments, etc.). Inclusion of such transfers might easily produce his empirical result as a pure retirement phenomenon (i.e., the higher one's previous wage—and hence current benefits—the more likely one would be to withdraw from the work force). He does not correct for this spurious channel of causation in his study. Dropping the requirement that an individual receives a transfer would be interesting, but Vroman does not report estimates from such a procedure. However, Vroman notes that most of the recent growth in dropouts comes from *younger* blacks (whose wages are lower, on average, than all blacks) and *older* whites. *Assuming* that dropouts earn between 85 and 100 percent of the median earnings (an assumption that is not based on any evidence), Vroman estimates that 25 percent of the black male relative income gain may be due to the dropout phenomena. The most serious problem—the exclusion of marginal black workers from the social security and CPS data—is not discussed or even noted by Vroman. His other evidence on the relationship between labor force participation and transfer programs is at best casual.
7. Smith and Welch (1986) compare the wages in previous periods of nonworkers with the wages of workers in current periods. Like Vroman, they ignore the point that an important reason for persons not to work is that they receive low offered wages. Their comparisons are thus biased toward rejecting the importance of the labor market dropout hypothesis by imputing too high a wage to nonworkers.
8. Margo (1986) disputes Smith's analysis, noting an important distinction between years of schooling attended and grades completed in schooling data collected at the turn of the century. Under certain assumptions about school retention rates disputed by Smith (1986), Margo presents a new series on years of schooling by cohort that contradict Smith's numbers (recorded in Table 3.8) by demonstrating a monotone secular *narrowing* in schooling completion levels by cohort. The exchange between Smith and Margo calls into question the basic quality of the educational statistics utilized by Smith (1984). These authors do not dispute the data presented in Tables 3.10 and 3.11 that document sharp racial disparity in schooling expenditure.
9. This is my interpretation and not Smith's. Smith (1984) does not perform an analysis of regional aggregates although Smith (1986) notes that part of the growth in white educational attainment relative to nonwhite attainment in Table 3.8 is due to a reduction in foreign-born white migration into the North.

References

Becker, G., 1981. *A Treatise on The Family.* Cambridge: Harvard University Press.

Bound, J., and R. Freeman, 1987. "Black Economic Progress: Erosion of the Post-1964 Gains in the 1980s?" Unpublished paper, University of Michigan (April).

Brown, C., 1984. "Black–White Earnings Ratios Since the Civil Rights Act of 1964: The Importance of Labor Market Dropouts." *Quarterly Journal of Economics* 99, no. 1: 31–44.

Butler, R., and J. Heckman, 1978. "The Government's Impact on the Labor Market Status of Black Americans." In *Equal Rights and Industrial Relations,* ed. L. J. Hausman. Madison, Wisc.: Industrial Relations Research Association, pp. 235–281.

Danziger, S., and P. Gottschalk, 1985. "Social Programs—A Partial Solution to but Not a Cause of Poverty: An Alternative to Charles Murray's View." Unpublished paper, University of Wisconsin, Institute for Research on Poverty (April).

Darity, W., 1983. "The Goal of Racial Economic Equality: A Critique." *Journal of Ethnic Studies* 10 (Winter): 51–70.

Darity, W., and S. Myers, 1980. "Changes in Black–White Income Inequality, 1968–1978: A Decade of Progress?" *Review of Black Political Economy* 10 (Summer): 355–379.

Farley, R., 1985. *Blacks and Whites.* Cambridge: Harvard University Press.

Freeman, R., 1973. "Changes in the Labor Market for Black Americans." *Brookings Papers on Economic Activity* 1 (Spring): 67–120.

Hamilton, H., 1959. "Educational Selectivity of Migration from the South." *Social Forces* 38 (October): 38–42.

Haveman, R., and B. Wolfe, 1984. "The Decline in Male Labor Force Participation: Comment." *Journal of Political Economy* 92 (June): 532–541.

Heckman, J., and Brook Payner, 1989. "Determining the Impact of Government Policy on the Economic Status of Blacks: A Case Study of South Carolina." *American Economic Review* 79: 138–177.

Holt, C., F. Modigliani, R. Muth, and H. Simon, 1960. *Planning Production Inventories and Work Force.* Englewood Cliffs, N.J.: Prentice-Hall.

Kousser, J. M., 1974. *The Shaping of Southern Politics.* New Haven: Yale University Press.

Leonard, J., 1984a. "The Impact of Affirmative Action on Employment." *Journal of Labor Economics* 2 (October): 439–463.

———, 1984b. "Employment and Occupational Advance under Affirmative Action." *Review of Economics and Statistics* 66 (August): 377–385.

Lillard, L., J. Smith, and F. Welch, 1986. "What Do We Really Know about Wages: The Importance of Non-Reporting and Census Imputation." *Journal of Political Economy* 94 (June): 489–506.

Margo, R., 1986. "Race and Human Capital: Comment." *American Economic Review* 76 (December): 1221–1224.

Murray, C., 1984. *Losing Ground.* New York: Basic Books.

Parsons, D., 1980. "The Decline in Male Labor Force Participation." *Journal of Political Economy* 88 (February): 117–134.

Smith, J., 1986. "Race and Human Capital: Reply." *American Economic Review* 76 (December): 1221–1224.

———, 1984. "Race and Human Capital." *American Economic Review* 74, no. 3: 685–698.

Smith, J., and F. Welch, 1986. "Closing the Gap: Forty Years of Economic Progress for Blacks." Santa Monica, Ca.: The RAND Corporation.

———, 1978. "Race Differences in Earnings: A Survey and New Evidence." Santa Monica, Ca.: The RAND Corporation R–2295.

U.S. Commission on Civil Rights, 1986. "The Economic Progress of Black Men in America." Clearinghouse Publication no. 91. Washington, D.C.

Vroman, W., 1986. "The Relative Earnings of Black Men: An Analysis of the Sample Selection Hypothesis." Washington, D.C.: Urban Institute.

Wattenberg, B., and R. Scammon, 1973. "Black Progress and Liberal Rhetoric." *Commentary* (April): 32–41.

Welch, F., 1973. "Education and Racial Discrimination." In *Discrimination in Labor Markets,* eds. O. Ashenfelter and A. Rees. Princeton: Princeton University Press.

Wilson, W., 1980. *The Declining Significance of Race.* Chicago: University of Chicago Press, Second Edition.

SAMUEL L. MYERS, JR.

Chapter 4. How Voluntary
Is Black Unemployment
and Black Labor Force Withdrawal?

O N S E V E R A L dimensions of economic well-being, black males lag behind the rest of the U.S. population. Their unemployment rates are more than twice that of whites; they earn only about 75 percent of what white males earn; and they are far less likely than white males to be found in highly skilled, well-paying jobs that offer the promise of upward mobility. Like white males, black males have experienced a rapid decline in labor force participation over the past two decades, but their labor force participation rates have fallen much more sharply than that of white males.

The diminishing labor supply among black males accompanies other devastating trends: one of these, the reduction in the supply of eligible husbands for growing numbers of unwed black mothers (Darity and Myers 1984); another, the total withdrawal of men from the noninstitutionalized population via black-on-black homicide and incarceration in the nation's growing prisons and mental hospitals (Darity and Myers 1987). Whether one measures well-being by conventional earnings or labor market variables or by social indices of family stability and personal freedom, the plight of the black male appears quite bleak. Indeed, an apt term to describe the condition of life for many young black males today is "marginalized."

In stark contrast with the gloomy picture of hopelessness and marginalization among black males in America is a decidedly optimistic vision. Smith and Welch (1986) and Freeman (1973) portray black men as overcoming overwhelming labor market barriers erected in an earlier era. One view presumes that this feat is a consequence of self-improvement via education. Another view presumes it is a consequence of opened doors and opportunities via government antidiscrimination efforts.

James Smith and Finis Welch contend that perceptible improvements in the economic well-being of black males have been realized since the early years of migration from the agricultural South to the industrial North. They also contend that earnings differentials in many higher-skilled occupations have virtually disappeared as a consequence of improved education and that increases in human capital investment among blacks is the source for the narrowing of racial wage differentials. While they admit that some blacks may have lagged behind, Smith and Welch see this less as a repudiation of their thesis than as a challenge for future efforts to narrow the remaining racial disparity in incomes.

Richard Freeman, along with several of his colleagues, thinks that government antidiscrimination policy is at the root of black gains. His analysis suggests that civil rights laws that ban employment discrimination have raised the demand for minority workers and thus have increased wages. This view, which praises the past progress of many blacks, is ambivalent about future prospects for further narrowing of the racial earnings gap.

Has the status of black males deteriorated or advanced? Are their futures bleaker or brighter now than they were several decades ago? Are they being removed in increasing numbers from or drawn into the mainstream of economic life? Has there been a significant improvement in relative well-being of many blacks who have finally overcome the poverty and oppression of a bygone era?

The emerging consensus is that each of these questions must be answered by a qualified yes to deterioration, growing bleakness, removal from the economic mainstream, but yes also to an improvement in the well-being of many blacks. There is no doubt that declining labor force participation and growing unemployment are signals of increased marginalization of at least one significant segment within the black community, the black "underclass." This "underclass" has become the epitome of superfluous labor in the sense that its members are neither wanted nor needed for the efficient operation of contemporary job markets. Increasingly, these people—who disproportionately populate the prisons, drug-abuse clinics, mental hospitals, and other repositories for the unwanted and disenfranchised of the world— have become the literal hemorrhoids of domestic policy making. Uncomfortably burdensome in their initial stages, these hidden inconveniences eventually erupt into painful reminders of failed policies and social neglect.

At the same time a very visible and vocal black middle class has evolved, led by lawyers, academics, Wall Street investment bankers and brokers, successful entrepreneurs, and public officials who demonstrate, however precariously, that the fruits of economic success have not eluded all within the black community. These representatives of what Freeman (1977) calls the "Black Elite" and what Darity (1983) terms the "managerial elite" enjoy earnings, levels of educational attainment, occupational prestige, and labor market tenure that are beyond the imagination, let alone the reach, of their less fortunate brothers and sisters.

How does one reconcile these conflicting visions? Does the improvement of the lucky few obscure the deterioration of conditions among the masses? Is the putative improvement among those fortunate enough to have a job an illusion created by the withdrawal of others from the mainstream of the economy? A host of hypotheses reject the "dramatic improvement" argument. These include the possibility that affirmative action and similar government efforts to improve the labor market position of blacks have resulted in creaming and other selective employment practices that actually make blacks, collectively, worse off than they would be in a market without the added push from the government (Sowell 1981). Another possibility is that government transfers and welfare payments have induced the lowest-wage workers to withdraw from the labor market and thereby to leave in their place higher-wage workers who contribute to the artificially raised mean of the resulting earnings distribution (Butler and Heckman 1977). Or, that other social processes, such as the rise of crime and imprisonment, have siphoned off the least productive and most redundant of the black labor supply, resulting in a work force unrepresentative of the vast majority of black people (Darity and Myers 1987).

These hypotheses share the conclusion that the presumed convergence of black and white male earnings is far less real than the optimistic view suggests. The last two hypotheses, while almost identical in their assessment of the impacts of withdrawal from the labor market on earnings inequality, differ fundamentally in their understandings of the processes generating the withdrawal from the labor market. One perspective views the withdrawal in terms of the rational choices of individualistic, self-interested decision makers, such as unemployed workers who are posited to experience longer spells of unemployment in response to higher unemployment benefits. The other views the withdrawal in a more deterministic sense: when employment opportunities dwindle and public policy shifts toward containment and exclusion of the least productive workers, withdrawal from the labor market becomes an aggregate consequence of these forces. Quite simply, the difference is one of voluntary against involuntary nonemployment.

It is this difference that gives rise to the preoccupation of the present chapter. The aim is not simply to debate whether black unemployment or labor market withdrawal is voluntary or involuntary, but rather, by probing the mechanics of movements in and out of the labor force, to explore the evidence that links public welfare transfers to the changing status of black males and that, in turn, has led certain commentators to conclude that welfare has contributed to the rise of poverty and the deterioration of life among blacks because of its built-in disincentives to work (Murray 1984). If life has become so harsh for blacks, in other words, is it because they have brought it upon themselves by choosing the public dole?

Notions of voluntary unemployment are discussed here as a backdrop for a review of evidence on the determinants of changing patterns of nonemployment among black males. That evidence will highlight the difficulties of differentiating between voluntary and involuntary aspects of labor force withdrawal. Nonetheless, an assessment can be made about the logical consistency of the voluntary withdrawal argument as it relates to welfare and other cash transfers that demonstrates that despite a statistical correlation between AFDC benefits and black labor force participation, this correlation does not always operate in a manner consistent with the illusory-progress hypothesis. At best only weak support for the voluntary withdrawal hypothesis can be marshalled.

The conclusion emerges that the involuntary component of the significant withdrawal from the labor market among black males may be far more important in contributing to the shifting economic fates of black males than is the voluntary component. Future research will have the burden of documenting the distributional aspects of this involuntary nonemployment, but conventional wisdom does suggest that it is the lowest strata of black life that suffers the harshest consequences of forces contributing to the truncation of the earnings profile within the black community. The findings are consistent with a contention that economic progress has been but an illusion for the masses of blacks and particularly for black males.

Why is it important to know whether unemployment or labor force withdrawal is voluntary or not? There are several reasons: (1) there are possible work disincentive effects of cash government transfers such as AFDC benefits; (2) the choice of policies for combating aggregate unemployment depends upon the presumed rationality of labor market behavior; and (3) there is the aforementioned interpretation of statistics that shows significant narrowing of earnings disparities between blacks and whites.

The work disincentive concern begins with the presumption that transfer recipients are rational decision makers: rational actors will work less if you pay them not to work. One of the major objections to conventional means of redistributing income and/or reducing poverty through income maintenance relates to this reduction in work effort due to transfer payments. If transfers work to reduce labor force participation or to extend periods of unemployment, it is plausible that recipients can end up receiving lower earnings after the transfer than before. This possible reduction in work effort is viewed with alarm by policy analysts and decision makers because it means higher levels of transfers may be needed to reach a given poverty-reduction target. It also means that welfare recipiency may increase and may last for longer durations. And this means higher welfare costs. Whether these dire consequences follow, however, depends critically upon the "rationality" of responses to these policy changes. In other words, do poor people voluntarily reduce their work effort and labor force participation as welfare becomes more attractive?

Optimal policies for combating unemployment also depend upon what amount of unemployment is frictional (and therefore voluntary) and what amount is structural (and thus involuntary). Frictional unemployment is viewed as desirable because the process of quitting and searching for better work is seen as necessary if the imperfect market is to gravitate toward equilibrium. Of course, the labor market is the one market that fails too frequently to make the necessary adjustments for movement toward competitive equilibrium; that failure suggests that not all unemployment is frictional. But even when one lives in a rational world of simultaneously unemployed workers and job vacancies in equilibrium, where one is faced with nontrivial search costs and informational asymmetries characteristic of labor markets, all unemployment need not be voluntary.

Salop (1979) proves this point elegantly. If there are two labor markets, an internal one where experienced workers are paid an identical wage and an external one from which new workers are hired, the requirement that both markets clear cannot always be met. This world can generate permanent structural involuntary unemployment in the short run where price adjustments fail to absorb the stock of idle persons willing to work at the going wage but for whom there are no jobs. In the presence of this structural unemployment, Salop demonstrates, moreover, that there always will be disguised unemployment; some people never enter the market because the external market does not clear. This theoretical insight suggests that rational decisions in imperfect markets can generate both involuntary and voluntary unemployment. The existence of search unemployment or of apparently "voluntary" labor market withdrawal is insufficient to establish that such unemployment or nonlabor force participation is frictional.

Even when the unemployment is totally voluntary, the disincentive effects of transfer and insurance schemes are not necessarily operative. As Dale Mortenson (1970, 1977), one of the leading scholars in search theory, has shown, the impacts of unemployment payments on labor supply are theoretically ambiguous. There are two offsetting effects of the unemployment benefits in a realistic world where payments are of limited duration: on one hand, the payments increase search and therefore unemployment because they reduce the cost of search; and, on the other hand, they reduce the cost of subsequent unemployment and thereby increase the probability of employment if one is near the end of the eligibility period.

Translating these findings to a world of welfare recipiency, one sees an immediate ambiguity of the impacts of AFDC on labor supply. Welfare payments to unemployed parents initially reduce the cost of unemployment to these parents and thus increase the likelihood of nonemployment. But an opposing tendency suggests that persons whose eligibility has expired or who currently are ineligible for these welfare benefits temporarily may take low-paying jobs because the cost of subsequent unemployment is reduced by the welfare benefit. Therefore, the net employment impacts of these welfare provisions are ambiguous.

The voluntary choice to withdraw from the labor force, moreover, does not imply that the recipient is necessarily worse off. In the standard microeconomic analysis of labor–leisure choices, the determination of the net impacts on the recipient's well-being rests upon a balancing of two often opposing impacts: the increase in utility from increased leisure and consumption via the transfers versus the substitution between leisure and consumption that could lead to lower levels of work. In the simplest microeconomic world of single-period decisions under perfect certainty, the private benefits always exceed the private costs when transfers are provided, given relatively innocuous assumptions about the shape of the welfare recipient's preferences.

Of course, it is not the excess of private benefits over private costs that determines policy makers' concerns. It is the public costs—including the nontrivial expenditures associated with the mere administrative transfer of funds from taxpayers to welfare recipients—that dominate the concerns about work disincentives and rising welfare rolls. If labor force withdrawal or unemployment is purely voluntary, then these costs can be controlled by the transfer parameters to which recipients respond. The adverse responses to the inducements of welfare can be controlled, at least theoretically, if the behavior to be affected is voluntary.

Voluntary labor force withdrawal and unemployment also can be described in conventional job search models. The classic explanation for the long spells of unemployment and the high rates of labor force withdrawal among black teenagers is that their "reservation wages" are too high. The reservation wage equates the marginal cost of additional search with the marginal benefit of search. As the marginal cost of search falls or the marginal benefit of search rises, the reservation wage increases. There is a positive relationship between the probability of remaining unemployed and the reservation wage. The higher the reservation wage, the higher the chances that the unemployed worker will continue to search.

Some analysts contend, without proving it rigorously, that illegal income, welfare, unemployment insurance, and transfers generally work to increase the reservation wage and therefore to reduce the probability that a given wage offer will be accepted. However, through time, reservation wages are presumed to decline. Thus, longer search should be associated with higher probabilities of job matches. This reasoning has been put to several tests and provides another angle from which to explore the voluntary nature of nonemployment. The key question of interest is whether differences in the willingness or ability to work explain the higher levels of unemployment and the lower rates of labor force participation among blacks as compared to whites. Blacks who have alternative sources of income and who shun low-wage menial work will have lower labor force participation rates and higher search unemployment if motivations, expectations, and aspirations are the sole determinants of labor market behavior. In contrast, if opportunities are more important in affecting labor supply, then unemployment and labor force withdrawal might be more appropriately understood in the context of external forces rather than voluntary choices.

The view that reservation wages are too high has been tested using data from the National Longitudinal Survey (NLS) and the National Bureau of Economic Research's (NBER) survey of inner-city youth. The latter, a specially designed survey of black youth in several inner cities, examined motivations, aspirations, participation in illegal activities, earnings from crime, and a host of standard labor market indicators.

Several important findings emerge. First, indirect evidence indicates that alternative sources of income, such as illegal earnings, do affect labor force behavior. Although Viscusi's (1986) analysis reaches this conclusion, it is marred by the inattention to several model specification issues well-known among researchers in the economics-of-crime area (Myers 1983; Schmidt and Witte 1985).

A second bit of evidence comes from Holzer (1986). Using the NLS and NBER data he concludes that:

1. The reservation wages of blacks are too high in the sense that their earnings expectations for the jobs that they seek are unrealistic.

2. For low-wage jobs—the bulk of the jobs for which the blacks in the sample are qualified—their reservation wages are lower than those among whites.

3. There are strong positive impacts of reservation wages on the duration of unemployment. The higher the reservation wage, the longer the duration of unemployment and/or periods out of the labor force.

4. Blacks aspired for jobs that are comparable to the jobs sought by whites, but these higher-skilled jobs are out of the reach of the vast majority of the black youth in the NBER sample.

The Holzer conclusions offer the strongest evidence to date for the hypothesis that black–white differentials in nonemployment can be attributable to the unrealistically high reservation wages of black youth. This evidence is the cornerstone of the view that the long and intermittent periods of unemployment among blacks, coupled with their high rates of labor force withdrawal, are the result of their own bad decisions. Like Murray and other conservative pundits who blame the victim—along with the government that aids the victims—for their poverty, those who see Holzer's results as support for the "reservation wage hypothesis" discover the fault among the disadvantaged. Black youth have high rates of unemployment because they refuse to accept the wage employers are willing to offer.

The obvious flaw with extending the Holzer results to the extreme conclusion that black unemployment is totally voluntary is that Holzer's model makes no attempt to estimate separately the wage offers of employers and the reservation wages of workers. That task is rendered nearly impossible by the nature of the data sets used and the well-known econometric snags in the identification of simultaneous equations such as offer and reservation schedules.

There is a further complication in that reservation wages generally are not observed. Researchers like Kiefer and Neumann (1979) demonstrate that inferences about the shape of the reservation wage curve are tenuously dependent on frequently untested assumptions about functional forms, model specification, and the like. One advantage of the NLS and NBER data sets is that reservation wages are observed, at least to the extent that workers are asked what wage they would accept for a given job. The question is "If you were offered a job as a _____ would you accept it at $_____/hr?" But this wording provokes the fundamental query, "What does the 'reservation wage' measure?" Does it measure the lowest wage that an individual is willing to accept for a given job, as the theory would require, or does it measure something else? Perhaps it measures wage expectations and is, in reality, a response to the question, "What is this job worth?"

The evidence that Holzer offers seems to raise concerns, which he acknowledges, about the meaning and interpretation of the empirical measure of reservation wages used in the NLS and NBER data sets. For example, Holzer finds that the reservation wages for menial or unpleasant jobs are lower than those for similar unskilled jobs. He interprets this as a demand for "compensating differentials." An alternative interpretation, consistent with the compensating variations view, but not dependent upon the acceptance of the wage measure as an indicator of a reservation wage, is that this response captures the worker's perception of the amount that he or she must be paid in order to forego leisure to work. As Kiefer and Neumann point out, that wage is indeed a sort of reservation wage, but not the reservation wage of search theory that equates the marginal cost of search with the marginal benefits. Instead, it measures what respondents think the job is worth and not what they believe they can earn in the job. The very fact that it is a response to a hypothetical question and not a schedule of wage offers and wage reservations further underscores the ambiguity of the Holzer findings. The reservation wage measure is sufficiently confounded by the wage expectations that policy conclusions from these results must be approached with great caution. For example, theory suggests that a worker will accept a job if the reservation wage is less than or equal to the offer wage. Yet, for individuals who actually were employed in the NBER sample, the mean reservation wage for *all* jobs exceeded the acceptance wage.

The reservation wage hypothesis for explaining the high rates of nonemployment among black youth is inherently a difficult one to test. Moreover, the results tell little about the process that leads to labor force withdrawal. The model begins with the assumption that nonemployment is voluntary and then sets forth to predict the differential effects of reservation wages on unemployment and labor force participation. A finding of no effect of reservation wages on the duration of nonemployment could be used to challenge the assumption of the voluntary nature of unemployment. But a finding of a direct effect of reservation wages on unemployment duration leaves untested the assumption of voluntary behavior. This also leaves unsettled the nature of the mechanism that induces the withdrawal of black males from the labor market.

Tests of the reservation wage hypothesis tell so little because unmeasured and unobservable variables are a part of the theory but are necessarily absent from the empirical work. For example, lack of information about wage offers induces rational labor market participants to search in the first place. Information about the market is imperfect because of the limited abilities of participants to process and synthesize the multiple attributes of a vast array of job opportunities; it is imperfect also because of the costs associated with such information in retrieval and dissemination and because much of that information only can be obtained "from the inside," or on the job. Especially with regard to smaller firms, there are few outlets for learning about the nonpecuniary qualities of a job except by actually taking the job.

Then there is the problem of the correlation of these unobservables with both the duration of nonemployment and the reservation wage. Information is presumably inversely related to the reservation wage. The more an individual knows about the available offers, the qualities of the job, and other intrinsic attributes of the job, the lower the reservation wage will be for a given duration of search. Better-informed people will have reservation wages that are closer to the wage offer distribution than uninformed people. They also should have shorter durations of unemployment. This complicates matters because information quality is unobserved in the reservation wage and the duration of unemployment equations. The impact of this unobservable is to bias upward the observed effect of reservation wages on the duration of nonemployment.

Not surprisingly, earlier evidence on the impact of reservation wages on black unemployment provided only ambiguous conclusions. For example, Stephenson (1976) found that while black youths' reservation wages were actually lower than white youths', blacks' relative reservation wages, or the ratio of the reservation wage to the previous wage, were higher than whites'. So low were the black youths' received wages that they always seemed to fall below the amount that the youths claimed was the lowest amount that they would accept. In any event, no one seems to have much of an explanation for these anomalous findings, and when these models are estimated, they generally fail to garner much explanatory power.

The reservation wage hypothesis that rests upon the voluntary nature of unemployment and nonemployment behavior, thus, has enough ambiguities associated with it to leave in doubt whether unrealistic aspirations or labor market expectations are the "cause" of the racial gap in employment.

It is useful to examine the trends in earnings inequality and transfer receipt to set the stage for our examination of the evidence on voluntary versus involuntary labor market withdrawal and unemployment. Table 4.1 illustrates the conventional evidence supporting the "dramatic improvement" hypothesis. Black earnings relative to white earnings rose in the decade from 1968 to 1978 from .6272 to .7914. That is, in the entire United States, black wage and salary income

TABLE 4.1. *Black–White Mean Earnings Ratio (Population in Labor Force)*

	1968	1970	1973	1975	1976	1985
Northeast						
Total	.7169	.7253	.7891	.8341	.8591	.7965
Male	.7018	.6856	.7190	.7868	.7802	.6892
Female	.9078	.9624	1.1214	1.0948	1.1797	1.0761
North Central						
Total	.8410	.8703	.8874	.9170	.9388	.7695
Male	.8168	.7405	.8375	.9057	.8771	.6720
Female	1.0330	1.0686	1.1331	1.1302	1.2286	1.0484
Southeast						
Total	.4955	.5718	.6462	.6329	.7052	.7016
Male	.4914	.5570	.6019	.5830	.6491	.6319
Female	.5776	.6832	.8370	.8376	.9093	.9052
Southwest						
Total	.5756	.5840	.6363	.6638	.7172	.6384
Male	.5846	.6040	.6436	.6729	.6786	.5826
Female	.6689	.6468	.7728	.7641	.9047	.8282
West						
Total	.8191	.7898	.8225	.7685	.9514	.7967
Male	.7834	.7527	.7663	.7572	.8498	.6993
Female	1.0597	1.0485	1.1326	1.0140	1.2702	1.0330
U.S.						
Total	.6272	.6652	.7246	.7346	.7914	.7273
Male	.6154	.6451	.6805	.6982	.7257	.6463
Female	.7706	.8296	.9584	.9412	1.0473	.9559

Source: Author's computations from Current Population Survey tapes.

increased from almost 63 percent of white wage and salary incomes in 1968 to more than 79 percent of white earnings in 1978.

The impressive earnings gains made by blacks, however, were eroded during the 1980s, as evidenced by the drop in the ratio of black to white earnings by 1985 to .7273, not much larger than the 1973 ratio. "Dramatic improvement" ceased to exist by the 1980s, as Table 4.2 suggests. This table displays the ratio of black-to-white median weekly earnings of full-time employed workers. Relative earnings by this measure deteriorated for both black men and black women during the 1980s.

During the 1970s black women experienced greater gains than black men, and the percentage improvements for black men and women were larger in the South than they were in the North or West, according to Table 4.1. In recent years, moreover, as racial earnings ratios have de-

TABLE 4.2. *Median Weekly Earnings Ratios, Full-Time Wage and Salary Workers, 1979–1985*

Year	Black–White total	Black–White males	Black–White females
1979	.8153	.7607	.9305
1980	.7910	.7649	.9158
1981	.8041	.7612	.9292
1982	.7792	.7356	.9139
1983	.8182	.7571	.9094
1984	.8006	.7550	.8993
1985	.7803	.7290	.8968

Source: Statistical Abstracts of the United States, annual.

clined, black men have slipped faster than black women (see Table 4.2).

What happened in the 1970s to explain the apparent narrowing of black–white wages and then in the 1980s to reverse this improvement? Note that both sets of figures relate to workers in the labor force. Could changing work behavior explain what happened? Tables 4.3 and 4.4 address these questions; they display weeks worked and weeks unemployed for blacks and whites over several years. Table 4.3 shows one aspect of employment: weeks worked. The ratio of black to white weeks worked for labor force participants remained flat for much of the period under scrutiny. For males the black–white employment ratio remained the same at about .92, whereas females experienced an upward swing of the black–white employment ratio at the end of the decade. While black and white women worked on average almost the same number of weeks out of the year, there was a nearly 7 to 8 percent difference in weeks worked by white and black men throughout the seventeen-year span. Although there were regional variations in this flat pattern of relative employment among men, there were no strong and consistent movements to suggest that the U.S. aggregate masked local improvements. For example, in the Northeast, there was a 3 percent difference in weeks worked by black and white men in 1978. This came after more than a half dozen years of relative improvements in black male employment. By 1985 the difference increased again to about 5 percent. In contrast, in the West there was a minor initial decline in the ratio of black to white weeks worked, after which a period of unchanged relative employment ensued. Thus, Table 4.3 provides few clues as to the sources of the decline in wage inequality.

Table 4.4, in contrast, reveals important shifts in the relative unemployment between blacks and whites. There is a sharp drop in the

TABLE 4.3. *Black–White Mean Ratio Weeks Worked*
(Population in Labor Force)

	1968	1970	1973	1975	1978	1985
Northeast						
Total	.9716	.9626	.9527	.9526	.9834	.9705
Male	.9372	.9535	.9288	.9420	.9730	.9491
Female	1.0425	.9979	1.0052	.9842	.9976	.9983
North Central						
Total	.9421	.9658	.9326	.9234	.9584	.9526
Male	.9377	.9486	.9090	.9302	.9430	.9246
Female	.9677	1.0086	.9802	.9364	.9934	.9882
Southeast						
Total	.9085	.9049	.9326	.9148	.9542	.9639
Male	.9063	.9087	.9131	.8975	.9303	.9411
Female	.9315	.9195	.9756	.9512	.9972	.9953
Southwest						
Total	.9204	.8926	.9073	.9084	.9419	.9597
Male	.9286	.9060	.8964	.8986	.9155	.9179
Female	.9402	.9020	.9554	.9473	.9923	1.0142
West						
Total	.9761	.9672	.9549	.9532	.9417	.9530
Male	.9328	.9369	.9414	.9474	.8970	.9135
Female	1.0378	1.0358	1.0028	.9725	1.0089	1.0047
U.S						
Total	.9352	.9330	.9379	.9275	.9599	.9634
Male	.9243	.9277	.9196	.9180	.9369	.9360
Female	.9753	.9628	.9834	.9579	1.0023	.9992

Source: Author's computations from Current Population Survey tapes.

ratio of black weeks unemployed to white weeks unemployed, a drop more pronounced and consistent among men than among women. This table reveals that for males in the United States the ratio of black to white weeks unemployed fell to 2.0452 in 1973 from a high of 2.1409 in 1968. In 1975 the black–white male unemployment ratio dropped again to 1.9444. Three years later, in 1978, it descended to 1.7770. By 1985 it had plunged to 1.2905. This steady drop in relative unemployment among male labor force participants is entirely consistent with systematic withdrawal of the more unemployable and therefore lower-wage workers; what is ambiguous, however, is whether *unwilling* or *unable* workers withdrew. The crux of the matter is that this evidence is consistent with both the voluntary and the involuntary unemployment arguments.

Adding to the ambiguity over the nature of the drop in relative un-

TABLE 4.4.   *Black–White Mean Ratio Weeks Unemployed*
              (Population in Labor Force)

	1968	1970	1973	1975	1978	1985
Northeast						
Total	1.9422	1.3526	1.5855	1.8757	1.4900	1.2722
Male	2.4454	1.5182	1.8068	1.9024	1.4246	1.3680
Female	1.3882	1.1671	1.3512	1.8870	1.6260	1.1629
North Central						
Total	2.7938	2.9712	3.0185	2.3954	2.3761	1.3885
Male	2.4481	2.7718	3.2539	2.3220	2.1398	1.4181
Female	3.3352	3.3268	2.7260	2.5151	2.8076	1.3701
Southeast						
Total	2.1942	2.5197	2.3681	1.9953	1.9202	1.2457
Male	2.0825	2.4671	2.1231	2.1328	1.9122	1.3008
Female	2.4807	2.5614	2.7749	1.8489	1.9409	1.1511
Southwest						
Total	2.8629	3.3352	2.9464	2.7405	2.1177	1.1585
Male	2.5703	3.5937	2.6140	2.8309	1.9581	1.2109
Female	3.3403	3.0245	3.2910	2.6673	2.3440	1.0882
West						
Total	1.7552	1.5968	1.9382	1.7801	2.2490	1.2627
Male	1.8587	1.7806	2.1013	1.6410	2.2943	1.2409
Female	1.6463	1.4106	1.7866	1.9904	2.2110	1.2547
U.S.						
Total	2.1228	2.1308	2.0218	1.9277	1.8693	1.2524
Male	2.1409	2.1157	2.0452	1.9444	1.7770	1.2905
Female	2.1380	2.1707	2.0194	1.9370	2.0242	1.2011

Source: Author's computations from Current Population Survey tapes.

employment among black men in the labor force is the variation in this ratio across regions. In the North Central region, for example, the ratio of black to white male weeks unemployed actually increased in the first half of the decade. In the South, there were erratic year-to-year movements in the ratio. In the Northeast region, there was a fall in the ratio of black to white weeks worked among males from 1968 to 1970, a rise from 1970 to 1975, and another decline from 1975 to 1985. These variations in the relative unemployment work themselves out to give the appearance of a national leakage of the lower-productivity blacks from the labor market, but nonetheless, it is unclear how and where these selective withdrawals were taking place.

In any event, a very powerful explanation for these selective withdrawals has been offered by Butler and Heckman (1977). The inducements of government transfers are supposed to trigger the voluntary mechanism leading to sample selection. Welfare and social security

TABLE 4.5. *Black–White Per Capita Welfare Income Ratio (Individuals 14+)*

	1968	1970	1973	1975	1978	1985
Northeast						
Total	7.3417	7.6561	8.0387	6.1069	6.3578	4.9522
Male	3.0973	3.3017	4.6182	2.9448	4.2779	2.5175
Female	8.6661	9.4382	8.9249	6.6752	6.4142	5.3679
North Central						
Total	9.2892	8.2430	7.7507	8.8240	9.5445	7.2856
Male	2.4575	3.3747	4.4783	6.7625	7.8292	4.9319
Female	12.5623	10.1536	8.5633	9.1534	9.3123	7.6050
Southeast						
Total	3.3796	4.6394	6.1440	4.5237	8.5213	7.7024
Male	3.6275	3.0400	3.0056	3.1253	2.3276	3.7403
Female	3.2536	5.3459	7.3026	5.0985	9.4335	8.6650
Southwest						
Total	3.6672	4.4173	6.4370	4.4000	10.3437	7.0009
Male	3.9440	4.0064	4.0796	1.9279	3.3567	2.0979
Female	3.4901	4.5338	7.1460	5.4316	11.4926	7.4429
West						
Total	5.9873	3.8039	4.3702	4.4377	6.1647	4.9291
Male	4.3268	4.4274	2.6038	3.4468	3.7403	2.7891
Female	6.4786	3.4588	4.8695	4.7813	6.6337	5.1987
U.S.						
Total	5.2302	5.1136	5.5986	4.9584	5.9186	4.8634
Male	3.5539	3.1604	3.1363	3.2750	3.5905	2.9519
Female	5.8130	5.8784	6.3262	5.3888	6.0990	5.0810

Source: Author's computations from Current Population Survey tapes.

benefits are thought to offer attractive alternatives to remaining in the work force. If these inducements are to work differentially upon blacks, then it is useful to inquire whether blacks have benefited relative to whites in the receipt of these transfers. Table 4.5 documents the welfare incomes of blacks relative to whites in the decade in question. The ratio of per capita public assistance incomes received by black females to that received by white females rose slightly during the 1970s and fell sharply in the 1980s. Among males it fell slightly during the early 1970s, rose in the late 1970s, and fell again in the 1980s, averaging out to an almost trendless pattern which bears little correspondence to labor supply fluctuations.

The pattern in the North Central region is exceptional. Here, there was a sharp rise in the black–white welfare income ratio among males during the 1970s. So sharp was this rise that by 1978 the black–white

TABLE 4.6. *Black–White Mean Ratio Social Security and/or Railroad Retirement Compensation (Individuals 14 +)*

	1968	1970	1973	1975	1978	1985
Northeast						
Total	.4866	.3865	.5148	.7334	.6427	.5878
Male	.5066	.3179	.5536	.8054	.6507	.6574
Female	.4735	.4512	.4845	.6783	.6379	.5327
North Central						
Total	.7898	.6197	.6963	.7146	.7704	.6465
Male	.8332	.5806	.6827	.6731	.8224	.6645
Female	.7507	.6655	.7151	.7641	.7297	.6315
Southeast						
Total	.7031	.6429	.7387	.7169	.8694	.6467
Male	.6307	.5916	.6911	.6638	.7940	.6354
Female	.8018	.7070	.7905	.7754	.9388	.6589
Southwest						
Total	.7525	.7354	.9014	.8484	.8980	.8265
Male	.7655	.7727	.8635	1.0045	.9026	.8786
Female	.7396	.7050	.9743	.7186	.8973	.7832
West						
Total	.5468	.7486	.5279	.7707	1.0947	.4238
Male	.5054	.5565	.5463	.8325	1.1120	.3744
Female	.5973	.9681	.5171	.7081	1.0730	.4746
U.S.						
Total	.6587	.5921	.6829	.7371	.8260	.6502
Male	.6540	.5493	.6703	.7449	.8099	.6647
Female	.6593	.6414	.7016	.7344	.8434	.6389

Source: Author's computations from Current Population Survey tapes.

welfare income ratio among males approached the ratio among females. In 1968 black men received about two and a half times as much welfare income as white men; by 1978, the welfare income of black men was nearly eight times that of white men. In the latter year, the ratio of mean welfare income received by black women was but a little more than nine times that received by white women in the North Central region. Although this region fell to about five by 1985, it was still well above the national average.

The other major transfer program is social security. Table 4.6 highlights the changes in the ratio of black to white mean social security income from 1968 to 1985. Again there are perceptible regional variations that diverge from the national trend. In the country as a whole, black men began to reach parity with whites in receipt of social security and railroad retirement income during the 1970s. By the 1980s the racial gap in these transfers widened again. The ratio rose from .65 in 1968, dropped briefly to .55 in 1970, rose again to .67 in 1973, and continued to improve thereafter, reaching .81 by 1978. But by 1985 the ratio had returned to .66, little above the 1968 level. On the regional level the patterns imperfectly match the national improvement. In the West, for example, there was a spectacular jump in the ratio among males from .50 in 1968 to 1.11 in 1978, but a devastating decline to .37 in 1985. By contrast in the North Central region, the ratio began in 1968 at .83, dropped in the mid-decade to .68, rose to .82 in 1978, and fell again to .66 in 1985.

The upshot of this investigation, then, is that the operative mechanism that is driving the effects of transfers on the withdrawal of the least productive black workers from the labor market is ambiguous at best. It is unclear whether the regional variations are separate "local stories" that make the aggregate U.S. picture seem overly simplistic, or whether they are deviations from a general national pattern. In any event, the weak trends in racial differences in weeks worked do not lend themselves well to the voluntary withdrawal argument while the strong trends in unemployment are consistent with either interpretation of labor market behavior.

More recently, another factor has entered the debate about voluntary versus involuntary withdrawal from the labor market. This concerns the degree to which labor market inequality has been masked by the allegedly voluntary withdrawal of the lowest-earning workers from the labor market. We now take a closer look at this phenomenon.

The best-known version of the argument that voluntary labor force withdrawal has created an illusion of racial economic progress is the work of Butler and Heckman (1977). They take the stance that, in general, there has been no change in the gap in the average productivity between blacks and whites. They suggest that the apparent improvement in the status of blacks has resulted from the removal of low human capital blacks from the labor market while the most productive blacks remained. This leads to raised ratios of black to white earnings and, in turn, to the illusion of black economic progress.

Various attempts to test this sample selection process have challenged the hypothesis. Hoffman and Link (1984) attempt to estimate population earnings equations from CPS data that primarily constrain estimates of earnings functions to those obtained for individuals with work experience. They "correct" for selection bias by using a procedure suggested by Heckman (1979). Focus is on those individuals with a positive employment probability in the sample year. Large standard errors are reported for the selection effect for young blacks and whites, suggesting to Hoffman and Link that the role of labor force withdrawal in driving up the relative wage ratios may be negligible.

They do find, as Donald Parsons (1980) did in an earlier study, that older workers—both black and white—experience significant reductions in labor force participation relative to other workers. This labor market withdrawal was found to contribute significantly to the determination of the population earnings estimates. Among older workers, the sample selection effect was operable. Hoffman and Link find that sample selection reduces the racial earning differential by nearly 22 percent and that the omission of the zero earners significantly biases upward the measure of black to white earnings. Many of these older workers cite health problems as the reason for their withdrawal from the labor market. Thus the selection process may not have been voluntary after all.

Although they do not report estimates of transfers on the selection probability, Hoffman and Link do refer to Parsons's estimates in explaining their results. Parsons reasoned that the decline in labor force participation among older men was attributable to availability of social security disability benefits and similar transfer payments; older men may withdraw from the labor market to avail themselves of the sometimes attractive benefit packages for which they may qualify. Among younger workers, Hoffman and Link found no such selection bias, and from that they infer that for young workers the earnings gap must be real.

Charles Brown (1984) also has examined the effect of zero earners on the racial earnings gap. Using aggregate data and correcting the median earnings for truncation, most of the earning gains by blacks remained after "correction" for zero earners was made. He concluded that sample selection may be a less important contributor to the observed increases in black earnings than the Heckman school would have one believe.

In a similar attempt to subject the Heckman hypothesis to a rigorous test, Wayne Vroman (1986) combines the CPS tapes on current earnings with the earnings histories from the Social Security Administration's earnings record data. Here the focus is on comparing the prior earnings of current transfer recipients. Amazingly, Vroman discovers that the effect of removing from the sample those people who subsequently become transfer recipients lowers the median earnings and does not raise it. It is not the people of lowest productivity who withdraw from the labor market in favor of receipt of transfers; it is the higher-earning ones who withdraw, according to Vroman. Not surprisingly, the transfers that induce men to withdraw from the labor market are not AFDC or similar welfare benefits but disability and retirement transfers.

Vroman casts further doubt on the Heckman argument by demonstrating that during the period when black–white earnings inequality narrowed the most, 1964–1973, there were no unusually large labor supply reductions. The facts as he sees them are the following: there were significant and sizable reductions in labor force participation among younger black males, but they were no larger in the period of the major reduction in earnings inequality than in later years; there was a rapid surge of transfer recipiency among black and white males in the era after the 1960s, but much of this was the receipt of retirement and disability funds; and finally, recipiency of transfers did affect measures of earning inequality, but not in the direction predicted by Heckman. Instead of selecting out the lowest-productivity workers, the transfer recipiency process led to the exclusion of higher-income workers. Quite simply, Vroman concludes, transfers could not have caused the observed change in relative earnings by race.

Smith and Welch (1986) also examine the Heckman argument. Their technique is to link adjacent years of the CPS where identical individuals can be found due to the sample rotation method used by the census enumerators. Since half of the sample entered in a given year remains in the next, it is possible to compare the previous earnings of dropouts with current labor force participants. Smith and Welch conclude that more than half of the racial earnings improvement from 1970 to 1980 among 25-to-30-year-old males can be accounted for by labor force withdrawal. Among older age groups, however, less than 10 percent of the wage gains by blacks can be so accounted. Moreover, in their optimistic assessment, Smith and Welch conclude that overall sample selection has played a minor and insignificant role in raising the measure of black economic well-being.

A more sophisticated attempt to account for labor force withdrawal, by Darity and Myers (1980), estimated simultaneously labor force participation and earnings equations for blacks and whites. These equations used a unique data set compiled from the Current Population Survey, using age, race, region, and sex cohorts for 1968 and 1978. One compilation used only individuals with positive incomes in those years; another computed the mean earnings for each cohort using all observations and included those not working. This amounts to assigning a zero wage to nonworkers, the antithetical strategy to assigning the earners' wage to nonworkers. In the positive income sample, welfare, public assistance, and other transfers significantly reduce the weeks worked among blacks and increase weeks unemployed. The nonemployment effects for blacks were greater in 1978 than in 1968 and larger than the estimated effects for whites. Thus transfers appear to reduce labor force participation among blacks when the sample is restricted to positive income earners.

When focus is placed on the "potential" labor force—that is, those in the labor force and those without earnings who are, nevertheless, in the noninstitutionalized civilian population—then the results are quite different. The impacts of transfers on weeks worked are considerably larger for whites than they are for blacks. Welfare and public assistance benefits, for example, reduce white weeks worked by more than twice that of blacks. While the influence of welfare on weeks unemployed is slightly larger for blacks than for whites, the negative impact of social security benefits on weeks worked continued to be larger for whites than blacks and actually fell for both between 1968 and 1978.

Furthermore, the Darity and Myers findings suggest that the effect of labor force participation on earnings is *stronger* among white workers than it is among black workers. Thus, although declines in labor force participation have lowered both black and white wages among potential labor market participants, the net impact of these declines is to widen the racial earnings gap among these potential workers, rather than narrow it.

These findings provide a completely different twist to the sample selection hypothesis. Although a systematic labor force withdrawal impact of transfers is not uncovered, the impact of welfare transfers and social security transfers on weeks worked and weeks unemployed is shown to be larger for whites than for blacks. Moreover, any apparent effect of labor force withdrawal on earnings is larger for whites than it is for blacks, when the sample of potential labor force participants is examined.

Our results do confirm that there may be a sample selection process that reduces black–white earnings ratios among those with *positive* earnings. But this reduction is not the result of blacks of low productivity withdrawing from the labor market. It is attributable, instead, to the reduction in labor force participation of whites of higher productivity. Indeed, this proposition gains added support in light of data that shows that young whites with higher levels of education did experience reduced weeks worked from 1968 to 1978 along with higher levels of unemployment. Intriguingly then, the Heckman argument is turned on its head to suggest that it is the voluntary withdrawal of more-productive whites and not less-productive blacks that has contributed to the observed declines in racial earnings inequality during the 1970s. Furthermore, this interpretation helps clear up the confu-

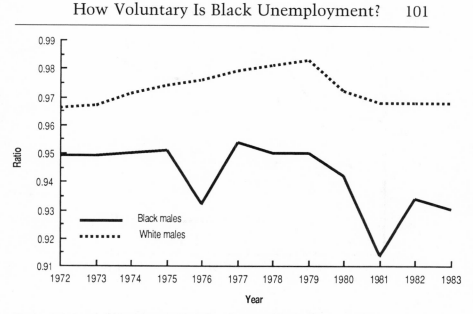

Figure 4.1. Ratio of Noninstitutionalized to Total Population by Race
Source: U.S. Department of Labor, Bureau of Labor Statistics, *Handbook of Labor Statistics*, Bulletin 2217, June 1985.

sion about how and why racial earnings gaps have again widened in the 1980s.

Current Population Survey data from 1972 to 1984, along with data from the Social Security Administration, provide another glimpse at the transfers/nonemployment nexus. Figure 4.1 displays the decline in the noninstitutionalized civilian male population in the United States. There has been a significant decline in the ratio of noninstitutionalized black males to the total of black males in the resident population. There were two sharp dips in this measure of withdrawal from the civilian population: one occurring in 1975–1976, the other occurring in 1980–1981. Both of these periods of substantial withdrawal of black men from the major sphere of economic life coincide with significant growth in the black prison population. Indeed, in the period of 1970 to 1985, the prison population in the United States more than doubled, with the black prison population increasing more rapidly than the white prison population (Myers 1986).

When one examines the fraction of individuals in the civilian noninstitutionalized population among males over age 16 not in the labor force, a more prominent result is apparent. This fraction of labor market nonparticipants has been rising for both blacks and whites throughout the 1970s and is substantially higher among blacks than among whites. The gap between the two widens in the downturn, thus

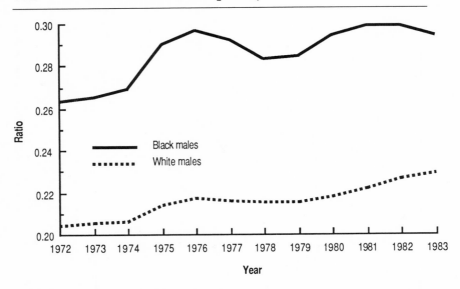

Figure 4.2. Ratio of Labor Force Nonparticipation to Noninstitutionalized Population, 1972–1983
Source: U.S. Department of Labor, Bureau of Labor Statistics, *Handbook of Labor Statistics*, Bulletin 2217, June 1985.

mirroring the major drops in the fraction of the black resident population outside of institutions observed for the mid-1970s and the early 1980s.

Therefore, Figures 4.1 and 4.2 reveal that both black and white males have been withdrawing from the labor force over the past decade and that the abruptness of that withdrawal, especially in 1976 and 1981, was more evident among blacks than whites. If blacks were withdrawing more rapidly from the labor market than whites, then what was the source of this withdrawal? Could it have been the inducements of AFDC? When real (in 1982 dollars) AFDC monthly benefits per recipient are mapped against black and white noninstitutionalized populations relative to the resident population, just the opposite is observed. Real AFDC benefits were declining sharply in the late 1970s, and yet withdrawals from the noninstitutionalized population continued. Moreover, a positive association is observed in the early part of the decade, with growing AFDC benefits accompanied by reductions in withdrawals from the noninstitutionalized population. These findings hardly provide support for the view that welfare induces black men to abandon the work world to live off of the dole.

In all fairness, Figure 4.3 does not examine withdrawal from the labor market, but merely withdrawal from the "potential" labor mar-

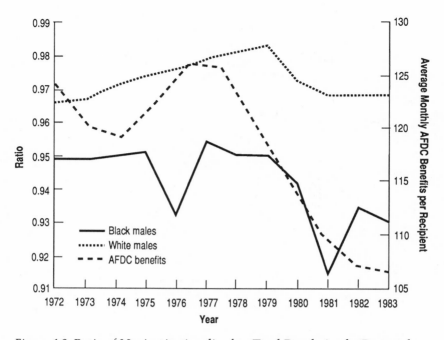

Figure 4.3. Ratio of Noninstitutionalized to Total Population by Race and
AFDC Benefits (in 1982 Dollars), 1972–1983
Sources: U.S. Department of Labor, Bureau of Labor Statistics, *Handbook of Labor
Statistics,* Bulletin 2217, June 1985; *Social Security Bulletin,* Annual Statistical
Supplement.

ket. Figure 4.4 captures the more conventional notion of labor force
participation. It measures the ratio of labor force nonparticipants to
the civilian, noninstitutionalized population over age 16. One minus
this ratio is the commonly referenced labor force participation rate.
Figure 4.4 reveals that the labor force nonparticipation rate has been
rising for blacks and whites. Again, in the early 1970s, a positive association occurs between the nonparticipation rate and the real AFDC
benefits. This is especially true for blacks. But the apparent support
for the welfare-induced labor force withdrawal vanishes after 1978,
when AFDC benefits turned sharply downward even as the black male
labor force withdrawal continued to increase. The evidence here is not
consistently supportive of the voluntary withdrawal hypothesis.

Quarterly labor force statistics provide another means for assessing
how voluntary labor force withdrawal is. Those individuals in the noninstitutionalized, civilian population not working and not looking for
work were asked whether they wanted to work. The fraction of those
not in the labor force who said that they did not want to work might
be regarded as voluntarily out of the labor force. These people included
men who had retired, those who were attending school, and the presumably lazy and unmotivated to whom so much attention has been

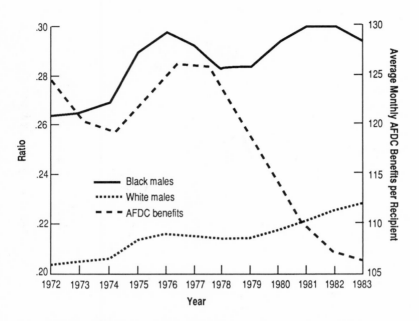

Figure 4.4. Ratio of Labor Force Nonparticipation to Noninstitutionalized Population and AFDC Benefits (in 1982 Dollars), 1972–1983
Sources: U.S. Department of Labor, Bureau of Labor Statistics, *Handbook of Labor Statistics*, Bulletin 2217, June 1985; *Social Security Bulletin*, Annual Statistical Supplement.

addressed by critics of the welfare system and social programs. Although this fraction of those who do not want to work is high for both blacks and whites, interestingly, it has been falling steadily among black males while remaining virtually constant among white males over the decade. This finding underscores the fact that larger fractions of white men are "voluntarily" out of the labor force than black men.

Figure 4.5 maps real AFDC benefits per recipient family against our measure of voluntary nonparticipation in the labor force. There is a strong correlation in the trend and fluctuations between AFDC benefits and black male "voluntary" withdrawal. As real AFDC benefits per recipient family fall, the fraction of black male nonparticipants in the labor force who voluntarily withdraw also falls. Thus, those who say that AFDC is correlated with voluntary withdrawal from the labor market are almost correct. However, the positive association between real AFDC benefits and voluntary withdrawal from the labor market fails to explain the decline in black labor force participation during those years when real AFDC benefits were falling.

In summary, labor force participation and unemployment decisions are probably in some respect voluntary. Indeed, a pattern of labor force

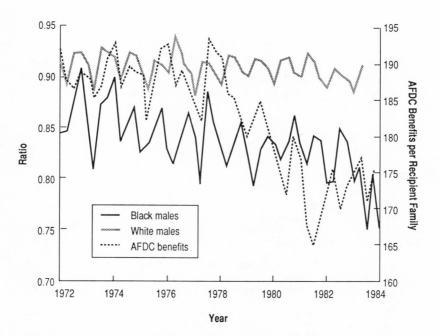

Figure 4.5. Ratio of Those Who Do Not Want to Work to Those Not in the Labor Force and AFDC Benefits, 1972–1984
Sources: U.S. Department of Labor, Bureau of Labor Statistics, *Handbook of Labor Statistics,* Bulletin 2217, June 1985; *Social Security Bulletin,* Annual Statistical Supplement.

withdrawal may be associated with family receipt of AFDC benefits. So, also, men who were in the noninstitutionalized, civilian population who did not work and who indicated that they did not want to work, may represent a group of voluntary withdrawals. But most voluntary withdrawals are not recipients of AFDC. They may receive social security or disability benefits, but their nonparticipation is unlikely to be stimulated by welfare. Instead, among whites and blacks, most voluntary withdrawals are because of school enrollment, retirement, or disability.

Fewer blacks than whites are voluntary withdrawals. The upshot is that the voluntary withdrawal perspective creates more puzzles than it resolves. It does not describe much of the labor force behavior of blacks, and when it does, it suggests patterns directly opposite those implied by Butler and Heckman (1977). The inducements of welfare do not explain the withdrawal of black men from the labor force in recent years; welfare has become less attractive precisely in the era when their labor force participation has fallen most rapidly.

Involuntary labor force withdrawal plays a more conspicuous role than voluntary withdrawal. The processes leading to the institutionalization and involuntary withdrawal of black men from the labor force should be explored more carefully. Understanding that process will prove essential in gaining new insights about black–white inequality.

References

Berger, Mark C., and Barry T. Hirsch, 1983. "The Civilian Earnings Experience of Vietnam Era Veterans." *Journal of Human Resources* 18 (Fall): 455–479.

Bianchi, Suzanne, M., 1980. "Racial Differences in Per Capita Income, 1960–76: The Importance of Household Size, Headship, and Laborforce Participation." *Demography* 17 (May): 129–143.

Bishop, John H., 1980. "Job, Cash Transfer, and Marital Instability: A Review and Synthesis of the Evidence." *Journal of Human Resources* 15 (Summer): 301–334.

Borjas, George, J., 1984. "Race, Turnover, and Male Earnings." *Industrial Relations* 23 (Winter): 763–789.

———, 1983. "The Measurement of Race and Gender Wage Differentials: Evidence from the Federal Sector." *Industrial and Labor Relations Review* 37 (October): 79–91.

Brimmer, Andrew F., 1984. "Long-Term Economic Growth and Black Unemployment Opportunities." *Review of Black Political Economy* 13 (Summer–Fall): 61–73.

Brown, Charles, 1984. "Black–White Earnings Ratios Since the Civil Rights Act of 1964: The Importance of Labor Market Dropouts." *Quarterly Journal of Economics* 32 (February): 32–43.

Butler, Richard, and James H. Heckman, 1977. "The Government's Impact on the Labor Market Status of Black Americans: A Critical Review." In *Equal Rights and Industrial Relations*, eds. Leonard J. Hausman, et al. Madison, Wisc.: Industrial Relations Research Association, 235–281.

Cook, P., 1975. "The Correctional Carrot: Better Jobs for Parolees." *Policy Analysis* 1 (1): 11–55.

Darden, Joe R., 1983. "Racial Differences in Unemployment: A Spatial Perspective." *Review of Black Political Economy* 12 (Spring): 93–105.

Darity, William, Jr., 1983. "The Managerial Class and Surplus Population." *Society* 21 (November–December): 54–62.

Darity, William, Jr., and Samuel Myers, Jr., 1987. "Is There a Crisis in the Black Community? The Problem of Family Structure, Earnings Inequality, and the Marginalization of Black Men." Unpublished paper presented at the National Economic Association Meeting, Chicago (December).

———, 1984. "Does Welfare Dependency Cause Female Headship? The Case of the Black Family." *Journal of Marriage and the Family* 46 (November): 765–779.

———, 1983. "Changes in Black Family Structure: Implications for Welfare Dependency." *American Economic Review* 73 (May): 59–64.

———, 1980. "Changes in Black–White Income Inequality, 1968–78: A Decade of Progress?" *Review of Black Political Economy* 10 (Summer): 365–379.

Eisenger, Peter, 1982. "Black Employment in Municipal Jobs: The Impact of Black Political Power." *American Political Science Review* 76: 380–392.

Freeman, Richard, 1977. *Black Elite*. New York: McGraw-Hill.

———, 1973. "Changes in the Labor Market for Black Americans, 1948–72." In *Brookings Papers on Economic Activity*, eds. Arthur M. Okun and George L. Perry, 67–131.

Hamilton, Earl G., 1984. "Long-Term Economic Growth and Black Employment Opportunities: Comments." *Review of Black Political Economy* 13, no. 1 and 2 (Summer–Fall): 74–79.

Heckman, James J., 1979. "Sample Selection Bias as a Specification Error." *Economet-rica* 49 (January): 153–162.

Hoffman, Saul D., and Charles R. Link, 1984. "Selectivity Bias in Male Wage Equations: Black–White Comparisons." *The Review of Economics and Statistics* 66 (May): 320–324.

Holzer, Harry J., 1986. "Black Youth Nonemployment: Duration and Job Search." In *The Black Youth Employment Crisis*, eds. Richard B. Freeman and Harry J. Holzer, 23–73. Chicago: University of Chicago Press.

Iden, George, 1980. "The Labor Force Experience of Black Youth: A Review." *Monthly Labor Review* 103 (August): 10–16.

Kiefer, Nicholas M., and George R. Neumann, 1979a. "An Empirical Job-Search Model with a Test of the Constant Reservation-Wage Hypothesis." *Journal of Political Economy* 87 (February): 89–107.

———, 1979b. "Estimation of Wage Offer Distributions and Reservation Wages." In *Studies of the Economics of Search*, eds. S. Lippmann and J. McCall, Amsterdam: North-Holland.

Killingsworth, Mark R., and Cordelia W. Reimers, 1983. "Race, Ranking, Promotion, and Pay at a Federal Facility: A Logit Analysis." *Industrial and Labor Relations Review* 37 (October): 92–107.

Krumm, Ronald J., 1984. "Regional Wage Differentials, Labor Supply Resources, and Race." *Journal of Regional Science* 24 (August): 431–442.

Lenihan, K. J., 1974. *Financial Resources of Released Prisoners*. Washington, D.C.: Bureau of Social Science Research, Inc.

Leonard, Jonathan S., 1985. "What Promises are Worth: The Impact of Affirmative Action Goals." *Journal of Human Resources* 20 (Winter): 3–20.

———, 1984a. "Antidiscrimination or Reverse Discrimination: The Impact of Change in Demographics, Title VII, and Affirmative Action on Productivity." *Journal of Human Resources* 19 (Spring): 145–174.

———, 1984b. "The Impact of Affirmative Action on Employment." *Journal of Labor Economics* 2 (2): 439–463.

———, 1984c. "Employment and Occupational Advance Under Affirmative Action." *Review of Economics and Statistics* 66 (August): 377–385.

———, 1967. "Dismissal for Off-the-Job Criminal Behavior." *Monthly Labor Review* 90 (November): 21–27.

Mallar, D. C., and C. D. Thorton, 1978. "Transition Aid for Released Prisoners: Evidence from Life Experience." *Journal of Human Resources* 13: 208–235.

Malveaux, Julianne, 1984. "Employment and Training Policy for Black America: Beyond Placebo." *Review of Black Political Economy* 13 (August, Summer–Fall): 138–144.

Miller, N., 1979. "A Study of the Number of Prisoners with Records of Arrest and Conviction in the Labor Force: Policy Implications for the U.S. Department of Labor." *Technical Analysis Papers* 63: 1–43.

Mortenson, Dale T., 1977. "Unemployment Insurance and Job-Search Decisions." *Industrial and Labor Relations Review* 30: 505–517.

———, 1970. "Job Search, the Duration of Unemployment, and the Phillips Curve." *American Economic Review* 60: 847–862.

Murray, Charles, 1984. *Losing Ground*. New York: Basic Books.

Myers, Samuel L., Jr., 1986. "Black Unemployment and Its Link to Crime." *The Urban League Review* 10 (Summer): 98–105.

———, 1983. "Estimating the Economic Model of Crime: Employment Versus Punishment Effects." *Quarterly Journal of Economics* 98 (February): 157–166.

Parsons, Donald O., 1980. "Racial Trends in Male Labor Force Participation." *American Economic Review* 70 (December): 911–920.

Piliavin, I., and R. Gardner, 1980. *Supported Work: Impact for Ex-Offenders*. Madison: University of Wisconsin Press.

Portnay, B., 1970. "Employment for Former Criminals." *Cornell Law Review* 55 (January): 306–320.

Pownal, George A., 1971. "Employment Problems of Released Prisoners." *Manpower* (January): 16–31.

Rossi, P. H., R. A. Berk, and K. J. Lenihan, 1980. *Money, Work, and Crime.* New York: Academic Press.

Salop, Steven C., 1979. "A Model of the Natural Rate of Unemployment." *American Economic Review* 69 (March): 117–125.

Schmidt, Peter, and Ann D. Witte, 1984. *An Economic Analysis of Crime and Justice: Theory, Methods, and Applications.* New York: Academic Press.

Shapiro, David, 1984. "Wage Differentials Among Black, Hispanic, and White Young Men." *Industrial and Labor Relations Review* 37 (July): 570–581.

Shulman, Steven, 1984. "The Measurement and Interpretation of Black Wage and Occupational Gains: A Reevaluation." *Review of Black Political Economy* 212 (Spring): 59–69.

Smith, James P., and Finis Welch, 1986. *Closing the Gap: Forty Years of Economic Progress for Blacks.* Santa Monica, Ca: RAND Corporation.

———, 1984. "Affirmative Action and Labor Markets." *Journal of Labor Economics* 2 (April): 269–301.

Sowell, Thomas, 1981. "Poverty, the Distribution of Income and Social Policy." In *The Limits of Government Regulation,* ed. James F. Gatti, 35–56. New York: Academic Press.

Stephenson, Stanley P., 1976. "The Economics of Youth Job Search Behavior." *Review of Economics and Statistics* 58 (February): 104–111.

Swinton, David H., 1983. "Orthodox and Systemic Explanations for Unemployment and Racial Inequality: Implications for Policy." *Review of Political Economy* 12 (Spring): 9–25.

Taggart, Robert, 1972. "Manpower Programs for Criminal Offenders." *Monthly Labor Review* 95 (August): 17–24.

Viscusi, Kip W., 1986. "Market Incentives for Criminal Behavior." In *The Black Youth Employment Crisis,* eds. Richard B. Freeman and Harry J. Holzer, 301–346. Chicago: University of Chicago Press.

Vroman, Wayne, 1986. "Transfer Payments, Sample Selection, and Male Black–White Earnings Differences." *American Economic Review* 76 (May): 351–354.

JAMES P. SMITH

Chapter 5. Career Wage Mobility

J OB CAREERS are not static. Fresh with their diplomas, most work-ers enter their chosen professions as little better than raw recruits with limited practical knowledge about the necessary skills. They spend their first months and years on the job partly as learners, investing considerable money and time in acquiring job-related skills. Most then transit into junior membership in their occupations; later still, the more successful move into full professional status. In the dynamics of occupational careers, some are more able, more ambitious, or luckier than others, and careers diverge among people who start the race at the same point. But the general tendency is for productivity and wages to rise the longer workers are on the job. For example, the earnings of men with twenty years of labor force experience typically run 80–90 percent higher than those in the first five years of work, and in some occupations the differentials are much higher.

These large wage differentials associated with labor market tenure raise an issue of the relative career prospects for black and white work-ers. The confinement of blacks to dead-end jobs is often thought to be a quantitatively important cause of the racial wage gap. Many have argued that blacks fall successively behind white workers in a variety of dimensions as their careers proceed. According to this view, black men have been systematically excluded by discriminatory forces from jobs with high career growth potential. Here I take a fresh look at this issue by examining the empirical evidence on male racial differences in occupational and wage mobility over labor force careers.

This chapter is organized into three sections. In the first section I recapitulate the principal empirical data—the less-rapid black wage growth with age—that gave rise to the idea that blacks have been con-fined to relatively dead-end jobs. The two main theoretical explana-tions for this age relationship—the secondary labor market and vin-tage hypotheses—are also outlined. The selective literature review in the second section summarizes the major empirical evidence. Finally, I report certain new results, derived from the 1940–1980 census, that document actual racial differences in career wage growth in far more

109

TABLE 5.1. *Black Male Wages as a Percentage of White Male Wages, 1940–1980*

Years of market experience	Census year				
	1940	1950	1960	1970	1980
1–5	46.7	61.8	60.2	75.1	84.2
6–10	47.5	61.0	59.1	70.1	76.6
11–15	44.4	58.3	59.4	66.2	73.5
16–20	44.4	56.6	58.4	62.8	71.2
21–25	42.3	54.1	57.6	62.7	67.8
26–30	41.7	53.2	56.2	60.6	66.9
31–35	40.2	50.3	53.8	60.0	66.5
36–40	39.8	46.9	55.9	60.3	68.5
All	43.3	55.2	57.5	64.4	72.6

Source: Public use tapes of the decennial censuses, 1940–1980.

detail than was previously possible. These new results present a far different historical record of male racial differences in career prospects than was thought to be the case.

The question is deceptively easy to pose: do black men enjoy salary increases and promotions equal to those of white men?[1] The instinctive reply of most Americans to this question would undoubtedly be in the negative, and until recently most economists would have given the same response. Such reactions apparently received widespread empirical confirmation since cross-sectional data indicated that black–white male income differences diverged sharply with age. This divergence spawned theories of labor market discrimination that asserted the existence of one key form of discrimination: that blacks as a group are forced into sectors of the economy where little career wage growth is possible. This theory dominated thinking on racial job mobility for decades, but it now appears to be, by and large, false.

The empirical origins of the theories that blacks in similar occupations do not progress as rapidly as whites over their careers date back at least to the 1940 census. It was the first census to include information on income; the large size of the sample allowed detailed decomposition of income differences between the races. Age-stratified income data from the 1940 census contained the first evidence based on national data that the wage gap between the races expanded systematically with age.[2]

To illustrate the typical cross-sectional pattern, Table 5.1 depicts black–white male weekly wage ratios from each of the decennial census tapes between 1940 and 1980. To highlight life-cycle patterns, these ratios are listed for five-year intervals of years of work experience.[3]

One pattern that characterizes all five census years in Table 5.1 is that black–white wage ratios decline with years of work experience. For example, in 1950, among men who had spent 36 to 40 years in the labor market, black wages were 47 percent of white. In the same year, among men in their first five years of work experience, black wages were 62 percent of white. This pattern, that younger blacks fare better in comparison to whites than their older counterparts, is a feature common to all cross-sectional studies.

How should we interpret this less-rapid black male wage growth with age in Table 5.1? A natural interpretation of the expanding wage differentials with age was the life-cycle interpretation actually assigned to it. Among a group of blacks and whites of similar education, region, and initial wage or job, over the course of a career blacks will fall further and further behind whites in earnings and job advancements. For a long time, the cross-sectional decline in wage ratios with experience, as depicted in Table 5.1, was the principal statistical evidence that led to widespread scientific and popular acceptance of a particular theory of labor market discrimination. This theory, labeled the "secondary" or "dual" labor market theory, viewed labor markets as stratified, with some markets being less upwardly mobile than others. Because of discrimination, blacks tended to be relegated to these secondary markets and to jobs with little potential for career advancement.

However, this cross-sectional increase in black wages with age is also consistent with an alternative "cohort" or "vintage" hypothesis that recognizes that each individual in a cross section is a member of a distinct birth cohort captured at a single point in his or her life cycle. In the cohort view, the observed cross-sectional decline in relative black–white wages with job experience simply reflects the fact that less-experienced workers are simultaneously members of more recent birth cohorts. For example, in Table 5.1, the 47 percent ratio for the 36–40 years experience interval may be lower than the 62 percent ratio for the first five years of experience in 1950 because the more experienced workers were born thirty-five years earlier. Relative to contemporary whites, these older blacks had less schooling and attended poorer quality schools than their black successors would 35 years later. If more rapid improvement in schooling quality and home environments had occurred over time for blacks, blacks and whites would be closer in terms of ability in the 1906–1910 cohorts than they were in the 1886–1895 cohorts. In the cohort view, the cross-sectional decline with age in black–white earnings does not reflect differential life-cycle effects, but rather the movement across age groups from younger to older cohorts.

The secondary labor market and cohort theories offer very different bases for adjusting the past trends and predicting the future trends in black–white income disparities. The life-cycle view is basically pessimistic. For any given group of workers, conditions will deteriorate for blacks relative to whites as they get older. Moreover, there is no reason to presume that when the next group of workers starts their work careers, blacks will fare any better relative to whites than previous generations did. In the cohort view, however, the relative position of a given group of black and white workers will not change over the work careers, but as each new cohort arrives on the scene, black wages will be higher relative to whites. Moreover, if the future course of differences among cohorts conforms to the past, the cohort hypothesis tends toward the more optimistic view that wage differences between blacks and whites will continue to narrow over time.

It should be clear that both the life-cycle and cohort hypotheses are consistent with the data presented in Table 5.1. In fact, any single cross-sectional data source, such as the census, is incapable of distinguishing between the cohort and life-cycle hypotheses since virtually by definition more experienced workers must be simultaneously members of older cohorts. In order to differentiate between the two hypotheses, we must be able to follow a given cohort of workers who entered the labor market at the same time over their life-cycle careers as they age. Researchers apply two techniques to accomplish this. The first involves using successive cross-sectional data sets in different calendar years to create synthetic cohorts. The second relies on longitudinal data sources that explicitly follow a given individual as he or she ages. The evidence from both points to the same conclusion— by and large the data reject the secondary labor market theory and confirm the cohort or vintage hypothesis.

Before reviewing the evidence, the reader should bear in mind that a finding that black wages do not rise as rapidly as white wages over life cycles would not alone be a confirmation of the secondary labor market hypothesis. Less-rapid black wage growth could reflect other factors that have little to do with the depiction of the labor market inherent in the secondary labor market view. For example, less on-the-job investment among black men would also lead to less-rapid salary increases for them.[4] Indeed, such prominent human capital adherents as Becker (1975) and Mincer (1974) assigned precisely this interpretation to the smaller age coefficients in black earnings functions. This lower rate of black job investment could reflect a number of factors: (1) an inability of blacks to finance such investments because of lower wealth and more limited access to capital markets; (2) a higher black discount rate for future income; or (3) a higher investment cost by blacks, possibly due to a higher cost of learning associated with lower schooling quality. All three factors have some plausibility, so that less-rapid black male wage growth is not necessarily evidence in favor of secondary labor markets. However, the reverse is not true. I have argued here that the belief that black wage and occupational mobility is less than that of whites has been critical to a strong acceptance of a racial component to secondary labor markets. What is the existing evidence on this issue?

For a long time, most researchers agreed on a life-cycle interpretation of the expanding racial wage disparities with age. Research centered instead on the mechanisms producing this empirical "fact." Especially important in this regard was the vast amount of literature subsumed under the label of the secondary or dual labor market hypothesis.[5] More recently, studies have relied on longitudinal data to trace life-cycle wage differences between the races.

Before discussing the secondary labor market studies, I must point out that I am focusing exclusively on a narrow and specific racial question of the dual labor market hypothesis. That is, do black and white men enjoy similar career wage growth? I think a fair reading of scholars adhering to the dual labor market view is that they assert that black men fall well short of the salary increases enjoyed by whites. But the dual labor theory deals with many more issues than this specific racial question. One can only be impressed when reading this literature with its grand vision, its richness in descriptive detail, and its historical scope. Such a complex theory can neither be accepted nor dismissed in its entirety with such simple tests as I pursue here. I make no claim to address the theory in its full scope. But it remains true that this literature contains an identifiable racial dimension. Dual labor market theorists invariably argue that blacks are disproportionately in the secondary labor market. If so, on average, black salary advances should be less than those of whites.

The beginning of the dual labor market view is a separation of the labor market into two parts: the primary and the secondary markets. Piore (1971) gives a classic discussion of the difference:

The primary market offers jobs which possess several of the following traits: high wages, good working conditions, employment stability and job security, equity and due process in the administration of work rules, and chances for advancement. The . . . secondary market has jobs which, relative to those in the primary sector, are decidedly less attractive. They tend to involve low wages, poor working conditions, considerable variability in employment, harsh and often arbitrary discipline, little opportunity to advance. (Piore 1971, 92)

As this quotation indicates, the good jobs with high salaries and promotion possibilities are in the primary sector; jobs in the secondary labor market are inherently unstable and low wage, and they have flat wage-seniority profiles.

The critical element of the dual market theory is not this dichotomy, but instead concerns mobility between the two sectors. The assertion that gives the theory its special content is that jobs in the primary sector are rationed. Opinions vary about underlying reasons for this rationing. This diversity is at the core of many of the competing views within the segmented labor market school. Some assign it a distinctly Marxist interpretation with an emphasis on class conflict; others emphasize the technological emergence of an industrial economy, with internal labor markets in large firms. Finally, others assert that discriminatory forces are the primary reason for this rationing. These disputes need not concern us here. What is essential is the simultaneous pressure of two markets—a primary market with high payoffs to education and seniority and a secondary market where laborers are largely unrewarded for personal attributes, including education and experience. Second, whatever the cause of the rationing, blacks are disproportionately in the secondary market.

Tests of the dual labor market as applied to race take a variety of forms, and it is difficult to characterize them succinctly. A common approach divides jobs into those thought to be in the primary or those in the secondary sector. The rules that guide this division have been a source of dispute even within the secondary labor market camp. One well-cited example is that of Osterman (1975), who candidly admits to the subjectivity in his work. He employed his own judgment to divide jobs into sectors, a judgment guided by the idea that the secondary sector "contains occupations characterized by low wages, instability of employment, and similar factors" (Osterman 1975, 5B). Other researchers employ more explicit rules.[6]

Given the separation into these markets, the next step is to look at the nature of the labor market within each. A standard procedure would be to estimate earnings functions in each market. It is hypothesized that the secondary labor market will have low estimated returns to education and experience. As a typical example, Osterman (1975) estimated such earnings equations based on the 1967 Survey of Economic Opportunity. Consistent with his expectations, neither age nor education had a statistically significant impact on earnings in the secondary labor market. Blacks, of course, were more likely to be in this secondary market.

The criticism of this empirical design is now standard, with Cain

(1976) as the main citation. The basic point made by Cain concerns sample selection bias. Put simply, he argues that, if we essentially divide the sample into low-wage and high-wage sectors, it should come as little surprise that the wage increments to anything in the truncated low-wage sector are small.

An example of an alternative approach is followed by Rumberger and Carnoy (1980). Using 1970 census data, they also separate markets into two groups. An attractive feature of their study is that they track actual mobility for individuals rather than deducing that mobility from an age coefficient. They report that blacks were less likely than whites to move from the secondary to primary sector between 1965 and 1970, but blacks were also more likely to fall from the primary to secondary sector over that period.

However, this procedure suffers from considerable problems. Essentially, Rumberger and Carnoy posit a line, with all occupations above the line being in the primary sector and all those below in the secondary. Crossing this line alone constitutes mobility. Within the secondary segment, blacks are in occupations further down from this crossing point than whites. Given their diverse starting points, even if there exists equal occupational mobility between the races, whites are more likely to cross the line simply because they are closer to it to begin with. An analogous argument holds within the primary sector. In this sector, whites have the better jobs and are further above the crossing line. Clearly, whites are less likely to traverse this line than blacks are. But that hardly constitutes a test of racial differences in occupational mobility.[7]

At first blush, it is surprising that so little empirical research has relied on panel data to test for differential career wage growth between the races. Panel data most directly monitor the actual wage changes associated with an additional year in the labor force. Unfortunately, existing longitudinal data quickly confront severe problems of adequate sample sizes, especially among black men. In addition, because of their recent availability, such data are limited largely to describing patterns of the last two decades. For these two reasons, panel data have proven to be far less useful for this issue than one would have hoped.

However, two studies use longitudinal data to estimate life-cycle wage profiles by race. Hoffman (1979) and Duncan and Hoffman (1983) both use the Panel Study of Income Dynamics (PSID) in their empirical work. Hoffman's work, the more directly relevant, was motivated precisely to address the issue of racial differences in career wage growth. He starts with the familiar observation that cross-sectional estimates of black career wage growth might bias severely downward the actual wage improvement black men enjoyed as their careers proceeded. The central purpose of his analysis was to contrast the cross-sectional wage profile with that obtained from actually following a group of workers over time.

In Hoffman's work, individuals are followed across the eight-year period 1967–1974. The PSID sample is divided into men aged 20–29 in 1967 and men aged 30–39 in that year. As a consequence, life-cycle wage histories up to age 46 are traced. These actual life-cycle wage histories are then contrasted to those predicted by a 1967 cross-sectional wage equation.

Hoffman's study points to a number of conclusions. Most important is its demonstration once again that vintage effects are quite strong for black men. Because of the rapid improvement in economic opportunities across black birth cohorts, the cross-sectional data seriously bias downward predictions of actual career wage growth among black men. For example, evaluated at eight years of experience, an extra year of work enhanced black male wages by 1.75 percent, if the cross-sectional results are used. The true life-cycle wage growth was actually 3.53 percent per year.

For black men in both age groups, the estimated cross-sectional experience terms are at least half the size of the actual age-related wage growth. For example, cross-sectional estimates indicate essentially a zero wage growth for black men 30–39 years old while the "true" effect was that black wages grew by 3.96 percent per year with each extra year on the job. In contrast, the vintage effects for whites are small (i.e., the estimated cross-sectional and longitudinal estimates of experience are quite similar). Reliable estimates of the true career prospects for black men simply cannot be obtained from cross-sectional studies.

Given the unreliability of cross-sectional estimates, Hoffman turns to his longitudinal analysis to compare actual wage growth between the races. The results vary with the age class considered. In the younger age group (i.e., those initially aged 20–29 years old in 1967), estimates are sensitive to the number of years of work experience. Among men with ten or more years of work experience, black wage growth actually slightly exceeds that of whites.[8] In contrast, among workers with less than ten years of work experience, white wage growth is larger than that experienced by black men.[9] For example, evaluated at eight years of work experience, white male wages grow 1.5 percent more per year than do wages of black men.

The results are more clear-cut for men 30–39 years old. Within this age group, the actual life-cycle wage experience favors black men. Among men in this age group, blacks are favored in wage growth by 1.5 percent per year.

Hoffman summarizes his conclusions succinctly:

The results suggest that differences in earnings growth did exist in the first eight to ten years of work, but that thereafter, earnings differences were maintained or even reduced. For birth cohorts, the pooled and extrapolated results indicate a far more optimistic life-cycle situation than would be inferred from cross-sectional results. (Hoffman 1979, 864)

The second study, Duncan and Hoffman, used the PSID data over the twelve-year period 1967–1978. Although twelve years of the PSID are used, individuals are only followed for four years due to the separation of the data into these three segments: 1967–1970; 1971–1974; 1975–1978. Black–white hourly wage ratios are listed for men aged 25–54 and separately for men aged 25–34.

In large part, Duncan and Hoffman's findings parallel those reported earlier in Hoffman. Once again, the data overwhelmingly points to strong black vintage effects. In fact, according to Duncan and Hoffman, virtually all the improvement in black–white wages represents across-cohort improvement. Across the full sample of men aged 25–54, black–white males wage ratios remain essentially constant as the workers age.[10] Among younger workers, mixed results are obtained.[11] In two of the three cohorts, black–white male wages declined while wage ratios were constant at .81 during the 1975–1978 period.[12]

This brief and selective literature review indicates that the debate has not been settled conclusively. Recent studies have been largely confined to the last few decades, a period that many view as too special in America's racial history to allow historical generalizations. In addition, recent tests of alternative theories, while they offer much of value, have become intricate and subtle. These tests have lost sight of the simple and powerful empirical relation—the much more rapid white male wage growth with age—that gave rise to the notion of black confinement to secondary markets in the first place.

Some new evidence challenges the simple fact that gave birth to the racial dimension of the secondary labor market view initially. My evidence relies on long-term historical tracking of actual career-related wage disparities between the races. My data comes in two parts. The first long-term series presents life-cycle profiles throughout the twentieth century. The disadvantage of this series is that it is indirectly derived from occupational data. The second series relies on actual wage data from 1940 to 1980.

Let us turn first to the long-term series. Until recently, series that tracked relative career progress by race simply did not exist. One reason is that nationally representative income data was not available before 1940. In order to provide information on what happened before that date, it is necessary to rely on indirect methods. In this section, I summarize such estimates originally presented in Smith (1984).

My long-term series is derived from published census occupational distributions of the work force. These distributions were available by race, sex, and age for all decennial censuses from 1890 onward. Occupations were first aggregated into a consistent set of 133 categories that could be calculated in each census year. Each occupation was then assigned a race, sex, and age-specific average income based on mean incomes derived from the 1970 census. The occupation-based income series I derived from this procedure is presented in Table 5.2.

Table 5.2 is organized to facilitate tracking of black–white income ratios across work careers. The first column lists five-year birth cohorts starting with those born between 1826 and 1835. By reading across the rows, we are able to monitor life-cycle income ratios for those cohorts listed in the first column. Complete careers of birth cohorts who entered the labor force in the twentieth century are presented in this table, as well as partial segments of careers for those men who entered the labor force in the last half of the nineteenth century.

Before looking at the actual life-cycle paths, it is informative to use Table 5.2 to see what the cross-sectional data predicts. The cross-sectional age relationship can be obtained by reading down the column under any census year. The qualitative pattern is the same in all census years from 1890 to 1980. Each cross section indicates a deterioration in black–white income ratios with age. If we use the cross section to project, black men should fall progressively behind whites as their careers proceed.

Reality turns out to be quite different. If we consider men who entered the labor force during the twentieth century (for example, those born after 1886), black–white income ratios do not decline over life cycles. The cross-sectional decline apparently results from more-rapid cohort effects for blacks and not from differential life-cycle career paths. On the basis of this occupation-based income data, blacks do not fall behind whites as their careers unfold. Among men born before 1886, Table 5.2 does provide evidence of a less-rapid career income growth for black men, although obviously not as pronounced as the cross section would predict.

By construction, the ratios presented in Table 5.2 only can detect life-cycle decay in the relative economic status of blacks that have their

TABLE 5.2. *Estimated Black–White Male Income Ratios by Birth Cohorts*

Birth cohort	Census year 1890	1900	1910	1920	1930	1940	1950	1960	1970	1980
1956–60										.653
1951–55										.625
1946–50									.646	.624
1941–45									.608	.610
1936–40								.571	.583	.573
1931–35								.561	.582	.593
1926–30							.555	.555	.577	.583
1921–25							.542	.546	.571	.554
1916–20						.501	.532	.537	.562	.583
1911–15						.488	} .516	.536		
1906–10					.509	.480		.526		
1901–05					.500	.482	} .508	.524		
1896–1900				.515	.498	.483		.519		
1891–95					.494	.478	.503			
1886–90				.494	.492	.469	.501			
1881–85					.481	.465				
1876–80		} .488			.458	.445				
1871–75		} .463		} .387	.452					
1866–70	} .472				.438					
1856–65	.454	.451								
1846–55	.435	.428								
1836–45	.417	.398								
1826–35	.397									
All Ages 10–75	.433	.442	.455	.476	.479	.474	.516	.542	.590	.611
Ages 20–64	.439	.449		.484	.486	.479	.522	.543	.585	.605

Source: Smith (1984).

origin in movements across occupations. This table does demonstrate the important point that any cross-sectional decline in relative incomes of blacks due to different occupational distributions for men of different ages is a cohort and not a life-cycle phenomenon. However, within occupations, incomes of blacks may be falling relative to whites, or more white-intensive occupations may exhibit faster career wage growth, even if race income neutrality prevails within occupations. If either of these two events occurs, relative income ratios of blacks will decline with age, but we would not capture it in Table 5.2. To find out about such possibilities, we must turn to actual income data.

One of the great advantages of the 1940 and 1950 census data is that long-term career changes can be monitored. For the first time, we can observe what actually happens to work careers across a forty-year period. A second advantage is that relative racial careers across many diverse decades can be followed. Many researchers have claimed that the 1960s and 1970s were a special time. If so, these decades may not be an appropriate period to test hypotheses that center around racial differences in career progression. All agree that these decades were a period of rapid black economic progress, and many viewed them as quite unusual. For example, other confounding forces, including the implementation of the major civil rights employment discrimination legislation, offered to some a plausible alternative explanation of racial progress. In the remainder of this section, I report some new research results derived from the 1940–1980 census files.

Table 5.3 isolates the actual labor market experiences of labor market cohorts by rearranging the items in Table 5.1. This rearrangement involves centering the original data by the initial year of labor market entry. For example, men in their first five years of work in 1940 first entered the labor market, on average, in 1938. Among these men, blacks earn 46.7 percent as much as whites. These same men by 1950 had spent ten to fifteen years in the labor market; blacks in this cohort now earn 58.3 percent as much as whites. By reading across any row in Table 5.3, we can follow the actual life-cycle path of relative wages of the labor market cohorts indexed in the first column.

The message of Table 5.3 is unambiguous. In contrast to the cross-sectional implication of deterioration in the relative economic status of blacks across labor market careers, the reality is that, if anything, black men actually improve their situation relative to whites. In virtually every instance depicted in Table 5.3, black men narrow the gap between their incomes and those of their white contemporaries as their careers evolve. The cross-sectional decline in each census year

TABLE 5.3. *Black Male Wages as a Percentage of White Male Wages by Labor Market Cohort*

Median year of initial labor market work	Census year				
	1940	1950	1960	1970	1980
1978					84.2
1973					76.6
1968				75.1	73.5
1963				70.1	71.2
1958			60.2	66.2	67.8
1953			59.1	62.8	66.9
1948		61.8	59.4	62.7	66.5
1943		60.0	58.4	60.6	68.5
1938	46.7	58.3	57.6	60.0	
1933	47.5	56.6	56.2	60.3	
1928	44.4	54.1	53.8		
1923	44.4	53.2	55.9		
1918	42.3	50.3			
1913	41.7	46.9			
1908	40.2				
1903	39.8				
All	43.3	55.2	57.5	64.4	72.6

Source: Public use tapes of the decennial censuses 1940–1980.

that characterized Table 5.1 is not the result of any increasing life-cycle differentiation by race. Instead, improvement in the quality of black workers relative to white workers across successive birth cohorts accounts for the cross-sectional decline.

A useful historical summary is provided by combining these census profiles with those obtained from the yearly CPS tapes between 1968 and 1982. The results of that blend are presented in Table 5.4.[13] This table lists for all work cohorts (beginning with those who started work in 1928) black–white male ratios of weekly wages for given accumulation of years of work experience.[14] In this table, reading down a column follows a work cohort across their careers.

The patterns in Table 5.4 are remarkable. Instead of blacks falling progressively behind whites, black men typically enjoy larger wage increases than white men do. For example, among men who entered the labor market between 1946 and 1948, black wages are initially 57.6 percent of whites. When we observe this group thirty-five years later, black men are earning 62.4 percent of whites. The problem blacks

TABLE 5.4. *Cohort Specific Black Male Wages as a Percentage of White Male Wages*

Years of labor market experience	Birth cohort								
	28–30	31–33	34–36	37–39	40–42	43–45	46–48	49–51	52–54
0–1					46.1	51.7	57.6	63.0	62.8
2–4				47.7	52.4	57.1	61.8	62.2	61.9
5–7			48.1	51.4	56.1	60.7	61.1	61.1	61.1
8–10		48.1	51.3	55.0	59.6	60.1	60.4	59.4	60.4
11–13	46.6	51.0	54.5	58.7	59.2	59.6	59.6	59.9	61.4
14–16	49.4	53.7	57.6	58.4	58.8	59.0	60.0	61.0	59.9
17–19	52.3	56.5	57.5	58.1	58.4	59.2	61.1	59.0	60.7
20–22	55.1	56.7	57.3	57.9	58.7	60.0	59.2	60.6	62.9
23–25	55.2	56.8	57.1	58.2	59.4	59.5	60.4	62.8	67.0
26–28	55.3	56.9	57.6	58.9	59.0	61.1	64.0	66.3	65.7
29–31	55.4	57.0	58.6	58.2	61.8	64.8	65.9	65.7	
32–34	55.8	57.3	58.3	61.7	64.7	65.5	62.4		
35–37	56.2	57.6	61.6	64.2	66.8	64.5			
38–40	56.5	59.9	62.3	66.4	67.2				

Years of labor market experience	Birth cohort								
	55–57	58–60	61–63	64–66	67–69	70–72	73–75	76–78	79–81
0–1	61.4	60.6	65.0	69.5	73.9	82.4	81.5	81.8	81.7
2–4	61.6	61.3	64.4	67.4	73.6	76.9	75.1	77.2	
5–7	61.1	63.2	65.2	69.6	72.7	73.0	76.4		
8–10	62.8	64.8	67.7	71.4	73.1	74.7			
11–13	62.2	65.2	69.3	72.8	70.1				
14–16	62.6	66.3	71.0	69.6					
17–19	64.6	69.7	70.9						
20–22	68.6	70.5							
23–25	68.4								

Source: Current Population Surveys.

face is clearly the large wage disparities that exist at the beginning of their labor market careers, not what evolves over labor market careers.

The only real exception to this rule takes place in the 1970s. Especially during the first five years of work experience, black wages do not rise as rapidly as whites' do. For example, the relatively high initial black male wages for the 1970–1978 work cohorts are not maintained over the first five years of work experience. This was the same period studied by Hoffman and Duncan (1983), using the longitudinal PSID data. They also reported that the only case in which black wages fail to keep up with those of whites is in the first five to eight years of work.

The interpretation of this recent divergence from the more common historical pattern remains open. But, note that this initial-year relative wage base in the early 1970s is sharply above that only five years earlier. In other work, I argue that this wage bubble in the early 1970s was an effect of affirmative action but that the gains were short-lived.[15] In the early stages of affirmative action, covered firms were desperately attempting to increase the number of black workers they employed. To achieve this aim, they bid up the wages of young black workers, the age group where most of the new hiring was taking place. Wages of young black workers increased dramatically from 1967 to 1972, but these wage gains had been eroded by 1977.

In my view, the evidence is overwhelming that once we go past the first five years of work experience, black and white men experience similar career-related wage growth. This conclusion is warranted whether we use longitudinal data on individuals or follow synthetic cohorts. The conclusion is also supported for all groups of workers in the forty years since 1940 and far earlier into the twentieth century if we can rely on occupation-based wage series. There seems to me little room for ambiguity here.

The remaining issue of legitimate debate should concentrate on the first five years of work. Even here, my actual historical wage profiles show little favoritism for whites. However, during the early 1970s, my data, as well as the longitudinal studies that cover this period, indicate that black men were unable to maintain their historically high initial wage ratios. I believe that this period represents a special case, reflecting a reaction to affirmative action pressures by covered firms. If so, the early 1970s should not serve as a predictor of future events. However, other interpretations are possible. Additional research on the early phase of the career is definitely warranted.[16] Yet, there is little doubt that the overall conclusion of similar career wage advancement between the races is the correct one.

Notes

1. I will concentrate exclusively on racial differences for men. The more complicated life-cycle labor force histories for women, with career interruptions associated with childbearing being the most notable characteristic, raise too many ancillary issues.
2. For the first extensive use of the 1940 census data to investigate career wage growth, see Zeman (1955).
3. Years of market experience is defined as current age − assumed age at leaving school. The mapping from years of schooling completed and school leaving age is as follows: ed 0–11 = age 17, ed 12 = age 18, ed 13–15 = age 20, ed 16 or more = age 23.
4. More precisely, less investment as a proportion of total income. See Mincer (1974) for a detailed exposition of the human capital approach to job investment.
5. For two readable and more lengthy literature reviews by a critic and a sympathizer of the dual labor market theories, see Cain (1976) and Reich (1984).
6. Andrisani's (1973) separation is based on median earnings in occupations. Those below the 33 percentile are in the secondary labor market.
7. It should be pointed out that using a more continuous definition of occupational mobility and without this separation into two segments, Leigh (1976) finds little evidence of black–white differences in occupational mobility.
8. Hoffman reports that for workers with ten or more years of work experience, the eight-year growth rate is 18.2 percent for blacks and 15.1 percent for whites.
9. However, small sample sizes suggest caution in reaching conclusions for this age group. Hoffman reports, for example, that there are only four blacks in the PSID sample with four years of experience or less.
10. For the first period, the wage rate is .64 in 1967 and .65 in 1970. During the second four years the ratio is .71 in 1971 and .69 in 1974. Finally, the wage ratio is .75 in 1975 and 1978.
11. The usefulness of the Duncan-Hoffman study for testing life-cycle evaluation is seriously marred by a change in sample definition between their first descriptive table (Table 1) and the remainder of their analytical work. In their descriptive table, they impose the restriction that a man had to work at least 500 hours in a year of the four years of the panel. However, in the analytical work, their restriction is that the man is in the sample if he worked 500 hours in a given year no matter what he worked in any other year. Thus, none of their analytical work follows identical individuals over time because only the descriptive table is used. Another major problem with the Duncan-Hoffman study is that age rather than experience stratification is used. Those aged 25–34 vary a good deal in work experience depending on the education level achieved. The whole debate centers on comparing blacks and whites at the same point in their work careers.
12. The ratio declines from .75 to .70 between 1967–1970, and .81 to .73 from 1971 to 1974.
13. The CPS numbers were derived from yearly Current Population Survey public use tapes. The census numbers were derived by centering the numbers in Table 5.3 in the experience midpoint and linearly interpolating between those midpoints. Similarly, intercensal years were also derived by linear interpolation. Whenever CPS and census data are both available, CPS numbers were used. The CPS and census series matched up very well when they met. As a result of all these interpolations, the simulations in Table 5.4 should be regarded mainly as illustrative.
14. A work cohort is defined by the year of initial labor market entry.
15. See Smith and Welch (1986).
16. Care must be exercised in this part of the career. Part of the wage growth we are witnessing represents a transition from the part-time teenage and often transitory labor market into full-time career jobs. It seems clear that black–white wage disparities are much smaller in this "teenage" labor market. To the extent that early career

wage profiles include part of that transition, it would not be surprising to see black–white wage ratios fall. However, the issues addressed in this chapter do not refer to that transition but rather to wage growth after the first full-time job is achieved. This same care must be exercised in empirical work to make certain that career wage growth represents only the period after achieving the first full-time job.

References

Andrisani, Paul J., 1973. *An Empirical Analysis of the Dual Labor Market Theory.* Columbus: Center for Human Resource Research, Ohio State University.

Becker, Gary S., 1975. *Human Capital.* Chicago: University of Chicago Press.

Cain, Glen G., 1976. "The Challenge of Segmented Labor Market Theories to Orthodox Theory: A Survey." *Journal of Economic Literature* 14 (December): 1215–1257.

Duncan, Greg J., and Saul D. Hoffman, 1983. "A New Look at the Causes of the Improved Economic Status of Black Workers." *Journal of Human Resources* 17 (2): 268–282.

Hoffman, Saul D., 1979. "Black–White Life-Cycle Earnings Differences and the Vintage Hypothesis: A Longitudinal Analysis." *American Economic Review* 69 (December): 855–867.

Leigh, Duane, 1976. "Occupational Advancement in the Late 1960s: An Indirect Test of the Dual Labor Market Hypothesis." *Journal of Human Resources* 11 (Spring): 155–171.

Mincer, Jacob, 1974. *Schooling, Experience and Earnings.* New York and London: National Bureau of Economic Research, Columbia University Press.

Osterman, Paul, 1975. "An Empirical Study of Labor Market Segmentation." *Industrial and Labor Relations Review* 128 (July): 508–523.

Piore, Michael J., 1971. "The Dual Labor Market." In *Problems in Political Economy,* ed. David J. Gordon, 92. Lexington, Mass.: D.C. Heath and Co.

Reich, Michael, 1984. "Segmented Labour, Time Series Hypothesis and Evidence." *Cambridge Journal of Economics* 8: 63–81.

Rumberger, Russell W., and Martin Carnoy, 1980. "Segmentation in the U.S. Labor Market: Its Effects on the Mobility and Earnings of Whites and Blacks." *Cambridge Journal of Economics* 4: 117–122.

Smith, James P., 1984. "Race and Human Capital." *American Economic Review* 74 (September): 685–698.

Smith, James P., and Finis R. Welch, 1986. *Closing the Gap: Forty Years of Economic Progress for Blacks.* Santa Monica, Ca.: The RAND Corporation, 4-3330-DoL.

Zeman, Morton, 1955. "A Comparative Analysis of White–Nonwhite Income Differentials." Unpublished dissertation, University of Chicago (September).

STEVEN SHULMAN

Chapter 6. A Critique of the Declining Discrimination Hypothesis

T HE FIRST accomplishment of the civil rights movement was to break the back of Jim Crow. The elimination of American apartheid and the establishment of color-blind law as a national principle signaled a new role for the federal government. Starting with the 1964 Civil Rights Act, Washington guaranteed black Americans their elementary rights of citizenship even if this conflicted with the will of local white majorities. Henceforth the exercise of "democracy" could no longer extend to the denial of legal, political, and economic equality.

With the principle established, the attention of the civil rights movement (and later the "black power" movement and the urban uprisings) turned to the achievement of substantive equality. Again the effort was directed toward pressing the federal government to end discrimination in housing, schooling, political representation, and employment and to provide social programs to counter the effects of generations of segregation and deprivation. These efforts, however, encountered a resistance more pervasive, though often less visible, than the drive for formal citizenship rights. While the latter frequently provoked violent and hateful responses by local white communities, Jim Crow could be isolated as a regional phenomenon which clearly contradicted the national credo of democracy. Race laws were an "American dilemma" (Myrdal 1944) because a democracy that denied some citizens their democratic rights contravened its own principle of existence. Jim Crow was thus clearly "wrong" in the sense that it was an ideological anathema to the American self-image. Hence it was possible to build a national consensus for full equality before the law.

Moving beyond the juridical sphere proved to be more problematic. For several reasons, the goal of economic equality is more contentious

This essay is a revised version of a chapter from the author's Ph.D. dissertation. Richard Edwards, Herbert Gintis and Daniel Clawson made helpful comments on earlier drafts.

than that of legal equality. First, antidiscrimination and affirmative action efforts trespass upon the apparently interior realm of private property. Forcing businesses to stop discriminating in sales is significantly less costly and threatening than forcing them to stop discriminating in production (hiring, allocation, pay, promotion, and discharge). The right of the government to interfere with internal business decisions has never had the same legitimacy as its right to control the legal system. Equalizing the rights of persons as citizens before the law is in one sense merely a matter of consistency; resolving a conflict between person-rights and property-rights in favor of the former is much more radical, for in essence it subordinates capitalism to the discourse of liberal democracy. Taken to its logical extreme, the extension of person-rights into the workplace would break down the control of capital over the production process. In this sense, civil rights and affirmative action legislation constitute a radical expansion of the state as a legitimate domain of progressive struggle. Furthermore, such legislation sometimes comes into conflict with the hard-won gains of the labor movement. This is particularly the case with the rights of referral unions to control hires and with seniority systems that have institutionalized black marginality. Additionally, economic equality itself can be a problematic goal, especially in a period of slow growth. Equalizing opportunity means increasing the competition for a limited set of rewards. Economic inequality is often thought to be just and necessary, and hence not analogous to legal inequality. So, too, the goal of economic equality sometimes is ironically seen to contradict that of legal equality, i.e., "reverse discrimination," even though formal equality itself may become a mechanism for the perpetuation of substantive inequality (Maguire 1980). For these reasons, the goal of economic equality has never enjoyed the same mass support among whites as has the goal of juridical equality (Wellman 1977).

It is thus hardly surprising that the economic advances of black Americans have encountered a backlash that their legal advances have not. Aside from a spate of "reverse discrimination" suits, blacks now confront quite widespread attitudes that they "have it made," that their economic advances are undeserved, that they are not qualified for the jobs they have been "given," that they are systematically preferred over whites, and that their poverty and unemployment are a matter of choice (Gill 1980; Jones 1977). Considering also the unabated persistence of housing and social segregation, community conflicts (e.g., busing), urban decay, and white mob/police/vigilante violence, it would not be an overstatement to say that race is still, over two decades after the Civil Rights Act, America's most explosive social division.

It it in this context that the debate over the "decline of discrimination" takes on its particular significance. Changes in social attitudes, increased access to educational resources, and some commitment by the government to prevent discrimination have improved the economic situation of some blacks. At the same time, widespread income and employment disparities persist, so that the standard of living for blacks as a group remains far beneath that of whites. Since some changes have occurred for some individuals, however, a body of literature has appeared arguing that the continuity of group differences must be due to factors aside from racial discrimination (e.g., class background, family structure, educational inadequacies, cultural peculiarities, or the effects of past discrimination). What I call the "declining discrimination hypothesis" has several versions, but all agree that whatever are the problems blacks face in today's labor market, discrimination is not one of them.

Although much of the debate has been confined to academia, the declining discrimination hypothesis clearly has important policy implications, implications that the Reagan administration at least was not slow to note. It provides ammunition for those who would end federal intervention against discrimination and the use of federal resources in any racially directed manner. Some of this literature has been widely publicized. William J. Wilson's *The Declining Significance of Race* (1980) was previewed in the *New York Times*, received the Spivak Award from the American Sociological Association, and was the subject of a major conference. The *New York Times Sunday Magazine* made a cover story out of the debate entitled "Race Versus Class" (Clark and Gershman 1978) and followed up with another cover story tellingly entitled "The Black Middle Class: Making It" (Brashler 1978). The popularization of the declining discrimination hypothesis may partially account for the fall in the fraction of all whites who believe that blacks experience discrimination in their efforts to achieve equality from three-quarters in 1970 to one-third in 1977 (National Urban League 1978; Appendix A). Roger Wilkins notes that

The New York Times/CBS News polls on racial attitudes indicate that most whites believe either that the battle for racial justice in the United States has been won or that it is too costly in terms of the sacrifices white people have to make for the visions that the 60s spawned to come true. (Wilkins 1978, 26)

From such a perspective, the persistence of inequality can only be attributed to deficiencies among the black population itself.

This paper explores the logical and factual content of the various versions of the declining discrimination hypothesis and develops an empirical and theoretical critique. My focus is on the 1970s since black gains over that decade occurred in the context of slow economic growth and as such are said to provide strong support for the declining discrimination hypothesis (Freeman 1981). I conclude with a discussion of developments in the 1980s and their implications for the economic analysis of discrimination.

The various versions of the declining discrimination hypothesis differ from each other in their explanations of how the decline occurred; they agree with each other that the convergence of black and white labor market outcomes proves that it has occurred. In this section, I will first discuss the concept of discrimination which typifies these theories, then summarize the evidence used to show that it has declined, and lastly describe the different explanations of the purported decline.

Richard Freeman, the original proponent of the declining discrimination hypothesis, has defined labor market discrimination as "differences among similarly qualified workers in wages, employment, and occupational position that can be traced to the bias of employers, employees, unions, or consumers" (Freeman 1978, 53). Any attribution of discrimination, then, must do two things: it must show that comparable blacks and whites experience divergent labor market outcomes, and it must causally connect this divergence to the actions of other economic agents. Wilson has, additionally, argued that discrimination is inversely related to class stratification. Since racism should affect everyone whose skin is black, a wide variation in black labor market experience would indicate that race *per se* is ceasing to be a factor in the determination of labor market outcomes. In other words, "as influence of race on minority class stratification decreases, then, of course, class takes on a greater importance in determining the life chances of minority individuals" (Wilson 1980, x). Thus a decline in discrimination would be indicated not only by growing similarities between blacks and whites but also by growing differences among blacks.

Certain indicators suggest that at least the first of these changes has been occurring since 1964, the most important development being the relative improvement in the occupational distribution. As can be seen from Table 6.1, black concentration in the professional, technical, managerial, and administrative categories more than doubles from 1960 to 1980, whereas the white concentration increases much more slowly. Laborers, household workers, and farmworkers as a share of total black employment fall concordantly. But it is also important to note that despite these improvements, the occupational gap remains severe. The percentage of blacks employed as professional, technical, managerial, and administrative workers by 1980 is less than the percentage of

TABLE 6.1.   *Percentage Distribution of Employed Persons by Race and Occupational Group*

	1960		1970		1980	
	W	NW	W	NW	W	NW
Prof., tech.	12.1	4.8	14.8	9.1	16.5	12.7
Man., admin.	11.7	2.6	11.4	3.5	12.0	5.8
Sales	7.0	1.5	6.7	2.1	6.8	2.9
Clerical	15.7	7.3	18.0	13.2	18.6	18.4
Crafts	13.8	6.0	13.5	8.2	13.3	9.6
Operatives	17.9	20.4	17.0	23.7	13.5	19.4
Nonfarm lab.	4.4	13.7	4.1	10.3	4.3	6.9
Service	8.2	17.5	9.4	18.3	11.3	19.9
Household	1.7	14.2	1.3	7.7	.8	3.2
Farm	7.4	12.1	4.0	2.9	2.9	1.8

Source: USBC 1981, Table 672.

Note: W refers to white and NW to nonwhite. This tends to understate the black–white differential because nonwhites include Asian-Americans. Columns may not add to 100.0 due to rounding.

whites so employed in 1960. Reynolds Farley notes that for both men and women, the percentage of blacks holding white-collar jobs was about the same in 1982 as it was for whites in 1940. He concludes nonetheless that "with regard to the occupations of employed workers, there is unambiguous evidence that blacks are gradually catching up with whites" (Farley 1984, 50).

One summary statistic of occupational change is what Freeman (1976) has called the "index of structural differences," or ISD. It is the sum of the absolute percentage point differences in occupational distributions, that is,

$$ISD = \sum |O_i^b - O_i^w|$$

where O_i^b is the proportion of blacks employed in the ith occupation and O_i^w is the like proportion of whites. The smaller the ISD, the closer the black and white occupational distributions. The index as computed from Table 6.1 falls from 67.1 in 1960 to 50.4 in 1970 to 36.4 in 1980 (though the level would be higher and the rate of decline slower if more detailed occupational categories were used). The primary cause of this fall, as noted above, is the decline in agricultural and household labor in conjunction with the increasing concentration of blacks in white-collar occupations.

Occupational distributions vary quite a bit by sex and age, and so does the black–white comparison when broken down in this manner. Table 6.2 lists the ISD separately for men and women by three age groups in 1980. The ISD does increase sharply with age, though with-

TABLE 6.2. *Index of Structural Differentiation*
by Sex and Selected Age, 1980

Age	Men	Women
16–19	28.1	19.1
25–34	42.6	26.0
45–54	53.8	61.8

Source: Computed from USBLS 1982, Table B-18.
Note: Nonwhite *vs.* white.

out further analysis it is unclear if this is due to better white access
to promotional ladders (which would tend to widen the gap over time)
or to decreased discrimination that benefits primarily younger black
cohorts. The fantastically high unemployment rates experienced by
black teenagers make it difficult to accept at face value the latter
explanation of their low ISD. The male–female contrast is striking:
the female ISD is about two-thirds that of the male among the younger
cohorts. This primarily reflects the shift from household labor into
clerical work by black women, in conjunction with the limited occupational mobility evinced in the aggregate by white women. Gender
differences in the ISD should not be interpreted to mean that black
women suffer less from racial discrimination than black men (e.g.,
Wilson 1980, 178), but rather that they have less distance to traverse
to catch up to white women than black men do to white men. Racial
and sexual discrimination interact in terms of the experiences of families as well as individuals and cannot be meaningfully distinguished
by "adding up" inequalities. Black women as a group experience a
much lower standard of living than white women because of residential segregation, unemployment rate differentials, poverty rate differentials, and differences in family incomes. Racial differences among
women persist in terms of occupations as well: Barbara Jones notes
that "black women suffer a more severe penalty for limited schooling
and only with four or more years of college does their [occupational]
distribution look like that of white women" (Jones 1985/86, 23). The
odd notion that racism affects women differently than men requires
more theoretical explanation and empirical justification if it is to add
to our understanding of the dynamics of racial and sexual inequality.

Both the positive and negative aspects of these findings are not
surprising. Unless two decades of civil rights activity have had no
effect, one would expect the black and white occupational distributions to become more similar. That the occupational distribution
among women is so much closer than among men is also not surprising given the wide gulf separating white men and women. Nonethe-

TABLE 6.3. *Black/White Earnings and Income Ratios*

	1964	1969	1979
Males			
Median wages and salaries			
All workers	.59	.67	.72
Year-round full-time	.66	.69	.76
Median income by age, year-round full-time			
20–24	.64	.82	.77
25–34	.61	.72	.74
35–44	.59	.68	.78
45–54	.55	.68	.59
Females			
Median wages and salaries			
All workers	.58	.79	1.01
Year-round full-time	.69	.82	.94

Source: Freeman 1981, Table 1.

less, occupational inequities along the lines of race continue to constitute a fundamental feature of the American economy. This qualified narrowing of the occupational gap between blacks and whites, especially among women and young adults, throughout the slow-growth years of the 1970s as well as the boom years of the 1960s, is the first and most fundamental piece of evidence for the declining discrimination hypothesis.

The second piece of evidence most commonly referred to is the decline in income and earnings differences. Table 6.3 summarizes data compiled by Freeman (1981) that show steady relative income and earnings gains among employed persons, with especially great relative gains recorded by black women. By 1972 wage incomes for all working black women actually exceeded those for white women. Freeman (1976) also reports that relative income gains were particularly rapid among blacks with college degrees and in high-level occupations. Smith and Welch (1986) show that younger blacks with more than a high-school education fared particularly well in terms of relative wages. And though younger, well-educated blacks have benefited the most, income differentials also have narrowed within all age cohorts. Racial differentials in the returns to schooling and in the impact of race on earnings have persistently declined; however, it is notable that differentials in the returns to experience among men are severe and have increased over time (Farley 1984). This latter finding may be attributable to the small fraction of black men who receive on-the-job training (Duncan 1984), itself indicative of less-rapid occupational convergence than that suggested by the gross statistics (or of differential treatment within the same occupations). These findings show that the occupational developments described here have generally been translated into income and earnings improvements among all black workers, and particularly among young college graduates.

The narrowing of the occupational and income gaps between employed blacks and whites indicates an important (even if mixed) trend toward convergence in labor market experiences. That change has occurred, however, should not be taken to mean that blacks and whites have become economic equals, or that it is a given that positive change will continue automatically. If black men, black women, and white women had possessed the same characteristics as white men and had worked the same number of hours, they respectively would have been paid 88 percent, 64 percent, and 58 percent as much in 1979 (Farley 1984). These figures represent an upper boundary since they exclude the relative probability of underemployment. Relative income gains for black men were generally slower in the 1970s than in the 1960s (see Table 6.3). Nonetheless, though the rate of change may be too slow (based on postwar trends—an optimistic calculation—Michael Reich [1981] estimates that racial inequality among men will not disappear until the year 2070), the direction of change would appear to be unmistakable.

While a shrinking of the economic gulf between employed blacks and whites appears unambiguous, the same cannot be said for the second postulate of the declining discrimination hypothesis, i.e., that class distinctions within the black population are increasing. Farley (1984) reports that the evidence on this question is mixed. Educational attainment has become more evenly distributed among blacks, a trend opposite to that of class polarization. Furthermore, the distribution of family income among blacks has remained surprisingly constant over the last thirty years, with the richest 5 percent receiving about 16 percent of total income. On the other hand, the occupational distribution has become more polarized, particularly if persons unemployed and out of the labor force are counted as being on the bottom rung. And income inequality between female-headed households and husband–wife households has increased. The evidence on class polarization thus appears to be inconclusive.

However, education, occupation, and income are only correlated with class position. The fundamental dividing line between the classes is the ownership or nonownership of capital, with earnings correspondingly originating as profits and interest as opposed to wages (Wright 1979). Because a black capitalist class has never fully emerged, the black class structure has never been bifurcated like the white class structure. In 1984, 14 percent of whites, but only 4 percent of blacks, owned their own business or profession. Twenty-two percent of whites owned stocks or mutual fund shares, as compared to 5.4 percent of blacks. Among asset owners, whites had a median net worth over 11 times greater than blacks. On the other side of the fence, 8.4 percent of white households had a zero or negative net worth, as compared to 30.5 percent of black households (USBC, 1986). Consequently, the black class structure is more restricted and skewed downward than that of whites, with corresponding implications concerning the economic and political power its elite has been able to wield.

The class polarization postulate suggests that blacks are becoming more similar to whites in that their opportunities are being determined by impersonal economic forces (i.e., class position) rather than racism. But this argument only circumvents the issue of the differential determination of class position. Erik Olin Wright (1979), for example, finds that most of the differences between blacks and whites in the returns to education disappear when he controls for class position (in the Marxian sense). He concludes, however, that "It would be a mistake to interpret the results . . . as indicating that all racial discrimination is really disguised class oppression. . . . The most obvious way in which racism intersects class relations is in the social processes which distribute people into class positions in the first place" (Wright 1979, 197). Racial inequality is only expressed—not explained—by class differences between blacks and whites.

The developments described here form the empirical foundation of the declining discrimination hypothesis. The decline in discrimination is taken to be the precondition of the growing parity in labor market outcomes between blacks and whites. Much of the debate has then come to center not on whether such a decline has occurred, but rather how it has occurred.

There are four competing views of how the relative improvements in black economic status have come about. The first is a segmentationist perspective based on barriers to competition between blacks and whites. Wilson (1980) argues that labor market discrimination occurs either when capitalists have the opportunity to exploit black workers or when white workers are forced into competition with them. He contends that political and legal developments now prevent capitalists from paying blacks less than whites for the same work or from formally instituting a racial division of labor. At the same time, blacks in different labor market segments are insulated from job market competition with whites. In the low-wage sector, blacks do not compete with whites because jobs are plentiful and undesirable (unemployment is due to high turnover rates). Blacks in the primary sectors are insulated from competition by affirmative action, credentialism, and the prevalence of institutionalized rules structuring labor relations, such as seniority systems. In the absence of racial exploitation or job competition, the material basis for discrimination has eroded. This, in conjunction with rising skill levels among blacks, has resulted in the relative occupational and income gains described previously.

Freeman's view complements Wilson's but focuses less on labor market structure than on federal antidiscrimination activity. Freeman (1973) argues that civil rights/affirmative action legislation has reduced the "demand for discrimination." He shows that Equal Employment Opportunity Commission (EEOC) expenditures are positively correlated with the post-1964 increase in black incomes (after accounting for cyclical and secular economic trends and educational changes). He also argues that blacks have responded to these new opportunities by increasing their educational and skill attainments (Freeman 1976). The changes in the demand for black labor, and the consequent supply adjustments, have resulted in the improved occupational and income positions.

James Smith and Finis Welch (1978, 1986), the principal proponents of a third version of the declining discrimination hypothesis, argue that the improvements in relative black incomes are primarily due to quantitative and qualitative improvements in black schooling levels. Racial differences in the returns to schooling have declined steadily over the course of this century so that rising black educational levels have been translated into rising relative income levels. The drop in governmental discrimination in the provision of education thus plays a major role in explaining the narrowing of the black–white income gap. As opposed to Freeman's institutional explanation, Smith and Welch employ a traditional human capital framework. Their work stands sharply in contrast to Wilson's, since his view is that the decline in discrimination is due to the absence of competition whereas they believe that the movement toward equality has resulted precisely from the normal workings of a competitive labor market.

The fourth view, also rooted in a human capital framework, differs in its explanation of how the skill composition of the black labor force has changed. Richard Butler and James Heckman (1977) argue that Freeman's view that federal antidiscrimination activity has improved occupational opportunities for blacks does not square with the persistent decline in the participation rates of prime-age black men. They further hold that Freeman's association of EEOC expenditures and rising black incomes is spurious because there was no relative income growth for either men or women in the West or Northwest. The income growth in the South began around 1960, four years before the Civil Rights Act was passed. Only the trend in the North Central region supports Freeman's hypothesis, and this trend disappears by 1975. Market mechanisms, not governmental policies, have resulted in the trend toward income convergence. While Butler and Heckman do not disagree with Smith and Welch's educational thesis, they argue that the latter have given insufficient weight to changes in the composition of the black labor force in their explanations of rising black skill levels. They show that a negative correlation exists between welfare expenditures and participation rates, which they conclude is due to the impact of public assistance programs on the black reservation wage. Thus, "by removing the lowest wage blacks from the labor force, social transfer programs can manufacture wage growth by simply subtracting the least productive blacks from the population base used to measure wages and earnings" (Butler and Heckman 1977, 236).

It is not my intent to evaluate the particular points of contention between the proponents of the declining discrimination hypothesis. Rather, I will establish that the assumption that they all share—that labor market discrimination has declined—is more empirically and theoretically problematic than they would have us believe. This is the task of the next two sections.

Empirical criticisms of the declining discrimination hypothesis can be grouped into the following categorical statements: (1) that the continued low living standard of much of the black population makes the idea that discrimination has declined absurd; (2) that the movements of other relative variables do not reveal a convergence of the black and white economic situations; (3) that the evidence of the declining discrimination hypothesis is correct but has been misinterpreted; and (4) that the evidence itself is faulty.

The first type of response is characteristic of organizations and individuals concerned with eradicating racism and racial inequality. It is an understandable political response, but tends not to address the intellectual issues. While it may be useful rhetorically and certainly appeals to common sense given the history of U.S. racism, it constitutes a simple denial of the question, i.e., why do blacks as a group remain impoverished and oppressed in the contemporary United States. No one denies that discrimination caused racial inequality in the past, but it does not necessarily follow that discrimination is the cause of racial inequality in the present. To make such an assumption would be to deny that the institutional and attitudinal changes of the past quarter-century have been meaningful. This may well be the case, but the problem is to prove it rather than assert it. If such a proposition were self-evident, this book would be unnecessary.

The second response deals more directly with the issues. Other indices of relative labor market outcomes aside from individual incomes and occupational attainment show no pattern of convergence. This is taken to contradict the declining discrimination hypothesis. The measures most commonly referred to are the black–white differentials in family incomes, unemployment rates, poverty rates, and labor force participation rates.

Black family incomes were 55 percent of white family incomes in 1965, 60 percent in 1975, and 57 percent in 1980. Charles Vert Willie (1979), in a direct response to Wilson, argues that this differential is determined by race, and proves that discrimination is not on the decline. Wilson responds that

A correct explanation of the overall decline in black family incomes since 1969 must include the fact that the proportion of black families with female heads has correspondingly increased during this period—from 28 percent in 1969 to 37 percent in 1976 to 39 percent in 1977 and finally to a startling 40 percent in 1978. And when one considers that in 1978 the median income of black female-headed families ($5,888) was $9,690 less than the median income of black male-headed families ($15,678), it does not take a great deal of imagination to understand why the recorded income ratio of black to white families has declined in recent years. (Wilson 1980, 158)

Freeman (1978, 54) makes the same point when he argues that family income comparisons are appropriate for evaluating economic well-being but inappropriate for understanding labor market discrimination. Smith and Welch concur: "The lack of recent improvement in black family incomes is a reflection of a growing problem in the black family, not of a decline in black labor market prospects" (1986, 106).

These authors are clearly correct that family income differentials cannot provide direct measures of discrimination without taking into account factors such as family structure. Their criticism, however, is flawed in that it assumes family structure to be independent of labor market status. Yet the distribution of householders by race and gender is in part a function of socio-economic pressures, including discrimination. Black households are more likely to be female-headed because black men are more likely to be dead, sick, or incarcerated; because lower black male incomes reduce the economic incentive for black women to marry; because birth control is less available in low-income areas; and because blacks face more stress than whites as a result of bigotry, poverty, unemployment, segregation, and ghettoization. If it is admitted that family structure is itself dependent upon social and economic experiences, including discrimination, then to that extent the impact of family structure on relative family incomes can be taken to reflect discrimination. Though the interaction makes quantification of the racial aspect difficult, it should nonetheless qualify the attribution of family income differentials simply to the greater incidence of female-headed households among blacks.

The unemployment rate differential is the other variable most commonly mentioned as a rejoinder to the declining discrimination hypothesis. Blacks have traditionally been twice as likely to be unemployed as whites, and the "long-term trend [is] toward a larger racial difference" (Farley 1984, 40). Freeman (1981, 1) parenthetically admits that young black workers "made unprecedented economic gains compared to whites in wages, occupational attainment, and earnings (but not in the chances of being employed)" in the late 1960s and early 1970s. Robert B. Hill (1978) uses cross-tabulations to show that comparable black and white youth experience vastly different unemployment rates and that over the 1970s black unemployment worsened relative to white unemployment, particularly for women. I show elsewhere (Shulman 1987) that discrimination is a significant determinant of the relative and absolute probability of black employment.

The failure of the unemployment rate differential to fall constitutes an anomaly for all versions of the declining discrimination hypothesis. The Smith/Welch and Butler/Heckman human capital explanations presume that the rise in relative black wages is due to improvements in the relative productivity of the black labor force. If this were the case, black unemployment also should have fallen relative to white unemployment because rising skill levels would have increased the hire rate (as the cost of on-the-job training declined) and reduced the layoff and quit rates (as the cost of turnover increased to both the firm and the worker). If human capital theory is consistently applied, unemployment rate differentials should move in the same direction as wage differentials. Freeman's government policy explanation for the drop in wage differentials is that the demand for black labor has increased. If this were the case, black employment also should have risen with black wages. Wilson's segmentationist explanation presumes that highly educated blacks are moving into the corporate and government sectors; consequently, the fall in the black–white educational gap (Farley 1984, 16–22) should reduce aggregate black unemployment as more blacks experience upward occupational mobility. The persistence of the black–white unemployment rate differential is therefore a substantial puzzle for the declining discrimination hypothesis.

Another variable frequently used to rebut the declining discrimination hypothesis is the labor force participation rate differential. Between 1960 and 1979, the nonwhite male participation rate falls from 83 percent to 71.9 percent, while the white male rate falls from 83.4

percent to 78.6 percent. The decline for black men is precipitous in all age groups, whereas for white men the rate stays stable or actually rises in all age groups except those 45 years old and over (USBLS 1980, Table 4). The decline for black men would thus appear to reflect declining employment opportunities, whereas for whites it seems to indicate a fall in retirement age. Farley (1984, 42) also concludes that "declining employment prospects and the resulting discouragement . . . account for the decline in the proportion of nonwhite men aged 25–54 who have jobs." Among women, participation rates have risen faster for whites than for blacks. Yet, as Jones (1985/86) argues, changes in the variables that influence labor supply decisions among women would lead one to expect the opposite to be the case. She concludes that the sluggish growth in the black female participation rate is due to a lack of employment opportunity for women with fewer than four years of college. Thus, for both black men and black women changes in participation rates appear to be closely connected to relative shortfalls in employment opportunities. If this were the case, it would not accord well with the notion that discrimination has declined (and relative opportunities for blacks have thereby improved) in the labor market.

Butler and Heckman (1977) and Smith and Welch (1986) attribute the participation rate differential to work disincentives created by transfer payments. Michael Reich (1981) attacks this assertion for failing to control for the demand for black labor, and hence being unable to establish the direction of causality. He further notes that

A demand-driven explanation of falling participation trends is in fact more consistent with the observation that the relative growth of transfer payments has been small in magnitude and that it occurred after the decline in participation rates. Moreover, welfare expenditures are related inversely to the level of economic activity, indicating, therefore, that welfare status often represents a response to inadequate demand for labor. (Reich 1981, 36)

This argument suggests that the rise in participation rate differentials is symptomatic of a shortfall in labor market opportunities for blacks. Such a conclusion also follows from the sizable participation rate differentials existing within most sex–age–education cohorts (USBLS 1979, Table F). Yet the work disincentives argument that participation rate declines are voluntary is in essence one of the distribution of blacks and whites between cohorts: whites, after all, do collect welfare and therefore face the same temptations to drop out of the labor market as blacks.

The last variable seen to contradict the declining discrimination hypothesis is the poverty rate. The poverty rate among black families has remained at triple that among white families over the past two decades. Nearly one-half of all black children live in poverty. Black poverty has variously been attributed to discrimination and the lack of opportunity (Harrington 1984), the increase in female-headed households among blacks (Farley 1984), and the impact of welfare on work incentives and marriage rates (Murray 1980). These causes are difficult to separate empirically. Mary Jo Bane (1986) shows that the bulk of the black–white poverty rate differential is due to higher poverty rates *within* family types. Black poverty is concentrated among female heads of households due to a reshuffling of the already poor into such households, as opposed to the creation of poverty from the formation of such households. Duncan (1984, 84) concludes that "there are no major effects of AFDC on family composition decisions." Reich (1981), as noted above, argues that increasing transfer payments are not the cause of falling participation rates and that both represent a response to an inadequate demand for labor. These findings suggest that the cause of black poverty lies in poor job prospects rather than family structure or work incentives. Overall, the persistence of widespread poverty and low family incomes among the black population in conjunction with rising differentials in the probability of employment have cast understandable doubt on the thesis that black opportunities have improved relative to white opportunities as discrimination has declined.

The third category of empirical responses to the declining discrimination hypothesis disputes its interpretation of the evidence of income and occupational convergence. Reich argues that the improvement in black incomes primarily reflects cyclical forces and the decline of the agrarian South. Since the movement out of the South is a one-time structural shift, he concludes that it is overly optimistic to assume that changes in black economic status will inevitably continue to follow their recent trends. This conclusion is buttressed by his demonstration that black–white income inequality has persisted within metropolitan areas and within cities. Since a "variety of demographic, economic, and political shifts of the last few decades . . . ought to have exerted a significant upward pressure on the relative incomes of blacks" (Reich 1981, 11) within as well as between economic sectors, countervailing forces producing inequality are too strong to assume that they will simply disappear. Reich (1981) also notes that the disappearance of income differentials among employed women is qualified by the fact that the earnings position of white women has declined relative to white men and that black women are likely to work more hours than white women. Thus, while the decline in income differentials is a valid observation, the conclusion that discrimination has declined is based upon an invalid interpretation of the causes of the convergence.

To my knowledge, none of the declining discrimination theorists have responded to Reich's study. Perhaps the most obvious possible rejoinder is that black gains continued through the 1970s. Freeman is particularly impressed by this:

Since the latter part of the 1970s, in particular, was a period of sluggish overall economic performance, whereas 1969 was a peak boom year, the continued positive trend in [the] black economic position occurred despite cyclical forces operating against blacks, which makes the 1970s trends particularly impressive as indicative of substantial underlying economic changes. (Freeman 1981, 5)

Since all of Freeman's measures only include employed persons, however, and black unemployment and labor force participation relatively worsened over the 1970s, his optimism about "substantial underlying economic changes" may be overstated. The 1970s record is a mixed one. For example, Diane Westcott notes that the number of black professional and craft workers increased about half as fast over the 1970s as compared to the 1960s. Although proportionately more blacks than whites moved into white-collar occupations,

few penetrated the higher salaried professional and managerial professions. In fact, the black-to-white earnings differential was unchanged for professional and technical workers between 1973 and 1980, and, even more importantly, black earnings relative to those of whites fell in the fast-growing clerical field. (Westcott 1982, 37)

While one would expect a relative increase in the number of entrants to widen intraoccupational wage differentials, the slowdown in the black entry rate over the 1970s should have allowed the earnings gap to narrow as 1960s entrants moved up promotional ladders. That this did not occur may be a consequence of excessively high black unemployment and/or excessively low black on-the-job training.

The fourth empirical counterattack contends that the income measures of black progress are intrinsically flawed. William Darity, Jr. (1980) notes that the measures commonly used to display black–white income convergence are based on samples restricted to persons with positive incomes. He argues that the exclusion of persons with zero incomes presents a misleadingly positive picture of black economic well-being due to disproportionately high black unemployment rates and disproportionately low black participation rates. His income ratios for all persons 14 years old and over (the "potential labor force") as compared to those for persons with positive incomes show, as one would expect, that the dramatic decline in income differentials is enormously slowed when persons with zero incomes are included.

In response, James Smith (1980) argues that this procedure is flawed because the assignment of a zero wage value to persons not in the labor force confounds the analysis of wage differences. If such an assignment is made, one cannot tell whether wage differences are falling because of wage rate changes or participation rate changes. Consequently, it is an inappropriate method for studying movements in the black–white wage differential. Smith's point is well taken if the sole issue of interest is wage inequality. However, one cannot conclude from a decline in wage differentials alone that the labor market is operating in a racially neutral fashion when other differentials (e.g., employment) fail to follow the same path. On this basis the conclusion of a general convergence of outcomes—and hence of a decline in total discrimination—cannot be drawn. Darity's index may be inappropriate for the isolated analysis of wage rates, but it tells a revealing story about overall changes in inequality when the narrowing of the wage gap is considered in conjunction with the widening of the employment gap.

In sum, the confidence with which Wilson, Freeman, Smith and Welch, and others conclude that labor market discrimination has declined appears to be empirically unwarranted. Other variables do not display the same pattern of convergence, the variables which do converge are subject to other interpretations, and the degree of their convergence is overstated because the sample base is skewed. These facts, of course, do not speak against the observation that important changes have occurred in the economic status of blacks, but they do imply that a "decline of discrimination" may be an overly optimistic and simplistic explanation of them.

Each of the versions of the declining discrimination hypothesis postulates the existence of some force that should erode discrimination. Turning now to the theoretical issues, I will argue that they fail to consider conditions that would inhibit or deflect the antidiscriminatory force and that they fail to consider other forces that would tend to perpetuate discrimination. The result is that they cannot comprehend racism as a complex entity. This means, in particular, that racism (1) can create both benefits and costs for the same economic agents, (2) can be weakened in some respects but not in others, and (3) can decline but then rise if the factors that have set it back cease to be effectively operative.

The view consonant with human capital theory is that competitive market forces have eroded discrimination. Job discrimination is costly for employers because it forces them to forego hiring needed employees or else to search longer or to offer higher wages to attract a larger pool of qualified applicants. Nondiscriminatory employers thus have a cost advantage over discriminators and so should drive them out of the market. Discrimination could persist only if the entire white race were organized into a cartel to enforce racist employment standards. However, this is hardly feasible since individuals have incentives to violate such an agreement, and the cost of such collusion is generally prohibitive (Sowell 1981, 36–39). Thus Milton Friedman believes that

> there is an economic incentive in a free market to separate economic efficiency from other characteristics of the individual. A businessman or entrepreneur who expresses preferences in his [sic] business activities that are not related to productive efficiency is at a disadvantage compared to other individuals who do not. Such an individual is in effect imposing higher costs on himself than are other individuals who do not have such preferences. Hence, in a free market they will tend to drive him out. (Friedman 1962, 109–110)

Two conditions necessary for the market to work in such a manner are absent or severely constrained in the contemporary United States: full employment and product competition. When there is an excess supply of labor, the additional hiring costs imposed by discrimination are reduced and conceivably eliminated. The hiring of qualified workers need not be foregone, search time need not be appreciably expanded, nor wages raised if the competition for jobs is severe enough. Such was certainly the case in the 1970s and the first half of the 1980s. Furthermore, giant corporations dominate important sectors of the economy. With restricted barriers to entry, the possibility that any loss in productive efficiency from discrimination will result in a loss of market share is dubious. This analytical framework is simply not very relevant in the conditions of today's labor market.

Other authors have developed models displaying compatibility between discrimination and profit maximization in competitive conditions (Reich 1981; Bowles 1985). Thus it is conceivable that discrimination may persist even in perfectly competitive conditions. These models assume that racism lowers the wage bill by dividing workers and weakening their bargaining power relative to capital. Furthermore, though these models concentrate on the benefits to capital, a higher profit/wage ratio need not mean a lower standard of living (compared to a situation of no racism) for white workers since racism also reduces job instability and competition. For this reason, the union movement has consistently refused to fight discrimination and, indeed, has often cooperated in the maintenance of a racial division of labor (Hill 1982). Thus, even if competition created costs for discriminators, other incentives would still exist for the persistence of discrimination on the part of both employers and white workers.

The argument that discrimination increases the costs of production also must be placed in the context of the possible cost increases from ceasing discrimination due to changes in the social organization of production. These costs can arise from violating traditional patterns of association and authority; increasing class conflict; increasing the wage bill; changing the established rules of internal labor markets; increasing training costs; and/or lowering team efficiency (Shulman 1985). Thus, even if it is the case that discrimination reduces technical efficiency, ceasing discrimination may still increase unit labor costs. Since discrimination can both increase and decrease costs, the firm's decision to continue or stop discriminating cannot be theoretically preordained.

Freeman's view that discrimination has been reduced by government intervention is logically similar to the market mechanism story and thereby suffers from some of the same defects. Government intervention, like diminished efficiency, raises the price of discrimination and thereby lowers the demand for it. Whether or not this has actually occurred has been the subject of an acrimonious debate (Freeman 1976; Smith and Welch 1978; Butler and Heckman 1977) that need not detain us here. The argument as it stands is subject to the same criticisms as the market mechanism story, i.e., that even if it is the case that government intervention raises the costs and risks of discrimination, the firm also faces certain costs from ceasing to discriminate, and how it responds is more a matter of its concrete situation than abstract structural imperatives. The uncertainty of the firm's response is particularly telling in this case, for whereas the market may be presumed to continue operating indefinitely into the future, federal intervention against discrimination, particularly since Reagan, cannot. Thus, given the cost and income incentives that sustain discrimination, there would not be much cause for optimism about the decline in discrimination as a secular trend. Furthermore, a variety of state activities have reduced the welfare of blacks over this same period. Housing, urban development, transportation, police, and military policies have worked, as Charles Payne (1979, 123) has noted, "disproportionately to the disadvantage of Blacks." The idea that federal intervention has caused discrimination to decline thus must be counterbalanced against the ways in which federal intervention has perpetuated black oppression and contributed to the deterioration of their labor market status.

Wilson holds that changes in class relations, not the market or the government, are responsible for the decline in discrimination. Because capitalists are prevented from superexploiting their black workers, and because job competition between black and white workers is obstructed, neither white workers nor capitalists have a motive to discriminate. Hence, race has ceased to be a factor in the determination of labor market outcomes.

Wilson's view ascribes racism solely to the self-interested actions of classes. But racism can be perpetuated through institutional mechanisms that remain in effect even without clear-cut class beneficiaries. These mechanisms develop out of the adaptive responses of the institution to its social environment. For example, a national survey of over four thousand employers disclosed several types of exclusionary practices rooted in the biases that result from social segregation and that employers have little incentive to change (Braddock and McPartland 1987). Thus, even if the class basis for discrimination has been undermined, it does not necessarily follow that discrimination has declined. Institutions suffer from inertia and conservatism because their behavioral rules, once in place, are frequently costly and difficult to change. Doeringer and Piore (1971, 136) for example, argue that disrupting the established channels of recruitment, screening, allocation, training, and wage setting can "raise the inefficiency of the labor force adjustment process, at least in the short run, thereby imposing costs on both the employer and society. Only where the effect of discrimination has been to create a grossly inefficient internal labor market will there be any offsetting benefits."

In this case, however, it is not clear that the initial motivation is no longer operative: job competition intensifies in recessions and can be exacerbated by some of the very forces Wilson contends obstruct it (e.g., affirmative action) while capitalists can have other motives than superexploitation to discriminate (e.g., an increasing need to divide their opposition as working-class resistance to a declining standard of living intensifies). Class and race relations are more difficult to separate out than Wilson's causal sequence suggests. As Wright (1979, 197) notes, "The empirical problem is to sort out the complex interplay of racism and class relations, not to obliterate the former in the latter."

The end of discrimination has been repeatedly heralded throughout this century (Reich 1981). But given the long and bitter history of U.S. race relations, the common response of skepticism has been understandable and even justified. Today, unfortunately, is no exception. The declining discrimination theorists need to tell a stronger story than they have if we are to accept that the course of U.S. history has so dramatically changed. Theoretically as well as empirically, their arguments are subject to many criticisms. Though much of this research has advanced our knowledge, it is still reasonable to conclude that discrimination remains a force to be reckoned with in today's labor market.

The declining discrimination hypothesis presumes a convergence of labor market outcomes between blacks and whites. We have seen that the evidence for this convergence is less than clear-cut. Nonetheless, the decade of the 1970s witnessed continued relative progress for *employed* blacks and in this sense provided support for the contention that discrimination was declining as a critical factor in the determination of opportunities for black Americans.

Unfortunately, the same cannot be said for the first half of the 1980s. From 1980 to 1986, the black–white ratio of median weekly earnings for full-time year-round workers fell from 0.77 to 0.73 for men and from 0.91 to 0.89 for women. The black–white ratio of median family incomes fell from 0.58 to 0.57. The percentage of black children below the poverty line rose from 42.1 to 42.7. Although total unemployment was virtually the same in 1986 as in 1980, the black–white unemployment rate ratio rose from 2.27 to 2.42 (USBC 1987). The black–white ratio of percentage employed as white-collar workers stagnated at 0.72. It was a poor half-decade for black progress in almost every respect.

Despite the slack labor markets characteristic of this period, one would not expect relative black progress to grind to a halt if discrimination were on a secular decline. In the first place, there is no automatic reason why unemployment should hinder the ability of blacks to catch up to whites. Black progress did not stop in the slow-growth years of the 1970s. As Barbara Bergmann points out,

The fallacy of the "just no jobs" argument is that it ignores the fact that even in a year of no growth, there are millions of hirings and millions of promotions. For example, between 1979 and 1980, total employment in manufacturing fell by about 700,000 jobs. Yet during that period, about 7,500,000 jobs were filled by hiring new people. Labor turnover goes on in good times and bad times. (Bergmann 1981, 33)

Aggregate unemployment, in other words, will hurt blacks (as well as whites) absolutely, but given a decline in discrimination and a narrowing of the human capital gap, there is no reason it should foreclose continued relative progress. Although a full-employment policy is often—and correctly—advocated as one of the best means of reducing racial inequality, the presumption behind such a policy is that relative black progress can only begin after white aspirations have been satisfied. If it takes full employment to move toward racial equality, then the propensity to discriminate has not declined but only has been offset by the pressures generated by an excess demand for labor.

In the second place, if aggregate unemployment is to blame for the lack of black progress, the racial distribution of unemployment must itself be explained. Black unemployment rates are at least double those of whites across most age/education cohorts, including younger, college-educated persons (USBLS 1983, Table B-13). Yet young, highly educated blacks are alleged to have benefited the most from the decline in discrimination (Freeman 1976). In the absence of a racial hiring queue, why should blacks and whites of similar ages and levels of educational attainment experience systematically different probabilities of employment?

Third, the failure of inequality to continue to fall over the 1980s is an unexpected finding for every version of the declining discrimination hypothesis. The deficiencies of the human capital explanation are the most glaring in this regard. If increased acquisition of human capital among blacks explains the drop in inequality over the 1960s and 1970s, there is little reason for the 1980s to display a different trend. Inequality if anything should decelerate even more quickly over the 1980s as the work experience accumulated over the previous decades begins to pay off. The government policy explanation, in contrast, can explain the failure of inequality to decline in terms of the Reagan administration's efforts to dismantle civil rights and affirmative action regulations and enforcement. However, the implication is then that the "demand for discrimination" never declined but was only offset by policy, thus reappearing in full force when that policy changed. The deeper question is why this should be the case. Finally, the class relations explanation is of little value in this regard since the corporate and governmental sectors have hardly fallen as a share of the total economy. The changes in class relations that Wilson believes have undermined the material basis for discrimination have not suddenly reversed in the current period, and consequently they cannot explain why the trend of declining racial inequality has reversed.

The failure of racial inequality to continue to decline over the 1980s in conjunction with the mixed record of progress over the preceding two decades suggest that the declining discrimination hypothesis is an overly simplistic explanation of the changes wrought by the civil rights movement. Certainly the passage of antidiscrimination legislation, the narrowing of the educational gap, the growth of transfer payments, and the emergence of a black middle class have been important (and in some sense unprecedented) developments in Afro-American history. But the context in which they occurred made their impact too complex to be captured by the optimistic vision of a permanent decline in discrimination.

The key factors offsetting these developments were the emergence of long-term slack labor markets in the context of a decline in civil rights enforcement. Sustained high unemployment increases the benefits from discrimination at the same time that it reduces its costs. White workers place a higher premium on job security, while employers face an expanded pool of applicants. Employers can thus give preference to the employment needs of their white workers without increasing hiring costs. They are motivated to do so in order to maximize stability in a downturn and to minimize wages by reducing the bargaining power of labor. It is for these reasons that blacks disproportionately suffer from unemployment and its effects (Shulman 1987).

The mixed record of black progress over the 1970s is explained by these contradictory trends. The propensity to discriminate was driven down by government policies, educational achievements, and changes in social attitudes but was raised by increasing competition over jobs and the advantages employers and white workers could accrue from it. The latter effect is neither automatic nor arbitrary: it results from the refusal of white people, despite their expressed opposition to discrimination, to accept racial progress if it entails a decline in their own opportunities (Wellman 1977). When market mechanisms produce unemployment, they thereby reproduce discrimination. The problem is magnified when antidiscrimination policies are weakened and employment policies reduce the buffers between workers and the vagaries of the labor market (Shulman 1985). For this reason, the 1980s have seen a reversal in the (mixed) progress characteristic of the preceding decade. If progress toward racial equality cannot be guaranteed by full employment, it certainly will not be manifest in an economic climate that encourages discrimination and a political climate that tolerates it. No matter how well intentioned are white people nor how well educated are black people, discrimination will only decline if and when these economic and political trends are reversed.

References

Bane, Mary Jo, 1986. "Household Composition and Poverty." In *Fighting Poverty: What Works and What Doesn't*, eds. Sheldon Danziger and Daniel Weinberg, 209–231. Cambridge: Harvard University Press.

Bergmann, Barbara, 1981. "The Shibboleth of the Shrinking Pie." *The Civil Rights Quarterly* (Summer–Fall).

Bowles, Samuel, 1985. "The Production Process in a Competitive Economy: Walrasian, Neo-Hobbesian and Marxian Models." *American Economic Review* 75 (March): 16–36.

Braddock, Jomills Henry II, and James M. McPartland, 1987. "How Minorities Continue to Be Excluded from Equal Employment Opportunities: Research on Labor Market and Institutional Barriers." *Journal of Social Issues* 43 (1): 5–39.

Brashler, William, 1978. "The Black Middle Class: Making It." *New York Times,* December 3, 34.

Butler, Richard, and James J. Heckman, 1977. "The Government's Impact on the Labor Market Status of Black Americans: A Critical Review." In *Equal Rights and Industrial Relations,* eds. Leonard J. Hausman et al., Madison, Wisc.: Industrial Relations Research Association, 235–281.

Clark, Kenneth B., and Carl Gershman, 1978. "Race Versus Class." *New York Times Sunday Magazine,* October 5.

Darity, William A., 1980. "Illusions of Black Economic Progress." *Review of Black Political Economy* 10, no. 2 (Winter): 153–168.

Doeringer, Peter B., and Michael J. Piore, 1971. *Internal Labor Markets and Manpower Analysis.* Lexington, Mass.: D. C. Heath and Company.

Duncan, Greg J., 1984. *Years of Poverty, Years of Plenty: The Changing Fortunes of American Workers and Families.* Ann Arbor: Institute for Social Research, University of Michigan.

Farley, Reynolds, 1984. *Blacks and Whites: Narrowing the Gap?* Cambridge: Harvard University Press.

Freeman, Richard B., 1981. "Have Black Labor Market Gains Been Permanent or Transitory?" Cambridge: Harvard Institute of Economic Research, Discussion Paper No. 849, (September).

———, 1978. "Black Economic Progress Since 1964." *Public Interest* 52 (Summer): 52–68.

———, 1976. *Black Elite: The New Market for Highly Qualified Black Americans.* New York: McGraw-Hill.

———, 1973. "Changes in the Labor Markets for Black Americans, 1948–1972." *Brookings Papers on Economic Activity:* 67–131.

Friedman, Milton, 1962. *Capitalism and Freedom.* Chicago: University of Chicago Press.

Gill, Gerald R., 1980. *Meanness Mania: The Changed Mood.* Washington, D.C.: Howard University Press.

Harrington, Michael, 1984. *The New American Poverty.* New York: Penguin Books.

Hill, Herbert, 1982. "The AFL–CIO and the Black Worker: Twenty-five Years After the Merger." *The Journal of Intergroup Relations* 10, no. 1 (Spring): 5–78.

Hill, Robert B., 1978. "The Illusion of Black Economic Progress." *Social Policy* 9, no. 3 (November–December): 14–25.

Jones, Barbara A. P., 1985–86. "Black Women and Labor Force Participation: An Analysis of Sluggish Growth Rates." *Review of Black Political Economy* 14, no. 2–3 (Fall–Winter): 11–31.

Jones, Faustine C., 1977. *The Changing Mood in America: Eroding Commitment?* Washington, D.C.: Institute for the Study of Educational Policy, Howard University Press.

Maguire, Daniel C., 1980. *A New American Justice: Ending the White Male Monopolies.* Garden City, N.Y.: Doubleday and Co.

Murray, Charles, 1984. *Losing Ground: American Social Policy, 1950–1980.* New York: Basic Books.

Myrdal, Gunnar, 1944. *An American Dilemma.* New York: Harper & Row.

National Urban League, 1978. *The State of Black America.* New York.

O'Hare, William P., 1985. "Poverty in America: Trends and New Patterns." *Population Bulletin* 40, no. 3 (June): 1–45.

Payne, Charles, 1979. "On the Declining—and Increasing—Significance of Race." In *The Caste and Class Controversy,* ed. Charles Vert Willie, 117–139. New York: General Hall Inc.

Reich, Michael, 1981. *Racial Inequality.* Princeton: Princeton University Press.

Shulman, Steven, 1987. "Discrimination, Human Capital, and Black/White Unemployment: Evidence from Cities." *Journal of Human Resources* 22 (Summer): 361–376.

———, 1985. "Competition and Racial Discrimination: The Employment Effect of

Reagan's Labor Market Policies." *Review of Radical Political Economics* 16 (Winter): 111–128.

Smith, James P., 1980. "Comments on Papers by Darity-Myers and Jeong." *Review of Black Political Economy* 10 (Summer): 384–390.

Smith, James P., and Finis Welch, 1986. "Closing the Gap: Forty Years of Economic Progress for Blacks." Santa Monica, Ca.: The RAND Corporation.

———, 1978. "Race Differences in Earnings: A Survey and New Information." Santa Monica, Ca.: The RAND Corporation.

Sowell, Thomas, 1981. *Markets and Minorities*. New York: Basic Books.

U.S. Bureau of Labor Statistics [USBLS], [1980] 1985. *Handbook of Labor Statistics*, Bulletin 2070. Washington, D.C.

———, [1979] 1983. Special Labor Force Report 240, 2159. Washington, D.C.

U.S. Bureau of the Census [USBC], 1986. *Household Wealth and Asset Ownership*, Series P-70, no. 7. Washington, D.C.

———, [1981] 1987. *Statistical Abstract of the U. S.* Washington, D.C.

Wellman, David, 1977. *Portraits of White Racism*. New York: Cambridge University Press.

Westcott, Diane Nilsen, 1982. "Blacks in the 1970s: Did They Scale the Job Ladder?" *Monthly Labor Review* 105, no. 6 (June): 29–38.

Wilkins, Roger, 1978. "Racial Outlook: Lack of Change Disturbs Blacks." *New York Times*, March 3, A20.

Willie, Charles Vert, ed., 1979. *The Caste and Class Controversy*. New York: General Hall Inc.

Wilson, William J., 1980. *The Declining Significance of Race*. Chicago: University of Chicago Press.

Wright, Erik Olin, 1979. *Class Structure and Income Determination*. New York: Academic Press.

PART TWO

Evaluating Affirmative Action

Chapter 7. Affirmative Action and Discrimination

IN TITLE VII of the Civil Rights Act of 1964 protection was extended against discrimination in employment on the basis of an individual's race, color, religion, sex, or national origin. The actions prohibited were broadly defined to include bias in hiring and discharge, compensation, terms, conditions, and privileges of employment, and included classifications of employees or applicants for employment that would segregate or limit them in any way—on the basis of their race, sex, or ethnicity—that would adversely affect their status as an employee. The act, which became effective in July 1965, at first covered most private-sector employers and by 1972 was extended to governments and educational institutions.

The Equal Employment Opportunity Commission (EEOC) was set up to monitor compliance.[1] Although its initial powers were adjudicatory, the EEOC was given the right to bring suit on behalf of plaintiffs by the 1972 amendment. Prior to that date, the EEOC only could investigate charges and attempt to resolve them by mediating between employer and employee and, if the issues were not resolved, it could give complainants a letter indicating their right to bring suit. When individuals had exhausted their recourse through the EEOC, they could proceed to the courts with or without the right-to-sue letter.

Executive Order 11246 was implemented in the fall of 1965 to create special pressure for nondiscriminatory behavior on the part of federal contractors. The order not only forbids employment discrimination in compliance with Title VII but adds a new wrinkle: the obligation to take *affirmative action* to ensure that applicants are employed and that employees are treated without regard to race or ethnicity. Although gender was not mentioned as a basis for prohibited discriminatory behavior in the initial order, it was added via Executive Order 11375.

A narrow reading of the executive orders would limit the contractor's responsibility to explicit attempts to ensure Title VII compliance. The

Support for this research is provided by a grant from the Sloan Foundation.

order, however, gave the secretary of labor fairly broad leeway in interpreting affirmative responsibility, and subsequent interpretations have called for a broader view.

It would be a mistake to think of federal contractors as a relatively small number of firms working primarily in defense-related industries. The fact is that most large firms and many smaller ones do enough business with the federal government to be classified as contractors.[2] Aside from governments and educational institutions, about one-half of all employees are in firms that provide annual statements to the EEOC which describe employee distributions by major occupational classifications by sex, race, and ethnicity. Roughly three-fourths of the employees described in reports to the EEOC are employed by federal contractors

Although affirmative action is the legally mandated responsibility of federal contractors, in popular use the term has become synonymous with all that followed on the employment front from the original civil rights act. My objective is to describe the responsibilities that arise from affirmative action as I see them, to characterize some of the criteria against which an employer's behavior is judged, and then to discuss some of the implications of compliance one might expect to observe. I conclude by presenting summary statistics showing recent changes in patterns of employment and compensation. The changes in employment—where minorities and women have shifted, within the private sector, to firms reporting to the EEOC and, among them, to federal contractors—are so stark that it is easy to infer that one is seeing significant effects of affirmative action. In contrast, the evidence for compensation is mixed. There were rapid changes in the early 1970s, but subsequent trends raise questions about their lasting effect. This is not to say that the relative income status of minorities—as summarized in my data on black men—has not improved. The improvement is clear. The issue is whether the improvement is different from what would have occurred in the absence of affirmative action. The data I summarize do not provide concrete answers.

Two theories of employment discrimination have dominated litigation. One refers to disparate treatment, the other to adverse impact. Proof under either theory requires comparisons of two or more groups that are defined on the basis of race, color, ethnicity, sex, or religion. The comparisons take as a given some measure of employment success, and it is necessary to establish that members of one group are more likely to be successful than members of another.

It is easy to see that statistics play a central role in comparisons of group success. When employees are stratified on any basis (except for very small groups), it will always be true that, even in a neutral environment, one group will, on average, be more successful than another. To establish a pattern of practice, it is necessary to show that differential success could not plausibly have occurred to the extent of the observed differential in an environment where group membership plays no explicit role.

Disparate treatment occurs when, within a pool of equally qualified candidates, members of one group are shown to be significantly more likely than members of another to be selected or when one group fares significantly better in compensation than another. Adverse impact occurs in a facially neutral environment where, for example, selection within the qualified candidate pool is equally likely for all groups yet the screen for admission to the qualified pool disproportionately limits the admission of members of one or more groups. Evidence of disparate treatment is sufficient for proof of discrimination, and intent is inferred from disproportionate representation among the successful. Adverse impact by itself is not sufficient for proof of discrimination. On the other hand, the adverse impact proof does not require an inference of discriminatory intent.

The adverse impact theory was first articulated by the U.S. Supreme Court in *Griggs* v. *Duke Power Company*. After Title VII took effect, the Duke Power Company imposed dual criteria for admission of its laborers into training programs for skilled craft positions. One criterion was a requirement of a high-school degree. The other was that candidates must receive at least national median scores on each of two general intelligence tests. The adverse impact was that blacks were less likely than whites either to be high-school graduates or to receive median scores.

The score requirement was disqualified with the observation that there had been no attempt by Duke Power to establish business necessity or even job relatedness. The company's argument that the score requirements would improve the overall quality of its work force was dismissed. The Court did not need an economist to point out that quality comes at a price and that higher quality per se is not a business necessity. The degree requirement was specifically invalidated with the observation that, prior to imposing the requirement, nongraduates had been promoted and had performed adequately.

The decision against Duke Power made no reference to the intent underlying the test and degree criteria that, insofar as the record shows, had been administered in a facially neutral way. The demonstration of adverse impact coupled with a failure to validate job relatedness was sufficient.

Tables 7.1 and 7.2 are offered as evidence that the laws and executive orders that prohibit employment discrimination have generated sig-

TABLE 7.1. *Summary Statistics for the Equal Employment Opportunity Commission (EEOC) and Office of Federal Contract Compliance (OFCC)*

A. EEOC

Year	Budget ($1,000s)	Resolved cases (1,000s)	Cases filed in federal courts under Title VII
1966	3,250	6.4	n/a
1970	13,250	8.5	340
1975	55,080	62.3	3,930
1979	111,420	81.7	5,480
1981	141,200	61.8	6,250
1982	144,739	57.2	7,689

B. OFCC

Year	Budget ($1,000s)	Positions
1970	570	34
1975	4,500	201
1978	7,190	216
1979[a]	43,214	1,021
1981[a]	48,189	1,232
1982[a]	43,150	979

Sources: EEOC budgets are from U.S. Executive Office of the President, *The Budget of the United States Government.* Washington, D.C.: Office of Management and Budget, various years. Title VII cases filed: *Annual Report of the Director,* EEOC, various years. OFCC data are unpublished data from the U.S. Department of Labor.

Note: n/a = not available.

[a]Beginning in 1979 these figures reflect consolidation of eleven agency offices with OFCC to form OFCCP.

nificant actions. It is sufficient to note that the growth in numbers of cases filed in federal courts during the 1970s accounts for almost all growth in federal civil litigation during the decade.[3]

A large number of the 1970s cases involved class actions. Because the stakes were high and the issues complex, there was a heavy reliance on expert witnesses who presented the results of their data analyses. It is not unusual for experts to play a central role in litigation. In issues of product liability, engineers, chemists, and biological and biomedical scientists are central. Statisticians analyze the appearance of patterns to determine whether chance factors can be precluded. In school desegregation cases, sociologists and social psychologists measure the extent of integration and discuss responses to alternative desegregation plans. Political scientists work on voting rights and discuss

TABLE 7.2. *EEOC Actionable Charges*

Year	Race	Sex
1965	0	0
1966	3,254	2,053
1967	4,786	2,003
1968	6,650	2,410
1969	9,562	2,689
1970	11,806	3,572
1971	15,394	5,820
1972	27,468	10,436
1973	29,370	13,692
1974	31,272	16,949
1975	33,124	20,205
1981	44,085	30,925

Source: Burnstein, 1979, derived from EEOC *Annual Reports.*

effects of reapportionment on voter representation. In antitrust litigation, economists address market theories. And in diverse actions they calculate market shares and monetary damages.

What is different in some respects about employment discrimination is that the requisite data analysis can be massive and the litigation can reach advanced stages before the data have been sufficiently digested to permit informed opinions.

Whenever an individual experiences an adverse employment outcome, it is only natural to suspect that something other than skill or job performance may be involved. It is often easy to point to more successful employees who are seemingly less qualified and to individuals of one's own group who have fared equally poorly. Add to this the simple facts that white men earn higher wages and, on balance, hold superior positions, and the seeds of doubt have been planted. Yet confirming or rejecting suspicions usually requires the compilation of data for a large number of employment actions, and when the simple comparisons of average rates of success show disproportionate results, the evaluation may be just beginning. At issue are questions of job histories, work experience, education, and training. The data demands are obvious, and the requisite data almost never reside in machine-readable form, cleaned and ready for a quick review.

Extensive data analysis is often required before opinions can be formed, and potential plaintiffs usually cannot even gain access to the data without filing a formal charge. Thus, the litigation runs ahead of the analysis. Experts are often retained in an advisory capacity to inform the litigants about the data and to testify if the litigation runs its full course.

As an economist who has been involved in many cases, I am often asked where students or interested observers can read about the criteria used in practice. It is to this end that the following discussion is offered as a minor diversion from my main objective. I will discuss the role of the statistician or economist who measures either disparate treatment or adverse impact, and not that of the validation expert. Validation is the domain of the job analyst who studies the hands-on requirements of jobs or of those who study the intersection of job requirements and eligibility criteria, like scored tests or unscored subjective criteria (e.g., a degree requirement or a suitable personality).

Validation is most likely to be required when a rigid criterion is imposed whose absence can serve as a knockout to limit entry into an eligibility pool. So-called edge factors like a high-school or college degree or previous occupational experience, which give one candidate an edge over another but do not serve as rigid requirements, are less likely to require extensive validation.

In analyzing charges of discrimination in *hiring*, an economist, given the freedom to ignore data constraints, would say that, at a given wage among the pool of willing applicants, a nondiscriminating employer will choose the most able workers. But when ability is not observed and is proxied by what may be rather poor correlates and when issues of the availability of information to prospective employees challenge the identification of those who are in principle willing, the jump from the hypothetical to the practical can be large. It is easy to speculate about the shortcomings of particular applications, but it is more difficult to find expedient alternatives.

Studies of discrimination in hiring always compare the representation of minorities or women among those hired to their representation in the relevant pool. Two approaches are used to identify candidate pools: the most common one relies on external availability and the other uses applicant flows.

The external availability measure always begins with an idea of the geographical spread of a market. In practice the geographic horizon can be inferred by examining residence patterns of job applicants or (when applications data are not available) of persons hired. The patterns are as one would suspect and are closely tied to wage rates. High-wage or skilled jobs often have a national market. Unskilled jobs draw over limited distances.

The relevant market is often defined with a simple boundary cutoff where, for example, all within a county, city, or metropolitan area are seen as potentially equally eligible. Alternatively, distance gradients can be introduced where those living closer to the firm or plant or those living nearer easily accessed commuting routes are assigned greater weight.

In computing external availability, cognizance of relevant skills is ordinarily taken in dimensions of ability and willingness. For example, for unskilled laborer positions, those whose occupations or training suggest a lack of interest would ordinarily be excluded. Similarly, in identifying the relevant pool for skilled crafts, one would exclude those in unskilled occupations.

Willingness and ability often can be inferred by examining the previous occupations and, perhaps, educational levels of successful applicants. Weighted pools are derived by mixing observed densities of previous occupations and residence with census measures of availability within occupations and geographic areas.

The external availability analysis typically results in a single number that describes the representation of the protected group of interest in the relevant area. This availability measure is then the criterion against which representation in hiring is judged. For example, suppose that an external availability calculation suggests that blacks constitute 30 percent of external availability. A firm whose hiring records show a statistically significant shortfall (i.e., less than 30 percent of those hired are black) is a candidate for a finding of discrimination in hiring.

The applicant flow methods use the applicant mix as the criterion against which hiring is judged. The advantage of the applicant flow method is that willingness is presumably demonstrated by filing an application. The disadvantage is that applicant records are not always retained. Moreover, information about job openings may not spread evenly among all who are potentially interested. Situations where information spreads by word-of-mouth are the most suspect.

A clear advantage of the applicant flow procedure is that information on previous work experience and training is sometimes available and models can be estimated that incorporate applicant qualifications.

One issue that arises in applicant flow analyses where, insofar as I know, the courts have given no guidance, involves the question of endogeneity of applicant mix.

It is hardly surprising that hiring generates applications. In one case that involved the hiring of unskilled laborers at a large steel plant, the applicant log showed as few as 10 to 20 applications per week during periods when there was no hiring. Yet, in periods of heavy hiring, there would be as many as 350 entries per week in the applicant log.

A regression study, in which separate equations are estimated to predict numbers of applications filed by blacks and by whites, shows that applications by whites are very sensitive to hiring but not to the racial mix of those hired.

In this case the plant was located in an essentially all-white residential area, and white applicants were drawn primarily from within a twenty-mile radius. Black applicants lived twenty-five to forty miles from the plant, and job openings were not advertised.

The regressions show a distributed lag pattern in which hiring begins to generate applications within one week, has a maximum response after three to four weeks, and then fades to zero at the end of six weeks. One extra hire ultimately results in about seven applications from whites. In contrast, if a white is hired, no new applications are filed by blacks but if a black is hired, 11.2 applications are filed by blacks.

In this case the applicant mix is clearly determined by the hiring mix. When no blacks are hired, the estimate is that less than 6 percent of the applications will be filed by blacks. When no whites are hired, the applicant mix will show increasing black representation as total hiring increases, reaching a maximum where about 60 percent of the applicants will be blacks. The functional form of the response equations that were estimated implies that the applicant mix is sensitive to the level and the mix of hiring. And simulations based on observed hiring levels show that the equilibrium, where representation of blacks among those hired is equal to representation among applicants, occurs when 45 percent of those hired are black.

The underlying data are that 26 percent of the entries in the applicant log refer to blacks and 23 percent of those hired were black. The two numbers are statistically different, and the court held that the employer had discriminated against blacks in hiring.

If the response equations were accurately estimated, then the inference is that the employer would also have discriminated if 26 percent of the hires had been black because applicant mix would have risen above 26 percent.

If it is generally true that the mix of applications responds to the mix of hiring, then the external availability and the applicant flow criteria are inconsistent. A logical implication of the external availability approach is that firms in the same market (wage, skill, and geographic area) have equal external availability and should, therefore, hire equal mixes of employees designated by Title VII group status. A logical implication of endogenous applications is that applicant flow equal-hiring-mix equilibria occur only alongside varied work force mixtures.

Aside from cases involving charges of discrimination in hiring, the actions most frequently challenged are initial placement and promotion. There was a time when cases involving charges of discrimination in pay were the most common. These cases are increasingly divided into their components of starting salary and pay progression, and can therefore be viewed as initial assignment and promotion. The advantage of the division is that cases have liability and remedy phases (which can occur either in separate or in mixed hearings). Remedy is usually restricted to actions that occurred no more than two years before the suit is filed. An employee's compensation incorporates actions that have occurred throughout his or her tenure, but the bifurcation into starting pay and pay change permits identification of the timing of decisions.

Studies of *initial assignment* compare starting jobs with qualifications of persons hired. A case involving a university, for example, might consider initial rank or tenure. The qualifying criteria would be previous rank and teaching and research experience. The statistical procedures used for dichotomous outcomes are usually logit or probit. Where more than two outcomes are involved, as with academic rank, and where order is clear, ordered logit or probit are used.

More frequently the number of slots where new hires are first placed is large, and a single-dimensional continuous representation of initial placement, such as starting salary, is used. These typically are regression studies where the starting wage is regressed on indicators that identify group membership (race, sex, etc.) and individual qualification criteria.

Students of wage discrimination who have been restricted to data in the public domain, such as the censuses, current population surveys, or the popular panel surveys, have only dreamed about data that approach the quality of the information that is sometimes available in these cases.

The information gleaned from résumés or application forms include education (schools attended, majors, and sometimes grade point averages or indications of honors) and prior job experience (previous employers, job titles, and dates). In cases involving charges of discrimination against women, interruptions or gaps in work careers can be inferred.

Cases where charges of discrimination in *promotion* are brought can be divided into those where opportunities are limited by the availability of openings and those where no such restriction is operable.

The second type refers to merit promotions or pay changes. The statistical analyses attempt to explain a dichotomous variable (promoted or not) or a scalar (annual salary change). The conditioning or control variables describe individual qualifications and characteristics of the current job.

When promotional opportunities are limited by the availability of openings, the statistical frame becomes identical to a study of hiring. These analyses consider series of competitions that each usually have only one winner. In some cases there are precisely defined eligibility pools, and there are often data that identify those who bid for posted openings.

The limited opening analyses are different from the analyses of unrestricted openings only if eligibility pools are defined and if the number of competitors or their quality varies from one competition to the next. The reason for the distinction is that, in the unrestricted case, one's own characteristics determine chances of success. In the restricted case, one's characteristics are contrasted with the characteristics of one's competitors: even slow horses can win in sufficiently poor fields.

As noted, discrimination on the basis of race, color, national origin, sex, or religion necessarily involves questions of patterns of practice, and the required proof is often statistical. Because the power of statistical tests increases with sample size, large firms are more likely to be successfully challenged than small ones. It may be true that the ink on Title VII had not dried before the term *small numbers defense* had been coined.

Private-sector establishments with more than 25 employees in firms with more than 100 workers and federal contractors with more than 50 employees are required to submit an EEO-1 form to the EEOC annually. The form describes numbers of employees in a matrix where the rows refer to nine occupational classifications and the columns divide workers by sex and within sex into the following categories: white; black; Hispanic; Asian; Native American; and other. This is the only requirement for reporting to the EEOC unless a charge has been filed.

The preceding discussion is intended as an overview of the kinds of constraints that Title VII imposes on employer behavior. Federal contractors face added constraints.

Since 1968 all federal contractors with at least fifty employees and annual contracts totaling $50,000 or more are required to produce an Affirmative Action Plan (AAP) and to update it annually. The plan must contain narrative discussion and numerical work-force analyses that compare the availability of minorities and women to their utilization within the firm.

The narrative parts of the plan must include programs to identify and eliminate discriminatory practices or practices with adverse impact, descriptions of plans to attain goals (and, if necessary, explanations of failure to reach earlier goals), and descriptions of internal audit and reporting systems.

The numerical part of the plan requires that workers be divided into job groups defined by similarity of skill, job content, wage rates, and promotional opportunities. Guidelines suggest that job groups contain at least fifty employees and that they not cross the boundaries for the nine occupational groups identified in the EEO-1 forms.

A work-force analysis must follow for each job group. It begins with calculations of percentage availability for women and for each minority whose population represents at least 2 percent of the population in the immediate labor area. Availability is calculated using an eight-factor analysis. The idea is that availability is calculated for eight criteria and a composite availability score is then computed as an average of the eight.[4] The eight factors are as follows:

1. the minority population of the labor area surrounding the facility;

2. the size of the minority unemployment force in the labor area surrounding the facility;

3. the percentage of the minority work force as compared with the total work force in the immediate labor area;

4. the general availability of minorities having requisite skills in the immediate labor area;

5. the availability of minorities having requisite skills in an area that the contractor may reasonably recruit;

6. the availability of promotable and transferable minorities within the contractor's organization;

7. the existence of training institutions capable of training persons in the requisite skills; and

8. the degree of training that the contractor is reasonably able to undertake as a means of making all job classes available to minorities.

The first factor is modified to labor force availability for women.

The OFCCP prefers that no factor receive weight in excess of 30 percent and that all factors receive positive weight.

After the availability analysis is complete, the contractor compares utilization (i.e., representation of minorities and women within the job group) to availability and is required to designate each job group where underutilization is determined.

The exact criterion for designating a job group as underutilizing a protected group is not defined. At various times, the OFCCP has argued alternatively that underutilization occurs if the deficit exceeds one percent and that it occurs if the utilization is less than 80 percent of availability. The courts, on the other hand, have accepted contractor arguments that the difference between utilization and availability must be statistically significant.

Where underutilization exists, the contractor must set goals and timetables for reaching those goals. The ultimate goal is presumed to be the availability estimate. The annual placement goal is expected to exceed availability to ensure that the ultimate goal is reached in less than a full employee generation. A "good faith" effort must be directed toward achieving the goal.

The regulations require that the contractor keep a copy of the AAP at each facility and that, along with supporting data, it must be produced on request. The only reporting requirement is that EEO-1 forms be filed annually.

The secretary of labor has the right to audit the employment practices of contractors. Compliance reviews are targeted toward specific firms and industries where minorities and women are seen as underrepresented or as being concentrated in lower-paying jobs.

Contractors who contest the OFCCP review findings can demand formal hearings before administrative law judges. These hearings are very similar to regular civil proceedings.

In addition to employees of federal contractors having ordinary rights under Title VII, the secretary of labor has the right to bar a firm from holding government contracts. The contractors' right of appeal is first to the secretary and then to federal courts.

As background for the empirical descriptions of effect that follow, in this section I develop a series of models of statistical discrimination and add my interpretation of effects of antidiscriminatory legislation.[5]

There is, of course, no shortage of economic theories of discrimination.[6] The majority of theories are taste based. They posit a simple preference of one group for another and can be classified either as employer or employee based. In either case the potential discriminator is willing to pay for the privilege of working with those he or she prefers. Whether a payment is necessary depends on available alternatives.[7] This general class of behavioral models can be described as taste based in the sense that responses are to individual preferences. It is clear that taste-based discrimination by employers is prohibited by Title VII.

The employee theories fall into two classes. In one, employees prefer and are willing to pay for the privilege of working with members of their own group, but physical productivity is not affected by employee mix.[8] In the second, employee productivity is affected. According to these theories, workers are less productive when they work in the presence of members of a less-preferred group.[9] Either theory results in a tendency toward segregated production in a freely competitive market. Presumably, in the modern litigative environment, employers of segregated facilities risk being found guilty of discrimination in hiring.[10]

Although, for practical purposes, taste-based discrimination is precluded by Title VII, the picture blurs when qualifications intervene, and it is this case that I examine. The models refer to statistical discrimination where actors do not have group specific preferences. Instead, when information of individual productivities is imperfect, group averages are exploited for their predictive power.

For simplicity, I consider two groups designated by the subscripts, 1 and 2. I assume that there is a simple ability, y, that is normally distributed within each group. Although the means are unequal, the variances are assumed to be equal. That is:

(1) $$y_1 \sim N(\mu_1, \sigma^2),$$

and

(2) $$y_2 \sim N(\mu_2, \sigma^2),$$

with $\mu_1 > \mu_2$ so that group 1 is stochastically superior.

In one case, I assume that y is a valid criterion for business decisions as is its correlate (defined later) x, so questions of validity do not arise. The relevant contrast in this case is between situations where productivity is observed, where productivity is observed only with (independent and additive) error, and where productivity is not observed but correlates are observed. An alternative view of the case where productivity is not observed is that a subjective assessment of productivity (e.g., supervisor ratings) is observed but its validity is uncertain.

There are two measures that I use for comparing the group densities of y. One refers to the probability that a randomly selected member of group 1 has a greater value of y than a randomly selected member of group 2. I call it the preference probability in the sense that, if an employer were to base selections on y only, the preference probability is the probability that a member of group 1 would be selected. The alternative comparison is relative availability or just availability. It is specific to y and at y it is the ratio of the group 1 to the group 2 density. The availability measure would be relevant if, for example, jobs were segregated by skill. If y were observable, then availability gives the expected group 1/group 2 employment ratio in a nondiscriminatory environment.

Assume first that y is observable. The assumption of normality with equal dispersion makes calculation of availability and selection probabilities easy.

Let $f_1(y)$ refer to the density of group 1 at y and let $f_2(y)$ be the corresponding measure for group 2. Thus, according to the normality assumption, availability at y is:

$$(3) \qquad \ln\left(\frac{f_1}{f_2}\right) = -\frac{1}{2}\left(\frac{\mu_1^2 - \mu_2^2}{\sigma^2}\right) + \left(\frac{\mu_1 - \mu_2}{\sigma^2}\right) y$$

and availability is a simple exponential function of y.[11] At $y = (\mu_1 + \mu_2)/2$ availability $= 1$. For values in excess of the mid-value, $(\mu_1 + \mu_2)/2$, group 1's availability exceeds group 2's, and vice versa.

Note

$$(4) \qquad y_1 - y_2 \sim N(\mu_1 - \mu_2, 2\sigma^2).$$

Let

$$(5) \qquad z \sim N(0, 1).$$

It follows that

$$(6) \qquad \text{Prob } (y_1 > y_2) = \text{Prob } [z > -(\mu_1 - \mu_2)/(2\sigma^2)^{1/2}].$$

In words, the probability that the y-value for a randomly selected member of group 1 exceeds the y-value for a randomly selected member of group 2 is the probability that the standard normal variable exceeds (the negative of) the expected differential normalized by its standard deviation.[12] This is all standard. We next turn to prediction when y is not observed.

The simplest case involves observation of y with error. The error, v, I consider normally distributed with zero mean and variance σ_v^2. Denote the error-laden observations $y^* = y + v$. It follows that:

$$(7) \qquad y_1^* \sim N(\mu_1, \sigma^2 + \sigma_v^2),$$

and

$$(8) \qquad y_2^* \sim N(\mu_2, \sigma^2 + \sigma_v^2).$$

Equations (3) and (6) can be revised in this case by substituting y^* for y and $\sigma^2 + \sigma_v^2$ for σ^2. The effect of observation errors is to blur the distinction between the groups. Relative availability continues to be unity at the mid-value, but the exponential gradient is reduced so that the population segregates less rapidly as y^* varies. In comparison to y, the error-laden observations understate group 1's availability at values of y^* in excess of $(\mu_1 + \mu_2)/2$ and the understatement increases as y^* increases. The reverse is true for values below the midpoint.

The group 1 selection probability is also understated when y^* is substituted for y. If, for example, $\sigma_v^2 = \sigma^2$ and if the population means differ by one standard deviation in y, they will differ by 0.71 standard deviation in y^*.

In practice, observational errors can be important and they may be asymmetric in the sense that the information available to enforcement authorities may be inferior to the information available to firms (i.e., σ_v^2 may be greater for enforcers than for firms).

I have noted procedures used in calculations of external availability in hiring cases, and the eight-factor analysis required by OFCCP makes the reliance on external availability calculations clear for assessing underutilization of women and minorities.

The availability calculations often rest on census labor force by occupation counts. To illustrate the observation error problem in these calculations, I have used a 1983/1984 matched file from the March annual demographic survey of the CPS (current population survey). The CPS is conducted by the U.S. Bureau of the Census and is the most important intercensus source of employment patterns.

The March CPS collects individual information of job and employer, which is then coded into three-digit detailed categories. Each survey gathers information of the current (i.e., March) job and of the primary job in the preceding year. The respondent is also asked whether he or she is now in the same job as the primary one in the preceding year. Although the response to this question is not released on public use tapes, the U.S. Bureau of the Census uses a machine-coding criterion that permits an inference of an affirmative response. If the respondent is now (in March) in the same job as for last year, the industry and occupational indicators are constrained by machine coding to be the same.

The CPS is a monthly survey, and the rotation format is that, after a household enters the survey, it is interviewed for four consecutive months. Then, after an eight-month interruption, a respondent from the household is again interviewed for four consecutive months. The result is that those who appear in, for example, the March 1983 survey should (with a fifty–fifty chance) have been either in the 1982 or the 1984 March survey. Practical considerations of nonresponse or of movement between households result in only about three-fourths agreement between potential and realized adjacent-year matches.

From the 1983/1984 matched files I selected a sample of men and women who should have had only one job during 1982, 1983, and at least until March 1984. The inclusion criteria were as follows:

1. In the 1983 survey the respondent must have indicated that he or she held only one job during 1982;

2. The March 1983 and the 1982 occupation and industry codes

TABLE 7.3. *Occupation and Industry Agreement within Matched Sample from March 1983–1984 CPS*

	Industry		
Occupation	Agree	Disagree	Total
Agree			
No. of observations	4,296	663	4,959
% of cell	53.6	8.3	61.8
% of row	86.6	13.4	
% of column	65.5	45.4	
Disagree			
No. of observations	2,265	798	3,063
% of cell	28.2	9.9	38.2
% of row	73.9	26.1	
% of column	34.5	54.6	
Total			
No. of observations	6,561	1,461	8,022
% of row	81.8	18.2	100.0

Source: U.S. Bureau of the Census, public use files, 1983 and 1984 (March). *Annual Demographic Supplement of the Current Population Surveys.*

must agree (for inference that the 1983 survey's current job is the same as the previous year's job);

3. In the 1984 survey the respondent must have indicated that he or she held only one job during the previous year (1983); and

4. From the 1984 survey the current job and previous year's occupation and industry codes must agree.

Table 7.3 gives a 2-×-2 layout showing the extent of occupational and industrial code agreement between the two surveys.

There are a total of 8,022 men and women in the matched survey that satisfy the four criteria. Of them, industry codes agree in the two surveys for 82 percent of the observations and occupation codes agree in 62 percent of the cases. Both occupation and industry are matched for only 54 percent of the observations, and neither matches for 10 percent of the people observed. A chi-square test of row/column independence is rejected, and it is clear that agreement for occupation increases the likelihood of an industry match, and vice versa. Even so, it is clear that there are large margins of error in occupational and industry coding.

Without additional data, it is not obvious that one should suspect frequencies of coding error to be correlated with sex or minority status.[13] Even if error frequencies are the same for all groups, their existence has predictable effects for measures like external availability.

Classification errors like those involved in coding occupation and industry do not, in general, satisfy the standard errors in variables format where errors do not change expected or average values.

The easiest way to see this is to consider a high–low dichotomy. Table 7.3 suggests a 20 percent error rate in coding occupation and a 10 percent error rate in coding industry.[14] I assume a hypothetical 15 percent coding error rate. Now consider two groups. In one, 75 percent of the members would correctly be classified as belonging to the higher of the two categories. The classification error will reduce this number to 67.5 percent (.85 of .75 plus .15 of .25). In the other group, 25 percent of the members shuld be classified as belonging in the higher category but erroneous classification yields 32.5 percent (.85 of .25 plus .15 of .75). Thus, classification errors bring the populations together and understate true differentials.

The second type of unobservable that I consider involves a case when y is not observed but a correlate, x, is observed. For simplicity, I assume that x is scaled in identically the same way as y (i.e., within each group it has the same mean and variance as y). I also assume that the correlation, ρ, between x and y is the same for each group. We have then the linear regression structure:

(9)
$$y_1 = (1 - \rho)\mu_1 + \rho x + \epsilon,$$

and

(10)
$$y_2 = (1 - \rho)\mu_2 + \rho x + \epsilon$$

where $\epsilon \sim N(0, [1 - \rho^2]\sigma^2)$.

Since y is not observed, the actors (decision makers in firms or enforcement authorities) are assumed to substitute predictions formed by deleting the unobservable, ϵ, from equations (9) and (10).

If predictions are denoted with ($\tilde{y}$'s) then we have the inference:

(11)
$$\tilde{y}_1 \sim N(\mu_1, \rho^2\sigma^2),$$

and

(12)
$$\tilde{y}_2 \sim N(\mu_2, \rho^2\sigma^2).$$

The effect of substituting a prediction, $\tilde{y}$, for the observation is precisely the opposite of substituting an observation with error. Predictions magnify group differentials. The group means do not change (just as they did not for observation errors) but predictions collapse on the means (i.e., variance is reduced). The ratio of the variance in the prediction to underlying or true variance is ρ^2 (or R^2 to those familiar with regression). The availability gradient is exaggerated, and the group 1 selection probability is increased. If, for example, $\rho = 0.5$[15] and if the groups were one standard deviation apart in y, they would be two standard deviations apart in $\tilde{y}$.

It is instructive to write equations (9) and (10) in compact form using a variable to identify group 2. That is,

(13) $$y = (1 - \rho)\mu_1 + (1 - \rho)(\mu_2 - \mu_1)\gamma + \rho x + \epsilon$$

where $\gamma = 1$ if the individual considered is from group 2 and $\gamma = 0$ if he or she is from group 1.

Since by assumption $\mu_2 - \mu_1 < 0$, equation (13) says that in forming predictions, if the individual is from group 2, subtract something. This is, of course, an artifact of predictions collapsing on means. It is clear from examining equations (9) and (10) that the statistically optimum predictor is nothing more than a weighted average of the individual's own observed characteristic and the group mean. Higher correlations assign more weight to the observation, and lower correlations assign more weight to the group average. The prediction illustrated in equation (13) exploits the information that (by assumption) group 2 is inferior to group 1 on average. Since y is imperfectly observed through the correlate x, information on group averages is incorporated into predictions.

The intent of Title VII is clear. Discrimination—read in this instance as the use of information—cannot be based on group identity where groups are specified on the basis of sex or minority status. This, then, leads us to a third type of prediction problem where information of group membership is suppressed.

Notice the linear regression format of equation (13). If y is observed but, for purposes of the present argument, is of questioned validity, say, "job performance," then equation (13) could be estimated as a linear regression of y on x and γ. The regression intercept (in probability limit and expected value) is $(1 - \rho)\mu_1$, the coefficient on γ is $(1 - \rho)(\mu_2 - \mu_1)$ and ρ is the coefficient on x.

Suppose, instead, that y is regressed only on x (i.e., the identifier, γ, is suppressed) to obtain

(14) $$\tilde{y}' = a + bx.$$

It follows that

(15) $E(b) = [\rho + f(1 - f)t^2]/[1 + f(1 - f)t^2]$, and $\text{plim } (a) = \bar{\mu}(1 - b)$

where $t = (\mu_1 - \mu_2)/\sigma$, f = fraction of individuals who are members of group 1, and $\bar{\mu} = f\mu_1 + (1 - f)\mu_2$. Since x is normal with means μ_1 and μ_2, it follows that:

(16) $$\tilde{y}'_1 \sim N(a + b\mu_1, b^2\sigma^2), \text{ and } \tilde{y}'_2 \sim N(a + b\mu_2, b^2\sigma^2).$$

The aggregate dominance or selection probability calculation is the same for $\tilde{y}'$ as for y. To see this, note that

(17) $$\tilde{y}_1 - \tilde{y}_2 \sim N[b(\mu_1 - \mu_2), 2b^2\sigma^2],$$

so

(18) $$\text{Prob}\,(\tilde{y}_1 > \tilde{y}_2 = \text{Prob}\left(z > \frac{b(\mu_2 - \mu_1)}{2^{1/2}b\sigma} = \frac{\mu_2 - \mu_1}{2^{1/2}\sigma}\right).$$

The availability calculation using $\tilde{y}'$ is different from the one using y.

(19) $$\ln\,[f_1(\tilde{y}')/f_2(\tilde{y}')] = -\frac{(\mu_1 - \mu_2)(2ab + \mu_1 + \mu_2)}{2b^2\sigma^2}$$
$$+ \frac{\mu_1 - \mu_2}{b\sigma^2}\tilde{y}'.$$

Relative availability is unitary when

(20) $$\tilde{y}' = a + \frac{1}{b}\left(\frac{\mu_1 + \mu_2}{2}\right).$$

Inspection of equation (15) shows that $0 < f < 1$, so the biased predictor shifts the point of equal availability to a value above the midpoint, $(\mu_1 + \mu_2)/2$. One facet of the biased predictor is that the availability gradient (in $\tilde{y}'$) exceeds the gradient for y. It is as if the function of calculating relative availability shifts downward and then rotates counterclockwise. The functions (19) and (3) intersect at the point

(21) $$y = \frac{2ab + (1 - b^2)(\mu_1 + \mu_2)}{2b(1 - b)}.$$

For lower scores, relative availability of group 1 is lower using $\tilde{y}'$ than it would be using y. For higher scores the opposite is true.

Before concluding this section, let us test another case. It considers the probability that a randomly chosen member of group 1 has a higher value of y than a randomly chosen member of group 2 who has the same value of x (the qualifying characteristic). Before turning to this calculation, however, consider the biased predictors, $\tilde{y}'$.

It is obvious that predictions like those formed by equation (14) contain error, so the presumption would be that

(22) $$\text{Prob}\,(y_1 > y_2 | x_1 = x_2) = 0.5.$$

That is, if specification (14) were appropriate, then the presumption would be that individuals from group 1 and group 2 who are matched in x would have equal chances (fifty–fifty) of dominating in y. Of

TABLE 7.4. *Relative Availability of Group 1*

Cases	Population mid-value $\mu_1 + \mu_2 = 1.5$	A difference of one standard deviation between the mid-value and the point of evaluation[a]	
		Low evaluation point	High evaluation point
1. *y* observed	1.0	.37	2.72
2. *y* observed with error	1.0	.49	2.02
3. Correlate *x* observed, unbiased prediction	1.0	.14	7.39
4. Correlate *x* observed with biased prediction	.07	0.3	.19[b]

[a] The standard deviation used is the within-group one.
[b] In this hypothetical case, relative availability is unitary at a point that exceeds the mid-value by 2⅔ standard deviations and the overtaking point (after which group 1 availability is overstated) occurs 6⅔ standard deviations above the mid-value.

TABLE 7.5. *Group 1 Selection Probabilities*

Cases	Unconditional	Conditional on equal values of *x*
1. *y* observed	.76	—
2. *y* observed with error	.69	—
3. Correlate *x* observed, unbiased prediction	.98	.66
4. Correlate *x* observed with biased prediction	.76	.50

course, by assumption, the underlying structure follows equations (9) and (10) from which,

(23) $\text{Prob}\,(y_1 > y_2 | x_1 = x_2) =$
$$\text{Prob}\{z > (1 - \rho)(\mu_2 - \mu_1)/[2(1 - \rho^2)]^{1/2}\sigma\}.$$

This section is long, and some of the algebra is tedious, so, as a summary, I consider a specific example where $\sigma = 1$, $\mu_1 = 2$, $\mu_2 = 1$ (i.e., the population means are one standard deviation apart, where the correlation of *y* with the qualifying characteristic, *x*, $\rho = 0.5$, and where the populations are equally sized, $f = 0.5$). I also assume for the observational error case that $\sigma_v = 1$.

It is clear from Tables 7.4 and 7.5 that the availability calculations are sensitive to incomplete or erroneous information. The biased prediction technique, however, results in an order-of-magnitude larger error than is associated with the other approaches.

The alternative calculation of stochastic dominance that I call the selection probability gives a different impression, however. There the problem of predicted distributions collapsing on sample means becomes clear when the number for the unbiased prediction is compared to the true population number in the row where y is presumed to be observed. The first column in Table 7.5 refers to observations as indicated and gives selection probabilities for unconditional random draws from the two populations. The second column refers to pairs of individuals who have equal values of the qualifying characteristic, x. The number in the row marked unbiased prediction assumes that both x and y are observed and is the conditional analogue to the unconditional probability in the first row. The conditional probability for unbiased prediction is reported for contrast with the conditional probability for biased prediction.[16]

Before examining some of the data that refer to the effects of affirmative action, I will review my earlier discussion of statistical discrimination alongside the issues of hiring, initial assignment, and promotion.

The most straightforward implications obtain for hiring where external availability criteria are used. We have seen from Table 7.3, and the discussion surrounding it, that classification errors in coding occupation and industry operate in exactly the same way as the availability measure when ability, y, is observed with error. The effect is to blur distinctions between groups. Thus, monitoring authorities who measure availability using coded occupational data (and, less frequently, industrial data) and firms who do the same—perhaps in compliance with the eight-factor analysis—will overstate minority availability at higher-level positions and understate it at lower-level positions. This, of course, assumes that, on average, minorities have fewer job skills than the majority groups with whom they are compared.

The effect of the availability calculation is a presumption of underutilization of minorities in jobs using greater skill and a presumption of overutilization in less-skilled jobs. It is easy to see that affirmative action can easily have a pro-skill bias in effects on minorities.[17] On the one hand it can create pressure for monitored firms to recruit the most skilled minorities. On the other, to protect against charges of shunting minorities into inferior jobs, external availability calculations can create pressure to avoid less-skilled minorities.

The implications for initial assignment and promotion are less obvious. Charges of discrimination in these areas are claims that similarly qualified minorities and women are not treated as favorably as white men. Here the analysis is strictly conditional on validated productivity correlates. When the correlation between observed indexes

TABLE 7.6.   *Percentages of White Men Employed in EEO-1 Reporting Firms*

	1966	1970	1974	1978	1980
All EEO-1	52.7	53.5	52.4	49.3	48.5
Federal contractors	n/a	39.2	38.9	37.4	36.2
Noncontractors	n/a	14.3	13.6	11.9	12.2

Note: Figures are derived as EEO-1 employment divided by *Current Population Survey* employment outside governments and educational institutions; n/a = not available.

of productivity, x in the preceding discussion, and the unobserved productivity measure, y, is held constant, the implication is what follows from a comparison of the biased prediction model with the unbiased prediction model. And, as is clear from the second column of Table 7.5, the comparisons create pressure for increased selection of minorities (again, assuming lower mean values of x and y) for openings where they otherwise would have been less favored.

An alternative interpretation is that the pressure is to collect better data (i.e., improved information of y correlates). The only distinction between the biased and unbiased prediction models arises from the assumption that the $x - y$ correlation is less than one.

This is not to say that affirmative action will have little effect in areas of starting assignment and promotion. The effects are first to shift decision criteria from subjective devices that are correlated with group membership to objective and verifiable criteria. The effect is also an increased incentive to keep better records. Rather than rely on group membership as a productivity proxy, the incentive is to identify alternative measures that, if they are in fact improved productivity correlates, will enhance minority selection probabilities.

If unbiased predictors are precluded by a strict interpretation of Title VII and OFCCP guidelines, it is clear from examples in the preceding discussion that the effects of antidiscriminatory legislation are homogenizing in an environment of imperfect data. I will now consider the evidence of employment effects and then turn to indirect evidence of wage responses.

The data for the discussion of employment effects is taken primarily from aggregates of EEO-1 reports provided to the EEOC. The numbers refer to firms in the private sector and are compared to totals for CPS employment outside governments and educational industries.

As a benchmark, I have calculated numbers of white men in firms reporting to the EEOC as a percentage of total employment in private industry. The percentages are given in Table 7.6 for selected years. Over the full period, 1966 to 1980, about one-half of employment is in firms reporting to the EEOC, and three-quarters of this employment is in

TABLE 7.7. *Representation of Protected Groups in Firms Reporting to the EEOC*

	1966	1970	1974	1978	1980
Black men	91.8	112.5	123.1	128.4	126.4
Black women	91.5	118.7	141.2	144.8	154.4
White women	90.1	93.4	95.8	97.6	96.7

Source: "Affirmative Action in Employment: An Overview and Assessment of Effects." In *Selected Affirmative Action Topics in Employment and Business Set-Asides.* U.S. Commission on Civil Rights, 1 (1985).

Note: Figures are percentages of protected workers in EEO-1 reporting firms divided by the corresponding percentages for white men. Ratios are multiplied by 100.

federal contractors. Note the declining fractions for white men after 1970. Part of this decline is the result of substitution that increased the representation of protected workers, but that is not the whole story. Patterns of employment growth during the 1970s show that the greatest increases are in industries where the smallest fractions of employees are in firms reporting to the EEOC.

In the tables that follow, I provide indices of representation for three protected groups: black men, black women, and white women. In each case, reference is to one of these groups. Employers are specified as either all EEO-1 reporting firms, federal contractors, or noncontractors. Job classifications include all employees, officials and managers, or professional and technical workers. The representation statistic is the number of protected workers in the job classification that work for the designated firms as a proportion of all protected workers in that classification, divided by the corresponding proportion for white men. The index is normalized so that a value of 100 means that the firms described employ the same fraction of protected group workers as of white men. An index value of 75 implies that only three-fourths as many protected workers are employed as would be predicted on the basis of the employment of white men.

Firms reporting to the EEOC are larger than others. Reporting firms are not distributed among industries in the same proportions as other firms nor do they have the same mix of occupations. It is, therefore, not surprising that the measures of representation usually differ from the 100 norm. The representation statistics are not particularly useful for determining whether firms or groups of firms intentionally opt for or against protected workers because of their minority status or whether the imbalance exists for other reasons. The value of the representation statistic is that it gives us a simple way of observing change (i.e., the numbers themselves are less interesting than the trends in them).

Table 7.6 gives employment shares for white men, while Table 7.7 gives shares for the three protected groups, black men, black women, and white women, as a percentage of the shares for white men. In

1966, 48.4 percent of the black men in private industry work for EEO-1 reporting firms. That number is 91.2 percent of the corresponding share for white men (52.7 percent). In 1966, employment shares of protected workers in firms reporting to the EEOC are 8 to 10 percent below their employment of white men. Note, however, the remarkable realignment between 1966 and 1970 for black men and women. In four years the firms reporting to the EEOC switch from having an under-representation of blacks to a disproportionately large representation.

For black men, the trend continues until 1974 and then apparently stabilizes, with the EEOC reporting firms employing a share that exceeds the share for white men by 25 percent. For black women, the growth is greater and has persisted. In 1980, EEO-1 reporting firms employed 48.5 percent of white men in private industry. These same firms employed 74.9 percent of the black women. Contrast this to the 1966 numbers of 52.7 percent for white men and 48.7 percent for black women.

The pattern for white women is qualitatively similar to that of the other groups, but the changes are smaller.

In fifteen years the employment picture shifts from one where protected groups are less likely to work for firms reporting to the EEOC to one where blacks are more likely and white women are about as likely as white men to work in these firms.

Although we cannot distinguish between federal contractors and others in the EEO-1 data in 1966, Table 7.8 provides this contrast for the later years. In addition to total employees, numbers are shown for the top two of the nine occupations contained in EEO-1 forms. Using 1970 as the benchmark, the first thing to observe is that protected workers are much more likely than white men to work for noncontractors. This contrast is sharper for women than for black men and is probably an artifact of occupational and industrial segregation.[18] The second thing to observe is that the representation statistics do not change much between 1970 and 1980 for noncontractors when all employees are considered. And, for the top two occupational groups, the patterns for change are erratic—perhaps showing a slight upward trend. The dominant changes are for federal contractors. Among all employees, representation increases between 1970 and 1980 by eighteen percentage points for black men, by forty-six points for black women, and by ten points for white women. The numbers for officials and managers and for professional and technical workers are more impressive.

The all-employee category necessarily refers to hiring, and the data show that federal contractors have recruited an increasing share of protected workers. These data also show that the bulk of the increase

TABLE 7.8. *Representation of Protected Workers in Firms Reporting to the EEOC by Contractor Status*

	1970	1974	1978	1980
A. All Employees				
Federal contractors				
Black men	105.6	118.3	125.7	123.5
Black women	88.2	112.1	121.9	134.5
White women	71.6	74.2	78.6	81.5
Noncontractors				
Black men	130.8	132.4	137.0	137.7
Black women	202.1	224.3	216.0	218.0
White women	154.5	157.4	157.1	142.6
B. Officials and Managers				
Federal contractors				
Black men	72.4	100.8	101.8	106.0
Black women	76.8	113.4	155.9	136.9
White women	52.6	57.0	64.1	62.8
Noncontractors				
Black men	100.0	112.9	99.0	109.4
Black women	180.2	227.6	248.5	209.4
White women	139.6	126.7	123.8	105.7
C. Professional and Technical Workers				
Federal contractors				
Black men	77.0	131.5	113.9	94.6
Black women	35.8	48.2	68.8	86.2
White women	42.9	43.9	52.8	57.8
Noncontractors				
Black men	108.6	167.2	133.3	113.2
Black women	184.3	252.9	274.3	235.7
White women	236.4	278.2	281.0	207.8

Source: Percentages of protected workers in EEO-1 reporting firms (by contractor status) relative to corresponding percentages for white men. Ratios are multiplied by 100. Underlying percentages in James P. Smith and Finis Welch, "Affirmative Action and Labor Markets," *Journal of Labor Economics* 2 (April, 1984).

is accomplished by 1974 for black men but continues throughout the period 1970–1980 for women.

In the wage comparison that follows, I will concentrate on black men. Although I recognize that the story for women (especially minority women) may be more striking, and is probably different, there are so many complications in wage contrasts of men and women arising from questions of interruptions in the work career that I have taken the easier route.

TABLE 7.9. *The Changing Representation of Black Men*

	Between:			
	1966 and 1970	1970 and 1974	1974 and 1978	1978 and 1980
All EEO-1	20.7	10.6	5.3	−2.0
Federal contractors	—	12.7	7.4	−2.2
Noncontractors	—	1.6	4.6	.7

Source: Tables 7.7 and 7.8.

It would be nice when interpreting wage comparisons if we could identify representation separately for federal contractors and for others reporting to the EEOC in 1966. Unfortunately, my data do not permit this calculation. Nonetheless, I assume that the 1966–1970 period was the one during which the greatest growth occurred. Consider the evidence from Tables 7.7 and 7.8. There are four component periods between 1966 and 1980 where changes in representation are observed: 1966–1970; 1970–1974; 1974–1978; and 1978–1980. In only the last three are differences between contractors and others known. In Table 7.9 I contrast changes in the representation of black men for all the EEOC-reporting firms with changes where the firms are distinguished by contractor status.

Notice after 1970 that changes for federal contractors are slightly larger but are otherwise similar to changes among all EEO-1 reports. Recall, in any case, that federal contractors account for about three-fourths of all EEO-1 employment. For the EEO-1 totals, representation of black men grows more between 1966 and 1970 than it does for any other period or combination of periods. Is it not reasonable to assume that most of this growth resulted from hiring by federal contractors?

Most comparisons of the earnings of black men and white men are based on age or years since leaving school and on level of education. I have distinguished five schooling levels: those who completed eight years of schooling; nine to eleven years; twelve years (high-school graduates); thirteen to fifteen years (one to three years of college); and sixteen or more years (college graduates).

The data are from the 1960, 1970, and 1980 U.S. censuses. These surveys are taken in April of the decennial census years and include information about individuals' age, education, and, for those who are employed by others, wages and salaries during the preceding calendar year (1959, 1969, or 1979). Numbers of weeks worked during the preceding year is also recorded, and, in most cases, I use average weekly

TABLE 7.10. *Earnings of Black Men as a Percentage of Earnings of White Men by Years since Leaving School, 1960, 1970, and 1980*

Years since leaving school	Annual earnings			Weekly earnings		
	1960	1970	1980	1960	1970	1980
1–5	58.4	70.5	76.2	61.1	74.6	80.8
6–10	54.9	65.1	71.3	58.8	68.1	75.0
11–15	54.8	63.1	69.2	58.6	65.2	72.4
16–20	54.7	60.7	67.1	58.4	62.9	70.0
21–25	55.0	59.8	65.4	58.3	62.2	67.8
26–30	53.4	58.4	64.5	56.8	60.7	67.1
31–35	53.3	57.8	65.0	56.1	60.1	66.7
36–40	54.0	58.7	66.6	57.2	60.5	68.5
All	55.3	62.7	70.9	58.6	64.9	73.5

Source: Individual records of wage and salaried employees from U.S. Bureau of the Census, public use files, 1960, 1970, and 1980, U.S. Censuses of Population and Housing.

earnings (earnings last year divided by weeks worked last year) for the comparisons.

The census does not tell us when people left school and began their work careers. The convention I use is to estimate time since leaving school (and beginning work) on the basis of age and education. For example, for those who did not complete high school, I assume the work career began at age 17. Those designated as in their first five years since leaving school, therefore, are those who were 17 to 21 years old when surveyed, provided that they did not graduate from high school. For high-school graduates, work is assumed to begin at age 18. For those who attended but did not graduate from college, work is assumed to begin at age 20, and at age 22 for college graduates. Thus, a 40-year-old college graduate is assumed to be in the eighteenth year out of school.

Table 7.10 gives earnings comparisons (by years since leaving school) from the three censuses.

The first thing to observe is that earnings ratios are higher in comparisons of average weekly wages than they are for those based on annual earnings. This reflects the fact that black men work fewer weeks per year on average than white men. The data for annual earnings are presented to make this point. The weekly earnings data are more closely related to wage rates, and I confine my comments to them.

Perhaps the most impressive numbers in this table are those in the bottom row, where averages are taken over all age groups. Between

1960 and 1980 weekly wages of black men rise from 58.6 percent of the earnings of white men to 73.5 percent. More than one-third of the black–white wage gap is closed during these twenty years. Part of this change occurred because schooling levels of blacks and whites are converging, but the largest part of the change is due to the fact that earnings of blacks are increasing relative to whites at the same schooling levels.

Earnings growth for blacks with the same schooling as whites could occur because the schools attended are increasingly similar in quality.[19] But the growth may also be attributable to improving job market opportunities for blacks.

If we choose a column in Table 7.10 and look down the rows, we see that the wage ratio is higher for younger than for older men. This partly reflects a narrowing black/white educational differential,[20] but it may also reflect superior job market opportunities for younger blacks.

The phenomenon of higher relative wages for young black men is often explained as an artifact of slower career progression. According to this argument, blacks and whites are most similar in realized earnings when they first enter the job market. As the career unfolds, blacks are disproportionately shunted into dead-end jobs while whites are promoted into higher-paying jobs. The obvious prediction is that relative wages of blacks fall as they age.

This view, which is called the dual or secondary market hypothesis, fails to explain why the wage profiles are higher in recent years than in 1960. Moreover, it simply misrepresents the data. Career progressions can be traced in Table 7.10 by reading on the diagonal.

For example, those who were one to five years out of school in 1960 were eleven to fifteen years out in 1970, and twenty-one to twenty-five years out in 1980. Starting with a relative wage of 61.1 percent in 1960, this cohort's wage increases to 65.2 percent in 1970 and to 67.8 percent in 1980. If you examine all such cohort comparisons in Table 7.10, you will see that there are a total of twelve changes to observe. Eleven of the twelve show rising relative wages for blacks as the career expands. The single exception is for those one to five years out of school in 1970 (and eleven to fifteen years out in 1980), for whom the wage ratio falls from 74.6 to 72.4 percent.

In Table 7.10, if we contrast 1960 and 1980 wage ratios, we see that the largest gains occur among the youngest groups. For example, relative wages for those one to five years out of school increase from 61.1 to 80.8 percent, or 19.7 percentage points. For the oldest group, relative wages increase from 57.2 to 68.5 percent (11.3 percentage points). As I will show, this pattern of greater growth for the younger groups only demonstrates more rapid growth in school completion in the recent

TABLE 7.11.   *Weekly Earnings of Black Men as a Percentage of Weekly Earnings of White Men in 1980 by Education and Years since Leaving School*

Years since leaving school	Years of school completed				
	8	9–11	12	13–15	16 or more
1–5	72.7	85.5	81.0	91.3	91.6
6–10	75.4	75.5	78.1	84.1	87.7
11–15	79.3	78.6	78.9	80.6	86.3
16–20	74.9	76.8	77.7	79.0	75.9
21–25	76.1	75.2	75.4	77.0	73.2
26–30	81.5	74.6	76.5	75.1	73.4
31–35	80.2	75.7	76.0	77.2	66.9
36–40	77.7	77.1	75.6	74.4	71.7

Source: U.S. Bureau of the Census, public use files, 1980.

period. Once changing educational levels are taken into account, a pattern of advance emerges that is fairly uniform across the age groups.

Notice that when the 1960 to 1980 changes are broken into two phases, 1960 to 1970 and 1970 to 1980, the greatest growth occurs for younger workers during the 1960s and for older workers during the 1970s. This contrast withstands adjustments for changing levels of education. I interpret it as suggesting that the impetus of affirmative action was on hiring in the 1960s but moved to promotion during the 1970s.

Because most newly hired workers are young (relative to the general work force), an emphasis on hiring creates a youth bias in wage change. An emphasis on promotion has no obvious youth bias.

In Table 7.11, I report wage ratios as of 1980 by time out of school and level of education. These ratios are generally higher than the ones reported in the earlier table, where black–white differences in schooling were combined with comparisons like those shown. One especially noteworthy feature of this table is that, at higher levels of schooling, younger black workers fare decidedly better in comparison to whites than do older workers. The reverse pattern appears for those with only eight years of schooling (i.e., those who did not attend high school). Another pattern of interest is that, among the youngest workers, relative wages of blacks increase as levels of schooling rise. This is an important departure from the familiar patterns of earlier times where earnings ratios for blacks declined as schooling increased. That familiar pattern—about which perhaps too much has been written—is exhibited for older workers in 1980.

There is a tradition in the economics literature of treating schooling

TABLE 7.12.   *Growth in Weekly Earnings of Black Men Relative to Weekly Earnings of White Men between 1960 and 1980, by Education and Years since Leaving School*

Years since leaving school	Years of school completed				
	8	9–11	12	13–15	16 or more
1–5	2.0[a]	9.0	10.8	16.2	19.9
6–10	1.6[a]	9.7	7.5	13.1	15.2
11–15	4.5[a]	12.3	12.1	14.6	17.8
16–20	6.1[a]	6.6	10.6	12.9	12.8
21–25	2.6[a]	5.9	7.7	14.0	19.1
26–30	9.2	9.5	10.3	10.2	13.9
31–35	9.7	8.9	11.1	21.1	14.0
36–40	7.6	11.9	15.0	19.1	16.6

Note: The figures in this table are 1980–1960 differences in earnings per week of black men as a percentage of earnings of white men.

[a] Not statistically different from zero.

as an investment in which students forego opportunities for current income and invest (via staying in school) in higher income for the future. A common practice in this tradition has been to compute rates of return to investments in schooling, just as rates of return are computed for alternative investments. A simple rule for comparing investments for two groups like blacks and whites involves observing whether income rises proportionately more for one of the groups as schooling increases. If it does, the rate of return is higher for that group. Using this rule for Table 7.11, we see that, for workers who have been out of school more than twenty years (i.e., those who left school before 1960), rates of return to schooling were lower for blacks than for whites. The opposite is true for more recent graduates. Investments in schooling are more lucrative today for blacks than for whites.

Table 7.12 shows earnings growth between 1960 and 1980. The numbers in this table are the differences between the numbers shown in Table 7.11 and a similar one (not shown) for 1960. When workers are grouped by age and education, we find in every case that wages of blacks are higher, relative to whites, in 1980 than in 1960.

The largest gains occur for the most educated. The smallest gains are found for those who are both the youngest and the least educated. When these changes are divided into those occurring during the 1960s and 1970s, an interesting pattern emerges. First, during the 1960s, the largest gain occurs among the youngest group at every level of education. Moreover, the change is greatest at the highest levels of schooling.

TABLE 7.13. *Average Growth in Relative Earnings of Black Men by Years since Leaving School (All Educational Levels)*

Years since leaving school	1960 to 1970	1970 to 1980	1960 to 1980
1–5	15.4	−2.9	12.5
6–10	8.2	1.9	10.1
11–15	8.1	5.0	13.1
16–20	5.6	4.5	10.1
21–25	5.9	2.9	8.8
26–30	3.5	6.7	10.2
31–35	3.9	8.0	11.9
36–40	6.9	6.3	13.2

Note: Figures are averages of changes within educational levels weighted by the (age specific) distributions of school completion for black men in 1980.

TABLE 7.14. *Average Growth in Relative Earnings of Black Men by Years of School Completed (All Ages)*

Years of school completed	1960 to 1970	1970 to 1980	1960 to 1980
8	2.0	4.3	6.3
9–11	5.7	3.5	9.2
12	7.3	2.8	10.1
13–15	12.0	2.4	14.4
16 or more	10.8	5.7	16.5

Note: Figures are averages of changes within age group weighted by the (education specific) age distributions of black men in 1980.

During the 1970s, relative wages of the youngest blacks fall at all levels of schooling except for college graduates.

I have tried to summarize the most salient features of these changes in Tables 7.13 and 7.14. Table 7.13 provides changes, averaged over schooling levels, for the groups designated by time since leaving school. Table 7.14 provides changes, averaged over time out of school, by level of schooling. Between 1960 and 1970, the largest increases in relative wages are found in the youngest groups. This pattern reverses between 1970 and 1980. Relative wages actually fall for those out of school five years or less and, for older workers, gains generally increase as age increases. When the periods are combined (in the third column of Table 7.13), no apparent pattern develops between time out of school and improvement in the relative wage of black men.

TABLE 7.15. *Average Weekly Wages of Black Men as a Percentage of Average Weekly Wages of White Men, Stratified by Schooling and Experience*

		Years of experience				
		1–5	6–10	11–20	21–30	31–40
A.	All schooling classes					
	1967–1968	69.5	66.1	61.9	59.7	57.7
	1971–1972	82.1	72.0	66.1	62.5	64.0
	1975–1976	81.4	74.0	70.2	67.8	68.8
	1979–1980	78.9	75.3	72.0	69.3	64.1
B.	Sixteen years of schooling					
	1967–1968	75.7	66.5	59.8	55.3	53.7
	1971–1972	101.1	84.6	65.3	62.0	69.5
	1975–1976	89.1	84.1	72.7	67.2	70.9
	1979–1980	92.3	86.1	77.9	69.9	64.5
C.	Twelve years of schooling					
	1967–1968	81.8	76.8	71.2	68.4	68.4
	1971–1972	90.7	82.3	76.2	71.0	73.8
	1975–1976	83.1	81.8	77.2	76.7	73.6
	1979–1980	79.5	78.1	78.4	77.8	76.2

Source: U.S. Bureau of the Census, yearly CPS public use tapes, various years.

In Table 7.14, we see a definite pattern of greater increases in the black–white wage ratio being associated with higher levels of schooling. There is no apparent pattern for changes during the 1970s. In the later period, the greatest change occurs for college graduates, and the second largest for those who did not attend high school. Of course (column three), the combined changes for the two decades show much larger gains for the most educated.

The three censuses give a broad overview of wage change, and it is clear from them that the relative position of black men has improved. They do not, however, distinguish between longer-run forces for wage convergence and the impact of affirmative action. With the time profile of employment responses as a benchmark, we can perhaps get a clearer idea of responses to affirmative action pressure by examining the time profile of wage change.

To this end I will compare ratios of weekly wages using CPS data from the March 1968–1981 surveys.[21] Table 7.15 summarizes the relevant ratios.

In each of the three panels, the individual rows summarize cross sections, and the pattern is the same as described for the censuses—namely, in comparison with whites the wages of young black men are high relative to wages of older black men. Further, as the second and third panels show, the difference between the relative wage of those with one to five years of potential experience and those with thirty-one to forty years is much higher for college than for high-school graduates.

The 1967–1968 cross sections also show higher relative wages for high-school than for college graduates. Yet the 1979–1980 cross sections show higher relative wages for young college graduates with ten or fewer years of experience than for high-school graduates. The ultimate reversal is, of course, implied by the more rapid attenuation of relative wages associated with increased experience in the earlier cross sections if the attenuation measures rates of cohort advance. No extrapolation from earlier periods would predict the kinds of patterns we find by reading down the first two columns of this table.

The abrupt jump in relative wages for young black men from 1967–1968 to 1971–1972, especially for college graduates, is remarkable. In isolation, it would be tempting to ascribe the change to affirmative action. First, the chance that firm and job specificity of skills increase with age makes it plausible that the young would be disproportionately affected. Second, to the extent that the greatest pressure for change accrues where blacks are least represented, effects should be sharper for college than for high-school graduates. Third, the employment effects are consistent with this timing.

There are two problems with this interpretation. One is that the change in wage patterns seems to have preceded the major enforcement and litigation activity described in Tables 7.1 and 7.2. The other is that the gain experienced between the first two cross sections seems to have been substantially lost in subsequent periods.

For college graduates, the end-point differentials achieved by comparing 1979–1980 and 1967–1968 are very large. Yet only for those with more than ten years of experience do the numbers seem to fall on a line of steady progress. For the six-to-ten-year group, the entire gain occurs between 1968–1969 and 1971–1972 with no subsequent change. And, for the new entrants (one to five years of experience) the incredible jump to 1971–1972 was followed by a drop (of one-half the magnitude of the increase) and subsequent stability.

The data for high-school graduates are less dramatic, but the patterns are similar in many ways. The most significant difference is that the end-point comparisons show no gain over the period. In fact, for high-school graduates, the 1979–1980 cross sections show relative wage profiles that are essentially independent of experience. This is in sharp contrast to all other cross sections for earlier years.

To summarize wage changes, there is a sharp departure from longer-run trends in the relative wages of black men—especially for the youngest and most educated—during the early days of affirmative action when representation of minorities was increasing more rapidly. Oddly, this change appears to have led the increase in compliance monitoring and litigation that occurred after 1972.

It is tempting to attribute the wage change that occurs between 1968 and 1972 to affirmative recruiting and placement behavior of federal contractors and other large firms that report to the EEOC. Much of the change appears to have been a wage bubble that had largely dissipated by 1980 when wages appear to return to their longer-run trends.

The 1972 to 1980 period is one of growing enforcement and litigation activity during which the representation of black men is approximately constant within the EEOC reporting firms.

In summary, I have tried to give an overview of the kinds of affirmative action pressures that firms face in the modern antidiscrimination environment. I have also tried to illustrate the kinds of issues that arise in empirical attempts to identify discrimination. As a general background I have traced through a series of simple models of statistical discrimination when productivity is not observed and correlates, including group membership, are substituted. The alternative to the statistical model of discrimination where the information of group membership is exploited is one where prediction is devoid of group identification. I call this model biased prediction, to reflect the fact that the exclusion of group membership results in prediction with greater error and overstates the average performance of groups with lower average ability while it understates the average performance of groups with higher average ability.

The biased prediction model corresponds with my interpretation of the type of model that a firm that does not discriminate, as discrimination is defined by Title VII, would use. That is, it would not exploit information of group membership in cases where groups are defined by sex or minority status.

If we knew the efficiency costs of erroneous decisions, it would be a simple matter to trace through the cost implications of the alternative models. I have not done so. Instead, I contrast the alternative models to infer the pressures entailed by compliance with Title VII. There are no surprises. The biased prediction model is homogenizing relative to the statistically discriminatory model in the sense that group differentials are reduced by reliance on the nondiscriminatory model.

With all this as background, I turn to the empirical record in summary form by examining changes in private-sector employment patterns and trends in wage contrasts between black and white men. The employment effects are unambiguous. Under affirmative action, employment of minorities and women has shifted dramatically to firms where monitoring is closest. The timing of the response is somewhat surprising in the sense that most of the change occurred soon after implementation of the relevant legislation and presidential orders—before monitoring agency budgets, the number of complaints filed, and subsequent litigation approached their current levels.

The wage response is even more perplexing. There is an apparent bubble coinciding with the period of rapid employment response, and subsequent trends suggest that the term *bubble* is appropriate. It is unclear for the most recent data whether current relative wages of black men reflect a lasting response to affirmative action. Closer examination of the data will, perhaps, provide added insight. For the present, it is clear that there has been long-run gain in the income status of black men.

A number of recent studies[22] have shown that the longer-run gain in relative earnings of black men can be attributed to three primary sources: rising levels of school completion, emigration from the rural South, and increasing value of additional schooling.

Affirmative action in labor markets is unlikely to have had a direct impact on migration or school completion. It may have affected the income advantage associated with extra schooling. The alternative explanation of growth in the value of schooling is quality enhancement, pure and simple. This is not the place to review the evidence on trends in the quality of schooling. It is sufficient to note that evidence exists—as measured by the fact that blacks and whites are increasingly likely to attend the same schools, as measured by the nominal trappings of schools such as teacher salaries or teacher/pupil ratios or days attended, or as measured by achievement test scores—that the quality of schooling is improving for blacks relative to whites. The case for a lasting wage effect as the result of affirmative action remains to be made.

Notes

1. In 1972, when protection was extended to federal employees under the Equal Employment Opportunity Act, the responsibility for compliance monitoring of federal agencies was given to the Civil Service Commission. Later the EEOC assumed the bulk of this responsibility as well.

2. The regulations require all firms with fifty or more employees and a contract or subcontract of $50,000 or more to have a written affirmative action plan.

3. In 1971 there were 6,710 civil cases tried in federal courts that did not involve issues of civil rights. In 1979 the number of noncivil rights cases was 7,100. Not all civil rights cases involved employment, but, by 1979, 41.2 percent of all civil rights cases filed were Title VII cases.

4. Construction contractors are not required to perform their own availability analysis. Instead, OFCCP performs it for them. For minorities, the OFCCP availability measure is constant within SMSAs and is the minority's labor force share in the area. The goal for women in contract construction is a national constant, 6.9 percent being the most recent number that I have seen.

5. I draw heavily on the earlier work of Phelps (1972) and Aigner and Cain (1977).

6. See, for example, Becker (1971) and Arrow (1972a,b).

7. See, in particular, the paper by Kreuger (1962) where discriminating monopsonists can gain and Becker (1971) where discriminatory intent results in segregated production without pecuniary effects.

8. See Becker (1971).

9. See Welch (1967).

10. I know of no case where it has been demonstrated that productivity is higher in segregated facilities. Presumably, a demonstration that this is true could result in a successful "business justification" defense.

11. An undesirable property of the relative availability calculation is that it is sensitive to scale. Consider, for example, the linear transform $C = \alpha_0 + \alpha_1 y$. Since $y \sim N$ (μ_1, σ^2) for $i = 1, 2$, it follows that $C \sim N (\alpha_0 + \alpha_1 \mu_i, \alpha_1^2 \sigma^2)$.

If we evaluate relative availability at a point on the y-line where y differs from one of the group means by $k\sigma$, we would expect that the availability under c at a corresponding point in one of the two densities would be the same. Instead, the two availability calculations give different results. Consider two points, $y' = \mu_i + k\sigma$ and c' $= \alpha_0 + \alpha_1\mu_i + k\alpha_1\sigma$. These points are equally dense in the reference population, $i =$ either 1 or 2. Yet the ratios of relative availability are:

$$\log f_1(c')/f_2(c') - \log f_1(y')/f_2(y') = [(\alpha_1^2 - 1)/\alpha_1^2](\mu_1^2 - \mu_2^2)/2\sigma^2.$$

Only when $\alpha_1 = 1$ (i.e., when scale is unchanged) do the two calculations give equal results. When $\alpha_1 < 1$, as in the examples that follow, group 1 availability is reduced by rescaling.

12. Notice that the selection probability refers to samples of size one for each population.

13. It is probable, however, that error frequencies are not the same for all groups. This is because occupational and industrial distributions differ and because it is likely that chances of error are not the same for all occupations and industries. Some are easier to code than others.

14. The error rates are approximate. Consider occupation to see how they are estimated. From Table 7.3 we have the result that 38.2 percent of the occupational codes disagree between the two surveys. For simplicity, I assume (contrary to fact) that agreement implies that both values are called correctly and disagreement occurs when at least one value is incorrect. If 80 percent of the values were coded correctly in the first survey and 80 percent of them were coded correctly in the second, there would be cross-survey agreement in 64 percent of the cases.

15. A correlation of 0.5 is about what one finds in correlating measured I.Q. in high school with grade point averages in college. The zero-order correlation between income and schooling of white men is about 0.3.

16. It is clear from equation (13) that the conditional probability is 1.0 if decisions for matched values of x are based on predictions only.

17. See my discussion (1981).

18. I do not intend for segregation to be viewed as discrimination; there is a long list of alternative explanations. Notice also that job categories like "officials and managers" or "professional and technical" are aggregates of many specific job titles. Occupational segregation, coupled with different occupational mixes between contractors and oth-

ers, will result in differences in representation of protected groups between these groups of employers.

19. For example, in 1960 black college graduates who were in their first five years out of school earned 72 percent as much as whites. In 1980 black college graduates in their first five years out of school earned 92 pecent as much as whites. These comparisons are of college graduates, 22 to 26 years old in 1960 and 1980. In the twenty years between 1960 and 1980, black college graduates were drawn increasingly from the same schools as whites. Twenty years earlier, recent black college graduates were much more likely to have graduated from traditionally all-black colleges, and the training received during college may have been less comparable than it was in 1980.

20. Average school completion levels of young black men are more similar to the educational levels of white men than is true for comparisons of older black and white men.

21. Each survey asks about earnings in the preceding year, and the convention I use is to refer to the income year rather than the survey year.

22. See, in particular, Welch and Smith (1986).

References

Aigner, Dennis J., and Glen G. Cain, 1977. "Statistical Theories of Discrimination." *Industrial and Labor Relations Review* 30: 175–187.

Arrow, Kenneth J., 1972a. "Models of Job Discrimination." In *Racial Discrimination in Economic Life*, ed. Anthony Pascal, 83–102. Lexington, Mass.: Lexington Books.

———, 1972b. "Some Mathematical Models of Race in the Labor Market." In *Racial Discrimination in Economic Life*, ed. Anthony Pascal, 187–203. Lexington, Mass.: Lexington Books.

Becker, Gary S., 1971. *The Economics of Discrimination*, Second Edition. Chicago: University of Chicago Press.

Burnstein, Paul, 1979. "Equal Employment Opportunity Legislation and the Income of Women and Nonwhites." *American Sociological Review* 44 (June): 367–391.

Equal Employment Opportunity Commission, various years. *Annual Report to the Director*. Washington, D.C.

Kreuger, Anne O., 1962. "The Economics of Employment Discrimination." *Journal of Political Economy* 71 (October): 481–486.

Phelps, Edmund S., 1972. "The Statistical Theory of Racism and Sexism." *American Economic Review* 62 (September): 659–661.

U.S. Executive Office of the President, various years. *The Budget of the U.S. Government*, Office of Management and Budget. Washington, D.C.

Welch, Finis, 1981. "Affirmative Action and Its Enforcement." *American Economic Review* 71 (May): 127–133.

———, 1967. "Labor Market Discrimination." *Journal of Political Economy* 75 (June): 225–240.

Welch, Finis, and James P. Smith, 1986. "Closing the Gap: Forty Years of Economic Progress for Blacks." Santa Monica, Ca.: The RAND Corporation, R-3330-DOL.

Chapter 8. Black Labor and Affirmative Action: An Historical Perspective

THE STUDY of working-class life in the United States reveals that race and ethnicity are of central importance in labor history because these forces have provided the basis for structures of group domination and subordination. Furthermore, ideologies and beliefs rooted in assumptions of racial privilege and white supremacy have sustained and perpetuated the patterns of discrimination within the labor force. Many observers who have stressed the economic aspects of collective action by workers have either ignored or misrepresented these patterns of discrimination, thus adopting an abstract ahistorical view that ignores social forces of great consequence. Among the most important of these is the primacy of race and ethnicity in the recomposition of the labor force after 1850, and more specifically, the use European immigrants made of labor unions to aid them in becoming assimilated and in developing as a privileged section of the working class at the expense of blacks and other nonwhite workers. Many labor unions emerged as the institutional expression of white working-class racism; their policies and practices resulting in unequal access, dependent on race, to employment and union membership.

Race consciousness and class consciousness were joined together. Racism was no less powerful than labor market and other economic forces, and white immigrants perceived their identity and interests in racial and ethnic group terms. According to the sociologist Herbert Blumer, "the view that industrialization moves ahead naturally to dissolve the racial factor is not borne out by the facts." He concludes that the "picture presented by industrialization in a racially ordered society is that industrial imperatives accommodate themselves to the racial mould and continue to operate effectively within it," and not *vice versa*.[1]

By the end of the nineteenth century the American working class was an immigrant working class. European immigrants held power and exercised great influence within organized labor. By 1900, Irish immigrants or their descendants held the presidencies of more than 50 of the 110 national unions in the American Federation of Labor (AFL).[2] Many other unions were led by immigrants or their sons; Germans followed the Irish in number and prominence, and the president of the AFL was a Jewish immigrant. Records of labor organizations confirm the dominant role of immigrants and their descendants in many individual unions and city and state labor bodies throughout the country at the turn of the century, and for decades later.[3] For the immigrant worker, advancement of the individual was dependent upon communal advancement. Participation in organized labor was a significant part of that process.

For blacks, both before and after emancipation, the experience was completely different; for them, systematic racial oppression, in the North and South, was the decisive fact of their lives.

Systems of racial oppression acquire their own dynamic. After discriminatory patterns have become established and after racial beliefs are constructed to justify social and economic inequality, the patterns and beliefs develop an independent life of their own. Thus racial stratification was sustained within the working class. Racism united white workers and was widely used as an effective organizing instrument by labor unions.

In the 1930s with the rise of the Congress of Industrial Organizations (CIO), the forms of discrimination sometimes changed, but the substance did not. Although CIO unions admitted blacks—in contrast to the craft unions of the AFL, which traditionally excluded them—CIO affiliates engaged in a variety of discriminatory practices after blacks had been admitted. Whether as a result of total exclusion by craft unions in some industries, or of segregated job structures under industrial union contracts in others, black workers were removed from competition for jobs reserved exclusively for whites.

During the period of the CIO organizing campaigns in the mass production sectors of the economy, thousands of black workers were for the first time enrolled as union members. But the great promise of the CIO, the promise of an interracial labor movement, was never realized. Some affiliates permitted segregated units and negotiated discriminatory provisions for job assignment, seniority, and promotion in union contracts. Black workers were rarely permitted to share power in major leadership positions, even in the most advanced unions. The

CIO policy was at best an expression of abstract equality in contrast to the pattern of exclusion and segregation that persisted within the AFL. By 1955, when the CIO and AFL merged and when the dynamic period of industrial organizing was over, the CIO policy on race had become an empty formality.

Interracial unions in which blacks were accepted as equal in the workplace and in leadership were rare in the history of American labor. Traditional racial patterns remained intact well into the second half of the twentieth century, the few exceptions in the main limited to some unions operating in the public sector where nonwhite workers constituted a large percentage of the labor force. The historical record suggests that unless there was a significant concentration of black workers in an industry and these workers had established their own leadership in advance of white-led union organization, then labor unions would engage in a broad range of discriminatory practices as they functioned primarily to advance the interests of white workers, to guarantee for themselves privileges in the labor market.

Although, by the early 1960s, decisions of the federal courts had created a new perception of law and public policy on civil rights issues, the long-established patterns of employment discrimination remained intact. By 1963, pressure had mounted for congressional enactment of a federal fair employment law as part of the drive for comprehensive civil rights legislation.

A broad national coalition emerged that sponsored the March on Washington of 1963, winning the support of many organizations and reflecting the high point of a brief national consensus that was responsible for passage of the Civil Rights Act of 1964. Notable for its absence from the list of participants, or even sponsors and supporters, of the march was the AFL–CIO. This was no accident or oversight. The executive council of the AFL–CIO, after extensive discussion and debate, refused to give its endorsement or even to recommend that affiliated unions give their support. The best they could do was to leave it to "individual union determination." Some unions, especially those with substantial black memberships, such as the United Auto Workers, did, in fact, actively support and participate in the March on Washington.

According to the veteran civil rights lawyer Joseph Rauh, who was a major strategist of the legislative struggle for passage of the Civil Rights Act, by 1964 the AFL–CIO "had just been so beaten for their racism that they wanted a bill, and then they could blame it all on the bill if it wasn't enforced."[4] Furthermore, failure to support the proposed act would have identified the AFL–CIO with blatant southern racism during a period of dramatic racial conflict and constituted defection from a liberal coalition under an activist Democratic president committed to adoption of the act. On behalf of the AFL–CIO, its president, George Meany, finally testified in support of the proposed law, and the federation was active in the lobbying effort to secure its adoption.

But despite the AFL–CIO's endorsement of Title VII, the employment section of the Civil Rights Act, many of its affiliates later repeatedly resisted compliance with the law. The low priority given to efforts to eliminate discrimination within affiliated unions was reflected in Meany's testimony when he stated that the AFL–CIO would not apply sanctions to unions that refused to comply with the employment provisions of the act, even though these sanctions had been applied in other contexts.

Meany's testimony is also revealing as it makes clear that the AFL–CIO leadership was unable to eliminate racial discrimination within its own ranks, not only because it refused to give a high priority to this issue, but also because it failed to understand the nature of such discrimination and how widespread it was. Meany repeatedly emphasized that there were only isolated instances of discrimination, as when he referred to the need for "mopping up." Other labor spokesmen often referred to "vestiges of discrimination," and the AFL–CIO in its publications acknowledged only "pockets of discrimination."[5]

Union discrimination, however, is not the result of a few isolated "pockets" of random, individual acts of bigotry. The denial of equal rights to blacks and other nonwhite workers within organized labor is the result of racist practices that have been institutionalized over many decades. But, the AFL–CIO and its affiliated unions, in refusing to move systematically against structures of discrimination, in insisting that each complaint was an ad hoc problem to be treated as an aberration, were in fact able to change little or nothing.

With the increasing judicial enforcement of Title VII, organized labor was transformed from a supporter of the law into an adversary of the law. It must be remembered that the AFL–CIO was willing to support the enactment of Title VII only if the law insulated established union seniority systems and only if the act would affect future discriminatory practices. The AFL–CIO, as a condition of its support, insisted upon the inclusion of Section 703(h) in Title VII, which they believed would protect the racial status quo of seniority systems for at least a generation. But the Equal Employment Opportunity Commission (EEOC) and the federal courts rejected this view.[6]

Even before the date that the EEOC was officially scheduled to begin operations, the AFL–CIO sought an agreement from the commission that, based on Section 703(h), the commission would not assert jurisdiction over seniority issues. On May 5, 1965, representatives of the AFL–CIO met with the EEOC to insist that the commission refrain from acting on complaints involving discriminatory job classification and promotion procedures based on seniority provisions in union contracts. In response, the commission requested that William Gould, then a professor of law at Wayne State University, conduct a study and formulate a report on the EEOC's authority and responsibility on this issue. Gould's report concluded "that most seniority arrangements locked blacks into segregated job departments and were, therefore, unlawful under the statute."[7] Later, Gould wrote that "the AFL–CIO policy of not agreeing to implement Title VII serves to postpone the effectuation of the statute's principles. Assertion of the leadership's innocence is simply the first in an arsenal of arguments that the AFL–CIO and its friends put forward to justify union misbehavior."[8]

During the first decade of Title VII litigation, federal courts repeatedly rejected organized labor's interpretation of Section 703(h) and in response the AFL–CIO did not hesitate to join with anticivil rights forces to limit the effectiveness of the law after its adoption. When it became clear after 1966 that the private right-to-sue and the resulting federal court decisions made possible for the first time the enforcement of effective legal prohibitions against job discrimination, organized labor sought to destroy that right.[9]

As black workers and women began to litigate under Section 706 of Title VII and the federal courts ordered broad remedies directly affecting traditional labor practices in many unionized industries, organized labor not only resisted compliance with the law but also altered its attitude toward further legislation to eliminate job discrimination. Beginning in 1966, when bills were first introduced in Congress proposing to amend Title VII by giving the EEOC authority to issue cease-and-desist orders, the AFL–CIO refused to support such measures unless the private right-to-sue, the major means of enforcing the law, was eliminated from Title VII. When the act was amended in 1972, proposals to give the EEOC cease-and-desist power were defeated, but the private right-to-sue provision was retained intact at the insistence of civil rights organizations. This issue was to be the source of much conflict between the AFL–CIO and black interest groups.

The AFL–CIO became increasingly hostile to the law as many of their largest and most important affiliates were repeatedly involved as defendants in costly and protracted litigation under Title VII. Organized labor found to its great dismay that unlike the ineffective state fair employment practice laws,[10] Title VII was being interpreted and enforced by the U.S. courts and that these courts were ordering extensive changes in traditional union racial practices.

Organized labor had enjoyed great freedom in negotiating seniority systems that restricted black workers to segregated promotional lines, thereby preserving desirable jobs for whites. Prior to the adoption of Title VII, courts were reluctant to disturb provisions in labor agreements established through collective bargaining. By overtly or covertly structuring systems of seniority and promotion on a racially segregated basis, many unions controlled the level of advancement and wages of black workers and formalized discriminatory practices. Wherever segregated seniority lines existed, investigation has invariably shown that blacks were limited to unskilled or semiskilled classifications and that whites were assigned to higher-paying, skilled jobs. Federal court decisions under Title VII involving seniority have had a profound impact on these practices, and as many industrial unions defended their discriminatory agreements, this issue was to become a major area of conflict and litigation.

In many industries and trades, including jobs in the public sector such as in police and fire departments, white workers were able to begin their climb on the seniority ladder precisely because nonwhites were systematically excluded from the competition for jobs. Various union seniority systems were established at a time when racial minorities were barred from employment and union membership. Obviously, blacks as a group, not just as individuals, constituted a class of victims who could not develop seniority status. A seniority system launched under such conditions inevitably becomes the institutionalized mechanism whereby whites as a group are granted racial privilege. In these and related seniority cases the federal courts repeatedly found labor unions to be in violation of Title VII and ordered new and sweeping remedies to eliminate the present effects of past discrimination.

During the congressional debate on the Civil Rights Act, the labor federation stated that Title VII "... *does not upset seniority rights already obtained by any employee....* The AFL–CIO does not believe in righting ancient wrongs by perpetrating new ones. ... It [Title VII] will take nothing away from the American worker which he has already acquired."[11]

A "Legislative Alert" issued by the federation's Industrial Union Department in May of 1964 stated that Title VII "... has nothing to do with the day-to-day operation of business firms or unions or with seniority systems."[12] The AFL–CIO also issued a pamphlet entitled "Civil Rights: Fact vs. Fiction," which sought to assure union members that Title VII would not interfere with union-negotiated seniority structures. In this publication and in many other statements by union officials it was clearly assumed that Title VII would not be retroactive and would not require unions and employers to make changes in "established" seniority systems.[13] Quite clearly, the leaders of organized labor, especially those of the industrial unions with a "liberal" reputation, never anticipated the extent to which labor unions would come under attack once Title VII went into effect.

In the first Title VII case to deal with the seniority issue, *Quarles* v. *Philip Morris, Inc. and the Tobacco Workers International Union*,[14] a federal court held that

The plain language of the Act condemns as an unfair labor practice all racial discrimination affecting employees without excluding present discrimination that originated in a seniority system devised before the effective date of the Act . . . the purpose of the Act is to eliminate racial discrimination in covered employment. Obviously one characteristic of a "bona fide" seniority system must be lack of discrimination . . . a departmental seniority system that has its genesis in racial discrimination is not a *bona fide* seniority system.

This approach was confirmed soon thereafter by the decision in *United States* v. *Papermakers Union, Local 189*,[15] and by many other cases in both northern and southern states. A new body of case law was soon to emerge, and by 1968 courts had begun to order changes in those collectively bargained seniority structures that systematically denied black workers equal employment and promotion opportunities.

In case after case, not only did AFL–CIO affiliates defend traditional forms of union discrimination that were found by the federal courts to violate the law, they also tried to narrow the interpretation of Title VII and prevent the application of the law to major problems of racial discrimination. In *U.S. Postal Service* v. *Aikens*,[16] for example, a case argued before the Supreme Court in 1983, the AFL–CIO joined with the Chamber of Commerce and the Reagan Justice Department in attacking the rights of minority workers under Title VII. The labor federation argued for new, more stringent standards that would make it more difficult for workers to prove they were the victims of racial discrimination. Although no unions were involved in this case, the AFL–CIO sought to undermine the position of black workers seeking legal remedies for job discrimination.

As a result of the Civil Rights Act and the lawsuits that followed, racist and sexist employment practices lost all legal sanction. The historical record shows that litigation under Title VII and other statutes has been the decisive factor in altering discriminatory patterns in many industries and occupations. It is significant that the compulsion of law was necessary to eliminate the traditional racist practices of many labor unions and that organized labor's long resistance to the changes required by civil rights law has been a major characteristic of its history in the years since the merger of the AFL and the CIO in 1955.

The unique development of the American working class after the middle years of the nineteenth century was marked by divisions and conflicts between immigrant and native born, Catholic and Protestant, skilled and unskilled, between ethnic communities, and most important, between racial groups. Workers defined themselves primarily according to race and ethnicity, and manifestations of class consciousness that transcended such loyalties were rare and episodic.

From the 1860s to the contemporary period, as workers became more union-conscious they also became more race-conscious, and as labor organizations became more successful they intensified their racist practices. The failure of labor historians to confront the extraordinary record of working-class racism has resulted in the failure to develop an adequate theory regarding the connection between race and class in American history.

From John R. Commons in the early years of the twentieth century to the work of Philip Taft in the 1960s, labor history was really union history. With few exceptions, it consisted of institutional studies of labor organizations based largely on an examination of union records. If traditional labor historians and economists such as John R. Commons, Selig Perlman, and Philip Taft mention black and other non-white workers at all, it is as a problem for white labor organizations and solely within the context of the institution of the labor union. In reaction to this traditional school, a group of younger labor historians began to emerge in the late 1960s. Critical of traditional methods, Herbert Gutman and David Montgomery, among others, developed what is essentially a neo-Marxian social history, proposing to "study the people": in short, to do for American labor history what E. P. Thompson did in his magisterial *The Making of the English Working Class* (1963). Much more sophisticated in their view of social processes than their predecessors, this group introduced important correctives to the Commons–Taft school. Still, it also is characterized by an *a priori* commitment to class consciousness as the decisive force in American labor history; while acknowledging some relative significance to race consciousness, it fails to recognize its central dynamic.

Race and racism were crucial factors in determining the characteristics of organized labor as a social institution, especially in its formative years during a period of white supremacy that continued for many decades and left a permanent mark on the development of American society. Furthermore, the historical record reveals that the embrace of white supremacy as ideology and as practice was a strategy for assimilation by European working-class immigrants, the white ethnics who were to constitute a major part of the membership and leadership of organized labor in the United States. While white ethnics experienced much hardship, they also benefited from the far more pervasive and brutal discrimination against Afro-Americans.

The occupational patterns of discrimination suffered by generations of nonwhites were different in kind from those experienced by European immigrant workers. One consequence is that current opposition to affirmative action is based on perceived group interest. What appears on the surface to be philosophical argument about "quotas" and "reverse discrimination" is in reality an extensive effort by white ethnics to maintain their preferential position.

Wages, and the status derived from steady work, could only be obtained by entering the permanent labor force, and labor unions were most important in providing access to the job market for many groups of immigrant workers. In contrast to the white ethnics, generations of black workers were systematically barred from employment in the primary sectors of the labor market, thereby denied the economic base that made possible the celebrated achievements and social mobility of white immigrant communities.

Early in their respective histories many individual unions, as well as the American Federation of Labor itself, adopted a policy based on the assumption that since non-Caucasian workers could not be assimilated, they therefore should be denied union membership on a racial basis and systematically denied employment in unionized occupations. This assumption was, of course, a self-fulfilling prophecy. Since nonwhites could not be Americanized, they were disqualified from employment and status and assigned to a permanent position as marginal laborers in unskilled and menial classifications at the lowest wages. If nonwhites found it difficult to improve their condition, it was because institutions like organized labor prevented them from doing so.

Whatever difficulties white immigrants initially experienced, they could eventually become naturalized, granted the rights of citizenship and full participation in the society. (The Naturalization Law of 1790 explicitly limited citizenship to "white" persons.) Success, however, necessitated a response to industrialization and to an ascendent bourgeois social order. For most white immigrants, the response was to seek acculturation and assimilation, a process that required the establishment of identity groups based on ethnicity as a means of progressing into the larger social order. *

---

* Joel Kovel (1970, 4) contends that racism was functional for this society in that it was a "stabilizing" element of culture. He writes that racism "defined a social universe,

For European immigrant workers, class consciousness was based on ethnic group consciousness; it did not mean proletarian solidarity with blacks and other nonwhite workers. Over time, the ethnic and racial divisions within the working class reinforced labor market segmentation and led to the development of a dual racial labor system. Contemporary racial patterns of employment represent the consequences and continuity of a process that has become a part of the historical experience of the white working class, an experience that was transformed into the organizational policy and practice of many labor unions. This phenomenon also explains why change in racial employment patterns is so bitterly resisted and why job inequality is so deep-rooted and routinely perpetuated. In the course of becoming "good Americans," the white working class reinforced its own divisions in the context of an emergent industrial division of labor.

The anti-Asian movement of organized white labor provided the context in which racist ideas were transformed into union policy and practice; race consciousness and union consciousness were mutually reinforced as craft exclusion and race exclusion were joined. Although from 1850 to 1870 the principal thrust of the anti-Asian movement was confined to the western states, it soon became a national issue. By obtaining the government's support in excluding a racially distinct people from entry and citizenship, organized labor laid an ideological groundwork that supported a racial perspective for exclusion. Racial arguments used against the Chinese could be and were invoked to exclude blacks. The arguments against the Japanese, that they possessed the racial traits of the Chinese and were, in addition, intrinsically dangerous, were a corollary to this rationale. Anti-Asian agitation, in effect, supplied a model of racial ideology applied by labor unions in the years after emancipation, when many national unions were formed.

For Samuel Gompers, president of the AFL from its founding in 1886 until his death in 1924 (with the exception of 1895, when John McBride of the United Mine Workers was president), membership in organized labor turned on the question of a people's assimilability. As he wrote in his autobiography:

I felt identified with the people of my new home and it was without a question that I accepted American customs and the American life. To my mind the foreigner was the one who did not identify himself with American life and

---

absorbed aggression, and facilitated a sense of virtue in white America—a trait which contributed to America's material success. Racism was an integral part of a stable and productive culture order." White immigrants and their descendants responded to these ideas, which were useful in diminishing the distinction between themselves and native-born "Americans" and were a significant element in the acculturative process. For a discussion of the historical antecedents of such beliefs see Takaki (1979, 11–15).

purposes. . . . The first step in Americanizing them [Bohemian workers] was to bring them to conform to American standards of work, which was a stepping stone to American standards of life. . . . By the beginning of the nineties, the racial problem in the labor movement was beginning to assume serious proportions. Our problem was part of the larger national problem, for the majority of immigrants no longer came from Western Europe where language, customs, and industrial organizations were similar to those of the United States but from the countries of Eastern Europe where lower standards of life and work prevailed. As these immigrants flooded basic industries they threatened to destroy our standards. . . . [A]s the number of immigrants rapidly increased and the admixture of various races was too rapid for assimilation, I could not escape the conclusion that some way must be found to safeguard America. . . . I have always opposed Chinese immigration not only because of the effect of Chinese standards of life and work but because of the racial problem created when Chinese and white workers were brought into the close contact of living and working side by side. . . . There was a sort of complacent confidence that America was a melting pot in which all manner of diverse nationalities could be gathered and inevitably, without planning or consideration on our part, Americans would finally emerge. In the absence of constructive efforts on the part of the community, the trade union movement had undertaken to teach foreign workers the economic bases of American standards of life, work, and ideals.[17]

The Chinese, Japanese, and Afro-Americans were "unassimilable," hence proscribed. Gompers was a Jewish immigrant who came to the presidency of the AFL from the leadership of the Cigar Makers' International Union. Under his leadership the federation and most of its affiliated unions organized European immigrant workers, excluding Asians and later black workers from the ranks of organized labor. From the start, the organized cigar makers were in the forefront of labor's assault on the Chinese. In California in 1874 they developed an ingenious method for forcing Chinese workers out of the trade, adopting a white label to indicate that the cigars were made by white union men.[18] On the cigar box was a reproduction of the union label with this pointed message:

> Buy no cigars except
> from the box marked
> with the trade-union label,
> thus you help maintain the
> white as against the Coolie
> standard of life and work.[19]

The facsimile of the label showed the union mark and the words "White Labor, White Labor." By 1875 St. Louis cigar makers followed suit with a bright red label. At their general convention three years later, the

Cigar Makers' International Union chose a blue label.[20] Thus, the tradition of the union label had its origin in a racist stratagem.*

The policy of the Cigar Makers' together with other craft unions at that time was to organize skilled workers exclusively, leaving the unskilled and disadvantaged to fend for themselves. An "aristocracy of labor" emerged. Cigar makers, workers on the railroads and in the printing trades, brewery workers, iron molders and those in other skilled occupations obtained benefits unavailable to the rest of the work force, which had no leverage in the open market.[21]

In 1884 the Cigar Makers' International Union established Local 228 in San Francisco, "the first step," writes Alexander Saxton, "of a long-range plan for driving Orientals out of the trade."[22] The campaign was successful. By the end of November 1885, the large producers capitulated to the demands of organized labor. The Chinese were to be forced out of the industry and replaced by white workers. The target date of January 1, 1886, was not met, but the Chinese were in time eliminated completely.[23] Similar campaigns were conducted in the boot and shoe trade and elsewhere. The process of racial occupational displacement was well underway. The predecessor of the AFL, the Federation of Organized Trades and Labor Unions, at its first convention in 1881, condemned the Chinese cigar makers of California and recommended that only union label cigars be purchased.[24]

The Wisconsin school of labor economists, such as John R. Commons, Selig Perlman, and, more recently, Philip Taft, argued that anti-Asian sentiment among white workers was a response to the great economic threat Chinese labor posed for whites. According to Selig

---

* Racism had become the essential component of a crude and reactionary class consciousness, as many labor organizations during this period conducted union label campaigns. The United Mine Workers of America, for example, tried assiduously to educate its membership in the origin and meaning of the union label. An article in the *United Mine Workers Journal* reprinted from the *American Federationist* disclosed that the white cigar makers of San Francisco had decided upon the label in the 1870s as a way of agitating "against the employment of the Chinese" and "decrying the purchase of goods of their making as well." And so, to "distinguish the products of the Caucasians a white label was placed upon each cigar box." The label stated "that the cigars were made by white men, and it was requested that white men should buy no other. This was the first union label" (*United Mine Workers Journal*, February 2, 1905, p. 5). The union label, then, was the mark of white labor consciousness. As the *Journal* put it: "Our weapons are the union and the stamp (label) of the union. They are not so deadly as powder and ball, but they are no less effective when employed in trading with people of our own race, whose thoughts we share and whose aspirations find response in every fiber of our being. . . . Help us, men and women of our race, to win this fight; help the people of your own kind to battle for the full possession of this land which God intended should be ours, and our children will take our places and will commend our work" (*United Mine Workers Journal*, March 5, 1903, p. 3). For a detailed study see Hill 1988.

Perlman: "The anti-Chinese agitation in California, culminating as it did in the Exclusion Law passed by Congress in 1882, was doubtless the most important single factor in the history of American labor, for without it the entire country might have been overrun by Mongolian labor and the labor movement might have become a conflict of races instead of classes."[25]

This analysis is derived from nineteenth-century labor sources (i.e., from the words and writings of union leaders and members, who assumed a priori that the Chinese represented a direct economic danger to white workers, and moreover, that the existence of "cheap coolie labor" was largely responsible for the depressed condition of the American economy after 1873).[26] Yet all available evidence indicates that Asian labor was not an economic threat to white workers nationally. The Chinese, in 1870, numbered only 368 outside of the West.[27] Even the most racist labor politician could not argue that Chinese labor was responsible for the depressed conditions of white workers. Three political groups after 1873 kept the Chinese question alive as a national issue: the Workingman's party, under the leadership of Dennis Kearney (an Irish immigrant) in San Francisco; the national Democratic party, attempting to revive itself after the Civil War;[28] and the Knights of Labor.[29]

By 1876, the Republicans also were prepared to support Chinese exclusion. Two key developments were responsible: (1) the failure of radical Republican policy to use blacks against the resurgence of the southern Democrats, both locally and nationally and (2) the Compromise of 1877, which forced blacks out of the political arena and led the Republicans, who had always been a minority party (Lincoln did not receive a majority in 1860) to look elsewhere for political support. Republicans concluded that workers were the key to any successful national coalition.

Adoption of the Chinese Exclusion Act of 1882 was only a partial victory for labor. With national politicians turning "anti-Coolieism" to their own purposes, the act as it finally stood was more sop than real solution. It did bar all future Chinese laborers from entering the United States after 1882, but it did not address itself to the Chinese who were already here. Labor's reaction to the passage of the bill was mixed. Labor leaders vigorously supported the bill: Terence V. Powderly had put the entire national Knights of Labor structure to work lobbying for it in 1882.[30] At the same time leadership of organized labor kept their anti-Chinese position alive after 1882. Powderly, for example, called for the total exclusion of all Chinese from the United States at the end of 1882, even while he and other union leaders simultaneously celebrated passage of the Exclusion Act as a labor victory.[31] (In 1892, the act forbidding naturalization of Chinese residents was renewed for another ten years, and in 1902 it was extended indefinitely. Not until 1943, 1946, and 1952 were a token quota of Chinese, Filipinos, and Japanese, respectively, granted the right to become U.S. citizens.)

After adoption of the Chinese Exclusion Act, organized labor reasserted its position as the vanguard of the anti-Asian campaign, as it had in the 1870s.[32] This new stage of agitation corresponded to a period of national economic decline, much as the activities of the Workingmen's party movement corresponded to decline in 1876. Although after 1876 the Chinese had not flooded out of the West into eastern industry as had been feared in 1870 (there were still only 3,663 Chinese living outside of the western states in 1880), the national political system in the 1870s and the 1880s had made anti-Chinese politics credible and acceptable.

At the end of the 1890s and into the twentieth century, the AFL and many of its affiliated national unions still continued to attack Asians in openly racist terms. The ideas of white supremacy they embraced would soon lead to similar attacks on Afro-Americans. The long and intense campaign against Asian workers provided the context in which "the driving emotions of racism could be woven into a pattern of economic rationalization. The conclusions drawn would then apply analogously to the Negro."[33]

Gompers, president of the AFL, and the fellow union leaders for whom he had increasingly come to speak, expanded their reach to include all nonwhite workers. In the *American Federationist* of February 1898, Gompers published an article titled "The Negro: His Relation to Southern Industry," by Will H. Winn, an AFL organizer in Georgia, that "explained" that blacks were not racially qualified to be union members because of "certain well known traits of Negro character," and because they were "of abandoned and reckless disposition." Negroes did not possess "those peculiarities of temperament such as patriotism, sympathy, sacrifice, etc., which are peculiar to most of the Caucasian race, and which alone make an organization of the character and complexity of the modern trade union possible."[34]

The Negro, Winn said, had an advantage over the white worker because he could work on farms for as many hours as required and for whatever wages offered and still be "the happiest and most contented individual imaginable."[35] Therefore, the Negro had no motivation to support unionism, a movement of the discontented. Since Negroes were passive and could not be organized, Winn proposed colonization as "a practical and mutually agreeable solution of the Negro-Labor problem."[36] Once the Negroes depart for Cuba, where they would "thrive and prosper," the white worker would be freed from "disorganizing competition" and would receive just compensation for his labor.

Gompers agreed with Winn's article. He wrote a letter to Winn praising him for having given the labor movement a good and fair statement of the subject.[37] Later, Winn, who opposed unionization of Negro workers, was chosen as one of three AFL organizers to lead the federation's southern organizing campaign. None of the organizers selected for the southern campaign was a Negro. One reported that he, a "full blooded Irishman," was "up against a hard proposition" in having to confront "jews and niggers," for the "Nigras there is the most ignorant people in the world."[38] When Gompers, asked by a newspaper reporter why the South had not been organized, gave three reasons, the first he named was "the fault of the Negroes."[39]

In 1905, in a statement in the official AFL publication, Gompers informed union members that "Caucasian civilization will serve notice that its uplifting process is not to be interfered with in any way."[40] He assured his readers that "The Caucasians are not going to let their standard of living be destroyed by negroes [sic], Chinamen, Japs, or any others."[41] Later, in a public address, he alluded to the difficulty in organizing Negro labor and recalled the "present unpreparedness" of the Negro for "fully exercising and enjoying" the possibilities of the labor movement.[42] In his autobiography, Gompers sought to justify these beliefs as necessary because "maintenance of the nation depended upon maintenance of racial purity."[43]

The federation's affiliated unions translated such concepts of racial inferiority into organizational practice. The discriminatory racial pattern, now firmly established, would persist in many forms as policy and practice for many decades.

It may be objected that the racial views of Gompers and his colleagues merely reflected the *Zeitgeist* of the American culture. From the end of the Civil War to the First World War, white Americans in general attributed the spectacular emergence of the United States as an industrial, military, and imperial power to racial superiority. Why should labor be singled out for criticism for sharing such views?

The AFL, which spoke for the overwhelming majority of organized workers from the 1890s on, was even more militantly racist than Americans in general. The responsibility for what the AFL did lay with the organization itself. It could have practiced what its leaders occasionally preached, namely, that all workers are equal, that no person should be treated as a commodity, that capital is the common enemy of all workers. Instead, it opted for the practice of racial discrimination based on the conviction that non-Caucasians deserved to be treated as commodities, that race transcended differences of class or wealth or power.

America's official party of the left at this time, the Socialist Party of the United States, held much the same position on racial issues. Its executive committee gave the party's seal of approval to racial exclusion laws. Morris Hillquit, an immigrant, and one of American socialism's chief theoreticians, supported measures to restrict the influx of "backward races." Victor Berger, also foreign born, the party's leader in Milwaukee and one of its major national figures, later its first congressmen, went much further. On the issue of race he was as extreme as Madison Grant or Lothrop Stoddard, whose book, *The Rising Tide of Color Against White World Supremacy* published in 1920, set forth an uncompromising white racist position.[44] Berger was vehement about keeping the United States a "white man's" country; he feared that it might be too late to prevent the United States from degenerating into a "black-and-yellow country within a few generations." For him at least this was a life-and-death struggle, a "fight for my wife and children . . . for all your wives and children."[45] Jack London's novels and short stories, as well as his essays were characterized by racist attitudes: "I am first of all a white man and only then a socialist," he said.[46]

Not every American socialist, of course, subscribed to such views. The radical wing of the party tended to take its universalist principles more seriously. One such radical was Louis Boudin (like Hillquit, a Russian-born Jew). Boudin was among the delegates at the 1907 congress of the Socialist International at Stuttgart, Germany, where an American proposal favoring the exclusion of "undesirable" immigrants was defeated. Boudin, who argued against the proposal, later explained why nearly all the delegates of twenty-two countries rejected it out of hand. They were not going to "establish the principle of dividing immigrants along racial lines into 'organizable' and 'unorganizable' " nor to "lay down as a rule of socialist policy, based on such principle of division, the demand for the exclusion of the so-called 'unorganizable' races." The socialist parties of the world were convinced, Boudin went on, that the "principles and demands formulated in our resolution are a snare and delusion, and cannot possibly result in any permanent good to the working class of this country or of the world. These principles and demands are unsocialistic, that is to say, they are repugnant to the permanent and lasting interests of the working class."[47]

Cameron H. King, Jr., on behalf of the Socialist party's national executive committee, couched the racist theme in the language of Marxian socialism. The logic proceeded as follows: The Socialist party must be the party of the working class, the party dedicated to Marx's "material conception of history," and just as an "organization becomes stronger the more accurately it meets the material interests and economic necessities of the people," it also becomes weaker when it falls "into the morass of impractical schemes while pursuing the beautiful but illusory ideals of altruistic utopianism."[48] The workers through their unions have "declared for the exclusion of Asiatic labor,"[49] therefore the Socialist party must adopt a similar position. Only by doing so will it be true to Marx's teachings. King condemned the socialists of other countries for failing to sympathize with their American brethren. He made it very clear that in the event of a conflict between race consciousness and class consciousness, socialists must choose the former lest they cut themselves off from the proletariat. In language reminiscent of Jack London's, King concluded that

The time has come for the Socialist Party to decide what its relation shall be to the working class. Are we going to bend the knee in worship of the idealistic phrase, "The Brotherhood of Man," or are we going to affirm our solidarity with American labor and prevent the destruction of its hard won standards of life? In short, are we to remain idealists out of touch with the red-blooded, self-assertive life, or are we to take our place in the workingmen's struggle for existence, organizing his forces and always fighting for advances in his means of life.[50]

Between 1860 and 1914 more than 25 million European immigrants arrived in the United States, and by 1890 the working class was largely composed of new stock immigrants. In many cities North and South, where blacks had once been employed in a great variety of occupations, skilled and unskilled, the process of black displacement was well underway by the last years of the century. Trade unions frequently were the instrument that forced black workers out of jobs they had traditionally held by replacing them with immigrant white workers.[51]

In 1898, John Stevens Durham, a white social reformer and journalist, described how the Negro worker's industrial advancement had been "checked by the interference of the labor organizations."[52] The Negro's "fate is involved in this struggle," he said, presenting extensive data to prove that as union organization progressed, Negro exclusion "became more and more prominent." In the past ten years "there has been no racial utterance from any leader of authority of unions advocating equality of opportunity for the Negro." The labor movement, he said, "distinctly denies equality to the colored workman."[53] He noted that the Negro was restricted to the lowest-paying menial jobs as a result of labor union practices in many crafts and industries, North and South. He cited Washington, D.C., as an example:

At one period, some of the best buildings were constructed by colored workmen. Their employment in large numbers continued some time after the war. The British Legation, the Centre Market, the Freedmen's Bank, and at least four well-built school houses are monuments to the acceptability of their work under foremen of their own color. Today, apart from hod-carriers, not a colored workman is to be seen on new buildings, and a handful of jobbers and patchers, with possibly two carpenters who can undertake a large job, are all who remain of the body of colored carpenters and builders and stone cutters who were generally employed a quarter of a century ago.[54]

Durham proceeded to give example after example of how labor unions prevented Negroes from working in many occupations, including those of baker, confectioner, printer, cooper, painter, and carpenter. He wrote: "A Negro working in the Government Printing Office can stay on as long as he is government employed, but once out of public service he cannot secure work as a printer on a union newspaper or in a union office. The Negro, whatever his record, finds all doors closed against him. Thus, in our national capital may be observed the effects of discrimination of labor organizations against the Negro."[55]

Negro stevedores had worked on New Orleans wharves, Durham wrote, but "the effective organization of white laborers was closely followed by the driving of Negroes from the levees at the muzzles of loaded rifles." In the iron industry, where the "union develops effective strength the black workmen must put down the trowel and take up the tray." Thus, ability to work, "the Negro's sole heritage from slavery and his only hope as a freedman, does not secure him opportunity."[56]

Extending his inquiry into the North, Durham found the effects of the racial exclusion policy there even "more manifest." In Philadelphia in 1838, The Society of Friends had compiled a directory of occupations in which free Negroes were employed, including such skilled jobs as cabinet maker, plumber, printer, sail maker, ship's carpenter, stone cutter, and many others. By the end of the 1890s, Negroes had been forced out of most of these and other craft occupations. In Philadelphia and other northern cities at the turn of the century, where work opportunities were in general expanding, the Negro experienced severe job curtailment and was increasingly limited to menial and service occupations. Durham observed that "today one may safely declare that practically all the trades enumerated . . . are closed against the colored workman."[57]

By the turn of the century the process of black job displacement that had begun in the South also prevailed in the North. Although economic expansion and the quickened pace of industrialization had yielded new and more attractive jobs, blacks were denied entry to these new jobs. At the same time, emerging labor unions that excluded blacks on the basis of race hastened the displacement of northern blacks from skilled jobs.

These trends were accelerated by fluctuations in business cycles. In times of industrial expansion, when labor was scarce, the black "labor reserve" was utilized. But the concomitant losses in periods of recession more than canceled the short-term gains, and blacks were increasingly limited to casual and unskilled jobs in the unorganized sector of the economy.[58]

When employers sought to hire blacks, white workers frequently protested. Between 1882 and 1900 at least fifty strikes were organized by whites in protest against the hiring of blacks.[59] Although some of these strikes failed, the success of a number of others led to the effective barring of blacks from almost all the higher-paid skilled work in many industries. In addition, white labor unions organized strikes and engaged in other actions to force the displacement of black workers from jobs they had long held. In 1890 the Brotherhood of Locomotive Trainmen petitioned the Houston and Texas Central Railroad to replace all black workers with whites,[60] and in 1909 white workers struck against the Georgia Railroad to protest the company's practice of hiring black firemen.[61] Ten black railroad workers were killed in 1911 during a strike organized to remove blacks employed by the Cincinnati, New Orleans, and Texas Pacific Railroad.[62] Similar events occurred elsewhere in the railroad industry over a period of many years.[63]

George S. Mitchell (co-author with Horace Cayton of *Black Workers and the New Unions*) noted in 1936 that "the Southern trade unionism of the last thirty odd years has been in good measure a protective device for the march of white artisans into places held by Negroes."[64] The white worker and his trade union displaced black labor on street railways, removed Afro-American firemen on railroads, took the jobs of black switchmen and shop workers, replaced blacks in construction work and shipbuilding, and forced them out of tobacco manufacturing and other industries. Mitchell wrote that the "typical city central labor body of Mobile or Savannah or Columbia or New Orleans or Richmond was a delegate meeting of white men drawn from white locals, jealous of every skilled place held by Negroes." The occasional all-black segregated local received little or no help from its international union or the AFL. As a result, black workers who through years of service had acquired the skill needed for craftmen's work were denied membership in white unions and forced out of skilled and semiskilled employment. The machinists, boilermakers, carmen, and other AFL unions, according to Mitchell, "absolutely forbid Negro membership."[65]

The experience of black workers in Birmingham, Alabama, and in Boston in the early 1900s is indicative of the national pattern. The movement of large numbers of European immigrants into the Birmingham steel mills eliminated the concentration of black workers in many trades.[66] In Boston, Irish immigrants displaced, and hence economically surpassed, blacks at the turn of the century.[67]

Unions affiliated with the AFL and the independent railroad brotherhoods attained their racially restrictive goals by a variety of methods, including exclusion of blacks and other nonwhites from membership through racial provisions in union constitutions or in the ritual bylaws of local unions; exclusion by tacit agreement in the absence of written provisions; establishment of racially segregated units that admitted only blacks; separate racial lines of seniority and promotion in labor contracts; union control of licensing boards; refusal to admit nonwhites into union-controlled apprenticeship and other training programs; negotiation of discriminatory labor agreements that adversely affected black workers while excluding them from union membership; and denial of access to hiring halls and other union-controlled job referral systems.

A typical example of early exclusionary racial practices is to be found in the 1865 constitution of the Cigar Makers' International Union. Article IX stated that "unless said person is a white practical cigar maker," he could not belong to the union. The Constitution of the Brotherhood of Railway Carmen specified that to qualify for membership, one had to be a "white person between the ages of 16 and 65 years."[68] The Wire Weavers Protective Association required that a member be a "Christian, white, Male of the full age of 21"[69] and the Masters, Mates, and Pilots union demanded that an applicant for membership be a "white person of good moral character."[70]

In 1871 the Cigar Makers' International Union convention transferred the racial exclusion provision from the national union's constitution to the admission ritual of the local union, where it performed the same function.[71] The International Typographical Union resorted to the same device, as did other unions later, including the Iron Molders Union, the National Association of Machinists, the National Carpenters Union, and the Bricklayers and Masons Union. Frank E. Wolfe's study of union membership exclusion summed up the racial practices of this period: "Indeed, all available evidence supports the conclusion that Negroes were seldom admitted into a union in any part of the country."[72]

After 1900, when black workers were admitted into some AFL unions, they were usually limited to segregated or auxiliary units, a policy sanctioned by Article XII, Section VI, of the Constitution of the American Federation of Labor as revised in 1900:

Separate charters may be issued to central unions, local unions, or federal labor unions, composed exclusively of colored workers, where in the judgment of the Executive Council it appears advisable.[73]

Union officials soon enforced segregated units as a matter of common practice, and this became the prevailing pattern within the federation. The Blacksmiths Union's constitution, for example, stated:

Where there are sufficient number of colored helpers they may be organized as an auxiliary local and shall be under the jurisdiction over that territory. Colored helpers shall not transfer except to another auxiliary local composed of *colored members, and colored members shall not be promoted to blacksmiths or helper apprentices, and will not be admitted to shops where white helpers are now employed* (emphasis in original).[74]

Other labor organizations, such as the Sheet Metal Workers Union, engaged in similar practices. Article IV, Section I of that union's 1918 constitution provided that separate charters for black sheet metal workers would

be granted only with the consent of the white local union established in the locality . . . where there are a sufficient number of Negro sheet metal workers, they may be organized as an Auxiliary Local and shall come under the jurisdiction of the White Local Union having jurisdiction over said locality. Members of Auxiliary Locals composed of colored sheet metal workers shall not transfer except to another Auxiliary Local composed of colored members.[75]

Segregated locals often functioned under restrictions and standards imposed by the same international unions that refused to admit black workers. Thus, in 1903, the International Brotherhood of Electrical Workers stated in its official publication that "we do not want the Negro in the International Brotherhood of Electrical Workers, but we think they should be organized into locals of their own."[76] A major purpose of creating segregated locals and auxiliary units was to prevent blacks from protecting their own interests in the collective bargaining process.

Total exclusion or segregation was enforced as national policy by most labor unions in the early decades of the twentieth century, when the goal of white labor organizations to confine black workers to the lowest rungs of the job ladder was increasingly successful. In the September 1905 issue of the *American Federationist*, Gompers wrote that, although the organization desired no controversy with Negroes, "if the colored man continued to lend himself to the work of tearing down what the white man has built up, a race hatred far worse than any ever known will result."[77] Another typical article, "Packingtown Conditions," written by John Roach in the August 1906 issue of the *American Federationist*, refers to "hordes of ignorant blacks" with "but few of those attributes we have learned to revere and love . . . huge strapping fellows, ignorant and vicious, whose predominating trait was animalism."[78]

Among the most powerful of the labor organizations at the turn of the century were the railroad unions, with a membership of more than one million by the early 1900s and the capacity for coordinated national strikes. The railroad labor unions, a vanguard of the organized American working class, were also among the most militantly racist.

The constitution of the Brotherhood of Locomotive Engineers provided that "no person shall become a member of the Brotherhood of Locomotive Engineers unless he is a white man 21 years of age."[79] The constitution of the Brotherhood of Locomotive Firemen and Enginemen, founded in 1873, and the Brotherhood of Railroad Trainmen, founded in 1883,[80] both limited membership to white males. The constitutional provision on membership in the Brotherhood of Locomotive Firemen and Enginemen stated these qualifications: "He shall be white born, of good moral character, sober and industrious, sound in body and limb, his eyesight shall be normal, not less than eighteen years of age, and able to read and write the English language."[81] In 1925 their constitution was amended and the following was added: "Mexicans, Indians, or those of Indian or Spanish-Mexican extraction are not eligible. . . . Natives of Italy are eligible to membership."[82] In 1928 the constitution added a special dispensation for the admission of American Indians to membership, to be granted only by the president of the International Union.[83] The Brotherhood of Railroad Trainmen also required membership applicants to be "a white male, sober and industrious."[84]

In 1949, Charles H. Houston, general counsel for the Association of Colored Railway Trainmen and Locomotive Firemen, summarized the racial practices of the railroad unions:

[T]he Big Four Brotherhoods have been using every means in their power to drive the Negro train and engine service worker out of employment and create a "racially closed shop" among the firemen, brakemen, switchmen, flagmen, and yardmen.[85]

A similar history of aggression by the railroad labor unions against black firemen and brakemen occurred also in northern states. Action was taken by the railway brotherhoods to force black workers out of jobs on the Michigan Central as early as 1863, and on the New York,

New Haven, and Hartford Railway; the Baltimore and Ohio; and other lines during the First World War.[86]

During the Second World War, the Brotherhood of Locomotive Firemen and Enginemen distributed a strike ballot to prevent the hiring of black firemen on the Atlantic Coast Line Railroad, and President Franklin D. Roosevelt's Committee on Fair Employment Practices held public hearings in 1943 on the racial employment pattern in the railroad industry. The unions, holding firm to their policies and practices, successfully defied the committee. Houston, a member of the committee, concluded that the operating railroad brotherhoods had established "the Nordic closed shop" on American railroads.[87]

Among the many unions that enforced a rigid policy of nonwhite exclusion into the modern period was the AFL's Seafarers International Union. The leader primarily responsible was Andrew Furuseth, a Norwegian immigrant and a major figure in the early organization of seamen, who was also one of the most militant white supremacists of his time. Furuseth frequently invoked racist arguments against non-Caucasian workers, as in his warnings before a congressional hearing in 1915 that whites would be forced from the sea if blacks and Asian workers were employed on American ships. For a decade Furuseth had lived the brutalized life of a seaman before becoming a union organizer and seeking, by the sheer force of his personality, to persuade Congress to improve working conditions on American merchant ships. Thanks mainly to his efforts, the LaFollette Seamen's Act was passed in 1915.[88]

Historians and biographers have duly acknowledged Furuseth's achievements.[89] But excluding non-Caucasians from American ships was no less important to him than improving the lot of seamen. His racism was buttressed by a far-ranging ideology. The power of the white race, he claimed, rested on its mastery of the seas. That control over the world which the white race—or a segment of it—had maintained unimpaired for three thousand years now stood in jeopardy because "Orientals" and other inferior people were replacing whites.[90] Furuseth called for adoption of a law that, in his words, "will mean safety to our part of the human race, national safety, and racial safety as well."[91] He wrote later in the Seamen's Journal, official publication of the Sailors' Union of the Pacific, that "self-respecting white men will not serve with Negroes."[92] Furuseth and his associates were responsible for a pattern of racial exclusion in the Seafarers International Union which continued into the contemporary period.[93] In 1905 Furuseth joined with other officials of the American Federation of Labor in San Francisco, including Patrick H. McCarthy (from Ireland), Olaf Tveitmoe (from Sweden), and Walter MacArthur (from Scotland), to establish the Asiatic Exclusion League.

In a 1930 study of the racial practices of labor unions Ira De A. Reid noted that even though some unions had removed racial exclusion provisions from their constitutions, they continued to exclude non-whites by tacit consent:

Tacit agreement, examinations and local determination of eligibility for membership serve as deterrents to Negro inclusion in many unions. The Plumbers have never made an issue of the question of admitting Negroes, though it is generally understood that they are not admitted. Despite persistent efforts of Negro plumbers in Philadelphia, New York, and Chicago to secure membership, they have not succeeded. . . . In Philadelphia, the licensing board will not grant licenses to Negro plumbers.[94]

Many construction unions had lobbied successfully in state legislatures and city councils for the enactment of statutes requiring that craftsmen such as plumbers, steamfitters, and electricians be licensed by state or municipal boards on which union representatives would sit. A 1905 letter from C. H. Perry, secretary of Local Union 110 of the Plumbers Union in Virginia, to the editor of the *Journal*, official organ of the Plumbers Union, revealed the purpose of such lobbying: to "entirely eliminate the black artisan . . . from the craft, especially in the southern district, as the Negro is a factor there."[95] By 1925 more than thirty states required licensing boards, which included union representatives, thus providing labor unions with the legal means to eliminate nonwhites from many trades.

Although racial issues were and are a crucial factor in American labor history, racist practices of labor organizations were either ignored or justified by dubious rationalizations in most of the important studies of that history, particularly in those works based in concept on the Commons–Taft tradition. John R. Commons himself was a frequent apologist for the racial policies of organized labor in general, and of Samuel Gompers and the American Federation of Labor in particular, and his statements on the Afro-American population are virtually a primer of racist thought similar to that expounded by the extreme advocates of white supremacy in the early years of the twentieth century. The following selection is typical:

Race differences are established in the very blood and physical constitution. . . . The improvidence of the negro [*sic*] is notorious. His neglect of his horse, his mule, his machinery, his eagerness to spend his earnings on finery, his reckless purchase of watermelons, chickens and garden stuff . . . these and many other incidents of improvidence explain the constant dependence of the negro. . . . The negro trade unionist has not as yet shown the organizing capacity of other races. . . . In some instances the negro is being organized by the white man not so much for his own protection as for the protection of the white workman . . . when the negro demands the same wages as white men, his industrial inferiority leads the employer to take white men in his place.

If a black cotton farmer succeeds it is only because he "is under the close supervision of a white landlord or creditor, who in self protection keeps control of him . . . the high mortality rate among colored people is owing to pulmonary consumption, scrofula, and syphilis, all of which are constitutional . . ." Commons approvingly quotes an alleged authority to explain that the high rate of infant mortality among southern blacks is "due to enfeebled constitutions and congenital diseases, inherited from parents suffering from the effects of sexual immorality and debauchery."[96]

Commenting on the Commons school of labor history, Alexander Saxton has written, "One of the several paradoxical aspects of the work of these Wisconsin scholars, was that while they had dedicated themselves to the pragmatic study of institutions in their actual functioning . . . none seems to have noted the institutional function of racism, nor to have detected its impact upon the psychology of any group, working class or otherwise. Doubtless, they did not note these things because they were not looking for them. What seemed a behavioral norm of American society required no special explanation."[97]

Data from cities, North and South, reveal the consequences of organized labor's efforts to remove nonwhite workers from many crafts and industries. In Cleveland, Ohio:

Union policies, both national and local, effectively kept most eligible Negroes out of the trade union movement. The Boilermaker's Union, the International Association of Machinists, and the Plumbers and Steamfitters Union had a national policy of excluding blacks. Other union locals in the city such as the Metal Polishers and the Paperhangers, barred Negroes on their own initiative. . . . In 1870 fully 31.7 percent of all black males in Cleveland had been employed in skilled trades; by 1910 this figure had dropped sharply to 11 percent. . . . The 1910 Census listed only five black plumbers in the entire city.[98]

In New Orleans there were 3,460 blacks listed in the city directory for 1870 as carpenters, cigar makers, painters, clerks, shoemakers, coopers, tailors, bakers, blacksmiths, and foundry hands. By 1904 the number was below 346, although the black population of the city had increased by more than 50 percent.[99]

Craft unions in the construction trades were a most important factor in the process of racial job displacement during the post-Reconstruction period. Prior to emancipation, there had been a concentration of black workers, both slave and free, in the building trades. The construction unions converted these jobs to "white men's work" and forced

Afro-Americans out. This process occurred in many cities along the eastern seaboard and throughout the southern states.

Data for New York City reveal that, between 1890 and 1910, when the percentage of the total immigrant white population reached 76 percent, black occupational eviction was intensified.[100] In the long-shore industry; in catering; as wagon drivers, coachmen, stable hands; as house painters, tailors, and brickmakers; as hotel and restaurant waiters; and in other trades, black workers were steadily forced out of employment. New York was a very active port in the early years of the twentieth century, but because stevedores were organized in labor unions and specific docks assigned on an ethnic basis to white immigrant workers, blacks were increasingly excluded from jobs on the water-front.[101]

As ethnic groups became occupationally concentrated, the ability of labor unions to provide a measure of job stability and advancement into the larger society for immigrant whites was instrumental in per-mitting them to expand their influence beyond the work place. By 1890 most labor organizations drew their members and leaders from white immigrant communities, which derived many benefits from the ethnic control of labor unions.

Where nonwhites were permitted to work, they were systematically limited to segregated jobs. The inferior status of blacks in the labor force made it possible for whites to receive higher wages and enjoy relatively better working conditions—individually and as a class. Dis-criminatory hiring practices and segregated seniority and promotional structures in manufacturing industries contributed to the relatively privileged position of white workers and the depressed condition of the black working class.

The greater rate of exploitation of the black worker, locked into an all-black labor classification, subsidized the higher wages of whites, a process repeated in many industries and codified into collective bar-gaining agreements. Thus, organized labor and management jointly created a severely exploited class of black labor, rigidly blocked from advancing into many all-white occupations. The permanent condition of poverty and social disorganization, which has characterized black life in the urban ghettos of the nation for many generations, is in large measure a consequence of the occupational displacement of blacks by white immigrants and the racial practices of organized labor.

Of course, white immigrants did not have an easy initial passage into all labor organizations. Hostility toward white foreign-born work-ers characterized some craft unions, especially in the building trades. A number of unions required citizenship or a declaration of intent as a condition of membership; others imposed high initiation fees, or required approval for admission by officers of the national organization or the presentation of a membership card from a foreign union.[102] Nevertheless, unions eventually admitted them. In time, these immigrant groups achieved control of certain trades and established an "ethnic lock" on jobs and union jurisdictions within their respective crafts, as in New York City where there was a Greek Furriers local, an Italian Dressmakers Union, and where locals of the Bricklayers Union were either Irish or Italian, and the Painters Union was largely Jewish. The Transport Workers Union was almost entirely Irish in its membership composition, the Brewery Workers Union German, as also the Bakery and Confectionary Workers Union, and a local of the Waiters Union was composed of Jewish workers. A similar pattern developed in other trades in many cities along the Atlantic seaboard and in midwestern communities with large ethnic concentrations. This process was in significant contrast to the permanent exclusion and powerlessness of black workers.

Widespread resentment at the preferential treatment given to white immigrants by labor unions led many blacks to believe that unions were instruments for the oppression of nonwhite workers by foreign-born workers. "The greatest enemy of the Negro," said one black leader from Indiana in 1899, "is the trade Unionism of the North."[103] Not surprisingly, the black press over a period of many years was filled with complaints against labor unions and immigrants. *

Henry C. Dotry, writing in the *Age* in 1891, reminded his black readers that "usually one of the first things foreigners learn after entering upon these shores is prejudice against the Afro-American, and they strive to bar him from various branches of labor." His predictions were grim indeed: "Experience of riots and distress, strikes and starvation . . . will soon begin to fall on America tenfold. . . . America has become the goal for the criminals and beggers" of Europe.[104]

The Colored American reported in 1898 and 1899 that labor unions were forcing black workers out of their traditional occupations—as barbers, coachmen, house painters, teamsters, and waiters.[105] Black workers increasingly perceived discriminatory labor unions as a conspiracy by foreigners against them. An editorial in *The Colored American* in 1903 said: "The first thing they do after landing and getting rid of their sea legs is to organize to keep the colored man out of the

---

* As early as 1853 Frederick Douglass wrote: "The old advocations, by which coloured men obtained a livelihood, are rapidly unceasingly and inevitably passing into other hands; every hour sees the black man elbowed out of employment by some newly arrived immigrant, whose hunger and whose color are thought to give him a better title to place; and so we believe it will continue until the last prop is levelled beneath us." (*Frederick Douglass's Paper*, March 4, 1853, p. 1.)

mines, out of the factories, out of the trade unions and out of all kinds of industries of the country."[106]

J. E. Bruce, a regular contributor to *The Colored American* under the pseudonym of "Bruce Grit" during the early 1900s, wrote on these themes again and again. In "Lessons of the Strike," commenting on a strike against the United Traction Company in Albany, Bruce said that "the leaders of the labor trust in America are largely men of foreign names and antecedents. . . . Who gave them the right to discriminate against the Negro in the labor market? To make him an industrial pariah when he is ready and willing to work?"[107] In 1902, he wrote that labor unions constituted "a gigantic closed corporation—a greedy, grasping, ruthless, intolerant, overbearing, dictatorial combination of half-educated white men." Finally, he declared flatly: "I am against them because they are against the Negro."[108]

The First World War, the corresponding increase in industrial production, and the drastic curtailment of European immigration offered a new opportunity to black workers in the North. The relatively small black migration to the North during the preceding fifty years, some Afro-American leaders later said, was a consequence of the large foreign immigration.[109] After immigration declined, the first wave of southern black migrants moved directly into industries and cities that had been filled by European immigrant labor: railroads, packinghouses, foundries, and automobile plants and steel mills, among others. Black workers were now moving into Cleveland, Chicago, Gary, Detroit, Milwaukee, Buffalo, and other manufacturing centers.[110] W. E. B. Du Bois, describing the movement northward as tentative and dependent on the war, added: "If for a generation after the present war European migration is restricted, the Negro will have an economic opportunity which no bourbonism can wholly close."[111]

European immigrant socialists were important in the development of several major unions and in the labor movement that emerged after the 1890s, though not in all sections since other groups, such as Irish Catholics, held divergent views on a variety of issues. German socialists, for example, were prominent within the AFL as leaders of the Brewery Workers International Union, the Bakery Workers, the Cigar Makers' and other unions with large German-speaking memberships.

One of the principal unions in New York City that developed out of the immigrant socialist tradition among Jewish workers was the International Ladies Garment Workers (ILGWU) founded in 1900. Sholem Asch, in his novel *East River*,[112] vividly describes the men and women from the villages of Russia and Poland who streamed into the sweatshop garment factories of New York's Lower East Side, driven to the United States by waves of anti-Semitic violence in the Czarist

Empire. Hundreds of thousands of Jews, among them many members of the revolutionary General Jewish Workers League, known as the Bund, struggled to establish labor unions.

From the 1890s, the garment industry in New York City absorbed successive waves of European immigrants. Many became skilled workers within an industry that offered stable employment and increased earnings; some eventually became small entrepreneurs employing immigrant workers themselves, while others moved out of the industry entirely to more desirable jobs in other sectors of the economy. As early as 1900, there were blacks working in the New York garment industry,[113] but for them such employment did not provide the means to escape from poverty and share in the economic and social progress enjoyed by white immigrant workers and their children. And for them, the ILGWU was to become part of the problem.

The experience of black workers was fundamentally different from that of European immigrants. For all their other problems, Jewish workers were white, and, together with other whites, they benefited from racial exclusionary practices and from the limitations on job advancement imposed on black workers because of their race. The theory that attempts to explain the problems of blacks in New York City as a consequence of their being the latest in a series of "newcomers" ignores history; ignores the fact that blacks were not immigrants, that they had been in the New York City area for many generations before the European immigration of the late nineteenth century; and ignores the factor of race that was decisive in determining their occupational status.[114]

Herman D. Bloch, the former Philip Murray Professor of Labor and Industrial Relations at Howard University, concludes in his study of black workers in New York, during the 1930s:

[B]oth the International Ladies Garment Workers Union (ILGWU) and the Amalgamated Clothing Workers of America had Negro Americans in their New York locals; it was disputable as to whether these unions practiced "egalitarianism." Both unions accepted the colored American primarily as a means of controlling the trade, but they restricted him to the least skilled trades (finishers, cleaners, and pressers). Control over these workers was essential to carry on effective collective bargaining in the industries. Secondly, the ILGWU accepted the bulk of its Negro American membership during organizing drives, taking the Negro American into the union in order to make a union shop . . .

Unionization of the colored Americans neglected a crucial issue: What occupations were open to these black Americans? What chance of upward economic mobility was available through a seniority system? The cutters' locals of both unions had no Negro American behind a pair of shears.[115]

Thirty years later the same pattern prevailed. Black workers were limited to the lowest-paying, unskilled job classifications within the ILGWU, and although their numbers had greatly increased, they were, with rare exception, excluded from the craft locals where wages were much higher. In the 1960s, however, blacks in New York as elsewhere increasingly struggled against the forces responsible for their subordinate and depressed condition. The emergence of a new body of constitutional law on race that developed after the 1954 decision of the U.S. Supreme Court in the school segregation cases, together with the dramatic confrontations with racism in the South, such as the Montgomery, Alabama, bus boycott of 1957, stimulated increasing black protest against many institutions engaged in discriminatory practices, including labor unions.[116]

In the ILGWU, the largest labor union in New York, the membership base had become increasingly black and Hispanic. But through a series of restrictive procedures (of doubtful legality under the Labor-Management Reporting and Disclosure Act of 1959), nonwhite workers were largely excluded from effective participation in the leadership of the union.[117] The general suppression of membership rights within the ILGWU, in conjunction with the extreme exploitation of nonwhite workers in the garment industry, the largest employer in the manufacturing sector of New York's economy, resulted in an increasingly restive labor force. The union was rigidly controlled by a self-perpetuating bureaucracy of white men whose base had been a Jewish working class that no longer existed and who were now increasingly in conflict with their nonwhite and female membership. In this context the pattern of discrimination was not the result of a conscious racist ideology but developed out of the interaction of an old Jewish union leadership with the changing social composition of the membership and the nature of the industry.

Although there had been earlier protest actions by the rank and file of the ILGWU, by the mid-1950s, such activity was occurring with greater frequency and involving larger numbers. A typical example was the demonstration of four hundred black and Hispanic workers in 1957 at the headquarters of the international union where a picket line was established to protest against "sweetheart contracts." Soon thereafter members of the ILGWU who worked in shops located in the Bronx filed a petition with the National Labor Relations Board to decertify the ILGWU as their collective bargaining representative.[118]

In 1958, Puerto Rican workers who were members of Local 62 held a public demonstration at the union's offices, carrying picket signs reading "We're tired of Industrial Peace. We Want Industrial Justice."[119] In that same year, black and Hispanic members of other ILGWU locals demonstrated at the headquarters of the international union to protest against the union's contracts.[120] The increasing discontent of black and Hispanic workers employed in the New York garment industry provided the context for the significant events that occurred in the 1960s on these issues.

A major factor in stimulating protest by nonwhite workers against the leadership of the ILGWU was the racial consequences of the union's policy of wage-suppression to keep the garment industry in New York City and thus to maintain the base of its economic and political power. A 1963 study, under the direction of economist Leon H. Keyserling and jointly funded by the ILGWU and employers, reported that, in real terms, the weekly and annual earnings of unionized garment workers in New York had declined during the preceding decade despite an increase in real productivity of at least 15 percent in the same period.[121]

Keyserling, documenting the consequences of the ILGWU's low-wage policy, concluded that wages for garment workers in New York lagged far behind those of workers organized by other unions and that conditions in New York garment manufacturing were among the worst of any unionized industry. His detailed analysis of payroll data had clear racial implications; he revealed that in union shops in Harlem, the Bronx, and Brooklyn, where significant numbers of black and Hispanic workers were concentrated, the relationship between percentage of workers and percentage of payroll corresponded more closely to the pattern prevailing in lower-wage areas outside of New York City than to wages in the central garment manufacturing district of Manhattan.[122] (This extensive study was never released by the union or the employers. The ILGWU acknowledged its existence in 1965, but reported that "Dr. Keyserling's recommendations were not practical in view of the special and unique nature of the garment industry."[123])

A study of wages in New York City released by the Bureau of Labor Statistics of the U.S. Department of Labor on June 27, 1962, indicated that the city had become a low-wage area and that between 1950 and 1960 wages for apparel workers there fell from second place among sixteen industrial categories to eleventh place and dropped below the national average for all manufacturing. The wage rates of unskilled and semiskilled garment workers, most of whom were nonwhite, were found to be below subsistence levels as indicated by the 1960 Interim City Workers Family Budget for New York City ($5,048) established by the Bureau of Labor Statistics.

In 1960 the average wage of all unionized garment workers in New York City was $2.40 an hour, in March 1963 $2.39, a decline in hourly wages of a penny an hour and a decline in real wages of nine cents an hour at 1959 price levels, according to data from the U.S. Bureau of Labor Statistics. It should be noted that the statistical data, significant as they are, are deceptive as far as blacks are concerned since the median income figure includes the wages of highly paid cutters and pressers who earned over $4 an hour and were almost exclusively white.[124] In 1963 between 15 and 20 percent of the ILGWU membership in New York City was earning less than $1.50 an hour.[125] All the available data indicate that this group consisted almost entirely of Negro and Puerto Rican workers. Thus, a significant percentage of Negro and Puerto Rican ILGWU members in the period between 1960 and 1965 not only experienced a drop in real earnings but also had an income that was below the figure that the U.S. Bureau of Labor Statistics rated as the poverty level for an average family in New York City.

The ILGWU's adoption and enforcement of a low-wage policy corresponded to the transformation in the racial composition of the labor force; that is, to the rapid increase of nonwhite workers in the garment industry. The nonwhite proportion of the population in New York City grew from 13 percent in 1950 to 22 percent in 1960.[126] By 1970, the nonwhite proportion of the population was 36.3 percent.[127] In 1980, blacks constituted 25.2 percent, Hispanics 19.9 percent and Asians 3.3 percent, and all the studies showed significantly higher labor force participation rates for these groups than for whites.[128] Since the end of the Second World War, the nonwhite and female labor force in the garment industry had been growing rapidly; by the 1960s it constituted a majority of the ILGWU's membership in New York City, but was concentrated in the lowest-paid job classifications with virtually no opportunity for advancement.

The ILGWU, the largest and most influential labor union in New York in the 1950s and 1960s, repeatedly opposed the adoption of a $1.50 hourly municipal minimum-wage law. Although actively supported by most other unions and civil rights organizations, the ILGWU threatened to withdraw from the AFL–CIO Central Labor Council in New York City if the council endorsed proposals for a city minimum wage.[129] Another union, publicly protesting the ILGWU's position, stated that "the ILGWU has a vested interest in the perpetuation of exploitation, low-wage pockets and poverty in New York City."[130]

On April 4, 1961, Ernest Holmes, a black worker who was a member of the National Association for the Advancement of Colored People (NAACP), filed a complaint with the New York State Commission for Human Rights against Local 10 of the ILGWU, charging discriminatory practices, including the refusal to admit on the basis of race, in violation of state law.[131] On May 18, 1963, twenty-five months later, in the case of *Holmes* v. *Falikman*,[132] the ILGWU entered into a consent agreement to comply with the law without admitting guilt. A year earlier a finding of "probable cause" was issued by the investigating commissioner, when the union failed to comply with the original order. The *New York Times* of July 2, 1961, reported, "With regard to the union, the decision found that 'the evidence raises serious doubt as to its good faith to comply with the State Law against Discrimination.' . . . "

On September 14, 1962, Investigating Commissioner Rupert Ruiz, in a letter to Emil Schlesinger, the attorney for Local 10, said that the commission had "repeatedly requested and for a period of eight months tried to obtain data pertinent to a resolution of the charges of discrimination against Amalgamated Ladies Garment Cutters Union, Local 10. These efforts were unsuccessful. The failure of representatives of that local to cooperate in the investigation, despite their promises to do so, left me no alternative but to find 'probable cause' to credit the allegations of the complaint."[133]

In defending itself before the New York State Commission for Human Rights, the ILGWU submitted many and various figures about the number of black and Hispanic members of Local 10, which controlled access to some of the highest-paying jobs in the industry. Local 10 was notorious for its exclusionary practices. Moe Falikman, manager of Local 10, is quoted in the *New York Times* of May 18, 1961, as stating that there were "more than 500 Negroes and Puerto Ricans" in the membership of the cutters local. Later, the ILGWU said that there were four hundred nonwhite members in this craft local, but subsequently the figure was reduced to three hundred and then to two hundred by representatives of the union. The commission repeatedly challenged the union to produce the names and addresses and places of employment of these alleged members, but such identification was never produced. (Individual union officers played their own "numbers game." For example, Gus Tyler, vice president of the ILGWU, wrote that "In Local 10, there are 199 known Negro and Spanish-speaking members."[134] Tyler explained that his figure includes "Cubans, Panamanians, Colombians, Dominicans, Salvadorians, Mexicans, etc., as well as Puerto Ricans."[135] But later Tyler said, "We had 275 black members in that local."[136])

Despite the commission's findings and conclusions, the American Jewish Committee, the Jewish Labor Committee, and other groups circulated statements asserting that "there are currently 250 Negro and Spanish-speaking cutters in Local 10." In response to the exact same assertion by the union earlier, the NAACP had informed the state commission that it would move to dismiss the complaint against the ILGWU if the union would identify such persons. The union failed to respond. The NAACP asked the American Jewish Committee, in a letter dated October 23, 1962, to provide such identification since it was now circulating the union's claim under its own name. That committee also failed to respond.[137]

The NAACP, conducting its own investigation, found no more than twenty-three nonwhite members of Local 10, which at that time had a membership of 7,531.[138] Most of these twenty-three were older men from Jamaica and other Caribbean countries who had been admitted into the ILGWU after the union had organized shops where they were already employed. Significantly, they were initially hired as cutters before the union became the collective bargaining agent at their place of employment.

On July 2, 1962, the *New York Herald Tribune*, in a front-page report headlined "ILGWU Condemned for Racial Barriers," summarized the history of this case:

The New York Cutters' local of the International Ladies Garment Workers' Union was judged guilty of racial discrimination in a report released yesterday by the State Commission for Human Rights. After a 15-month investigation, the commission found the union: Was indifferent to a worker's charge of mistreatment; Lacked a clear policy through which minority-group members could gain union membership; Showed 'reluctance' to disclose the racial composition of its membership to the investigators. The cutters are the most highly skilled and highly paid workers in the garment industry, and are represented in New York by Local 10, ILGWU. The union proudly proclaims the Socialist heritage of its leaders.[139]

The news report noted that wages for members of Local 10 "are roughly double that of other workers in the industry." This case received much public attention and led to a congressional investigation of the ILGWU's racial practices.*

---

* The ILGWU often distorted the history of the congressional investigation. Gus Tyler, vice president of the union, wrote, for example, that Adam Clayton Powell, chairman of the House Committee on Education and Labor, was "riding a little wave of anti-Semitism" and that the union was exonerated. According to Tyler, "There was no case. There was nothing. . . . We won the round. We won the war" (Tyler, 1982, 173–174). The official record directly contradicts Tyler's claim because there was no exoneration of the union. The ILGWU was greatly embarrassed by the exposure of its racial and other practices and received much criticism during the public hearings. See U.S. House 1962. Documentation in congressional files, together with extensive interviewing by the author of persons on staff during the investigation reveal that the ILGWU used its considerable political influence at the highest levels of government to stop the hearings. An announcement was made at the last session on September 21, 1962, that the hearings were "recessed, to reconvene subject to call." But they were never reconvened. After the union succeeded in making certain political arrangements, the congressional committee quietly abandoned the hearings, which were never formally concluded. For the author's testimony before the hearings see *Congressional Record—House*, January 31, 1963, pp. 1496–1499.

The ILGWU reacted by claiming that such criticism was motivated by anti-Semitism, and that these actions were a malicious attack upon the Jewish leadership of the union. Union officials, hard-pressed and embarrassed by the public exposure of the union's long-established treatment of nonwhite workers, tried to deflect attention from the central issue of racial discrimination by an intensive public relations campaign that focused on alleged anti-Semitism. These events anticipated later conflicts between Jews and blacks in other circumstances, demonstrating how immigrant groups, now integrated into American society, may defend their own privileges and power when confronted by a new black militancy.[140]

The criticisms of the ILGWU raised in the course of the Holmes case and in its aftermath charged the union with perpetuating a pattern that limited nonwhites to the least-desirable jobs by preventing their movement into skilled classifications and by routinely violating the basic requirements of internal union democracy. The ILGWU leadership was also charged with negotiating contracts that were more beneficial to employers than to nonwhite workers.

In these protest activities, a growing black and Hispanic working class had tried to open an avenue for advancement in an institution controlled by an established stratum of Jewish leaders anxious to preserve the privileges of their group within the industry and union—a stratum that by that time had more in common with employers than with the black and Hispanic members of the ILGWU. Black organizations understood that what nonwhite workers were doing in attacking the union leadership was precisely what Jews and other immigrant groups had done in the past. Indeed, the history of immigrants in America is a continuum of efforts in which ethnic groups, as they rose, fought as a bloc within institutions to advance their group interests, using the availability of particular occupations as a lever for their integrationist goals.

But, in the 1960s, Jewish organizations interpreted criticisms of the ILGWU as an assault upon the Jewish community. Thus, they responded *as a community* in defense of the ILGWU leadership and denounced representatives of the black workers as anti-Semites. The issue was not, however, a Jewish one, for in their own resistance to black aspirations, Jews were acting as assimilated Americans, just as gentile groups in the past had reacted to pressure from upwardly bound Jews.

Many national Jewish organizations became actively involved, sending out a torrent of correspondence, newsletters, bulletins, and press releases defending the ILGWU. The following is a small sample. The American Jewish Committee distributed an eight-page tract written by Harry Fleishman, a member of its staff, entitled "Is the ILGWU Biased?" (November 1962), and through its newsletter, *Let's Be Human*, repeatedly praised the ILGWU and denounced its critics.* The American Jewish Congress, on December 6, 1962, sent a statement signed by Shad Polier, chairman of the organization's governing council, to its members, defending the union and repeating Fleishman's distortions, including references to "Ernest Holmes, a Negro member of the International Ladies Garment Workers Union." It is a matter of record in sworn documents filed with the New York State Commission for Human Rights that Holmes, up to that date, had never been a member of the union. On December 7, 1962, Polier sent copies of his statement to ILGWU vice president Charles S. Zimmerman, who was also manager of its New York Dress Joint Board, along with a letter suggesting a meeting on "the ILGWU–NAACP controversy."[141]

The Anti-Defamation League of B'nai B'rith, the largest Jewish fraternal order in the United States, also came to the defense of the ILGWU. Oscar Cohen, national program director of the league, reported its efforts on behalf of the union to Zimmerman in a letter dated December 3, 1962. He writes, "We are terribly upset," and that by writing to people "around the country, . . . we are going to give this statement [from the union] wide distribution"; he closes by promising Zimmerman to "do as much as I can."[142]

The Jewish Labor Committee was extremely active on behalf of the union. The ILGWU provided major financial support to this organization, and many of its officers were leaders of the union. On October 11, 1962, the organization adopted a resolution denouncing the NAACP; it was distributed nationally and reported in the press. On October 31, 1962, Roy Wilkins, executive secretary of the NAACP, in a letter to

---

* A letter dated November 13, 1962, from John A. Morsell, assistant to the executive secretary of the NAACP, to Harry Fleishman, of the American Jewish Committee, provides a thoughtful response to Fleishman's assertions that are replete with many errors of fact. (Copy in author's files.) On January 15, 1963, David Dubinsky, president of the ILGWU, sent a copy of this letter, together with a covering note, to George Meany, president of the AFL–CIO. (Box 207, File 30, Dubinsky Collection, ILGWU Archives.) Data in ILGWU files make it evident that Fleishman was involved in formulating the union's public relations strategy. A memorandum from Will Chasan of the ILGWU staff to Charles S. Zimmerman, manager of the New York Dress Joint Board of the union, dated October 28, 1962, for example, makes reference to Fleishman's activities and to a letter he received from Herbert Hill, labor secretary of the NAACP, dated October 23, 1962. Chasan writes, "The awful thing about Hill's letter is that, on the whole, it is probably an accurate summary, and it exposes the awful idiocy of the way this situation was handled." (Box 26, File 8, Zimmerman Collection, ILGWU Archives.) Archival sources for documentation of this history are the Library of Jewish Information of the American Jewish Committee, New York, International Ladies Garment Workers' Union Archives, New York, especially the Dubinsky and Zimmerman papers, and the NAACP Collection in the Library of Congress, Washington, D.C.

Emanuel Muravchik, director of the Jewish Labor Committee, responded to that organization's statement:

We find the language of this resolution strange, indeed. It is as vituperative and unrestrained as any against which complaint has been lodged by some labor spokesmen in the past. . . . In addition to the language, there are the threats which can hardly be received with equanimity by an organization which has traditions of its own imbedded in a long history. Not a few chapters of that history detail the heartbreaking struggles through the decades against the icy indifference, the callous and active hostility or the lukewarm and opportunistic attitude of a vast body of trade unionists. When you declare in 1962 that the NAACP's continued attack upon discrimination against Negro workers by trade union bodies and leaders places "in jeopardy" continued progress toward civil rights goals or rends the "unity" among civil rights forces, or renders a "disservice" to the Negro worker, or raises the question "whether it is any longer possible to work with the NAACP" you are, in fact, seeking by threats to force us to conform to what the Jewish Labor Committee is pleased to classify as proper behavior in the circumstances. Needless to say, we cannot bow to this threat. We reject the proposition that any segment of the labor movement is sacrosanct in the matter of practices and/or policies which restrict employment opportunities on racial or religious or nationality grounds. We reject the contention that bringing such charges constitutes a move to destroy "unity" among civil rights groups unless it be admitted that this unity is a precarious thing, perched upon unilateral definition of discrimination by each member group. In such a situation, the "unity" is of no basic value and its destruction may be regarded as not a calamity, but a blessed clearing of the air.

In reply to the charge of anti-Semitism, Wilkins stated,

This is a grave charge to make. . . . We do not deign to defend ourselves against such a baseless allegation. Its inclusion in the resolution, as well as in the statements to the press by Mr. Zimmerman is unworthy of an organization like the Jewish Labor Committee which, in the very nature of things, must be conversant with the seriousness of such a charge and with the evidence required to give it substance. . . . Similarly, we do not feel that the general denials and outraged protests which have been the response of the ILGWU to our charges of discriminatory practices are in any way an adequate answer to those charges.[143]

The resolution of the Holmes case did not put an end to protest from nonwhite workers against discriminatory practices by the ILGWU. In its aftermath, black, Hispanic, and Asian-American workers began to organize dissident groups within various local unions. This activity led to the filing of complaints with federal agencies and to initiation of litigation on a variety of issues relating to race and violations of internal union democracy. Among these was the intervention in 1971 by the U.S. Department of Labor in the election proceedings within the 15,000 member Knitgoods Local 155 of the ILGWU in response to a formal complaint filed by a black and Hispanic caucus known as "the Rank And File Committee."[144]

The caucus charged that a series of illegal practices by the union violated federal law by preventing the election of black and Hispanic workers to leadership positions within the local. After investigation, the U.S. Department of Labor ordered a rerun of the election. At a press conference, the "Rank And File Committee" charged that ILGWU officials signed contracts that forced them to work "under sweatshop conditions," and claimed that black and Spanish-speaking workers constituted 75 percent of the membership of Local 155 but were denied any voice in determining union policies. In its press release, the committee protested racist characterizations of its members in *The Jewish Daily Forward*, the leading Yiddish language newspaper in New York. The committee said that articles in the *Forward* reporting on the conflict within Local 155 contained "racist insults and slanderous lies . . . such as calling black and Spanish-speaking members of the Rank And File Committee a 'gang,' 'marijuana smokers,' 'drug addicts and pushers,' and 'bewildered children.' " Such "slanders" were "a vicious and obvious attempt to whip up race hatred between the younger workers and our older, mostly Jewish coworkers in the shops. . . . We are not anti-Semites. . . . We struggle with all workers, Black, white and Spanish-speaking, of all religions, for a strong local."[145]

On February 17, 1971, a *Jewish Daily Forward* story headlined "Knitgoods Local 155 and the Elections," by Y. Fogel, reported that the "Communist Rank and File" are involved in a "Communist web of intrigues," and identified the black and Hispanic caucus as the work of "Communist agents." The article concluded with the explanation that "the communists only really want to take over the locals and the Union and offer them up on a Red tray to the Stalin inheritors who, together with El-Fatah, want to eliminate Israel."[146]

Another example of conflict between the ILGWU and nonwhite workers involved the union's financing of a segregated housing project. On May 25, 1983, black, Hispanic, and Asian-American members of the ILGWU demonstrated at the headquarters building of the international union to protest the exclusion of nonwhite union members from the ILGWU-financed East River Houses. One union member, Margarita Lopez, was quoted in the *New York Daily News* as saying, "How could this happen? How could this happen in a union that is supposed to be so liberal. The blacks, the Hispanics, the Chinese are the workers. The dues come from those people, but the housing is all white and middle class. These were union pension funds. They give union funds but union workers who are black and Hispanic and Chinese cannot live in those houses."[147]

In 1977, after a group of nonwhite workers had filed a lawsuit, Federal Judge Robert L. Carter found that there was indeed a pattern of unlawful racial exclusion in the ILGWU East River Houses.[148] Documentation introduced into the court record revealed that the ILGWU had contributed more than $20 million of union funds to subsidize a housing development for middle-class whites who were not ILGWU members, adjacent to a vast area of substandard housing inhabited mainly by racial minorities. This was to become a major issue among nonwhite ILGWU members in the New York area; several thousand workers signed petitions demanding an end to the racist pattern in the union's East River Houses, also known as ILGWU Co-operative Village.[149]

When Title VII went into effect, many complaints were filed against the ILGWU with the Equal Employment Opportunity Commission. In some of these cases the EEOC sustained charges of race and sex discrimination against the International Union as well as its locals and in *Putterman* v. *Local 155, ILGWU, and the International Ladies Garment Workers Union*,[150] a federal court in New York found "willful" and "intentional" violations of the legal prohibitions against race and sex discrimination by both the local and international unions. Among the many EEOC charges filed against the ILGWU were cases in Chicago, Philadelphia, Cleveland, Atlanta, New York, and other cities.[151]

With the rising affluence of the Jewish population and its assimilation into American society, the foundations of Jewish radicalism disintegrated. Many descendants of the Jewish immigrant worker, who had been obsessed by history and discontented with capitalism, now were upwardly mobile professionals or corporate managers with a stake in the perpetuation of existing social institutions. The troubled intellectual inquisitiveness cultivated by previous generations of radicalized Jews gave way to an acceptance of the legitimacy and indeed the virtue of existing American values and institutions. The unprecedented transformation of Jewish life in the United States and its implications required analysis and explanation within the Jewish community. Nathan Glazer's article, "Negroes and Jews: The New Challenge to Pluralism," that appeared in the December 1964 issue of *Commentary*, published by the American Jewish Committee, asserted that the crisis in the early 1960s between blacks and Jews occurred because these groups had "different capacities to take advantage of the opportunities that are truly in large measure open to all."[152] The American environment, Glazer said, is not prejudicial to one group or the other.

Jews, Glazer asserts, are able to take advantage of the "democracy of merit" that he believes characterizes contemporary American society, while the Negro personality and behavior are responsible for the Negro's incapacity to realize the opportunities available to all. Glazer views these patterns as cultural phenomena.

In his version of cultural pluralism, Glazer argues that Jewish resistance to new black militancy is based partly "on a growing awareness of the depths of Negro antagonism to the world that Jewish liberalism considers desirable." Jews, he wrote, lived a different kind of life in American society, with their own businesses, neighborhoods, schools, and unions; Jews never attacked social discrimination per se, and they never challenged "the right of a group to maintain distinctive institutions," but now Negro demands "pose a serious threat to the ability of other groups to maintain *their* communities." Negroes, Glazer complained, had no distinctive institutions of their own and wanted, therefore, to integrate all of American life. He reprimanded the Negro for wanting to enter on an "equal footing" into "Jewish business . . . the Jewish union . . . or the Jewish (or largely Jewish) neighborhood and school." The "force of present-day Negro demands," said Glazer, "is that the sub-community, because it either protects privilege, or creates inequality, has no right to exist." The separatism that "other groups see as a value," Glazer wrote, "Negroes see as a strategy in the fight for equal right." He also noted "the resistance of Jewish organizations and individual Jews to such demands as preferential union membership and preferential hiring."[153]

What union did Glazer have in mind? The only union regarded as a "Jewish union," one that had come under attack from blacks at that time because of discriminatory racial practices, was the ILGWU. In what ways could the ILGWU be classified as "Jewish"? Jewish immigrants founded the ILGWU, constituted a majority of its membership until the late 1930s, and Jews remained in control of the organization long thereafter. But two decades *before* Glazer wrote this article, the percentage of Jewish membership in the union had fallen to 30 percent and continued to decline steadily.[154] The Negroes accused of forcing themselves upon another ethnic group constituted—together with Hispanics in 1962—a far larger proportion of the union membership. In the central ILGWU membership base of New York City, where the garment industry and the union were concentrated, Negroes and Hispanics constituted a majority of the membership.[155] In this context, the "privileges" of the ethnic "sub-community" described by Glazer are in fact derived from the institutionalization of discrimination and the exploitation of subordinate groups. When the nonwhite victims of that arrangement attempted to advance themselves by doing what other groups, including Jews, had succeeded in doing, they were, according to Glazer, "challenging the very system under which Jews have done so well."[156]

Ironically, the goals and methods of the black struggle to which Glazer pointed with disapproval characterized the history of many Jewish organizations in their earlier efforts to realize Jewish aspirations. The result that blacks desired—according to Glazer, structural integration as a group into American society—was what Jews already had and what blacks could not have because of their well-known defects. Glazer advised blacks to forego that goal in the name of a nominally cultural theory.

In his influential 1975 book, *Affirmative Discrimination: Ethnic Inequality and Public Policy*, Glazer developed the ideas offered in his 1964 *Commentary* essay. In explanation of the opposition to affirmative action, he wrote: "The later white ethnic groups are strongly represented in the trade unions and the areas of construction, transportation, and manufacturing in which trade unions are powerful." Working-class ethnics have benefited from and are committed to established union procedures such as seniority, but "They see these principles now challenged and restricted by affirmative action and quotas for blacks and other groups."[157]

It is important to note that the economic data cited by Glazer were obsolete before the book was published. Glazer's major concern here is the social disequilibrium that he believes will ensue as a consequence of affirmative action programs. He constructs a three-tiered, unique, and successful American pattern of ethnic absorption, assimilation, and accommodation that does not require affirmative action. He is convinced that the consensus on racial equality that produced the Civil Rights Acts in the mid-1960s was in itself the remedy. In other words, the establishment of equal opportunity was achieved by the very proclamation of it.

In Glazer's argument, sometimes the word "ethnic" is used to include race, sometimes it is not; the blurring of the distinction plays an important role in his formulation. He locates, so to speak, the distinctive American ethnic experience in three sets of decisions that have expanded "the definition of those who may be included in it to the point where it now includes all humanity." These "sets of decisions" establish "that all may be included in the nation, that they may not establish new nations here, and that they may, nevertheless, freely maintain whatever aspects of national existence they are inclined to." Ethnicity (race?) is not a category forced on Americans: its "voluntary character . . . is what makes it so distinctive in the American setting."[158]

The chief danger to this distinctive American pattern of "accommodation of group differences came from establishment of a caste system in the United States," or, on the other hand, from "the demand that those accepted into American society become Americanized or assimilated, and lose distinctive group identity."[159] But according to Glazer, these threats are a thing of the past. The real problem is the race and group-membership identification called for by affirmative action programs. Such distinct identification by race or group will destroy the carefully calibrated social coherence achieved through the accommodative nature of the American ethnic pattern.

Glazer's journey through the ethnic-racial experience in America is filled with familiar signposts—"prejudice," "discrimination," "slavery," "racism"—but it is a strangely abstract landscape, devoid of people, one in which roseate patterns float free of any mooring in history. The subjugation of the black population in slavery and later in other forms of exploitation, the near extermination of Native Americans, the xenophobia of nativist movements, and the destructive violence of organizations like the Ku Klux Klan—all of these are seen as mere deflections from the mainstream of the American experience. To believe otherwise is for Glazer a wilfully misguided act based on "a selective misreading of American history. No one is now excluded from the broadest access to what the society makes possible; and . . . this access is combined with a considerable concern for whatever is necessary to maintain group identity and loyalty."[160]

If blacks and other minority groups and even the white poor do not feel that they have "the broadest access to what the society makes possible," are they suffering from a failure of perception or from moral defect? One is reminded of the logic of the 1896 decision of the U.S. Supreme Court in *Plessy* v. *Ferguson*, the leading case upholding racial segregation, overruled in the 1954 *Brown* decision:

We consider the underlying fallacy of the plaintiff's argument to consist in the assumption that the enforced separation of the two races stamps the colored race with a badge of inferiority. If this be so, it is not by reason of anything found in the act, but solely because the colored race chooses to put that construction upon it.[161]

To make the victims responsible for their condition is to reassure the sons and daughters of immigrants that they have no responsibility for continuing racism and inequality, while at the same time protecting and advancing the interests of their own communities. Glazer's theory not only denies any justification for affirmative action programs, but regards such measures as dangerous to the future of the Republic. A consequence of Glazer's theory is that there is no history, or history that he regards as having any significance, between the enactment of the Fourteenth Amendment in 1868 and the Supreme Court's decision in *Brown* v. *Board of Education*, in 1954.[162] (Glazer's argument is quoted in the brief of the Anti-Defamation League of B'nai B'rith submitted to the U.S. Supreme Court in opposition to affirmative action in the *Bakke* case.)

Arguments about the morality of "quotas" and denunciations of "reverse discrimination" repeated by the opponents of affirmative action are the artifice of public debate. In view of the tenacity of inequality and injustice, it is difficult to believe that affirmative action is more threatening to the social fabric than the persistent racism that continues to pervade much of American society.

An economic analysis of the comparative status of blacks and white immigrants since 1880 by Stanley Lieberson concludes:

The situation for new Europeans in the United States, bad as it may have been, was not as bad as that experienced by blacks at the same time. Witness, for example, the differences in the disposition to ban openly blacks from unions at the turn of the century, the greater concentration of blacks in 1900 in service occupations and their smaller numbers in manufacturing and mechanical jobs, the higher black death rates in the North and even the greater segregation of blacks with respect to the avenues of eminence open to them. It is a serious mistake to underestimate how far the new Europeans have come in the nation, and how hard it all was, but it is equally erroneous to assume that the obstacles were as great as those faced by blacks or that the starting point was the same.[163]

It must be recognized that whatever the problems experienced by European ethnic groups, they were white in a society acutely conscious of race. They and their descendants substantially contributed to the development of discriminatory patterns, just as they were the beneficiaries of such practices themselves. The idea that the suffering of white people is more important and worthy of attention than the suffering of black people, and that it is acceptable to obtain advantages at the expense of blacks, permeates much of American society.*

---

* American labor history is in the main characterized by such approaches. Jack Barbash writes that "the labor union offered a natural defense for the exploited Irish-Catholic workers in the cities, and the beginnings of permanent unions in many trades and industries are inextricably associated with the pressing needs of immigrant Irish workers for economic protection." He concludes that "the union has provided a meeting ground for people of diverse ethnic backgrounds and has resulted in submergence of ethnic rivalries in the interest of common goals. In short, the union has had a powerful 'Americanizing' influence" (Barbash 1952, 73, 81). The racial consequences of the domination of labor unions by white immigrants and their descendants, in this instance as in so many others, is ignored, although the same labor organizations that served the interests of European immigrants were responsible for sustained injury to generations

European immigrants greatly benefited from the exclusionary racial pattern because it gave them preferential status in gaining access to training and jobs reserved for whites only. Over time, this preferential status became an important factor in making possible the economic gains of ethnic communities, in contrast to the declining condition of black workers.

The elimination of traditional patterns of discrimination required by the Civil Rights Act of 1964 adversely affected the expectations of whites, since it compelled competition with black workers and other minority group members where no competition previously existed. White worker expectations had become the norm, and any alteration of the norm was considered to be "reverse discrimination." It is, in fact, *the removal of the preferential treatment traditionally enjoyed by white workers at the expense of blacks as a class* that is at issue in the affirmative action controversy.

Excerpts from two federal court decisions involving craft unions, one in Louisiana and the other in New York, reveal how the traditional preferential system for whites had been maintained. In *Vogler* v. *Asbestos Workers, Local 53*, in New Orleans, the Court of Appeals for the Fifth Circuit stated:

In pursuing its exclusionary and nepotistic policies, Local 53 engaged in a pattern and practice of discrimination on the basis of race and national origin both in membership and referrals. It was found to be Local 53's practice to refer white persons of limited experience and white journeymen of other trade unions as mechanic asbestos workers. It was also found to be its practice to refuse to consider Negroes or Mexican-Americans for membership and to refuse to refer Negroes for employment or to accept Negroes for referral for employment. This policy and various acts of discrimination, both prior to and after the effective date of the Civil Rights Act of 1964, were admitted at trial and on this appeal.[164]

---

of nonwhite workers. In this history the primacy of race is central. That the extensive record involving race and ethnicity and organized labor has been, for the most part, ignored or distorted is a function of assumptions that are incorporated in an implicit American racial ideology. Ideology is that set of beliefs so readily accepted that they do not have to be stated. Institutions as well as academic studies are often based on such unspoken beliefs. That this tradition continues in the work of certain younger scholars devoted to the "new labor history" is made evident in the much acclaimed study by Sean Wilentz (1984). In a book of more than 400 pages, Wilentz simply ignores the black working class; for him, they virtually do not exist. One perceptive historian has observed that Wilentz "invokes Herman Melville, but while Melville's work constantly reminds us that people of color were central to the culture of those who worked on or near water in nineteenth-century America, New York City's black workers—during part of the period discussed one New Yorker in eleven was black—appear twice in *Chants Democratic*, once in a footnote and again as victims of prejudice" (Roediger, 1986).

In *United States* v. *Lathers, Local 46*, in New York City, the district court found that

There is a deep-rooted and pervasive practice in this union of handing out jobs on the basis of union membership, kinship, friendship and, generally, "pull." The specific tactics, practices, devices and arrangements just enumerated have amounted in practical fact to varying modes of implementing this central pattern of unlawful criteria. The hirings at the site, the by-passing of the lists, the use of the hiring hall, when it was used at all, as a formality rather than as a place for legitimate and nondiscriminatory distribution of work all reflected the basic evil of preferring Local 46 members, relatives, friends, or friends of friends in job referrals. And since the membership of this Local has for so long been almost exclusively white, the result could have been forecast: the jobs, and especially the more desirable jobs, have gone disproportionately to whites rather than Blacks.[165]

Commenting on the union's practices in maintaining an all-white membership and restricting jobs, the court added a sharply worded statement:

Because courts may know what all the world knows, practices of nepotism and favoritism like those disclosed here could, and probably should, be condemned as inevitably discriminatory. . . . But there is no need in this case even for so modest a generalization. The whole story is here, in vivid and repetitive detail. Giving life and point to an impressive statistical demonstration, the Government has shown in case after case the preference of whites over Blacks on grounds of nepotism or acquaintanceship. The officers of the local did not merely acquiesce in this state of affairs; many, if not all, of them have been active participants in the pattern of favoritism and its inevitable concomitant, racial discrimination.[166]

Predictably, this labor union, which for more than half a century had systematically excluded blacks and Hispanics, proclaimed the court-ordered affirmative action remedy "reverse discrimination." But the U.S. Court of Appeals for the Second Circuit, rejecting the union's contention, sustained the order of the lower court.

Labor unions in diverse jurisdictions have attacked affirmative action programs that provide employment for blacks and women previously excluded from many job classifications. On January 18, 1973, the U.S. District Court in Philadelphia approved a consent decree that ended two years of hearings on discriminatory practices in twenty-three subsidiaries of the American Telephone and Telegraph Company (AT&T).[167] The company agreed to revise its promotion and job-transfer practices, to make changes in its testing procedures, and to pay $38 million in back-pay and other wage adjustments, a figure that was later increased to $80 million. Two years later the original agreement was modified when investigation by the government revealed that AT&T had failed to comply with the consent decree in certain specific classifications; a Supplemental Agreement was negotiated.[168] The new agreement signed by the company and the government on May 9, 1975, did not become effective at the time because of legal challenges by two AFL–CIO unions, the Communications Workers of America and the International Brotherhood of Electrical Workers, joined by the Alliance of Independent Telephone Workers. On August 20, 1976, a federal judge rejected the union's arguments and held that the negotiated hiring and promotion goals were an acceptable remedy under Title VII, the union contract notwithstanding.[169] The three labor organizations had succeeded in delaying the effective date of the agreement for more than a year and also filed grievances to prevent the implementation of the affirmative action program.

In another case, *Jersey Central Power & Light Co. v. IBEW, Local 327*,[170] the union succeeded in destroying a plan intended to provide equal treatment to victims of past discrimination. The company was found to be in violation of Title VII by engaging in discriminatory hiring practices; it agreed to an affirmative action program that resulted in the employment of women and racial minorities. When the company found it necessary to furlough about 10 percent of its 3,850 member work force, it agreed to comply with an EEOC conciliation agreement requiring a reduction of the work force in a way that would not disproportionately victimize the newly hired women and black workers. But in 1975 the International Brotherhood of Electrical Workers succeeded in overturning the conciliation agreement when it took its case to the Third Circuit Court of Appeals, which ruled that the union seniority system "will be sustained even though it may operate to the disadvantage of females and minority groups as a result of past employment practices."

The American Federation of Teachers (AFT), an affiliate of the AFL–CIO, has been among the most active opponents of affirmative action, even though a substantial part of its membership consists of women and blacks. The AFT filed a brief *amicus curiae* in opposition to affirmative action in the *Bakke* case before the Supreme Court,[171] and in *Chance* v. *Board of Examiners*,[172] its New York affiliate, the United Federation of Teachers, filed a brief against the black and Puerto Rican plaintiffs.

In *Chance* a federal court ruled that the City of New York must stop using its traditional examinations for selecting school principals because the test had the "effect of discriminating significantly and substantially against qualified black and Puerto Rican applicants." The court concluded that the procedures of the board of examiners, allegedly based upon the merit system, could not be justified as being reasonably related to job performance.

The American Federation of Teachers also intervened in the Boston school case decided by the U.S. Court of Appeals for the First Circuit in 1982.[173] Rejecting arguments by the Boston Teachers Union, an AFT affiliate, that U.S. District Judge W. Arthur Garrity, Jr., had ordered an affirmative action plan that amounted to a "forbidden racial preference," the appellate court said that the plan was a "reasonable response" and necessary to "safeguard the progress toward desegregation."

Since most black teachers in the Boston school system were hired later than the majority of white teachers, they would lose their jobs if layoffs were made on the basis of union seniority. Judge Garrity, responsible for enforcing federal court orders requiring the desegregation of the Boston school system, ordered an approach that would ensure that the level of black employment among Boston's 5,000 teachers did not fall below the then current figure of 19 percent.

In rejecting the arguments of the Boston Teachers Union, the circuit court stated: "Black children have a right to an education in a school system free of racial discrimination in the employment of teachers and staff." In response to the union's claim that the order of the district court violated its collective bargaining agreement, the circuit court ruled that "the contract alone cannot bar a federal court from granting effective relief for constitutional violations. . . . Once a court has found racial discrimination in a school case, race-conscious remedies not only are permitted they are said to be required where color-blind approaches would be inadequate."[174]

Other labor organizations have also been active in the legal effort to nullify affirmative action programs. Among the many cases are *Detroit Police Officers Ass'n* v. *City of Detroit, Tangren* v. *Wackenhut Services Inc., Zipes* v. *TWA, Minnick* v. *California Department of Corrections, U.S.* v. *City of Miami,* and *Baker* v. *City of Detroit.*[175] The attacks upon affirmative action by labor unions, together with their insistence upon the rigid application of "last hired—first fired" seniority provisions in union contracts, have been understood by civil rights advocates as a sustained effort to perpetuate the traditional privileged status of white workers.[176] Organized labor has repeatedly refused modifications in established seniority systems and with few exceptions rejects affirmative action approaches as a remedy to eliminate discriminatory patterns. The Reagan administration in the 1980s intervened on behalf of white workers and their unions in litigation attacking affirmative action programs in Boston, New Orleans, Memphis, Detroit, New York, and elsewhere.

Construction labor unions and the AFL–CIO have been most active in leading a national campaign against affirmative action. They have lobbied extensively in Congress against affirmative action requirements imposed by federal agencies on government contractors and used their political influence to cripple enforcement in the construction industry. The AFL–CIO Building and Construction Trades Department joined with employer associations in the legal attack against the Philadelphia Plan to provide jobs for minority workers in federally subsidized construction projects and filed briefs *amicus curiae* in other cases against affirmative action programs.[177]

George Meany, president of the AFL–CIO, was deeply involved in these actions. Meany's father, an Irish immigrant, had been president of a New York Plumbers Union local that functioned as a job protective association for Irish immigrants and their sons at the turn of the century. George Meany became its business agent.[178] While head of the AFL–CIO, he was also the de facto leader of the construction unions, the organizational base of his long career. During a press interview on August 28, 1975, in response to a reporter's question, Meany stated:

To say that I've got some responsibility to make up for discrimination that took place 125 years ago is nuts. . . . I don't buy that at all.
Reporter: Does anybody have a responsibility in contemporary American society? . . .
Meany: Not that I know of. . . . And to say that we've got to sacrifice our kids and our rights to take care of people who merely say that we've got to be employed because our skin is black, that is discrimination in reverse and we don't buy it.[179]

A significant factor in the intransigent resistance of building trades unions to the requirements of contemporary civil rights laws is the circumstance that local unions are often based largely upon ethnic communities. The leaders and members of such unions adamantly believe that the jobs they control "belong" to their ethnic group. (The larger local unions may consist of several nationality groups, each with their own leadership and a tacit distribution of work.)

The events leading to the first lawsuit filed by the Department of Justice under Title VII tell much about the racial practices of the AFL–CIO unions in the building trades. In response to repeated civil rights demonstrations during 1965 at the "Gateway Arch," a federally funded construction project in St. Louis, the U.S. government required each contractor to employ a minimum percentage of minority workers. When the general contractor engaged three fully qualified black plumbers who were members of an independent labor union, all workers belonging to the "lily-white" AFL–CIO construction unions walked off the job. At the request of the NAACP, the Department of Justice conducted an investigation of the work stoppage in light of Title VII and federal contract requirements.

In February 1966, the U.S. attorney general filed a Title VII suit against four of the unions involved in the walkout: Local 1 of the International Brotherhood of Electrical Workers, Local 36 of the Sheet Metal Workers, Plumbers Local 5, and Steamfitters Local 562. The AFL–CIO Building and Construction Trades Council of St. Louis was also named as a defendant.[180] The government charged that the unions refused to admit blacks; failed to operate their respective hiring-hall referral systems on a nondiscriminatory basis; and failed to organize employers who hired black workers. Prior to trial, the Plumbers and Steamfitters signed a consent decree that admitted the major allegations in the government's charges and agreed to some remedial action in the future. But, the U.S. Justice Department finally found it necessary to enforce the law by obtaining an injunction in federal court to stop the racially motivated strike.

Similar work stoppages by the building trades unions to prevent the employment of blacks on other publicly funded construction projects took place during this period at the Cleveland Municipal Mall, at the U.S. Mint project in Philadelphia, and at the building site of the New York City Terminal Market. These cases together with similar conflicts in many other cities led to extensive litigation in federal courts.[181]

As might have been expected from their history, the construction unions repeatedly resisted, evaded, and in some cases, defied the law, and it is not surprising that the first contempt citation issued by a federal court under Title VII was against a construction labor union, Local 189 of the Plumbers Union in Columbus, Ohio. Local 46 of the Lathers Union and Local 28, Sheet Metal Workers, both in New York City, were among the other construction unions held in contempt after violating agreements with the government to cease and desist in their racist practices.[182]

Instead of calling for compliance with civil rights laws and federal executive orders to eliminate the nationwide pattern of discrimination in the construction industry, the AFL–CIO and its affiliated building trades unions proposed voluntary "hometown plans," based on a variety of training activities and so-called outreach programs under union control. These plans were intended as a substitute for federal contract compliance and the enforcement of civil rights laws in the construction industry. They were vigorously pressed by the AFL–CIO as the alternative to government-imposed plans containing mandatory hiring goals and timetables.

The first, most publicized, hometown plan went into effect in Chicago in 1970, and by April 1971, the U.S. Department of Labor had approved and funded hometown plans for ninety-three cities. But years later it was evident that the hometown plans changed virtually nothing for black workers in the construction industry. On July 2, 1974, the U.S. Labor Department reported that 101 local construction unions had failed to make a "good faith effort" to meet the minimal requirements of their hometown plans.[183] By 1976, most of these plans were in great disarray and had ceased to function, and the U.S. Labor Department eventually phased out the entire program.[184]

The hometown plans made it possible for construction unions and contractors to violate with impunity the legal prohibitions against employment discrimination, and their history also calls attention to the contradictory role of government agencies in civil rights enforcement. In several cities where the U.S. Justice Department had initiated litigation against building trades unions for violation of Title VII, the U.S. Department of Labor had declared these very same labor organizations to be in compliance with the law by virtue of their participation in a hometown plan. The evidence in Chicago, Pittsburgh, San Francisco, New York, Boston, Atlanta, and in many other cities reveals that hometown plans and apprenticeship outreach programs did not eliminate or even diminish discriminatory job patterns in the building trades. Measured even by their own very limited expectations, they failed. In a survey of the Washington, D.C., plan, for example, the *Washington Post*, in an article subtitled "10 Year Effort Fails to Alter Racial Ratio in the Trades," concluded that "the white men's unions of 1970 remain the white men's unions of the 1980s."[185]

The conclusion is inescapable. Apprenticeship outreach programs, after more than twenty years of operation, have failed to eliminate the discriminatory racial pattern in the building trades; they have served the interests of restrictive labor unions but not the interests of blacks and other minority workers. Indeed, the data reveal that the present system of apprenticeship training constitutes an additional and formidable barrier to black workers. In *United States* v. *Local 638, Steamfitters*, the district court stated: "This practice of admitting whites by informal standards and without reference to apprenticeship programs while denying such admission to non-whites is discriminatory and unlawful."[186]

While there has been an overall increase during the past decade in nonwhite participation in apprenticeship training, there has been little change in the percentages of black journeymen admitted into unions controlling employment in the skilled occupations. Black construction workers remain concentrated in unskilled laborers' jobs, among carpenters, and in the trowel trades. Apprenticeship training is obviously not an end in itself. It is meaningful only if it leads to skilled employment and union membership, and it has failed to do so for most blacks seeking to enter the crafts.

The landmark decision of the U.S. Supreme Court on July 2, 1986, involving Local 28 of the Sheetmetal Workers Union,[187] in which the Court advanced affirmative action as an appropriate legal remedy, was a further development in almost four decades of struggle to end the overt racist practices of this union, which controls all hiring in its craft jurisdiction in New York City. Other cases involving unions in the building trades have a similar history, and after years of litigation are still pending in federal courts. Among these, for example, is *Commonwealth of Pennsylvania and Williams* v. *Operating Engineers, Local 542*,[188] in Philadelphia, where the black plaintiffs have returned to the courts thirty-one times to obtain fundamental rights guaranteed in the law. It tells much about race and the distribution of political power among contending groups in American society that labor unions in the construction industry have succeeded in maintaining the racial status quo.

Through the collective bargaining process organized labor has played a major role in institutionalizing discriminatory practices in many trades and industries. Labor–management agreements covering both craft and industrial jobs frequently codified and structured discriminatory racial patterns. As a result of codification in union agreements, especially in provisions relating to seniority and job-assignment practices, casual, informal discrimination in employment became more rigid and enforceable. It is for these reasons that a substantial body of litigation under Title VII of the Civil Rights Act involves unions as defendants or codefendants with employers in Title VII cases.

The United Steelworkers of America and other industrial unions that were formed by the CIO have repeatedly been found responsible for unlawful discriminatory practices by federal courts in both northern and southern states. In reporting the decision of a U.S. District Court in a 1973 steel industry case, the *New York Times* stated that "the system kept some lines of work reserved for black workers and some for white. The meanest, hottest, lowest-paying jobs, unsurprisingly, were generally reserved for the blacks."[189] Although black workers over a period of many years repeatedly protested the role of the Steelworkers Union in perpetuating discriminatory patterns,[190] the international union refused to modify contractual provisions resulting in segregated job lines until such practices were eliminated by federal court orders.[191]

Black workers were involved in early CIO organizing campaigns in the steel industry and played a most important role in the unionization of basic steel, but decades later their position in the industry was still uniformly inferior to that of white workers. A confidential survey by the Steelworkers Union in 1964 of the status of blacks in unionized steel plants in Youngstown, Ohio, described the disparity in the job status of white and black steelworkers and concluded that

given the same seniority and education, the white employee's chances for advancement are substantially greater than are the Negro's and this is true at all levels of seniority, at all levels of education, and at all job levels. Furthermore, each of the tables reveals that a white employee with little or no formal education has a better opportunity for advancement than a Negro high school graduate.

According to a study of black employment in the basic steel industry of Pittsburgh, made for the EEOC and released in April, 1968:

Negroes comprise 12.27 percent of the laborers, 12.93 percent of the service workers, and 10.86 percent of the semiskilled operatives, but only 3.21 percent of the craftsmen. They are, therefore, almost twofold over-represented in the lowest classification and equally disproportionately under-represented in the most skilled blue-collar work.[192]

This pattern was the result not of occasional acts of racial malevolence but rather the direct consequence of seniority and job-promotion provisions in collective bargaining agreements negotiated by the Steelworkers Union. It was typical of the status of black workers in many unionized industries.

In the decade between the 1955 merger of the AFL and the CIO and 1965, when Title VII of the Civil Rights Act went into effect, the federation and its affiliated unions had the opportunity to eliminate widespread patterns of racial discrimination within labor organizations. They could have taken seriously the complaints filed by black workers and the reports of civil rights agencies, and they could have responded by initiating a vigorous program of internal reform on racial problems and moved against recalcitrant local unions. But instead they treated the issue as a public relations problem.[193] As a result, when Title VII went into effect, labor unions were inundated with lawsuits and repeatedly, over a period of many years, they joined with employers against their own black union members in an effort to perpetuate discriminatory job practices, even though the federal courts had declared such practices to be unlawful.

Once Title VII went into effect, black workers who were members of industrial unions filed many charges with the EEOC and initiated lawsuits in the federal courts against the unions to which they belonged because they had learned that what exclusion was to the craft unions, separate lines of job promotion and seniority were to the industrial unions. These issues have been the subject of extensive litigation in the federal courts.

Typical of the many cases involving the United Steelworkers and other industrial unions was the 1970 decision of a federal court that found the union and the Bethlehem Steel Corporation in Lackawanna, New York, to be in violation of the law. The court stated that:

The pervasiveness and longevity of the overt discriminatory hiring and job assignment practices, admitted by Bethlehem and the union, compel the conclusion that the present seniority and transfer provisions were based on past discriminatory classifications. . . . Job assignment practices were reprehensible. Over 80 percent of black workers were placed in eleven departments which contained the hotter and dirtier jobs in the plant. Blacks were excluded from higher paying and cleaner jobs.[194]

Observing that discriminatory contract provisions were embodied in nationwide master agreements negotiated by the international union in 1962, 1965, and 1968, the court also noted that "The Lackawanna plant was a microcosm of classic job discrimination in the North, making clear why Congress enacted Title VII of the Civil Rights Act of 1964."[195]

On October 14, 1971, the court's decree defined as members of the affected class some sixteen hundred black steelworkers; entitling them to receive benefits as a result of the court's decision. It is significant that in the *Bethlehem Steel* case, the U.S. Court of Appeals for the Second Circuit stated that the job expectations of whites were based on past union seniority practices that

arise from an illegal system. . . . Moreover, their seniority advantages are not indefeasibly vested rights but mere expectations derived from a bargaining agreement subject to modification. . . . If relief under Title VII can be denied merely because the majority group of employees, who have not suffered discrimination, will be unhappy about it, there will be little hope of correcting the wrongs to which the Act is directed.[196]

Federal courts repeatedly found the Steelworkers Union guilty of violating Title VII, and in 1974, the union and major employers in basic steel manufacturing negotiated an industrywide consent decree in an effort to obtain immunity from future lawsuits brought by black steelworkers, especially since the courts were ordering extensive changes in union contracts and awarding substantial monetary relief to black plaintiffs. But the attempt to ward off judicial intervention in the racial practices of the steel industry only partially succeeded as litigation continued. Among the cases initiated after the consent decree was the class action race discrimination suit against the Steelworkers Union and the Lukens Steel Co. of Coatesville, Pennsylvania. In this case the U.S. Court of Appeals for the Third Circuit found that the union had violated both Title VII and the Civil Rights Act of 1866 by failing in the "affirmative duty . . . to combat discrimination in the workplace" by not processing grievances involving race.[197]

In addition to the Steelworkers Union, many other unions were defendants in employment discrimination cases under Title VII. Such litigation involved labor organizations in papermaking and communications, in the tobacco industry, in aircraft and automotive manufacturing (both the United Auto Workers [UAW] and the International Association of Machinists), in longshore, in public utilities, and in the transportation industry, among others. The U.S. Court of Appeals for the Fifth Circuit, for example, ruled that a union seniority system in the railroad industry that had been developed through fifty years of collective bargaining agreements was not immune to remedial measures intended to provide relief to black workers. In *U.S. v. Jacksonville Terminal Co.*,[198] the court held that work rules and other provisions in union contracts in the railroad industry were no less susceptible to court-ordered remedies and relief from racial discrimination than those in other industries. According to the appellate court, union agreements do not "carry the authoritative imprimatur and moral force of sacred scripture, or even of mundane legislation." Furthermore, in the legal context of Title VII, the railroad industry and its labor unions could not be deemed "a state within a state."[199] Appellate courts expanded the definition of unlawful seniority and job-promotion practices and provided extensive relief to black workers in a great number of cases involving many industries and unions.

In 1961, the U.S. Commission on Civil Rights, in a survey of black employment in the automotive industry, reported on manufacturing operations where the United Auto Workers Union was the collective bargaining agent:

In Detroit Negroes constituted a substantial proportion—from 20 to 30 percent—of the total work force, but . . . their representation in 'nontraditional' jobs was slight. . . . In Baltimore, each of the companies employed Negroes only in production work and not above the semiskilled level . . . in Atlanta, the two automobile assembly plants employed no Negroes in assembly operations. Except for one driver of an inside power truck, all Negro employees observed were engaged in janitorial work—sweeping, mopping, or carrying away trash.[200]

The Skilled Trades Department of the UAW had long been a "lily-white" enclave within the union as were the jobs classified under its jurisdiction in the industry. According to data presented at hearings of the U.S. Commission on Civil Rights in 1960, black workers constituted .07 percent of the skilled labor force in Detroit auto plants.[201] Of 289 workers in the automotive apprenticeship training program in the Detroit area, 1 was black.[202]

In response to increasing protest from its black membership, the UAW in 1963 conducted a survey to provide the union "with some impressions of the degree of progress being made with respect to the non-white membership."[203] The union's own report showed that within the UAW only 12.9 percent of the production workers surveyed were nonwhite, while only 1.4 percent of the membership in skilled trades were nonwhite. It found that out of twenty-nine states responding to the survey, only eight had a few nonwhite apprentices in training. Twenty states surveyed did not have a single nonwhite apprentice. It also found that 94.5 percent of all workers enrolled in either employee-in-training programs or employee-upgrading programs were white. Furthermore, the union's survey found only 54 nonwhite apprentices out of a total of 1,958 participating in the UAW's joint labor–management programs.[204]

By 1970, most large manufacturing plants within Detroit had black majorities. The former chief union steward at the Chrysler Jefferson-Kercheval plant (with 7,638 workers, the second largest Chrysler manufacturing facility) reported that in 1972, 65 percent of the UAW's membership in the plant were black.[205] A similar pattern was developing throughout the Detroit area, the heart of the UAW. By the spring of 1972, eleven UAW locals in Detroit had black presidents, and more than half of the Chrysler locals within the city had black majorities. Sixty-five to 70 percent of the more than 4,000 UAW members at the Eldon Gear and Axle workers were black, and in excess of 60 percent of the production workers at the Dodge main plant were black.

Significant black increases also occurred in some UAW locals outside of Michigan. For example, at the Ford plant in Mahwah, New Jersey, 21 percent of all workers were black in 1958. In 1970, blacks comprised more than 40 percent of the labor force.[206] Malcolm Denise, vice president for labor relations of the Ford Motor Company, stated, "Whatever some may feel about the black issue in general, we are in fact dependent, and will continue to be, on black people to make this company go."[207] Despite the dramatic increases in the black labor force within Detroit auto plants during the 1960s and early 1970s,[208] the EEOC found that in 1975, blacks were still concentrated in lower-level jobs.[209]

In the first nine years after Title VII went into effect, 1,335 charges were filed by members of the UAW with the EEOC against the union,[210] and throughout the 1970s and 1980s, the UAW continued to be a defendant in Title VII litigation initiated by its own nonwhite membership. Typical of these cases was the lawsuit filed in 1973 by black UAW members against the General Motors Corporation, Detroit Diesel Allison Division, the UAW International Union, and its Local 933 in Indianapolis.[211] The black plaintiffs charged both the company and the union with violating Title VII in regard to sex and race discrimination.

In an earlier period the UAW had supported the movement of blacks into assembly line jobs,[212] but by the 1950s the patterns of employment segregation had become rigid, and the union failed to attack the racial practices of the skilled trades. As the Reuther leadership consolidated its power and the internal political life of the UAW became increasingly monolithic, the position and influence of blacks within the union sharply declined. By the late 1950s, black discontent within the UAW began to emerge publicly with the organization of black caucuses and racial protest groups that repeatedly attacked the racism of both employers and union. The racial occupational pattern, the failure of the UAW to attack discriminatory practices, and the lack of black representation in policy-making positions within the union caused black workers in several major Detroit auto plants and elsewhere to engage in factory shutdowns and "wildcat" strikes led by such groups as the Dodge Revolutionary Union Movement (DRUM) and the League of Revolutionary Black Workers.[213] Extensive racial protest activities within the union led to the election in 1962 of Nelson "Jack" Edwards, the first black member of the UAW executive board, followed by the advancement of other blacks into leadership positions. The emergence of independent black caucuses within the UAW and other industrial unions in the late 1950s representing a broad spectrum of political beliefs was a significant development in the historical continuum of racial protest activities within industrial unions by black workers. In retrospect, it is evident that industrial unions, as well as craft unions, tend to institutionalize the racial status quo, while the basic premise of contemporary civil rights laws, and of black aspirations, is that the racial status quo must be altered.

Those industrial unions with a predominantly white membership that were controlled for many years by leaders loyal to the Communist party were substantively no different in their racial practices than other labor organizations. One such example was Local 1111 of the United Electrical, Radio, and Machine Workers Union. In 1968, the civil rights movement attacked one of Milwaukee's oldest and largest employers, the Allen-Bradley Company, which held lucrative federal government contracts and was well known for its racist employment practices. The company's overt policy of maintaining a virtually all-white labor force, against which mass demonstrations by local civil rights organizations were organized, led to intervention by the federal government. (Of 6,888 workers employed in 1964, 4 were black.[214]) The Allen-Bradley case received national attention and became a landmark in the history of federal contract compliance efforts.[215] On August 14, 1968, more than six hundred marchers wound their way through Milwaukee's streets towards the heavily guarded gates of Allen-Bradley's huge manufacturing facility. As the demonstrators, mainly black and Hispanic, marched through ethnic working-class neighborhoods, hostile crowds of whites threw rocks and bottles and shouted racist epithets. The police did little to protect the marchers, and according to newspaper reports, serious violence was averted only after the police department cordoned off an area and permitted the marchers to gather at the plant gates.[216]

In response to a government investigation and hearings held by the U.S. Department of Labor, as required by federal contract cancellation procedures, the company argued that any step to hire minority group members would mean preferential hiring of unqualified people and would violate seniority principles. The hearing panel found abundant evidence of systematic discrimination over a period of many years, and in an emphatic recommendation to the secretary of labor, urged that all government contracts with the Allen-Bradley Company be cancelled. After much delay and further negotiations, the company finally agreed to a series of remedial measures to comply with federal regulations and staved off the cancellation.[217]

What is most interesting about this case is that Local 1111, the recognized union holding collective bargaining rights at this plant, had repeatedly, over a thirty-year period, negotiated union contracts with Allen-Bradley without once making inquiry into the racial employment policies of the company. Why this union not only permitted the company to maintain a "lily-white" labor force, but was in fact a party to such practices is revealed in a letter to the *Milwaukee Sentinel* from a worker who explained that the union at Allen-Bradley "encouraged hiring policies under which the sons and nephews of union members were brought into the company before others were considered . . . this type of union hiring policy naturally excluded the vast majority of Negroes and Latin American residents of the area."[218] At this plant, as in so many others in industries across the nation, the union operated an effective network providing information about vacancies and access to jobs within ethnic working-class communities. The union functioned on behalf of white workers to protect their privileged position in initial hiring, and through the application of seniority, to maintain preferential access to job advancement.

Local 1111, founded in 1937, was one of the oldest and largest local units of the United Electrical, Radio, and Machine Workers, a union founded and dominated for many years by the trade union apparatus of the Communist party. The UE routinely passed resolutions denouncing discrimination, as did some other industrial unions, but these were part of an empty ritual rarely transformed into practice at the workplace. In September 1949, the leadership of the United Electrical Workers, anticipating the expulsion of communist-controlled unions from the CIO, disaffiliated from the CIO; the CIO expelled several such unions at its convention in November of 1949.

The pattern of discrimination at the Allen-Bradley Co. in Milwaukee was not exceptional. Other unions whose leaders had a long association with the Communist party were defendants in actions brought by black workers under Title VII of the Civil Rights Act. Among the most important of such cases were the charges filed in 1967 against the International Longshoremen's and Warehousemen's Union (ILWU) whose president was Harry Bridges.[219] In their lawsuit, black longshoremen charged that the ILWU in Portland, Oregon, used the union referral system to exclude blacks from desirable jobs as checkers and clerks (a pattern repeated in many other cities). This case demonstrates how labor unions, in this instance the ILWU, delayed relief to black workers for extensive periods by introducing complex legal challenges of a procedural nature. Although the union was eventually forced to alter its racial practices, it succeeded in postponing change on the Portland waterfront for a decade by creating delays in the courts.

On November 2, 1967, the first charge of racial discrimination was served on the ILWU. For the next seven years, the international union, together with its local affiliate and the employers association, succeeded in preventing the courts from considering the merits of the case. After a lower-court finding on procedural issues, the case was appealed to the U.S. Court of Appeals for the Ninth Circuit, which in June 1972 reversed and remanded. In November 1974, the black workers filed for a new trial, alleging falsification of records; the motion was denied, and the plaintiffs again appealed to the circuit court. In November 1976, the appeals court reversed and remanded, having found that black workers who attacked the system of hiring at the port had established a prima facie case of discrimination in violation of Title VII. (On the record the union's business agent "admitted the existence of racial discrimination prior to October 1967."[220]) Ten years after the filing of the original charge, this case was finally tried on the substantive issue of racial discrimination, and the ILWU was ordered to eliminate its discriminatory practices.

A close observer of the West Coast longshoremen's union writes that "despite the policy of the national union, reaffirmed in convention resolutions time after time . . . as recently as the sixties there were ports on the coast where for days you could watch ships being loaded without once seeing a black longshoreman. In some, a remote lumber port up in the Northwest like Coos Bay, you might believe the explanation that the port was all-white because there weren't any Blacks in the community. But in others—Portland and Los Angeles, for example—the lily-white labor force was obviously the product of a policy of exclusion."[221]

In conclusion, in reviewing the attacks upon affirmative action, it is necessary to note the argument of those who state that they are not against affirmative action, only against "quotas." Affirmative action without numbers, whether in the form of quotas, goals, or timetables, is meaningless; there must be some benchmark, some tangible measure of change. Statistical evidence to measure performance is essential. Not to use numbers is to revert to the era of symbolic gesture or, at best, "tokenism." When all the rhetoric about "reverse discrimination" and "quotas" is stripped away, it is clear that the opposition to affirmative action is in fact the continuing effort to perpetuate the privileged position of whites in American society.

White ethnic groups and labor unions frequently argue that affirmative action programs will penalize innocent whites who are not responsible for past discriminatory practices. This argument turns on the notion of individual rights and sounds very moral and highminded. But it ignores social reality. As has been demonstrated in many lawsuits, nonwhites have been denied jobs, training, and advancement not as individuals but as a class, no matter what their personal merit and qualification. Wherever discriminatory employment patterns exist, hiring and promotion without affirmative action perpetuate the old injustice.

It is significant that two historically interrelated groups, certain white ethnics and much of organized labor, have been in the forefront of the attacks against affirmative action.[222] Both vigorously oppose the most effective approach to eliminate employment practices that continue to victimize the nonwhite population. Yet before the emergence of affirmative action remedies, the legal prohibitions against job discrimination were for the most part declarations of abstract morality. Pronouncements of public policy such as state and municipal fair employment practice laws were mainly symbolic, and the patterns of job discrimination remained intact. Because affirmative action programs go beyond individual relief to attack long-established patterns of discrimination and, if vigorously enforced by government agencies over a sustained period, can become a major instrument for social change, they have come under powerful and repeated attack. As long as Title VII litigation was concerned largely with procedural and conceptual issues, only limited attention was given to the consequences of remedies. However, once affirmative action was widely applied and the focus of litigation shifted to the adoption of affirmative action plans, entrenched interests were threatened. And as the gains of the 1960s were eroded, the nation became more mean spirited and self-deceiving.

Racism in the history of the United States has not been an aberration. It has been systematized and structured into the functioning of the society's most fundamental institutions. In the present as in the past, it is widely accepted as a basis for promoting the interests of whites. For many generations the assumptions of white supremacy were codified in the law, imposed by custom, and often enforced by violence. While the forms have changed, the legacy of white supremacy is expressed in the continuing patterns of racial discrimination; for the vast majority of black and other nonwhite people, race and racism remain the decisive factors in their lives.

The nineteenth-century European migrations to the United States took place during the long age of blatant white supremacy, legal and extralegal, formal and informal. As the patterns of segregation and discrimination emerged North and South, the doors of opportunity were opened to white immigrants but closed to blacks and other non-whites. European immigrants and their descendants explain their success as the result of their devotion to the work ethic, ignoring a variety of other factors, such as the systematic exclusion of non-Caucasians from competition for employment. As white immigrants moved up in the social order, black workers and those of other nonwhite races could fill only the least desirable places in a marginal secondary labor market, the only places open to them.

The romanticized histories of the struggles of white immigrants and their labor unions repeatedly ignore the racial aspects of that history, neglecting the fact that white immigrants were labor competitors with blacks, that whites used labor organizations to exclude nonwhite workers from the primary labor force in many industries, and that they had the advantage of being white in a social order of racial subordination.

The current conflict over affirmative action is not simply an argument about abstract rights or ethnic bigotry. In the final analysis it is an argument between those who insist upon the substance of a long-postponed break with the traditions of American racism and those groups that insist upon maintaining the valuable privileges and benefits they now enjoy as a consequence of that dismal history.

Notes

1. Blumer 1965, 220–253.
2. Thernstrom 1980, 538.
3. For statistical data see Van Tine 1973, 9–28; Rosenblum 1973, 67–86. For an interesting discussion of the ethnic composition of Chicago's working class in 1890, see Keil 1983.
4. Rauh 1987, 5.
5. See U.S. Senate 1963, 151–152; Rustin 1971, 80. The Civil Rights Resolution adopted by the Eighth AFL–CIO Convention, October 1969, refers to "pockets of discrimination" (Publication no. 8F, 1969, Washington, D.C., unpaged).
6. At the end of its second year the EEOC stated that "in various Commission decisions during the fiscal year, certain broad principles were articulated which are applicable to a determination of whether a seniority system meets the requirements of section 703(h): (1). A seniority system which has the intent or effect of perpetuating past discrimination is not a bona fide seniority system within the meaning of section 703(h) of Title VII. (2). The fact that a seniority system is the product of collective bargaining does not compel the conclusion that it is a *bona fide* system." (*EEOC Second Annual Report*, June 1, 1968, 43). This approach was accepted by many courts in seniority cases for more than a decade. The Supreme Court in its decisions in *Moody* v. *Albemarle Paper Company*, 442 U.S. 405, 10 FEP Cases 1181 (1975), involving the Paperworkers Union, and *Franks* v. *Bowman Transportation Co.*, 424 U.S. 747, 12 FEP Cases 549 (1976), involving the Steel Workers Union, expanded the definition of unlawful seniority and provided extensive relief to black workers. See also *James* v. *Stockham Valves and Fittings Co.*, 559 F.2d 310, 15 FEP Cases 827 5th Cr. (1977).
7. Gould 1977, 72.
8. Ibid., 21.
9. See author's interview with Joseph L. Rauh, January 4, 1973, Washington, D.C., and 1968 letter to Rauh from Jack Greenberg, director-counsel, NAACP Legal Defense and Educational Fund, Inc., quoted in Hill 1977, 35–37.
10. During the congressional arguments on Title VII, proponents of the bill frequently invoked state fair employment practice acts. For example, Senator Leverett Saltonstall of Massachusetts, in discussing the relationship of conciliation to court enforcement of antidiscrimination laws, stated that "[i]n Massachusetts, we have had experience with an arrangement of this sort for 17 years; and, as I recall, approximately 4,700 unfair practices complaints have been brought before our Massachusetts Commission Against Discrimination. Only two of them have been taken to court for adjudication. One has been decided, and a second is now in court, but has not yet been decided. That procedure is the basis and theory of this part of the bill, and that is why I support it." 110 CONG. REC., 14, 191 (1964) reprinted in *EEOC, Legislative History*, 3311. Congressman Ogden R. Reid of New York, arguing for the passage of Title VII, placed in the record documentation showing the disposition of complaints filed with the New York State Commission on Human Rights from its inception and stated that "[f]rom 1945 to 1963—10,869 total complaints were filed—over 8,000 of these on employment—and the vast majority were settled voluntarily by conference, conciliation, and persuasion. Of the same 1 percent that finally went to public hearings only 12 today are still pending." 110 CONG. REC., 1635 (1964) reprinted in *EEOC, Legislative History*, 3346.
11. AFL–CIO press release, Washington, D.C., January 31, 1964.
12. Industrial Union Department, AFL–CIO, Legislative Alert, Washington, D.C., May 1964.
13. "Civil Rights: Fact vs. Fiction," Civil Rights Department, AFL–CIO, Washington, D.C., 1964.

14. 279 F. Supp. 505, 1 FEP 260 (E.D.VA. 1968).

15. 416, F.2d 980, 1 FEP 875 (5th Cir. 1969), cert. denied, 379 U.S. 919 (1970).

16. 665 F.2d 1057, 26 FEP 1151 (D.C. Cir. 1981) cert. granted, 455 U.S. 1015 (1982), 453 U.S. 902 (1983), Brief amicus curiae of the AFL–CIO.

17. Gompers 1925, 51–152, 161, 378.

18. Eaves 1910, 386.

19. Quoted from document in the archives of the California Historical Society, San Francisco, n.d. This material was not catalogued. A later version of the label is reproduced in Cross 1935, 172.

20. Eaves 1910, 386; Lorwin 1933, 367.

21. See Commons et al. 1918, 301–315.

22. Saxton 1971, 216.

23. For a detailed account, see Saxton 1971, 213–218.

24. Report of the Proceedings of the Federation of Trades and Labor Unions, 1881, 22.

25. Perlman 1922, 62. See also Commons 1907, 1-7, 141; Taft 1968, 166–188; Taft 1964, 301–304.

26. In California in 1860, the Chinese were 9 percent of the population; in 1870, 8.6 percent, and 1880, 7.5 percent. In 1882 when the Chinese Exclusion Act was passed, the total Chinese population in the United States was 105,465, with 71 percent living in California (U.S. Bureau of the Census 1982). Between 1870 and 1920 the combined Chinese and Japanese population in the United States never exceeded more than one-fifth of one percent of the total population. For data on the geographical distribution of the Chinese population in 1870 and 1880, see U.S. Bureau of the Census, 1882, 379. The Exclusion Law of 1882 drastically reduced the Chinese population. Since there were few Chinese females in the United States, the continued existence of the Chinese population depended on new immigrants. While the population of the nation and of California increased very rapidly after 1880, the Chinese population steadily declined. From 105,465 Chinese in the United States in 1880, their number had dropped to 90,000 in 1900 and by 1910 more than half of the male Chinese population in California were 45 years of age or older. On the issue of Chinese labor competition with whites in California, Mary R. Coolidge (1909, 399) concludes "that such Chinese competition as there was, was slight in degree and affected only a very small number of white wage workers." For detailed Chinese immigration statistics, see pp. 498–500 of Coolidge's book.

27. U.S. Bureau of the Census 1872. For additional data, see Coolidge 1909; Ping Chiu 1963; Lyman 1970.

28. Saxton 1971, 104–112.

29. See Somma 1952.

30. Ibid., 464–472.

31. Ibid., 30–39.

32. Gompers and his fellow labor leaders were to continue this activity into the twentieth century. His most comprehensive statement on the subject appeared in a pamphlet of which he was co-author entitled Some Reasons for Chinese Exclusion: Meat vs. Rice, American Manhood Against Asiatic Coolieism, Which Shall Survive? This was published by the AFL in 1901 and was brought out again in 1908. Gompers and his co-author, Herman Guttstadt, a representative of the Cigar Maker's Union in San Francisco, wrote that "the racial differences between American whites and Asiatics would never be overcome." The superior whites had to exclude the inferior Asiatics by law, or if necessary, "by force of arms." The Chinese were congenitally immoral: "The Yellow Man found it natural to lie, cheat, and murder and ninety-nine out of every one hundred Chinese are gamblers." According to Gompers, the Asiatic people were lecherous, loved to live in filthy surrounding and damp cellars, and thus the "instinct of the race remains unchanged." Although the Chinese servant may work faithfully in an "American household," explained Gompers, "he joyfully hastens back to his slum and his burrow to the grateful luxury of his normal surroundings—vice, filth, and an atmosphere of horror." Gompers conjures up a horrifying picture of how the Chinese entice white boys and girls into becoming "opium fiends." Condemned

to spend their lives in the backrooms of laundries, these lost souls are forced to yield their bodies to maniacal yellow men. "What other crimes were committed in these dark and fetid places," Gompers writes, "when the little innocent victims of the Chinamen's wiles were under the influence of the drug, are almost too horrible to imagine." Gompers is certain that where miscegenation has occurred, "the offspring have been invariably degenerate," that "the issue of Caucasian and Mongolian does not possess the virtues of either." He warns that the "peaceful invasion" of the United States by "Asiatic barbarians" is underway. History, Gompers reminds his readers, has given Americans an awesome responsibility. It is nothing less than to keep "our inheritance . . . pure and uncontaminated . . . we are the trustees for mankind." The 1904 AFL convention made a special point of condemning the "Japanese and all . . . Asiatics." (*Proceedings*, American Federation of Labor, 1904, 7–8). The pages of the *American Federationist* were full of alarums and excursions about the "Jap menace." In one notable instance (May 1904 issue of the *American Federationist*), Gompers denounced the Japanese socialist, Sen Katayama, then visiting the United States, as "this presumptuous Jap" with a "leprous mouth whose utterances show this mongrel's perverseness, ignorance and maliciousness."

33. Saxton 1971, 104.
34. *American Federationist* (February 1898): 269–271.
35. Ibid.
36. Ibid.
37. Gompers to Will H. Winn, January 19, 1898. (Material cited from archival correspondence is taken from Mandel 1955.)
38. F. L. McGruder to Gompers, October 4, 1899.
39. *American Federationist* (May 1899): 57.
40. Ibid., (September 1905): 636.
41. Ibid., 636–637.
42. Ibid., (January 1911): 34–37.
43. Gompers 1925, 160.
44. Stoddard 1920; Grant 1916.
45. Quoted in Kipnis 1952, 276–286.
46. Quoted in Foner 1947, 59.
47. Boudin 1908, 491.
48. King 1908, 661.
49. Ibid., 662.
50. Ibid., 669.
51. The literature on the black workers' experience with white organized labor during this period is extensive. Among the most important works are Du Bois 1902; Du Bois with Dill 1912; Wesley 1927; Spero and Harris 1931; Greene and Woodson 1930. For a critical study of some prevailing views, see Hill 1988.
52. Durham 1898, 222.
53. Ibid., 224.
54. Ibid., 225.
55. Ibid., 227. This pattern in Washington, D.C., similar to the national pattern of black exclusion from the printing craft unions and the printing industry, remained in effect until 1982 when unions and employers entered into a consent decree to cease discriminatory practices and develop a racially integrated labor force. See Consent Order, *EEOC* v. *Printing Industry of Metropolitan Washington, D.C., et. al.*, Civil Action No. 80–3213 (D.D.C.), January 19, 1982. This settlement was in response to a lawsuit filed in 1980 charging eight unions in the printing industry and fifty-four employers with discriminatory practices in violation of Title VII of the Civil Rights Act of 1964.
56. Ibid., 228.
57. Ibid., 230.
58. See Barron 1971.
59. *Sixteenth Annual Report of the Commission on Labor, Strikes and Lockouts* (Washington, D.C., 1901), 413–465.
60. *Locomotive Firemen's Magazine* (December 1890): 1094.

61. "The Georgia Railroad Strike," *Outlook*, June 5, 1909, 310; cited in Spero and Harris 1931, n. 42. 289.

62. Spero and Harris 1931, 291.

63. See Houston 1949; "Elimination of Negro Firemen on American Railroads" 1944; Hill 1985, 343–372.

64. Mitchell 1936.

65. Ibid.

66. See Worthman 1971, 185.

67. See Thernstrom 1973, 186–187.

68. Constitution of the Brotherhood of Railway Carmen of America, 1890, section 6, clause a.

69. U.S. Bureau of Labor Statistics 1929, 208.

70. Ibid., 104.

71. The meaning of the elimination in 1871 of Article IX, the exclusion clause in the constitution of the Cigar Makers' Union, is explained in *The Working Man's Advocate* (November 25, 1871): 1.

72. Wolfe 1912, 114.

73. *Proceedings*, AFL Convention, 1900, 12–13; see also 22–23, 117, 129.

74. U.S. Bureau of Labor Statistics 1929, 55.

75. Constitution of the Amalgamated Sheet Metal Workers International Alliance, article IV, section I, 1918.

76. *Electrical World* (April 1903): 102.

77. *American Federationist* (September 1905): 636.

78. Ibid., (August 1906): 534.

79. A copy of the union's constitution was introduced into evidence at *A Hearing To Hear Evidence On Complaints Of Racial Discrimination In Employment On Certain Railroads Of The United States*, President's Committee On Fair Employment Practices, Washington, D.C., September 15–18, 1943, p. 412, Record Group 228, Preliminary Inventory No. 147, Records of the FEPC, National Archives, Washington, D.C.

80. Constitution—Revisions and Amendments, presented at the First Annual Convention, Brotherhood of Railroad Brakemen of the Western Hemisphere, Oneonta, N.Y., October 20–25, 1884, Constitution of Subordinate Lodges, article 2, membership section 1, 9.

81. Constitution of the Brotherhood of Locomotive Firemen and Enginemen, 1906, section 162, 77–78.

82. Ibid., 1925, article 12, section 22(b), 158–159.

83. Ibid., 1937, article 13, section 22(b), 127.

84. Constitution—Revisions and Amendments, 1884. (See n. 80 above.)

85. Houston 1949, 269.

86. See *Brotherhood of Locomotive Firemen and Enginemen's Magazine* (June 15, 1917): 9, and (August 15, 1917): 11–12.

87. Houston 1949, 269.

88. See Auerbach 1961.

89. See, for example, Axtell 1948; Weintraub 1959; Taylor 1923; Goldberg 1957.

90. See Auerbach 1961, 347.

91. Ibid., 355.

92. *Seamen's Journal* (February 1929): 35.

93. See Hill 1985, 218–234.

94. Reid 1930, 38.

95. Quoted in Spero and Harris 1931, 477–478.

96. Commons 1907, 7, 39–62.

97. Saxton 1971, 269.

98. Kusmer 1976, 68–73.

99. Data given in Woodward 1951, 361.

100. U.S. Department of Commerce 1920, 27.

101. See Ovington 1906; Speed 1900; Tucker 1908; American Academy of Political and Social Science 1913; Baker 1907–1908.

102. See Wolfe 1912, 100–112.
103. Quoted in Kusmer 1976, 70.
104. *New York Age*, May 16, 1891, 1.
105. *The Colored American*, October 29, 1898, 1, and July 22, 1899, 1.
106. Ibid., May 23, 1903, 1.
107. Ibid., May 25, 1901, 1.
108. Ibid., October 18, 1902, 3.
109. See, for example, Du Bois 1917, 54; Haynes 1919, 170; Johnson 1927, 554–558.
110. Stouffer and Florant 1940, Chap. 1, 8; Florant 1942, 52; Woodson 1918.
111. Du Bois 1917, 54.
112. Asch 1946.
113. See Spero and Harris 1931, 337. For information on black workers in New York in the early 1900s, see Ovington 1911; Haynes 1912; Scheiner 1965, Chap. 2, 45–64; Bloch 1969, 97–115.
114. Among several studies are Scheiner 1965, 1–14, and Bloch 1969, 1–34. See also Johnson 1930; Osofsky 1966; Ottley and Weatherby 1967.
115. Bloch 1969, 107.
116. See Hill 1959, 1961, 1965.
117. For a detailed description of the restrictions on political activity within the union and of the eligibility requirements for union office, see Hill 1972a.
118. Interview with Daniel J. Schulder, president of the Association of Catholic Trade Unionists, New York, November 18, 1957, and examination of the data in the Association's files on this matter.
119. Braestrup 1958 (Oct. 8).
120. ILGWU *Report*, 30th Convention, 1959, 183; *Justice*, November 1, 1958, 2. See also Braestrup 1958 (Oct. 7).
121. Keyserling 1963.
122. Ibid., graphs 8A and 8C; see also graph 10E, Chap. 11A, and Chap. 12A.
123. Report of the General Executive Board to the 32nd Convention, ILGWU, Miami Beach, May 12, 1965.
124. U.S. Bureau of Labor Statistics 1966.
125. The shift in rank of average hourly earnings among industrial workers in Birmingham, Alabama, and New York City during the ten-year period from 1950 to 1960 was significant. In 1950 New York ranked tenth and Birmingham thirty-third among forty-six cities in relation to average hourly earnings of production workers. In 1960, New York City had fallen to thirtieth place and Birmingham was tenth. See U.S. Bureau of Labor Statistics 1962, 24, Table 6.
126. U.S. Bureau of the Census 1963.
127. U.S. Bureau of the Census 1973.
128. U.S. Bureau of the Census 1983. See also U.S. Equal Employment Opportunity Commission 1975a; U.S. Bureau of the Census 1978. For additional specialized data, see U.S. Bureau of Labor Statistics 1971; Jaco and Wilber 1975.
129. Among several accounts, see Myerson 1969; Witte 1962; Kempton 1962. See also Hill 1974a; Michaels n.d.
130. Statement of Joint Council 16, New York Locals of the International Brotherhood of Teamsters, May 1962.
131. This was not the first complaint filed with the New York State Commission against the ILGWU. In a 1946 case, (*Hunter* v. *Sullivan Dress Shop*, C-1439-46), a black woman charged that she was denied employment because of her race in jobs controlled by Local 89, the Italian Dressmakers unit of the ILGWU. Nationality based local unions became illegal in 1945 in New York under the State Anti-Discrimination Law. Title VII, the employment section of the Civil Rights Act of 1964, further required the elimination of such locals, and some unions moved to disband them. Although several labor organizations complied with state and federal law, the ILGWU continued to maintain two Italian locals in New York City: Local 89 designated as the Italian Dressmakers Union and Local 48 designated as the Italian Cloak Makers Union. According to the report of the General Executive Board of the ILGWU dated May 12,

1965, Local 89, the largest local in the international union, had a membership of 20,898 and Local 48 had a membership of 8,047 (pp. 116–122). After the state commission notified the ILGWU that the existence of nationality locals was a violation of state law, the union on January 27, 1947, entered into an agreement with the commission that it would not bar blacks, Spanish-speaking, or other persons from membership in the Italian locals. Despite the agreement, and in defiance of state and later federal law, the ILGWU maintained the two Italian locals for another three decades without a single black or Hispanic worker gaining membership in the two locals, which controlled access to some of the highest-paying jobs in the industry. In 1977, because of a declining Italian membership, the union finally eliminated the practice and restructured locals in the New York area. See *Report of the General Executive Board*, Thirty-Sixth Convention, International Ladies Garment Workers Union, 1977, p. 112.

132. *Holmes* v. *Falikman*, C-7580-61, New York State Commission for Human Rights, 1963.

133. *Holmes* v. *Falikman*, File, 1963, New York State Commission for Human Rights, (copy in author's files).

134. Tyler 1962, 7.

135. Ibid.

136. Tyler 1982, 173.

137. Herbert Hill, National Labor Secretary, NAACP, to Harry Fleishman, Director, National Labor Service, American Jewish Committee, October 23, 1962.

138. *Report* of the General Executive Board to the 32nd Convention, ILGWU, Miami Beach, Florida, May 12, 1965, p. 124.

139. Seldin 1962; see also Ferretti 1962.

140. In 1968, another version of black–Jewish conflict occurred involving the United Federation of Teachers in the Ocean Hill–Brownsville area of Brooklyn. The president of that union, Albert Shanker, who came out of a Jewish immigrant socialist background, used the issue of anti-Semitism as a response to black demands for decentralization and community control of public schools. Shanker was accused of circulating counterfeit anti-Semitic leaflets supposedly published by black community groups. His purpose was to provoke black–Jewish conflict, thereby stimulating support from the Jewish membership of the union and Jewish organizations during a strike called by the union. See Epstein 1968. According to Dwight Macdonald (1968), the United Federation of Teachers was doing "their best to increase fear and hatred driving Negro against Jew in this city." For a discussion of these issues see the exchange between Albert Shanker and Herbert Hill in Hall 1972, 218–235.

141. Polier to Zimmerman, December 7, 1962, Box 26, File 9, Zimmerman Collection, ILGWU Archives.

142. Cohen to Zimmerman, December 3, 1962, Box 26, File 9, Zimmerman Collection, ILGWU Archives.

143. Copy in author's files.

144. Mrs. Florence Rice, a black woman who was a member of Local 155, was warned earlier by a union official that if she gave testimony before the congressional committee she would never work again in the garment industry. She told the committee that "workers have been intimidated by union officials with threats of losing their jobs if they so much as appear at the hearing" (U.S. House 1962, 167). Soon after her appearance before the committee in open hearings, she was dismissed from her job and was not able to obtain employment thereafter as a garment worker. Mrs. Rice later became director of the Harlem Consumer Council and a community activist. Burton H. Hall, the attorney who represented the Rank and File Committee in the complaint filed with the U.S. Labor Department, described how the leaders of Local 10 and Local 155 conducted campaigns of intimidation and violence in their respective local union elections. (See Hall 1972). He also reports on the wage rates for union members in 1971 under contracts negotiated by Local 155: "The collective bargaining agreement currently in force between Knitgood Workers' Local 155 and the employers in New York City, New Jersey, and Long Island calls for weekly wages of $71.75 for

inspectors, hand sewers, finishers, crocheters, and floor girls, accounting for more than half the workers in the industry. Take-home pay is much lower, between $57 and $59 for a full week. Sweatshops have not disappeared; they are hiding behind an ILGWU union label" (Hall 1972, n. 1, 295).

145. Press release, Rank and File Committee of Local 155, February 24, 1971.

146. Fogel 1977.

147. Quoted in Caldwell 1983.

148. *Julio Huertas et al.* v. *East River Housing Corp. et al.*, U.S. District Court, Southern District of New York, 77 Civ. 4494 (RLC) 1977.

149. Interview with Frederic Seiden and Francis Goldin of the Lower East Side Joint Planning Council, New York, March 24–25, 1983. Sources that document the ILG-WU's role in financing and sponsoring the "$20,000,000 ILGWU Co-operative Village" are Danish 1957, 305–307; Dubinsky with Raskin 1977, 216–218; *Justice*, May 1, 1952, 1. See also Report of the General Executive Board to the 32nd ILGWU Convention, Miami Beach, May 12, 1965, 8.

150. U.S. District Court, Southern District of New York, Memorandum Opinion and Order, 78 Civ. 6000 (MJL), August 20, 1983.

151. The New York EEOC charges included charge TNY9-0648; TNY1-1413; 2-1463; 9-0059; and 1754. In charge YNK3-063, the International Union itself was a respondent. The charges filed outside of New York included Chicago (TCH8-0277); Kansas City, Mo. (TKC1-1101); Memphis (TME1-1091); San Francisco (TSF3-0853); Baltimore (TBA3-0084); Philadelphia (TPA2-0165); Cleveland (TCL1-0805); Atlanta (TATO-1245); Charlotte (TCT2-0468, 2-0043, 1-0002, 1-0004, 1-0006, 1-0008, 1-0010); and Birmingham (TB10-0954, 1-0357, 1-0195, 1-0873, 9-0098, 2-0875).

152. Glazer 1964, 32.

153. Ibid., 32–34.

154. See Seligman 1944; American Jewish Committee 1954; Helfgott 1961, 209.

155. Jacobs 1963, 116. In 1978, Local 23–25, with 25,000 members, was the largest local of the ILGWU in New York City, and its composition may be taken as a general indicator of demographic trends within the ILGWU membership. The membership of Local 23–25 was approximately 94 percent female and 6 percent male. Minorities represented 93 percent of this membership—94 percent of the overall female and 83 percent of the overall male population. Between 1972 and 1978, Asian membership increased by 349 percent, with a 16 percent increase in Hispanic members, and a 64 percent decrease in white union members. ("The Effects of Selected Union Policies . . . " 1981, 145–146). Two community activists, Peter Kwong and Jo Ann Lum, have described Local 23–25 of the ILGWU as "an ineffectual and decaying Union" (Kwong and Lum 1988, 314).

156. Glazer 1964, 32.

157. Glazer 1975, 186–187.

158. Ibid., 7, 28, 24.

159. Ibid., 7.

160. Ibid., 7.

161. 163 U.S. 537 (1896).

162. 347 U.S. 483 (1954).

163. Lieberson 1980, 383.

164. 407 F.2d 1047, 1 FEP 577 (5th Cir. 1969).

165. 328 F.Supp. 429, 3 FEP 457 (S.D.N.Y. 1971), *affirmed* 471 F.2d 408, 5 FEP 318 (2nd Cir.), *cert. denied*, 412 U.S. 939 (1973).

166. Ibid.

167. *Equal Employment Opportunity Commission, James D. Hodgson, Secretary of Labor, United States Department of Labor and United States of America* v. *American Telephone and Telegraph Company et al.* (Civil Action No. 73–149, January 18, 1973).

168. Supplemental Agreement, *Equal Employment Opportunity Commission, James D. Hodgson, Secretary of Labor, United States Department of Labor and United States of America* (Civil Action No. 73–149, May 13, 1975).

169. *EEOC* v. *American Tel. & Tel. Co.*, 556 F.2d 167, 14 FEP 1210 (3rd Cir. 1977), *cert. denied*, 438 U.S. 915 (1978).

170. 542 F.2d 8, 13 FEP Cases 762 (3rd Cir. 1976).

171. *Regents of the University of California* v. *Bakke*, 438 U.S. 265, 17 FEP Cases 1000 (1978). Brief *amicus curiae*, American Federation of Teachers, AFL–CIO.

172. 458 F.2d 1167, 4 FEP 596 (2nd Cir. 1972).

173. *Tallulah Morgan* v. *John D. O'Bryant*, U.S. Court of Appeals for the First Circuit, No. 81-1561, February 17, 1982. The A. Philip Randolph Institute joined with the Boston Teachers' Union and filed a brief as *amicus curiae* urging reversal of the affirmative action order.

174. Ibid.

175. 446 F.Supp. 979, 16 FEP Cases 1005 (E.D. Mich. 1978); D.C. Nev. 480 F.Supp. 539 (1979); U.S. Sup. Ct. (1982) 50 LW4238 (February 23, 1982); U.S. Sup. Ct. (1981) *cert. dismissed* 24:1809, 25 FEP Cases 1383; CA5 (1980) *order rehear en banc* 22:846, 23 FEP Cases 1510, 625 F.2d 1310; D.C. Mich (1978), 24 FEP Cases 1959, 458 F.2d 379.

176. An examination of briefs *amicus curiae* filed by ethnic and labor groups in the Supreme Court cases involving affirmative action reveal the following: In the *De Funis* case (1974), briefs attacking affirmative action came from the Anti-Defamation League of B'nai B'rith, the American Jewish Committee, the American Jewish Congress, and the Jewish Rights Council. The National Organization of Jewish Women filed a brief in support of affirmative action which was endorsed by the Commission on Social Action of the Union of American Hebrew Congregations. The AFL–CIO filed a brief against affirmative action, as did the National Association of Manufacturers. The United Auto Workers, United Farm Workers, and the American Federation of State, County, and Municipal Employees filed briefs in support, as did the United Mine Workers, an independent union. In *Bakke* (1978), among the groups which filed *amici* briefs against affirmative action were the American Jewish Committee, American Jewish Congress, Anti-Defamation League of B'nai Birth, Jewish Labor Committee, National Jewish Commission on Law and Public Affairs, UNICO National (the largest Italian-American organization in the U.S.), Italian-American Foundation, Chicago Division of UNICO, Hellenic Bar Association of Illinois, Ukrainian Congress Committee of America, Polish American Affairs Council, and Polish American Educators Association. All seven Jewish organizations filed briefs opposing affirmative action; the two Jewish groups that had supported affirmative action in the *De Funis* case did not file in *Bakke*. The American Federation of Teachers filed against affirmative action, while some other unions submitted a joint brief in support. In *Weber* (1979), five *amici* briefs urged the Supreme Court to decide against affirmative action; these were from the Anti-Defamation League of B'nai B'rith, the National Jewish Commission on Law and Public Affairs, the Ukrainian Congress Committee of America, and UNICO National. Several unions with large black memberships filed in support. In *Fullilove* (1980), the Anti-Defamation League of B'nai B'rith joined with employer groups and the Pacific League Foundation to argue against affirmative action. The Anti-Defamation League filed briefs in opposition to affirmative action in several lower court cases and has been among the most active of all groups in attacking affirmative action in the courts. In 1982, the ADL filed a brief against minority interests in the Boston Firefighters case (*Boston Firefighters Union, Local 718* v. *Boston Branch, NAACP*) with the Supreme Court, as did the AFL–CIO and the U.S. Department of Justice. On June 12, 1984, the Supreme Court in the Memphis fire-fighters case (*Firefighters Local Union No. 1784* v. *Stotts*) held that layoffs must be made on the basis of applicable union seniority rules, even if advances in minority employment as a result of court-ordered affirmative action are destroyed in the process. In this case, many labor unions and ethnic organizations joined with the U.S. Justice Department in urging the Court to rule against affirmative action. This was generally the pattern in the cases that followed. In addition to filing briefs *amicus*, ADL initiated its own litigation against affirmative action. (See for example press release, Anti-Defamation League of B'nai B'rith, New York, January 14, 1975).

177. For an analysis of the Philadelphia Plan and its history, see Jones 1970a; Hill 1974b.

For an account of civil rights protest activities in the construction industry, see Hill 1968.

178. Local 2 of the Plumbers Union in New York City was George Meany's "home local" all the years he was secretary-treasurer and then president of the labor federation. This union, which had systematically excluded nonwhites for decades, was the subject of a drama of great public significance during the 1960s involving the U.S. courts, the National Labor Relations Board, civil rights organizations, and municipal and state governments, as it defied efforts to racially integrate its membership and the labor force within its jurisdiction. See Hill 1983.

179. *News from the AFL–CIO*, press release, Department of Public Relations, August 31, 1975, 8.

180. *United States* v. *Building and Construction Trade Council*, 271 F.Supp. 447 (E.D. Mo., 1966).

181. Re Cleveland: *New York Times*, "Cleveland Union Protest," August 8, 1963; see also U.S. Commission on Civil Rights 1966, 443–444.

Re Philadelphia: "Building Unions May Walk Out in Bias Dispute," *Philadelphia Inquirer*, April 26, 1968, 1; see also *Philadelphia Inquirer*, May 8, 1968, for details of the racial work stoppage.

Re New York: *Official Report of Proceedings before the Trial Examiner of the National Labor Relations Board*, Local Union No. 2 of the United Association, AFL–CIO and Astrove Plumbing and Heating Corp. (Case No. 2-CB4024); *NLRB* v. *Local 2 United Association of Journeymen and Apprentices of the Plumbing and Pipefitting Industry of the United States and Canada*, 360 F.2d 428 (2nd Cir. 1966); see also, *New York Times*, May 1, 1964, 1; *New York Post*, May 16, 1964, 3: editorial, "The White Supremacy Plumbers," *New York Post*, May 3, 1964, 32; *New York Times*, May 2, 1964, 1.

182. *EEOC* v. *Plumbers, Local 189*, 311 F. Supp. 464 2 FEP 807 (S.D. Ohio 1970). *United States* v. *Wood Wire and Metal Lathers, Local 46*, 326 F.Supp. 429, 3 FEP Cases 457 (S.D.N.Y 1971). *EEOC* v. *Sheet Metal Workers, Local 638 . . . and Local 28*, 565 F.2nd 31, 15 FEP 1618 (2nd Cir. 1977). See also, Ronald Smothers, "Union and Employers in Contempt on Job Bias," *New York Times*, August 26, 1982, 1.

183. O'Brien 1974, 8.

184. At the end of the 1970s few if any voluntary hometown plans were in actual operation. This conclusion is based upon the field investigations of the author over a two-year period and was confirmed by the assistant secretary of labor for employment standards, Donald Elisburg, in an interview in Washington, D.C., April 16, 1979. For studies of the hometown plans, see Hill 1974c; U.S. Commission on Civil Rights 1975, 343–399; U.S. Commission on Civil Rights 1976, 173–206; U.S. Commission on Civil Rights 1977, 126–143.

185. Milloy 1981.

186. 401 F.Supp. 467, 12 FEP Cases 712 (S.D. New York, 1975), *affirmed as modified*, 532 F. 2d 821, 12 FEP Cases 755 (2nd Cir. 1976).

187. *Local 638 . . . Local 28 of the Sheetmetal Workers International Ass'n et al.* v. *EEOC et al.* (No. 84-1656).

188. 347 F.Supp. 268 (E.D. PA. 1979).

189. Shabecoff 1973.

190. See Fair Employment Practices Committee 1945, 81–82. For an example of the long history of futile protest by black steelworkers within the union, see the decertification petition filed with the National Labor Relations Board in the Atlantic Steel Company case, *Atlantic Steel Co. and United Steelworkers of America, Local No. 2401*, NLRB Case No. R-2964, Motion to Rescind Certification, October 29, 1962, especially "Affidavits and Memorandum Supporting Motion." This was a preliminary action to the later successful *Hughes Tool* case where the remedy of decertification on the basis of racial discrimination was first granted. *Independent Metal Workers, Locals 1 and 2*, 147 NLRB 1573, 56 LRRM 1289, (1964). For documentation of the black response to union discrimination in a southern local of the Steelworkers Union since the 1940s, see "Brief for Respondents" in a 1982 case, *Pullman-Standard* v. *Swint*,

456 U.S. 273, 28 FEP 1073. For discussion of this history, see Hill 1985, 24–25, 386. Over a period of many years the Civil Rights Department of the AFL–CIO failed to effect any change in response to complaints from black steelworkers on these and related issues, and increasingly the filing of complaints was regarded by workers as a futile exercise. An "Open Letter to the President of the United Steelworkers of America," distributed at the 1968 convention of that organization by a nationwide caucus of black steelworkers stated in part:

> The present director of the AFL–CIO Civil Rights Department has no involvement with Negro workers and their problems. He does not know of our problems. He does not represent us. He does not act in our interests. We believe we speak for many thousands of Negro workers not only in the Steelworkers Union but in other AFL–CIO affiliates with large Negro memberships when we demand the replacement of a white paternalist with a Black trade unionist who can honestly represent Negro workers and act on their behalf . . . For years Negro workers have stopped filing complaints with the AFL–CIO Civil Rights Department because experience has taught us that the Department is unable to function on our behalf. Most often it represents the discriminators in organized labor rather than the Black workers who are the victims of white racism within the house of labor (copy in author's possession).

191. See, for example, *U.S.* v. *Bethlehem Steel Corp.*, 446 F.2nd 652 (2nd Cir. 1971). As federal courts repeatedly rejected the defense of discriminatory seniority systems and ordered plantwide seniority to replace segregated departmental lines of promotion, unions seeking to ward off further judicial inquiry into their collective bargaining agreements, and also to protect union treasuries, entered into consent decrees to modify existing seniority practices. Among these was the steel industry agreement (*United States* v. *Allegheny-Ludlum Industries, Inc.*, 517 F.2d 826, 11 FEP 167 [5 Cir. 1975]) involving nine steel companies and the Steelworkers Union.

192. U.S. Equal Employment Opportunity Commission 1968, 16–17.

193. In 1959, the NAACP informed the AFL–CIO that it was "totally inadequate . . . to proceed from individual random complaints" and that it was necessary to take action against discriminatory patterns "on a systematic basis through each international union," but this approach was rejected (letter to Charles S. Zimmerman, chairman, AFL–CIO Civil Rights Committee, from Herbert Hill, labor secretary, NAACP, February 10, 1959). At least one AFL–CIO official questioned its policy and wrote in an internal memorandum that the labor federation "does not have a concise or even a reasonably clear civil rights inventory relating to our various AFL–CIO unions. For example, no one has the answer to these questions . . . which local unions have a separate line of job progression; which local unions have segregated meetings; which local unions have denied membership because of race; which local unions have separate personal facilities, etc., etc? . . . isn't this problem one that should be on the agenda of the AFL–CIO Executive Council for discussion?" (memorandum to Walter P. Reuther, from Jacob Clayman, executive director, Industrial Union Department, AFL–CIO, November 2, 1962, Folder 4, Box 504, Reuther Collection, Archives of Labor History and Urban Affairs, Wayne State University, Detroit). The "civil rights inventory" was never made and the position of the AFL–CIO on internal racial practices did not change. See Hill 1982.

194. *United States* v. *Bethlehem Steel Corp.*, 446 F.2d 652, 3 FEP 589 (2nd Cir. 1971).

195. Ibid., 655.

196. Ibid., 663.

197. *Goodman* v. *Lukens Steel Co. and United Steelworkers of America, AFL–CIO*, 777 F.2d 113 3d Cir. 1985), cert. denied.

198. 316 F.Supp. 567, 2 FEP 610 (M.D. FL, 1970), 451 F.2d 418, 3 FEP 862 (5th Cir. 1971), cert. denied 406 U.S. 906 (1972).

199. Ibid.

200. U.S. Commission on Civil Rights 1961, 65.

201. U.S. Commission on Civil Rights 1960, 87.

202. Report of the Negro American Labor Council, November 30, 1963. Data given in Bloch 1969, 53.

203. Memo to Walter P. Reuther from William H. Oliver, codirector, UAW Fair Practices Department, January 16, 1964.

204. Ibid.

205. Widick 1976, 58.

206. Interview with B. J. Widick, New York, March 27, 1972.

207. Quoted in Kremen 1972, 22.

208. See U.S. Bureau of the Census 1963, P.C. (2) 7A, Table 36, and 1973, P.C. (1) D24, Table 186; Bureau of Labor Statistics 1972, 14.

209. U.S. Equal Employment Opportunity Commission 1975, 6, 231.

210. UAW 1976, 205.

211. *Movement for Opportunity and Equality* v. *General Motors Corp. . . .* , CA No. 1P73-C-412 (D.C.S. Ind., Indianapolis Division, August 23, 1973). Black auto workers filed many complaints with federal contract compliance agencies against employers and the UAW during the 1950s in St. Louis, Kansas City, Atlanta, and elsewhere and with the EEOC after 1965. Investigative reports made by government agencies confirm this as does the litigation record. (See, for example, Memorandum from Jacob Seidenberg, executive director, President's Committee on Government Contracts, Subject: "Compliance Review Reports, Ford Assembly Plants, Atlanta, Dallas, Memphis, Chicago, Kansas City, Norfolk-Portsmouth, and Long Beach, California," April 22, 1957. See also Memorandum to Leonard Woodcock, director, General Motors Department, UAW, from Herbert Hill, labor secretary, NAACP, "re: Status of Negro Workers—General Motors Corporation, St. Louis Plant," June 3, 1957. This memorandum describes in detail the employment of "Negroes exclusively for menial jobs such as porter, sweeper and material handler, etc., and the limiting of nonwhites to janitorial departments."

212. See Hill 1985, 260–270.

213. See Geschwender 1977; Georgakas and Surkin 1975; Hill 1972; Gould 1969. For information on black caucus activity within the UAW from the inception of the union to the late 1960s, see Hill interviews 1967–1968.

214. *New York Times*, August 11, 1968, 41.

215. See Jones 1970b. As a matter of policy and practice, the Allen-Bradley Company filled most of its job vacancies through referrals from friends and relatives already employed by the company. In October 1967, under pressure from government agencies to employ nonwhites, the company agreed to delete from their employment procedures all references to "friends and relatives," but although they removed such questions from printed application forms, as late as May 1968, company representatives continued to ask job applicants if they were related to, or were friends with, anyone employed by Allen-Bradley. In addition to the issue of race discrimination, the company was also accused of practicing unlawful sex discrimination. In 1968, as a result of a lawsuit brought by four hundred women employed at Allen-Bradley who charged wage differentials based on sex, the company agreed to an out-of-court settlement that included compensatory payments for past wage discrimination, equal wages for women doing the same work as men, and the elimination of sex-based job classifications in the contract with the United Electrical Workers Union.

216. *Milwaukee Journal*, August 8, 14, 15, 21, 22, September 17, 1968; *Milwaukee Sentinel*, August 14, 20, 21, 1968; *New York Times*, August 11, 1968; *Business Week*, October 12, 1968.

217. Secretary of Labor Decision, *In Matter of Allen-Bradley Co.*, Office of Federal Contract Compliance, Docket No. 101-68, August 1969, cited in *Government Contracts*, Washington, D.C., paragraph 2746, June 14, 1972. See also Jones 1970b, 756–762; *Milwaukee Journal*, January 7, February 11, August 28, 1969; *Business Week*, January 11, August 16, 1969.

218. *Milwaukee Sentinel*, August 28, 1968, part 2, 16.

219. *Gibson* v. *ILGWU, Local 40*, 13 FEP Cases 997, 465 F.2d 108 (9th Cir. 1974).

220. *Gibson* v. *ILGWU, Local 40*, 543 F.2d 1259 (9th Cir. 1976).

221. Larrowe 1972, 366–367.

222. There is a long history of immigrant hostility against blacks. In Philadelphia, Irish-

led, violent attacks against the Afro-American community occurred in 1829, 1834, 1838, and 1849. Race riots occurred in Boston, St. Paul, Cincinnati, Toledo, and other cities during the Civil War. On March 6, 1863, the Detroit race riot, the major riot in the midwest, began. "Exploding racial conflict between immigrants—mostly Irish— and the black underlay the midwestern riots, as well as their counterparts in New York, Boston, and smaller New York cities of Brooklyn, Buffalo and Troy. As recent immigrants, the Irish manifested relatively little interest in the war to preserve the union; the sons of Eire were more concerned about the competition of black laborers for unskilled and service jobs" (Katzman 1973, 44–45). In a contemporary account of the race riot in New York in 1863, Joel Tyler Headley, describing those who attacked blacks, wrote: "A great proportion of these being Irish, it naturally became an Irish question, and eventually an Irish riot . . . the whole block on Broadway, between Twenty-eighth and Twenty-ninth streets, was burned down . . . while these fires were under full headway a new idea seemed to strike the mob . . . it now impelled by a strange logic sought to destroy the Colored Orphan Asylum on Fifth Avenue, extending from Forty-third to Forty-fourth street . . . the slaves were black, ergo, all blacks are responsible for the war. This seemed to be the logic of the mob, and having reached the sage conclusion to which it conducted, did not stop to consider how poor helpless orphans could be held responsible, but proceeded at once to wreak their vengeance on them . . . soon the massive structure was a sheet of flame" (Headley 1873, 149– 171). See also Moody 1958. Immigrant hostility was also a factor in the widespread violence against blacks in the early twentieth century as in East St. Louis in 1917 and Chicago in 1919. In 1951 the author observed the violence of Poles and other Slavic-Americans against blacks during the riots in Cicero, Illinois, and again in Chicago in 1966 against blacks who were participating in the marches led by Rev. Martin Luther King, Jr. In Boston, organized groups of whites based in ethnic communities demonstrated against school desegregation and repeatedly engaged in racial violence. Members and leaders of AFL–CIO building trades unions were involved in this activity in south Boston for many years. James Kelley, for example, a former official of the Sheet Metal Workers Union was head of the South Boston Information Center, the parent organization of a paramilitary racist group known as the South Boston Marshalls. The emergence of such organizations in working-class neighborhoods occurred in several cities involved in school desegregation efforts during the 1960s and 1970s.

References

American Academy of Political and Social Science, 1913. *The Negro's Progress in Fifty Years.* Philadelphia.

American Jewish Committee, 1954. *Jewish Labor in the United States.* New York.

Asch, Sholem, 1946. *East River.* Trans. A. H. Gross. New York: Putnam.

Auerbach, Jerold S., 1961. "Progressives at Sea, the LaFollette Act of 1915." *Labor History* (Fall): 346–357.

Axtell, Silas B., ed., 1948. *A Symposium on Andrew Furuseth.* Mass.: Darwin Press.

Baker, R. S., 1907–1908. "The Negro's Struggle for Survival in the North." *American Magazine* 65, 22.

Barbash, Jack, 1952. "Ethnic Factors in the Development of the American Labor Movement." In *Interpreting the Labor Movement,* ed. George Brooks, Milton Derber, David MacCabe, and Philip Taft, 48–64. Industrial Relations Research Association. Champaign, Ill.: Twin City Publishing.

Barron, Harold M., 1971. "The Demand for Black Labor." *Radical America* 5(2): 1–46.

Bloch, Herman D., 1969. *The Circle of Discrimination.* New York: New York University Press.

Blumer, Herbert, 1965. "Industrialization and Race Relations." In *Industrialization and Race Relations: A Symposium*, ed. Guy Hunter, 220–253. London: Oxford University Press.

Boudin, Louis, 1908. "Immigration at Stuttgart." *International Socialist Review* 8 (February).

Braestrup, Peter, 1958. "Life Among the Garment Workers." *New York Herald Tribune*, October 7 (p. 23), October 8 (p. 15).

Caldwell, Earl, 1983. "When a House Can't Be Your Home." *New York Daily News*, June 1, 4.

Commons, John R., et al., 1918. *History of Labor in the United States*. Vol. 2. New York: Macmillan.

———, 1907. *Races and Immigrants in America*. New York: Macmillan.

Coolidge, Mary R., 1909. *Chinese Immigration*. New York: H. Holt & Co.

Danish, Max D., 1957. *The World of David Dubinsky*. Cleveland: World.

Dubinsky, David, with A. H. Raskin, 1977. *David Dubinsky: A Life with Labor*. New York: Simon & Schuster.

Du Bois, W. E. B., 1902. *The Negro Artisan*. Atlanta: University Press.

———, 1917. "The Passing of Jim Crow." *The Independent*, July 14, 8–10.

Du Bois, W. E. B., with Augustus G. Dill, 1912. *The Negro American Artisan*. Atlanta: University Press.

Durham, John Stevens, 1898. "The Labor Unions and the Negro." *Atlantic Monthly*, February, 222.

Eaves, Lucile, 1910. *A History of California Labor Legislation: With an Introductory Sketch of the San Francisco Labor Movement*. Berkeley: University of California Press.

"The Effects of Selected Union Policies on Equal Opportunity in New York City," 1981. A study prepared for the U.S. Commission on Civil Rights. Washington, D.C.

"The Elimination of Negro Firemen on American Railroads—A Study of the Evidence Adduced at the Hearing Before the President's Committee on Fair Employment Practices," 1944. *Lawyers Guild Review* 4(1944): 321.

Epstein, Jason, 1968. "The Issue at Ocean Hill." *New York Review of Books*, November 21, 3.

Fair Employment Practices Committee, 1945. *First Report, July 1943–December 1944*. Washington, D. C.

Ferretti, Fred, 1962. "Crusading Negro Finds Road Is Rough." *New York Herald Tribune*, July 2, 8.

Florant, Lionel C., 1942. "Negro Migration 1860–1940." Revised draft of a memorandum for the Carnegie Corporation's study of the Negro in America (Myrdal Study). Schomburg Collection, New York Public Library.

Fogel, Y., 1977. "Knitgoods Local 155 and the Elections." *Jewish Daily Forward*, 1. (Translated copy in author's files.)

Foner, Philip S., ed., 1947. *Jack London*. New York: Citadel.

Georgakas, Dan, and Marvin Surkin, 1975. *Detroit: I Do Mind Dying*. New York: St. Martin's.

Geschwender, James A., 1977. *Class, Race and Worker Insurgency*. Cambridge, England: Cambridge University Press.

Glazer, Nathan, 1975. *Affirmative Discrimination: Ethnic Inequality and Public Policy*. New York: Basic Books.

———, 1964. "Negroes and Jews: The New Challenge to Pluralism." *Commentary*, December, 29–35.

Goldberg, Joseph, 1957. *The Maritime Story*. Cambridge: Harvard University Press.

Gompers, Samuel, 1925. *Seventy Years of Life and Labor: An Autobiography*. Vol. 2. New York: Dutton.

Gould, William B., 1977. *Black Workers in White Unions*. Ithaca: Cornell University Press.

———, 1969. "Black Power in the Unions: The Impact upon Collective Bargaining Relationships." *Yale Law Journal* (November): 46–84.

Grant, Madison, 1916. *The Passing of the Great Race.* New York: Scribner.

Greene, Lorenzo J., and Carter G. Woodson, 1930. *The Negro Wage-Earner.* Washington, D.C.: The Association for the Study of Negro Life and History.

Hall, Burton H., 1972. "The ILGWU and the Labor Department." In *Autocracy and Insurgency in Organized Labor,* ed. Burton H. Hall, 284–295. New Brunswick, N.J.: Transaction.

Haynes, G. E., 1919. "Effects of War Conditions on Negro Labor." *Proceedings of the Academy of Political Science* (February): 168–182.

———, 1912. *The Negro at Work in New York City: A Study in Economic Progress.* New York: Longmans.

Headley, Joel Tyler, 1873. *The Great Riots of New York: 1712–1873.* Indianapolis: Bobbs-Merrill, 1970.

Helfgott, Roy B., 1961. "Trade Unionism Among the Jewish Garment Workers of Britain and the United States." *Labor History* 2(2): 206–218.

Hill, Herbert, 1988. "Myth-Making as Labor History: Herbert Gutman and the United Mine Workers of America." *International Journal of Politics, Culture, and Society* 2(2): 132–200.

———, 1985. *Black Labor and the American Legal System.* Madison: University of Wisconsin Press.

———, 1983. "The New York City Terminal Market Controversy: A Case Study of Race, Labor, and Power." *Humanities in Society* 6 (Fall 1983): 351–391. (Reprint no. 255, Industrial Relations Research Institute, University of Wisconsin—Madison.)

———, 1982. "The AFL–CIO and the Black Worker: Twenty-Five Years After the Merger." *Journal of Intergroup Relations* 10(1): 5–78. (Reprint no. 241, Industrial Relations Research Institute, University of Wisconsin—Madison.)

———, 1977. "The Equal Employment Opportunity Acts of 1964 and 1972: A Critical Analysis of the Legislative History and Administration of the Law." *Industrial Relations Law Journal* 2(1): 1–96.

———, 1974a. "Guardians of the Sweatshop." In *Puerto Rico and Puerto Ricans,* eds. A. Lopez and J. Petras, 72–84. New York: Wiley.

———, 1974b. "Labor Union Control of Job Training: A Critical Analysis of Apprenticeship Outreach Programs and the Hometown Plans." Occasional Paper vol. 2, no. 1. Washington, D.C.: Institute for Urban Affairs and Research, Howard University.

———, 1972a. "The ILGWU Today: The Decay of a Labor Union." In *Autocracy and Insurgency in Organized Labor,* ed. Burton H. Hall, 147–160. New Brunswick, N.J.: Transaction.

———, 1972b. "Black Dissent in Organized Labor." In *Seasons of Rebellion—Protest and Radicalism in Recent America,* eds. Joseph Boskin and Robert Rosenstone, 55–80. New York: Holt.

———, 1968. "The Racial Practices of Organized Labor: The Contemporary Record." In *The Negro and the American Labor Movement,* ed. Julius Jacobson, 286–320. Garden City, New York: Anchor Books.

———, 1967–1968. Interviews: Joseph Billups, October 27, 1967; Hodges Mason, November 28, 1967; Shelton Tappes, October 27, 1967, and February 10, 1968; George W. Crockett, March 2, 1968; Robert Battle, March 19, 1968; Horace Sheffield, July 24, 1968. Transcripts in Archives of Labor History and Urban Affairs, Walter Reuther Library, Wayne State University, Detroit.

———, 1965. "Racial Inequality in Employment: The Patterns of Discrimination." *Annals of the American Academy of Political and Social Science* (January): 30–47.

———, 1961. "Racism Within Organized Labor." *The Journal of Negro Education* (2): 109–118.

———, 1959. "Labor Unions and the Negro." *Commentary,* December, 479–488.

Houston, Charles H., 1949. "Foul Employment Practices on the Rails" (based on a report to the Fortieth Annual Convention of the NAACP, Los Angeles, July 1949). *The Crisis,* October, 269–272.

Jaco, D. E., and G. L. Wilber, 1975. "Asian-Americans in the Labor Market." *Monthly Labor Review,* U.S. Bureau of Labor Statistics, July, 33–38.

Jacobs, Paul, 1953. *The State of the Union*. New York: Atheneum.

Johnson, C. S., 1927. "The American Migrant: The Negro." *National Conference of Social Work Proceedings*, 554–558.

Johnson, James Weldon, 1930. *Black Manhattan*. New York: Knopf.

Jones, James E., Jr., 1970a. "The Bugaboo of Employment Quotas." *Wisconsin Law Review* 1970(2): 341–403.

———, 1970b. "Federal Contract Compliance in Phase II—The Dawning of the Age of Enforcement of Equal Employment Obligations." *Georgia Law Review* 4 (June): 756–769.

Katzman, David M., 1973. *Before the Ghetto: Black Detroit in the Nineteenth Century*. Urbana: University of Illinois Press.

Keil, Hartmut, 1983. "The German Immigrant Working Class of Chicago, 1875–90: Workers, Labor Leaders, and the Labor Movement." In *American Labor and Immigration History, 1877–1920s*, ed. Dirk Hoerder, 157–176. Urbana: University of Illinois Press.

Kempton, Murray, 1962. "The Wage Fight." *New York Post*, August 21, 22.

Keyserling, Leon H., 1963. "The New York Dress Industry: Problems and Prospects." Manuscript, New York Public Library, main branch.

King, Cameron H., Jr., 1908. "Asiatic Exclusion." *International Socialist Review* 8 (May).

Kipnis, Ira, 1952. *The American Socialist Movement 1897-1912*. New York: Columbia University Press.

Kovel, Joel, 1970. *White Racism*. New York: Pantheon.

Kremen, Bennett, 1972. "No Pride in This Dust." *Dissent*, Winter, 753–758.

Kusmer, Kenneth L., 1976. *A Ghetto Takes Shape: Black Cleveland, 1870–1930*. Urbana: University of Illinois Press.

Kwong, Peter, and Jo Ann Lum, 1988. "Letter to the Editor." *The Nation*, October 10, 314.

Larrowe, Charles P., 1972. *Harry Bridges: The Rise and Fall of Radical Labor in the United States*. New York: Lawrence Hill.

Lieberson, Stanley, 1980. *A Piece of the Pie, Blacks and White Immigrants Since 1880*, Berkeley: University of California Press.

Lorwin, Lewis, 1933. *The American Federation of Labor*. Washington, D.C.: Brookings.

Lyman, Stanford M., 1970. *The Asian in the West*. Social Science and Humanities Publications no. 4. Reno: Western Studies Center, University of Nevada.

Macdonald, Dwight, 1968. "An Open Letter to Michael Harrington." *New York Review of Books*, December 5, 48.

Mandel, Bernard, 1955. "Samuel Gompers and the Negro Workers, 1886–1914." *The Journal of Negro History* 40(1): 34–60.

Michaels, Lance, n.d. "The Apparel Industry's Impact on New York City's Economy: An Analysis of Population Patterns Compared with Employment Opportunities." Manuscript, Office of the Mayor, New York City.

Milloy, Courtland, Jr., 1981. "Plan to Get More Blacks into Washington Construction Jobs Fails." *Washington Post*, March 10, 1.

Mitchell, George Sinclair, 1936. "The Negro in Southern Trade Unionism." *The Southern Economic Journal* 2(3): 27–38.

Moody, Richard, 1958. *The Astor Place Riot*. Bloomington: University of Indiana Press.

Myerson, Michael, 1969. "The ILGWU: Fighting for Lower Wages." *Ramparts*, October, 51–55.

O'Brien, Tim, 1974. "Minority Job Goals Stiffened." *Washington Post*, July 3, 8.

Osofsky, Gilbert, 1966. *Harlem, the Making of a Ghetto*. New York: Harper & Row.

Ottley, R., and W. Weatherby, eds., 1967. *The Negro in New York, 1626–1940*. New York: Praeger.

Ovington, Mary White, 1911. *Half a Man: The Status of the Negro in New York*. New York: Longmans.

———, 1906. "The Negro in the Trade Unions of New York." *Annals of the American Academy of Political and Social Science* (May): 64–75.

Perlman, Selig, 1922. *The History of Trade Unionism in the United States*. New York: A. M. Kelly, 1950. (Originally published in 1922.)

Ping Chiu, 1963. *Chinese Labor in California, 1850–1880: An Economic Study*. Madison: State Historical Society of Wisconsin.

Rauh, Joseph, 1987. Interview, July 25, Washington, D.C. Quoted in Helene Slessarev. "Organized Labor and the Civil Rights Movement in the Fight for Employment Policy." Paper presented at the Annual Meeting of the American Political Science Association, September 3–6, 1987, Chicago, 5.

Reid, Ira De A., 1930. *Negro Membership in American Labor Unions*. New York: National Urban League.

Roediger, David, 1986. "Labor in White Skin: Race and Working-Class History." Unpublished paper, author's files.

Rosenblum, Gerald, 1973. *Immigrant Workers, Their Impact on American Labor Radicalism*. New York: Basic Books.

Rustin, Bayard, 1971. "The Blacks and the Unions." *Harper's Magazine*, May, 80.

Saxton, Alexander, 1971. *The Indispensable Enemy: Labor and the Anti-Chinese Movement in California*. Berkeley: University of California Press.

Scheiner, Seth M., 1965. *Negro Mecca, a History of the Negro in New York City, 1865–1920*. New York: New York University Press.

Seldin, Joel, 1962. "ILGWU Condemned for Racial Barriers." *New York Herald Tribune*, July 2, 1.

Seligman, Ben, 1944. "The Jewish Labor Leader." *Contemporary Jewish Record*, December, 606–607.

Shabecoff, Philip, 1973. "Breaking Seniority Barriers." *New York Times*, May 6, D-1.

Shanker, Albert, and Herbert Hill, 1972. "Black Protest, Union Democracy and the UFT." In *Autocracy and Insurgency in Organized Labor*, ed. Burton H. Hall, 218–235. New Brunswick, N.J.: Transaction Books.

Somma, Nicolas, 1952. "The Knights of Labor and Chinese Immigration." Master's thesis, Catholic University, Washington, D.C.

Speed, J. G., 1900. "The Negro in New York." *Harper's Weekly*, December 22.

Spero, Sterling D., and Abram L. Harris, 1931. *The Black Worker*. New York: Columbia University Press.

Stoddard, Lothrop, 1920. *The Rising Tide of Color Against White World Supremacy*. New York: Scribner.

Stouffer, Samuel A., and Lionel C. Florant, 1940. "Negro Population Movements, 1860–1940, in Relation to Social and Economic Factors." Preliminary draft of a memorandum for the Carnegie Corporation's study of the Negro in America (Myrdal Study). Schomburg Collection, New York Public Library.

Taft, Philip, 1968. *Labor Politics American Style: The California State Federation of Labor*. Cambridge: Harvard University Press.

———, 1964. *Organized Labor in American History*. New York: Harper & Row.

Takaki, Ronald, 1979. *Iron Cages: Race and Culture in 19th Century America*. New York: Knopf.

Taylor, Paul S., 1923. *The Sailor's Union of the Pacific*. New York: Ronald.

Thernstrom, Stephan, ed., 1980. *Harvard Encyclopedia of American Ethnic Groups*. Cambridge: Harvard University Press.

Thernstrom, Stephan, 1973. *The Other Bostonians*. Cambridge: Harvard University Press.

Thompson, E. P., 1963. *The Making of the English Working Class*. New York: Pantheon.

Tucker, H., 1908. "Negro Craftsmen in New York." *Southern Workmen* 37.

Tyler, Gus, 1982. "The Intellectual and the ILGWU." In *Creators and Disturbers, Reminiscences by Jewish Intellectuals of New York*, ed. Bernard Rosenberg and Ernest Goldstein, 155–175. New York: Columbia University Press.

———, 1962. "The Truth About the ILGWU." *New Politics* 2(1): 7.

UAW, 1976. *Twenty-Seven Years of Civil Rights*. UAW Constitutional Convention Reports, 1947–1974, International Union. Detroit.

U.S. Bureau of the Census, 1983. *1980 Census of Population, Detailed Characteristics*.

———, 1982. *Population Reports, 1860 to 1980.*

———, 1978. *Current Population Reports: Characteristics of the Population Below Poverty Level, 1976.* Series P-60, no. 115; P-60, no. 110; P-20, no. 329.

———, 1973. *1970 Census of Population, Detailed Characteristics.*

———, 1963. *1960 Census of the Population, Detailed Characteristics; Occupational Characteristics.*

———, 1882. "Chinese in the United States by States and Territories." *Tenth Census of the United States.* Vol. 1.

———, 1872. *Ninth Census of the United States, Part 1.*

U.S. Bureau of Labor Statistics, 1972. "Black Americans: A Decade of Occupational Change." Bulletin 1760. Washington, D.C.

———, 1971. *The New York Puerto Rican: Patterns of Work Experience.* (Poverty Area Profiles, Regional Report no. 19.) New York.

———, 1966. "Occupational Earnings—Women's and Misses' Dresses." No. 66-176. August. Washington, D.C.

———, 1962. "Employment, Earnings, and Wages in New York City, 1950–1960." New York, Middle Atlantic Regional Office. June.

———, 1929. "Handbook of American Trade Unions." Bulletin 506. Washington, D.C.

U.S. Commission on Civil Rights, 1977. *The Federal Civil Right Enforcement Effort—1977, To Eliminate Employment Discrimination: A Sequel.* December. Washington, D.C.

———, 1976. *The Challenge Ahead: Equal Opportunity in Referral Unions.* May. Washington, D.C.

———, 1975. *The Federal Civil Rights Enforcement Effort—1974, To Eliminate Employment Discrimination.* Vol. 5. July. Washington, D.C.

———, 1966. Hearing before the Commission, April 1–7, Cleveland. Washington, D.C.

———, 1961. *Employment.* Report no. 3. Washington, D.C.

———, 1960. Hearings before the Commission, Detroit, December 14–15. Washington, D.C.

U.S. Department of Commerce, 1920. *Immigrants and Their Children.* Census Monograph no. 7. Washington, D.C.

U.S. Equal Employment Opportunity Commission, 1975a. "EEOC Report Summary by Industry, SMSA, New York–New Jersey, SIC23 Apparel." Washington, D.C.

———, 1975b. "EEO-1 Report Summary by Industry Within SMSA's, Detroit, Michigan." Washington, D.C.

———, 1968. "Job Patterns for Minorities and Women in Private Industry." April. Washington, D.C.

———, 1966. EEOC, *A Legislative History of Titles VII and IX of the Civil Rights Act of 1964.* Washington, D.C.

U.S. House, 1962. *Hearings Before the Ad Hoc Subcommittee on Investigation of the Garment Industry.* Committee on Education and Labor. 87th Congress, 2nd Session, August 17, 18, 23, 24, and September 21. Washington, D.C.

U.S. Senate, 1963. *Equal Employment Opportunity: Hearings Before the Subcommittee on Employment and Manpower of the Committee on Labor and Public Welfare.* 88th Congress, 1st session. Washington, D.C.

Van Tine, Warren R., 1973. *The Making of the Labor Bureaucrat, Union Leadership in the United States, 1870–1920.* Amherst, Mass.: University of Massachusetts Press.

Weintraub, Hyman, 1959. *Andrew Furuseth.* Berkeley: University of California Press.

Wesley, Charles H., 1972. *Negro Labor in the United States.* New York: Vanguard. New York: Russell & Russell: 1967.

Widick, B. J., ed., 1976. *Auto Work and Its Discontents.* Baltimore: Johns Hopkins University Press.

Wilentz, Sean, 1984. *Chants Democratic, New York City and the Rise of the American Working Class, 1788–1850.* New York: Oxford University Press.

Witte, Arnold, 1962. "Letter to the Editor." *New York World-Telegram & Sun*, October 5, 16.

Wolfe, Frank E., 1912. *Admission to American Trade Unions*. Baltimore: Johns Hopkins University Press.

Woodson, Carter G., 1918. *A Century of Negro Migration*. Washington, D.C.: The Association for the Study of Negro Life and History.

Woodward, C. Vann, 1951. *Origins of the New South, 1877–1913*. Baton Rouge: Louisiana State University Press.

Worthman, Paul, 1971. "Working-Class Mobility in Birmingham, Alabama, 1880–1914." In *Anonymous Americans*, ed. Tamara K. Hareven, 47–69. Englewood Cliffs, N.J.: Prentice-Hall.

Chapter 9. Why Should We Care about Group Inequality?

THIS ESSAY is about the ethical propriety and practical efficacy of a range of policy undertakings referred to as "affirmative action." These policies have been contentious and problematic, and a variety of arguments have been advanced in their support. Here I try to close a gap, as I see it, in this "literature of justification" that has grown up around the practice of preferential treatment, by offering what I term a "minimalist's argument" for departing from the color-blind standard. I consider how some forms of argument in support of preferential treatment not only fail to justify the practice but, even worse, work to undermine the basis for cooperation among different ethnic groups in the American democracy. As a practical matter the use of group preference can, under circumstances I detail, produce results far different from the egalitarian objectives that most often motivate their adoption.

It may seem fatuous in the extreme to raise as a serious matter, in the contemporary United States, the question "Why should we care about group inequality?" Is not the historical and moral imperative of such concern self-evident? Must not those who value the pursuit of justice be intensely concerned about economic disparities among groups of persons? The most obvious answer to the title question would seem, then, to be: "we should care because such inequality is the external manifestation of the oppression of individuals on the basis of their group identity."

Yet, this response, upon examination, is not entirely adequate. Why should the mere existence of group disparities evidence the oppressive treatment of individuals? There is little support in the historical record for the notion that, in the absence of oppression based upon group membership, all socially relevant aggregates of persons would achieve roughly the same distribution of economic rewards.[1] Indeed, to hold this view is to deny the economic relevance of historically determined and culturally reinforced beliefs, values, interests, and attitudes that define distinct ethnicities. Distinct cultures will necessarily produce distinct patterns of interest and work among their adherents. And while this need not be an argument against egalitarianism, since distinct interests and different work need not receive different remuneration, it does serve to shift our focus from disparities among groups per se to disparities in the rewards to the different types of activities toward which various groups' members incline.

In fact, a subtle logical problem haunts the idea of equality among groups. To the extent that the arguments for equal group results presuppose the continued existence of general inequality, they end up (merely) demanding an equality *between groups* of a given amount of inequality *within groups*. They leave us with the question: why is inequality among individuals of the same group acceptable when inequality between the groups is not? Indeed, there is "group inequality" whenever there is inequality—one need only take those at the bottom to constitute a "group." This is precisely what a radical, class analysis of society does. The unanswered question here is why the ethnic-racial-sexual identification of "group" should take precedence over all others. It is a question usually avoided in popular discussions of the need to equalize group disparities.

It is, of course, possible to hold that the very existence of distinct beliefs, values, interests, and so forth in distinct groups is evidence of oppression. And it is surely true that one major consequence of domination is to alter the conception of self held by the dominated. Women are socialized into the acceptance as natural or desirable of roles that undermine their competitive position in the world of work. Minorities, so this argument goes, do not aspire to those professions in which there are presently few persons like themselves to serve as role models, to illustrate that the opportunity for success is really there. In this view group disparities evidence oppression even when arising most immediately out of differences in "tastes" among persons, since those differences are themselves due to oppression.

But this argument, if it were valid, would prove too much. The differentiating effect of oppression has sometimes worked to make a group of persons *more* effective in economic competition. And the differences of beliefs and values among various groups sometimes reflect centuries of historical development, in lands far removed from that which they currently occupy. If group differences in beliefs and values bearing on economic achievement are the fruit of oppression, then why not also those group differences in cultural style so much celebrated by cultural pluralists? If, for example, poor academic performance among black students reflects "oppression," why should not outstanding athletic performance stem from the same source? We re-

main, then, with two questions: when does group inequality constitute a moral problem, and what may appropriately be done about it?

In contemporary American society such disparities are often taken
to constitute a moral problem and to occasion a public policy response.
The use of racial preferences in education, employment, or even politics, a frequent policy response, has been controversial; courts and
philosophers have sought to define the circumstances under which
such preferences might legitimately be employed. Recently, both in
the courts and in public discourse, questions have been raised about
the legitimacy of government efforts on behalf of women, blacks, and
other racial minorities. Some of these questions strike deeply at the
philosophical foundation of preferential policies.

It is a tenet of long standing in American liberalism that the use by
the state of ascriptive personal characteristics as a basis for discriminating among individuals, whether that discrimination be in their
favor or to their disadvantage, is wrong. Such practice stigmatizes the
individuals involved and reinforces private inclinations to make invidious distinctions based upon the same ascriptive characteristics.

The antidiscrimination principle, codified in so many statutes and
court rulings of recent decades, is founded upon such a world view.
Martin Luther King put it well when he said: "I have a dream that my
four little children will one day live in a nation where they will not
be judged by the color of their skin, but by the content of their character" (Broderick and Meier 1965). Plaintiffs' attorneys in the landmark *Brown* case and in oral argument before the U.S. Supreme Court
made similar representations when urging the Court to overturn the
"separate but equal" doctrine. Civil rights advocates in the legislature,
working for the passage of the Civil Rights Act of 1964, offered extensive assurances that they sought only to enforce on the private sector
such restrictions in their business practices as were consistent with
assuring color-blind hiring and promotion standards.[2] Throughout this
early history of the civil rights revolution, the classical liberal principle
of aversion to the use of racial (or religious or sexual) classification was
adhered to by the advocates of change. And this antidiscrimination
principle has a noble intellectual pedigree, harking back to the En-
lightenment-era challenge to hereditary authority and reflected in the
"anonymity axiom" of modern social choice theory.[3]

Yet, in a historically remarkable transformation, this position of the
liberal political community in our country has dramatically changed.[4]
Today, King's dream that race might one day become an insignificant
category in American civic life seems naively utopian. It is no small
irony that, a mere two decades after his moving oration, the passionate
evocation in public debate of his "color-blind" ideal is, for many, an

indication of a limited commitment to the goal of racial justice. The recalcitrant persistence of group disparity in the face of formal equality of opportunity has forced many liberals to look to race-conscious public action as the only viable remedy.

However, unlike the earlier antidiscrimination principle, color-conscious state action rests on rather less firm philosophical ground. The key court decisions supporting it are, in the main, closely divided ones. The arguments encountered in support of the practice seem, at least to this listener, to be more tortured and less compelling than those put forward on behalf of the color-blind principle.[5] Typically, these arguments demonstrate the invalidity of the notion that positions should be distributed according to the nebulous criterion of "merit" and follow that with a set of unsupported empirical claims about the benefits sure to flow from a more equal distribution of positions among groups.

There is, for example, a tendency in these arguments to obscure the distinction between group-conscious state actions whose main purpose is to prevent overt, but undetectable, private discrimination and those whose principal aim is to increase the representation of protected groups without any implication that their "underrepresentation" evidences illegal private behavior. The first set of policies, call them "enforcement-oriented," though requiring use by the state of what may be imperfect (i.e., color-conscious) means, aim to eliminate private practices and procedures that themselves violate the antidiscrimination principle. (They may be likened to the use of statistical market share data by antitrust authorities when seeking to determine whether a firm has engaged in illegal, but unobservable, business practices.) The second type of policies, call them "result-oriented," concern themselves with the outcome of private actions that may be wholly unobjectionable but that occur in the face of unacceptable de facto racial disparities. The two types of policies cannot be rationalized in the same manner. A coherent theory of the practice of affirmative action must be able to distinguish among them. How, if at all, can the "result-oriented" use of racial categories by the state be justified?

My "minimalist's" argument will, I hope, establish that a plausible specification of how multi-ethnic societies actually function will lead to the conclusion that *social justice is not consistent with a blanket prohibition on the use of group categories as a basis for state action.* I will rely on an intellectual tradition long familiar to economics—one that justifies departures from laissez faire when, due to some sort of market failure, the outcomes of private actions are socially undesirable. This market failure rests upon the very social behavior that induces distinct racial and ethnic groups, as a permanent structural matter, among which inequality might arise in the first place.[6]

I will inquire whether, in theory, we should expect the continued application of racially neutral procedures to lead eventually to an outcome no longer reflective of our history of discrimination. If the answer to this query were negative, then adherence to a policy of equal opportunity alone would condemn those whose rights have historically been violated (and their progeny) to suffer indefinitely from what most would regard as ethically illegitimate acts. Since, presumably, this would be an ethically unacceptable state of affairs, a (weak) case for intervention would thereby be made. There are reasons to believe that the consequences of apparently innocuous and ubiquitous social behaviors systematically and intrinsically pass on from one generation to the next that group inequality originally engendered by historical discrimination.

Thus, I propose that we take certain aspects of the dynamic performance of an unrestrained market economy as a standard in evaluating the ethical legitimacy of affirmative action. The choice between public policy limited to what Douglas Rae (1981) has called "prospect-regarding equality of opportunity" or extended to some sort of color-conscious intervention should depend upon the extent to which we are confident of the ability of markets to naturally erode historically generated differences in status between groups. One part of this puzzle can be resolved if we seek to identify precisely what it is about laissez faire that leads us to expect (as supporters of affirmative action typically do) that, even in the absence of ongoing economic discrimination, genuine equality might not be attained without special state actions.

Imagine an economic model in which persons compete for jobs in competitive labor markets—where job assignments are made under conditions of equal opportunity and are based solely on an individual's productive characteristics—and in which the markets for jobs operate without regard to individuals' ascriptive characteristics. Suppose, however, that the individual's acquisition of productive characteristics is favorably influenced by the economic success of the individual's parents. Equal opportunity does not extend to the realm of social backgrounds, and differences in background are permitted to affect a person's access to training resources.[7] This model is much like the world in which we live. Persons begin life with endowments of what might be called "social capital," nontransferable advantages of birth that are conveyed by parental behaviors bearing on later-life productivity. In such a world, the deleterious consequences of past discrimination for (say) a racial minority are reflected in the fact that minority young people have, on the average, less favorable parental influences on their skill-acquisition practices.

Further, imagine that families group themselves together into social clusters, or local "communities," and that certain "local public goods" important to subsequent individual productivity are provided uniformly to young people of the same community. These "local public goods" may be very general in nature. One thinks naturally of public education, but also important might be peer influences that shape the development of personal character, contacts that generate information about the world of work, and friendship networks that evolve among persons situated in the same or closely related "communities." What is critical is that these community "goods" (or, possibly, "bads") be provided *internally* to the social clusters in question and that outsiders be excluded from the consumption of such goods. I use the term *communities* to represent those private, voluntary associational behaviors common to all societies, in which persons choose their companions, often on the basis of common ethnicity, religion, or economic class. Since access to these "communities" could depend on parents' social status, this provides another avenue by which parental background influences offsprings' achievement—another source of social capital.

In order to pose the question most sharply, I assume that all individuals have identical preferences with respect to economic choices and that an identical distribution of innate aptitudes characterizes each generation of majority and minority workers.[8] Thus, in the absence of any historical economic discrimination, and notwithstanding the tendency for persons to cluster socially, we should expect the economic status of minority and majority group members to be equal, on average. I want now to inquire whether, in this idealized world, the competitive labor market would eventually eliminate any initial differences in the average status of the two groups that historical discrimination might have produced.

One can investigate this question by writing down a mathematical representation of this idealized world. The results obtained depend upon whether only family income or both family income and race influence the set of social clusters (i.e., "communities") to which a family may belong. When persons in society discriminate in their choice of associates on the basis of economic class, but not ethnic group, one can show (with a few additional, technical assumptions) that equal opportunity as defined here always leads (eventually) to an equal distribution of outcomes between the groups.[9] However, when there is social segregation in associational behavior along group as well as class lines, then it is not generally true that historically generated differences between the groups attenuate in the face of racially neutral procedures. Examples may be constructed in which group inequality persists indefinitely, even though no underlying group differences in tastes or abilities exist.

This inequality persists because, when there is some racial segregation among communities—that is, when race operates as a basis of social but not economic discrimination—the process by which status is transferred across generations does not work in the same way for minority and majority families. *The inequality of family circumstances generated by historical economic discrimination is exacerbated by differential access to the benefits of those quasi-public resources available only in the affiliational clusters or "communities."* A kind of negative intragroup "externality" is exerted, through local public goods provision, by the (relatively more numerous) lower-income minority families on higher-income minority families of the same communities. (Or, if you prefer, a positive intragroup externality is exerted by the relatively more numerous higher-income majority families on the lower-income majority families of the same communities.) And, because in a world of some social segregation the group composition of one's community depends in part on the choices of one's neighbors, this effect cannot be completely avoided by an individual's actions.[10] As a consequence, the ability of equal opportunity to bring about equal results is impaired by the desire of majority and minority families to share communities with their own kind. This social clustering of the groups is, of course, an essential feature of a multi-ethnic society such as ours. Indeed, in its absence, there would not be selective mating by racial groups, and in short order (two to three generations) the "problem" of group inequality would be submerged by wholesale miscegenation.

We cannot expect laissez faire to produce equality of results between equally endowed social groups if these groups have experienced differential treatment in the past and if among the channels through which parents pass on status to their children is included the social clustering of individuals along group-exclusive lines. On this argument, state action that is cognizant of groups is *legitimized* by the claim that, in its absence, the consequences of historical wrongs could be with us for the ages. It is *necessitated* by the fact that individuals, in the course of their private social intercourse, engage in racial distinctions that have material consequences. These distinctions are reflected in this model by the "choice of community"—with whom to spend one's time, in what neighborhoods to live, among which children to encourage one's offspring to play, to what set of clubs and friendship networks to belong, and with what sort of person to encourage one's children to mate. Such decisions, in our law and in our ethics, lie beyond the reach of the antidiscrimination mandate. They are private matters that, though susceptible to influence and moral suasion about the tolerance of diversity and the like, are not thought to constitute the proper subject of judicial or legislative decree. The freedom to act upon our own prejudices and discriminations that induce each of us to identify ourselves with and make our lives among a restricted set of our fellows is, for many if not most Americans, among those inalienable rights to life, liberty, and the pursuit of happiness enshrined in our Declaration of Independence.

There are two points I wish to stress about the "minimalist's" argument. First, it rests quite specifically on a conception of group differences in the transmission of status across generations and thus points to those state interventions that are intended to neutralize such disparities; racial preference is not defended here in the abstract, as a generalized remedy for racial inequality or repayment for past wrong. Rather, a specific mechanism that passes on, from past to present to future, the consequences of wrongful acts has been explicated. It is to neutralize *that* mechanism that "taking color into account" is legitimated. And, I would argue, any alternative justification for racial preference should be similarly grounded on an explicit delineation of the "fine structure" of social life that causes the need for such extraordinary state action to arise. The simple evocation of "two hundred years of slavery" or of "past discrimination against minorities and women" does not begin to meet this standard. The question remains: what have been the specific consequences of past deeds that require, for their reversal, the employment of racial classification? The attainment of equal educational opportunities through race-conscious public policy provides a good example. Racial criteria used in the siting or allocation of public housing units would be another. But those racial preferences that confer benefits upon minority group members who do not suffer background-related impediments to their mobility (e.g., minority business set-asides) only could be rationalized if the recipients' connection to their less-fortunate fellows would ensure a sufficiently large beneficial spillover effect on the social mobility of the poor. Many current practices would have difficulty meeting this empirical test.

Moreover, other remedies, not dependent on race-conscious action but intended to reduce severely for all citizens the differential advantages due to poor social background (such as early childhood education, employment programs for disadvantaged urban youths, or publicly financed assistance in the acquisition of higher education) might also be sufficient to avoid the perpetuation of past racial wrongs.[11] In other words, the type of argument that the late Justice William O.

Douglas made in his *DeFunis* dissent, which acknowledges the legitimacy of taking social background into account when making admissions decisions at a public law school but nonetheless rejects explicit racial considerations, might well suffice to meet the concerns raised here. Again, it becomes an empirical question, resolved by inquiry into the explicit mechanisms of social mobility, on which the legitimacy of explicitly racial intervention would turn.

The second, perhaps more important, point is that, in addition to providing a rationale for extraordinary state action intended to limit the degree of group inequality, the underlying behavioral premises of this model suggest that there are *limits* on what one can hope to achieve through the use of racial classification by the state. As noted previously, the reach of civil rights laws will be insufficient to eliminate all socially and economically relevant discriminatory behavior. Evidently we are not willing to undertake the degree of intrusion into the intimate associational choices of individuals that an equalizing redistribution of social capital would require.[12]

Indeed, people enter into enormously important contractual relationships, as a result of which their social and economic status is profoundly affected but among which racial discrimination is routinely practiced. Choice of marital partner is but the most obvious. People discriminate here by race with a vengeance. A black woman, for example, does not have an opportunity equal to that of a white woman to become the wife of a given white man. This inequality in opportunity cuts both ways, but because white men are on the whole better-off financially than blacks, one could imagine calculating the monetary damages to black women of this kind of racial discrimination. A class-action suit might be brought on their behalf, alleging harm based on invidious racial discrimination by white men! That such a notion strikes most people as absurd is mere testimony to the fact that we all basically accept the legitimacy of the practice of racial discrimination in the intimate, personal sphere.

The point, though, is much more general than love and marriage. While we seek to maintain integration through race-conscious allocation of public housing units, it is clear that such practices cannot prevent disgruntled residents from moving away when the racial composition of their neighborhood changes contrary to their liking. And while racial school assignments may be needed, it is also clear that busing for desegregation cannot prevent unhappy parents (those who can afford it!) from sending their children to private schools or moving to another, more ethnically homogenous district. How intrusive we choose to be in restricting such responses is ultimately a political question, though it would seem that eliminating this kind of discrimination altogether would not be a reasonable expectation in this society. Application of the nondiscrimination mandate has, in practice, been restricted to the domain of impersonal, public, and economic transactions (employment, credit, housing, voting rights); it has not been allowed to interfere much with personal, private, and intimately social intercourse.

Moreover, it seems likely that the state's use of racial classification will generally be insufficient in overcoming the economic consequences of this private discriminatory practice—for the fact that such exclusive social "clubs" do form along group lines has important economic consequences. There is an extensive literature in economics and sociology documenting the importance of family and community background as factors influencing a child's later success. Much evidence suggests that the social and economic benefits deriving from privileged access to the "right" communities cannot be offset easily through the state's use of racial classification.

Having offered a rationale for departure from the "color-blind" standard, one could ask at this point whether there are not unsound rationales for worrying about group inequality that have been offered in our public debates. I think this is decidedly so. As political theorists have long recognized, more is required in the achievement and maintenance of a just society than the writing of a philosophical treatise or a constitution that upholds essential principles of liberty and equality. It is also necessary to secure, as a practical matter, the means through which such principles might be lived by and followed in the everyday life of the polity. In a pluralist society such as ours, where distinctions of race and religion are deep and widespread, this is not a trivial matter. I would venture that, at this historical juncture, a sincere commitment in our government to reducing racial inequality is a necessary element of what is needed to establish a just political community in the United States. But this concern is not, by itself, sufficient to that task.

Indeed, certain features of our public discourse over the legitimacy of racial preferences undermine the maintenance of this kind of community. For example, affirmative action represents to many blacks not merely needed public action in the face of past wrong, but also a just recompense for that wrong. The distinction is vital. For many, affirmative action finds its essential rationale in an interpretation of history—i.e., in an ideology: that blacks have been wronged by American society in such a way that justice now demands they receive special consideration as a matter of right. This position can be contrasted with the means-end calculus that I have offered here as justification for the practice. The reparations argument, however, immediately raises a question: why do the wrongs of this particular group and not those of others deserve recompense? Such a question can be poisonous for the politics of a pluralistic democracy.

There is, of course, a favored answer to this question—slavery—but it is one that does not really satisfy anyone, black or white. No amount of recounting the unique sufferings attendant to the slave experience makes plain why a middle-class black should be offered an educational opportunity that is being denied to a lower-class white. Many Americans are descended from forebears who suffered discrimination and mistreatment at the hands of hostile majorities both here and in their native lands. Yet, and here is the crucial point, these Americans on the whole have no claim to the public acknowledgment and ratification of their past suffering as do blacks under affirmative action. The institution of this policy, rationalized in this specific way, therefore implicitly confers special *public* status on the historic injustices faced by its beneficiary groups and hence devalues, implicitly, the injustices endured by others.

The public character of this process of acknowledgment and ratification is central to my argument. We are a democratic, ethnically heterogeneous polity. Racial preferences become issues in local, state, and national elections; they are the topic of debate in corporate board rooms and university faculty meetings; their adoption and maintenance require public consensus, notwithstanding the role the judicial decree has played in their propagation. Therefore, the public consensus requisite to the broad use of such preferences results, de facto, in the complicity of every American in a symbolic recognition of extraordinary societal guilt and culpability regarding the plight of a particular group of citizens. Failure to embrace such practice invites the charge of insensitivity to the wrongs of the past or, indeed, the accusation of racism.[13]

But perhaps most important, the public discourse around racial preference inevitably leads to comparisons among the sufferings of different groups—an exercise in what one might call "comparative victimology." Was the anti-Asian sentiment in the western states culminating in the Japanese internments during the Second World War "worse" than the discrimination against blacks? Were the restrictions and attendant poverty faced by Irish immigrants to northeastern cities a century ago "worse" than those confronting black migrants to those same cities some decades later? And ultimately, was the Holocaust a more profound evil than chattel slavery?

Such questions are, of course, unanswerable, if for no other reason than that they require us to compare degrees of suffering and extent of moral outrage as experienced internally, subjectively, privately, by different peoples. There is no neutral vantage, no Archimedean point, from which to take up such a comparison. We cannot expect that the normal means of argument and persuasion will reconcile divergent perceptions among ethnic groups about the relative moral affront that history has given them. We must not, therefore, permit such disputes to arise if we are to maintain an environment of comity among groups in this ethnically diverse society. Yet some critics of affirmative action can be heard to say "Our suffering has been as great"; and some defenders of racial quotas for blacks have become "tired of hearing about the Holocaust."

These are enormously sensitive matters, going to the heart of how various groups in our society define their collective identities. James Baldwin, writing in the late 1960s in the face of Jewish objections to the use of quotas in New York City, declared what many blacks believe: "One does not wish to be told by an American Jew that his suffering is as great as the American Negro's suffering. It isn't, and one knows it isn't from the very tone in which he assures you that it is" (1985, 427). And when, in 1979, Jesse Jackson visited Yad Vashem, the Holocaust memorial in Jerusalem, he deeply offended many Jews with what he may have considered a conciliatory remark: "The suffering [of the Jews during the Holocaust] is atrocious, but really not unique to human history" (1984, 21). By forcing into the open such comparative judgments concerning what amount to sacred historical meanings for the respective groups, the public rationalization of racial preference as payment for the wrongs of the past has fostered deeper, less-easily assuaged divisions than could ever have been produced by a "mere" conflict of material interests.

So the legitimation of racial preferences is not simply a matter of whether *blacks* think our ancestors' brutalization under slavery exceeded—in its inhumanity, its scale, its violence—the evil of Hitler's ovens. By involving judgments arrived at through democratic processes, racially preferential treatment expresses the collective priorities of the nation as a whole. The special place of blacks in the practice of affirmative action is, therefore, doomed to be controversial, and in the end—should it become a permanent institution and its application continue to favor blacks of comfortable social backgrounds over whites of more modest circumstances—unacceptable to a majority of Americans. Individual citizens—be they Catholics, Jews, Armenians, blacks, or others—will ensure that their children are imbued with a keen sense of the wrongs done to their group in the past. It is important for many Americans to keep alive in the memory of successive generations what their ancestors endured; this is crucial to their knowing, fully, who they are. It is, however, another matter entirely when one group of citizens requires all others to share such a private understanding—when, as a matter of proper social etiquette, all others must share a sense of guilt about the wrongs a particular group has endured.

There is something tenuous, and ultimately pathetic, about the position of blacks in this regard. Do not recoil here at the use of the word *pathetic;* that, after all, is what this issue is all about—evoking the pity, and the guilt, of whites. But, for that very reason, the practice is inconsistent with the goals of freedom and equality for blacks. One cannot be the equal of those whose pity or guilt one actively seeks. By framing the matter thus, the petitioner gives to those being petitioned an awesome power. He who has the capacity to grant your freedom evidently has the ability to take it away—you are therefore dependent upon his magnanimity.

How long can blacks continue to evoke the "slavery was terrible, and it was your fault" rhetoric and still suppose that dignity and equality can be had thereby? Is it not fantastic to suppose that the oppressor, upon hearing the extent of his crimes, would, in the interest of decency, decide to grant the claimants their every demand? The direct sociological role of the slave experience in explaining the current problem seems to be quite limited. The evocation of slavery in our contemporary discourse has little to do with sociology or with historical causation. Its main effect is moral; it uses the slave experience to establish culpability.

Yet the question remains: why should others—the vast majority of whom have ancestors who arrived here after the emancipation or who fought against the institution of slavery or who endured profound discriminations of their own—permit themselves to be morally blackmailed with such rhetoric? How long can the failures of the present among black Americans be excused and explained by reference to the wrongs of the past? Would not one expect that nonblack Americans would eventually become inured to the entreaties of blacks who explain teenage motherhood, urban crime, and low SAT scores with the observation that blacks have been in bondage for 400 years? When pummeled with this rhetoric nowadays, most whites sit in silence. Dare we ask: what does that silence mean? (And, indeed, what does the constant repetition of this litany do to blacks themselves?) At some point, won't resentment, contempt, and disdain for a group of people that sees itself in such terms begin to rise? Consider the contradictions: blacks seek general recognition of their accomplishments in the past and yet must insist upon the extent to which their ancestors were reduced to helplessness. Blacks must emphasize that they live in a nation that has never respected their humanity, yet expect that by so doing, their fellow countrymen will be moved to come to their assistance.

I would now like to explore some of the deleterious side effects that can issue from the use of color-conscious methods in the public or private sectors. Reliance on affirmative action to achieve minority or female representation in highly prestigious positions can have a decidedly negative impact on the esteem of the groups because it can lead to the general presumption that members of the beneficiary groups could not qualify for such positions without the help of special preference.

If, in an employment situation, say, it is known that racial classification is in use, so that differential selection criteria are employed for the hiring of different racial groups, and if it is known that the quality of performance on the job depends on how one did on the criteria of selection, then it is a rational statistical inference to impute a lower expected quality of job performance to persons of the race that was preferentially favored in selection. Using racial classification in selection for employment creates objective incentives for customers, coworkers, and others to take race into account after the employment decision has been made. Selection by race makes race "informative" in the postselection environment.

In what kind of environment is such an "informational externality" likely to be important? Precisely when it is difficult to obtain objective and accurate readings on a person's productivity and when that unknown productivity is of significance to those sharing the employment environment with the preferentially selected employee. For example, in a "team production" situation (like a professional partnership or among students forming study groups), where output is the result of the efforts of several individuals and individual contributions cannot be separately identified, the willingness of workers to participate in "teams" containing those suspected of having been preferentially selected will be less than it would have been if the same criteria of selection had been used for all employees.[14]

Also, when the employment carries prestige and honor because it represents an unusual accomplishment of which very few individuals are capable (an appointment to a top university faculty, for example), the use of preferential selection will undermine the ability of those preferred to garner for themselves the honorary, as distinct from the pecuniary, benefits associated with the employment. (And this is true even for individuals who do not themselves require the preference.) If, for example, Nobel prizes in physics were awarded with the idea in mind that each continent should be periodically represented, it would be widely suspected (by those insufficiently informed to make inde-

pendent judgments in such matters, and that includes nearly everyone)
that a physicist from Africa who won the award had not made as significant a contribution to the science as one from Europe, even if the
objective scientific merit of the African's contribution were as great.
If law review appointments at a prestigious law school were made to
ensure appropriate group balance, students belonging to preferred groups
might never earn honor available to others, no matter how great their
individual talents.

An interesting example of the phenomenon I am discussing here
can be found in the U.S. military. Sociologist Charles Moskos (1986)
published an article in *The Atlantic* describing the results of his investigation of the status of blacks in the U.S. Army. He noted that
roughly 7 percent of all Army generals are now black, as is nearly 10
percent of the Army's officer corps. Moskos reports that among the
black officers he interviewed, the view was widely held that in the
Army blacks "[s]till . . . have to be better qualified than whites in
order to advance." That is, racial discrimination still exists there. One
senior black officer was "worried about some of the younger guys. They
don't understand that a black still has to do more than a white to get
promoted. . . . If they think equal effort will get equal reward, they've
got a big surprise coming" (1986, 64). Yet, despite this awareness of
racial discrimination, these officers were dubious about the value of
racially preferential treatment in the military. Black commanders tended
to be tougher in their evaluation of black subordinates than were white
commanders of their white subordinates. Even those officers who
thought affirmative action was necessary in civilian life disapproved
of its use in the military. According to Moskos: "They draw manifest
self-esteem from the fact that they themselves have not been beneficiaries of such [preferential] treatment—rather the reverse. Black officers distrust black leaders in civilian life who would seek advancement
through racial politics or as supplicants of benevolent whites."[15]

Further illustration of unintended consequence, combining both
the "team production" and "honor" effects, comes from the world of
corporate management.[16] Many of those charged with the responsibility of managing large companies in the U.S. economy today are
quite concerned with the state of their minority hiring efforts. The
advent of affirmative action masks some serious, continuing disparities in the rates at which blacks, Hispanics, and women are penetrating
the very highest ranks of power and control within these institutions.
While equal opportunity could be said to be working tolerably well at
the entry and middle-level positions, it has proven ineffective in help-
ing these "newcomers" to advance to the upper echelons of their or-

ganizations. The problem is so widespread that a name has been invented for it—the *plateau phenomenon.*

Increasingly, able and ambitious young women and blacks talk of taking the entrepreneurial route to business success, only to feel stymied by their inability to get on the "fast track" within their companies. Wall Street brokerage and law firms, though they have increased the number of young black associates in their ranks, still have very few black partners and virtually no black senior or managing partners.[17] Many large companies now have their complement of minority vice presidents and staff personnel (especially in the governmental relations and equal opportunity areas), but they continue to have very few minorities at the rank of senior vice president or higher and a paucity of nonwhites in those authoritative line positions where the companies' profits and future leaders are made.

The failure of women and minorities to penetrate the highest levels of an organization involves factors beyond the raw competence of the individuals involved. While people differ in their abilities, no one today would suggest that there are no blacks or women with the aptitude and dedication to succeed at the highest levels in the corporate world. The fact that so very few of them do succeed suggests that the problem may well stem from subtle aspects of interpersonal relations within companies in addition to old-fashioned racism. When a company determines to increase the number of women and minorities in its management ranks, the normal method is to make the recruitment and retention of such persons an organizational goal and to evaluate the performance of those with authority to hire, in part, by the extent to which they succeed in advancing this goal. The company actually encourages its personnel decision makers to use racial (or gender) classification in addition to other employment screens. This practice of goal setting is done with an explicitness and seriousness that, of course, varies from company to company. Yet, the inevitable result is to confer some advantage upon minority and women employees in the competition for entry and mid-level positions in the company. Even when such preferential treatment is avoided by management, the perception among white male employees, in this era of constant focus on the need to increase minority and female participation, is likely to be that the "newcomers" are getting some kind of break that is not available to them.

In addition, minority or female employees may be hired or promoted into jobs for which they are not ready; better-qualified nonminority personnel may, from time to time, be passed over for promotion. Here too, nonfavored employees will often *perceive* that mistakes of this sort are being made even when in fact they are not. Resentments and jealousies are likely to arise. Charges of "reverse discrimination" will, in all probability, be made more or less quietly among white men who see themselves as disadvantaged. It only takes one or two "disasters"— minority appointments that do not work out—to reinforce already-existing prejudices and convince many in the organization that all minority managers are suspect. *The use of racial or sexual employment goals is therefore likely to alter the way in which minority or women managers are viewed by their white male subordinates and superiors.*

Even though most minority employees may measure up to, or even exceed, the standards of performance that others in the firm must meet, the presence of just a few who do not casts an aura of suspicion over the others. Such uncertainty about so-called affirmative action hires—those who, it is suspected, would not have their jobs if they were not members of a minority or female—may only reflect the prejudice or bigotry of their coworkers. But, and this is crucial, to the extent that the suspicion is widely held, it can work to undermine the objective effectiveness of the minority manager.

Since competition for advancement from the lower rungs of the corporate ladder is sure to be keen, there is a natural tendency for those not benefiting from the organization's equal opportunity goals to see the progress of minorities or women as due in great part to affirmative action. If, to illustrate, four white men and one woman are competing for a position that ultimately is awarded to the woman, all four male employees may harbor the suspicion that *they* were unfairly passed over in the interest of meeting diversity goals, when in fact this supposition must be false for at least three of them.[18] When, as happens in many companies, the attainment of equal opportunity goals is seen as something that occurs only at the expense of productivity—as a price to be paid for doing business in the inner city or to "keep the feds off our backs"—these suspicions are given tacit confirmation by the organization's very approach to the problem of diversity.

Thus, the use of racial classification can entail serious costs. If not properly and carefully administered, it can create or promote a general perception that those minorities or women who benefit from the firm's interest in increasing diversity are somehow less qualified than others competing for the same positions. And when widely held, this general perception, whether well-founded or merely a reflection of prejudice, can work to limit the degree of success and long-term career prospects of minority and female managers. In a managerial environment, the productivity of an individual is not merely determined by the individual's knowledge, business judgment, industry, or vision. It depends as well on the ability of the manager to induce the cooperation, motivation, trust, and confidence of those whom he or she must lead. It depends, in other words, on the extent to which the manager can command the *respect* of his or her colleagues and subordinates.

This observation illustrates the fact that general suspicion of the competence of minority or female managerial personnel can become a self-fulfilling prophecy. When the bottom-line performance of a manager depends on his or her ability to motivate others, and when those others begin with a lack of confidence in the ability of the manager, then even the most technically competent, hard-working individual may fail to induce top performance in his or her people. And the fact that top performance is not achieved only serves to confirm the belief of those who doubted the manager's competence in the first place.[19]

This self-reinforcing cycle of negative expectations is likely to be a particularly significant problem in the higher-level and line, as distinct from lower-level and staff, positions in an organization. Here an individual's contribution to company profitability depends heavily upon leadership and interpersonal qualities: securing the confidence and trust of peers, motivating subordinates to achieve up to their potential. Managerial performance at this level depends rather less on individual, technical skills. Whether one becomes really "good" at these jobs is determined, in part, by how "good" others believe one can be.

Another critical factor at this level of an organization is self-confidence, which also may be undermined by the use of racial classification. Among the questions most frequently asked by minority and female personnel about to assume a post of unusual responsibility is: "Would I have been offered this position if I had not been a black (or woman, or . . .)?" Most people in such a situation want to be reassured that their achievement has been earned and is not based simply on an organizational requirement of diversity. And not only that, they want their prospective associates and subordinates to be assured of this as well. When appointments are being made partly on a racial or sexual basis, recipients' beliefs that they are as good as their achievements would seem to suggest are weakened. A genuinely outstanding person who rises quickly to the mid-level of an organization without ever knowing for sure whether this career advance would have taken place in the absence of affirmative action may not approach the job with the same degree of self-assurance as otherwise would be the case.[20] And this absence of the full measure of confidence can make the difference between success and failure in the upper managerial ranks.

All of these potentially detrimental effects that I associate with the use of preferential treatment of nonwhite and female employees within an enterprise are reinforced by the general discussion of racial and sexual inequality in our society. The constant attention to numerical imbalances in the number of blacks versus whites or women versus men who have achieved a particular rank in the corporate sector, in addition to placing what may be entirely warranted pressure on individual companies, serves to remind people—black and white, male and female—that such preferences are a part of their work environment. In order to defend affirmative action in the political arena, its advocates often seem to argue that almost no blacks or women could reach the highest levels of achievement without the aid of special pressures. Yet, this tactic runs the risk of presuming that all blacks and women, whether directly or indirectly, are indebted to civil rights activity for their achievements. And this presumption may reinforce the general suspicion about minority or female competence that already exists.

None of this discussion should be construed as an expression of doubt about the desirability of vigorously promoting diversity in corporate management or elsewhere in American society. What seems crucial is that, in light of the pitfalls discussed, the process of achieving diversity be *managed* with care, mindful of the dangers inherent in the situation. Affirmative action involves not simply the *rights* of individuals, as many lawyers are given to argue, but also the *prudence* of the particular means used to advance their interests. The plateau phenomenon, where able young minority or female managers find themselves unable to advance to the top ranks of their companies, undoubtedly reflects factors beyond those I have discussed. But it is the consensus of personnel managers with whom I have talked that the factors I have selected are involved in many cases. In particular, it seems quite probable that general distrust of the capabilities of minority and female managers will accompany and reinforce old-fashioned racist or sexist aversion to having "outsiders" join the "old boys network" within the organization. Such suspicions can, where occasionally validated by experience, provide the perfect excuse for preexisting prejudices, which are not merely "bad" behaviors that should be censured. They are a part of the environment in which these policies operate and may determine their success or failure.

In summary, I have suggested the need for a more rigorous justification of the departure from the simple "color-blind" interpretation of the antidiscrimination principle, which the contemporary practice of preferential treatment represents. I have tried to provide such a justification. My argument turns on the extent to which *social* discrimination among today's citizens will perpetuate indefinitely the group inequality engendered by past *economic* discrimination. Because the antidiscrimination principle does not extend into the most intimate of private, associational choices, it is compatible with the continued practice of racial discrimination in such choices. Yet this practice, together with a history of racial discrimination in the public sphere, will ensure that the consequences of past bigotry become a permanent part of the social landscape. To avoid this possibility, I argue, the use of group-conscious public action is justified.

Yet, I have recognized that such preferential policies may not be the only, or the best, response to persistent group inequality. And I have suggested that some of the arguments used to justify racial preferences seem likely to exacerbate, rather than diminish, the problems of racial conflict that continue to afflict our society. I have been particularly critical of the "reparations" argument, which justifies special treatment of today's blacks because of mistreatment of blacks in the past. I have noted that such public practice implicitly elevates the past suffering of blacks to a privileged position—above that held by the mistreatments endured by other ethnic Americans—and does so in a way likely to be particularly controversial. This problem seems especially severe when the preferential practices in question benefit blacks of comfortable economic circumstances at the expense of ethnic whites who are more poorly situated.

Finally, I have noted that, even where justified, the use of racial preference may not always be wise. This is a prudential argument that is meant to have only restricted applicability. There are certain types of environments in which the danger of negative unintended consequences of racial preference seems particularly acute. In these environments I urge that much greater caution be employed when efforts to increase "out-group" participation are undertaken because the use of differential standards for members of different groups can work to undermine the capacity of the intended beneficiaries to garner for themselves the full benefits of their achievements and can even objectively impede their functioning.

The debate over affirmative action has been left too much to lawyers and philosophers and has engaged too little the interests of economists, sociologists, political scientists, and psychologists. It is as if for this policy, unlike all others, we could determine a priori the wisdom of its application in all instances—as if its practice were either "right" or "wrong," never simply "prudent" or "unwise." If I accomplish anything here, I hope it is to impress upon the reader the ambiguity and complexity of this issue, to make him or her see that in this area there is the opportunity to do much good but also the risk of doing much harm. The impassioned pursuit of justice, untempered by respect for a reasoned evaluation of the consequences of our efforts, obviously is not an advance over indifference.

Notes

1. See, for example, Thomas Sowell (1983). Sowell chronicles numerous instances around the world in which group differences in economic status do not correspond to the presence or absence of oppression. Often, as with the Chinese in Southeast Asian countries or Indians in East Africa or Jews in Western Europe, those subject to oppression have done better economically than those in the role of oppressor.
2. Hubert Humphrey's speech to the Senate during the floor debate on the Civil Rights Act of 1964 is often cited in this regard.
3. For example, see Amartya Sen (1979). The anonymity axiom requires a social decision maker to be indifferent between two distributions of economic advantage that differ only in terms of who gets what reward but that have the same overall pattern of reward.
4. See, for discussion of this transformation, Bennett and Eastland (1976); and, with particular focus on the area of school desegregation, Wolters (1984).
5. I think here, for example, of Ronald Dworkin's (1977) essay "*DeFunis* v. *Sweat*," in which he attempts, with uncharacteristic inelegance, to distinguish between *DeFunis*, on the one hand, and *Sweat* v. *Painter* on the other. For a critical analysis of Dworkin's argument, see Michael Walzer (1981).
6. The following argument draws on my previous work. See Loury (1976, 1977, 1981, 1985a).
7. James Fishkin (1983) has discussed the philosophical implications of what he calls "background inequalities" for a liberal theory of status disparities. His notion of the "trilemma of equal opportunity"—an unresolvable tension between the ideals of equal opportunity, reward according to desert, and the autonomy of the family—is closely related to the argument offered.
8. In keeping with my earlier discussion, it would be possible to treat such differences in tastes that have economic consequences (e.g., occupational preferences, entrepreneurial inclinations) as a part of what is conveyed through parents' social capital.
9. See Loury (1977); for a rigorous mathematical treatment of this question, see Loury (1976).
10. See, for example, Schelling (1978), ch. 4, for an analysis of how even a very mild individual preference for association with one's own kind can lead, in the aggregate, to a highly segregated outcome. For instance, Schelling notes that if everyone would merely prefer to live in a neighborhood in which their group is in the majority, then only complete separation will satisfy the preferences of all members of both groups.
11. This, in essence, is what sociologist William Julius Wilson (1978, 1984) has been arguing with respect to the inner-city poor. He notes that the primary problems facing poor blacks derive from their economic plight and afflict poor whites as well. Moreover, he argues that political support for dramatic efforts to reverse these problems will be more readily had if those efforts are couched in racially universal terms.
12. The U.S. Supreme Court's decision in the Detroit cross-district busing case, *Milliken* v. *Bradley*, 418 U.S. 171 (1974), limiting the use of metropolitan busing to solve the "white flight" problem, gives a classic illustration of this point.
13. See Loury (1986) for more detail.
14. Recently, lawsuits have been brought by mid-level minority employees working in large bureaucracies, at IBM and the U.S. State Department, for example, alleging that they are not treated the same by supervisors and coworkers. Yet, if they were hired under different criteria than coworkers, they *are not* in fact the same on the average! Differential treatment, though regrettable, should come therefore as no surprise.
15. Indeed, in order to defend such programs in the private sector, it becomes necessary for advocates to argue that almost no blacks could reach the positions in question without special favors. When there is internal disagreement among black intellectuals, for example, about the merits of affirmative action, critics of the policy are

attacked as being disingenuous, since (it is said) they clearly owe their own prominence to the very policy they criticize. (See, for example, Cornel West 1986). The specific circumstances of the individual do not matter in this, for it is presumed that *all* blacks are indebted to civil rights activity for their achievements. The consequence is a kind of "socialization" of the individual's success. The individual's effort to claim achievement for himself or herself (and thus to secure the autonomy and legitimacy needed to deviate from group consensus) is perceived as a kind of betrayal. From the reasonable observation that all blacks are indebted to those who fought and beat Jim Crow, these intellectuals draw the conclusion that the group's most accomplished persons, by celebrating their personal achievements as being due to their ability and not to racial preferences, have betrayed their fellows!

16. The following account is drawn from an unpublished paper of mine, Loury (1985b).

17. Frank Raines, black partner in Lazard Freres, reported in an interview that there are only three black partners in Wall Street investment firms, two of whom handle public finance issues (local black governments being primary among their clients).

18. Psychological "incentives" exist for people to use this excuse even when it is not true. This gives them a good rationale for their own failure. As one colleague cleverly observed, "Affirmative action is a boon to mediocre whites—[it gives] them reason to think better of themselves than they otherwise could."

19. Consider the position of a female commander of troops in a combat situation. This person will be ineffective if, when issuing critical orders under duress, she is unable to inspire the obedience and confidence of her troops. Her troops' belief in her capacities is thus an objective determinant of her capacities. It would seem particularly unwise, in the face of widespread male suspicion of the performance capabilities of female commanders, to promote any woman into such a position who did not exhibit absolutely impeccable qualifications. That is, until the ability of women to function under combat conditions has been amply demonstrated, it would seem to be unwise to employ *preferential* criteria for the selection of women to such positions. To do so encourages precisely those beliefs that could undermine the effectiveness of the new commander.

20. Moreover, if you push too fast, good people may fail and be marked for life by that failure. Consider the case of the graduate student who would have done just fine at State U., but who ends up at the bottom of the class at Harvard.

References

Baldwin, James, 1967. "Negroes Are Anti-Semitic Because They're Anti-White." *New York Times Magazine*, April 9. Reprinted in Baldwin, James, 1985. *The Price of the Ticket*. New York: St. Martin's Press, 427.

Bennett, William, and Terry Eastland, 1976. *Counting by Race*. Ithaca: Cornell University Press.

Broderick, F., and A. Meier, 1965. *Negro Protest Thought in the Twentieth Century*. Indianapolis: Bobbs-Merrill, 404.

Dworkin, Ronald, 1977. "*DeFunis* v. *Sweat*." In *Taking Rights Seriously*, ch. 9. Cambridge: Harvard University Press.

Fishkin, James, 1983. *Justice, Equal Opportunity, and the Family*. New Haven: Yale University Press.

Jackson, Jesse, 1984. "The Blacks and American Foreign Policy." *Commentary*, April, 21.

Loury, Glenn C., 1986. "Behind the Black–Jewish Split." *Commentary*, January.

———, 1985a. "Beyond Civil Rights." *The New Republic*, October 5.

———, 1985b. "Equal Opportunity: Reality, Achievable Goal, or Elusive Dream?" Paper presented at symposium, Equal Opportunity in Corporate Management, organized by the Equitable Life Assurance Society of America in cooperation with the Institute for Leadership in Corporate Management at Morehouse College, New York, December.

―――, 1981. "Is Equal Opportunity Enough?" *American Economic Review. Papers and Proceedings* 71 (May): 122–126.

―――, 1977. "A Dynamic Theory of Racial Income Differences." In *Women, Minorities and Employment Discrimination,* eds. P.A. Wallace and A. LaMond, 153–186. Lexington, Mass.: Lexington Books.

―――, 1976. "Essays in the Theory of Income Distribution." Ph.D. diss., Department of Economics, M.I.T., ch. 1.

Moskos, Charles, 1986. "Success Story: Blacks in the Army." *The Atlantic Monthly,* May, 64.

Rae, Douglas, 1981. *Equalities.* Cambridge: Harvard University Press.

Schelling, Thomas, 1978. *Micromotives and Macrobehaviors.* New York: W.W. Norton.

Sen, Amartya, 1979. *Collective Choice and Social Welfare.* Amsterdam: North Holland Publishing Co., 68.

Sowell, Thomas, 1983. *The Economics and Politics of Race: An International Perspective.* New York: William Morrow and Co.

Walzer, Michael, 1981. *Spheres of Justice,* ch. 5. New York: Basic Books.

West, Cornel, 1986. "Unmasking the Black Conservatives." *The Christian Century,* July 16–23, 645.

Wilson, William Julius, 1984. "Race-Specific Policies and the Truly Disadvantaged." *Yale Law and Policy Review* 2 (Spring): 272–290.

―――, 1978. *The Declining Significance of Race.* Chicago: University of Chicago Press.

Wolters, Raymond, 1984. *The Burden* of Brown. Knoxville: University of Tennessee Press.

PART THREE

Culture, Competition, and Discrimination

SHERRIE A. KOSSOUDJI

Chapter 10. Pride and Prejudice: Culture's Role in Markets

IS CULTURE RESPONSIBLE for the inability of black workers
to achieve parity with white workers? This question, not a new one,
represents but the latest round of social theorizing on the source of
historical employment inequalities.[1] The current debate focuses on
the relative impacts of discrimination and black culture. Discrimination theory, which implies that white culture is the problem, has
fallen out of favor with many policy makers; cultural explanations are
on the rise in both policy circles and scholarly works.

Culture is usually thought of with pride because it connects images
of a people's past with their present. Individuals' experiences are en-
riched by their cultural associations, and socialization equips them
with the skills that make it possible in adulthood to satisfy their needs
(at least to the extent that the environment permits). Instead, in the
cultural approach, aspects of black culture and its associated socialization patterns are, in effect, said to limit experiences and sabotage
blacks' labor market opportunities. Its implications lead us to question
the efficacy of administered labor market policies. Not surprisingly,
the cultural approach was very popular with the Reagan administration because it provided a potent salvo against the concept of affirmative action.

The "culturalogical school" is still amorphous—at this point, it is
characterized by only the most general of ideas. Those who suggest
that culture explains labor market behavior take the view that black
culture, especially as it is manifested by the structure of black family
life, does not encourage the development of human capital skills and
attitudes that promote mobility in the labor market. The relationship
between welfare programs and black household structure leaves young
boys without stable role models, while premarital pregnancy inter-

I would like to thank Warren Whatley, William Darity, and participants of the Population Studies Center Brown Bag series for valuable comments and insights on the
work presented in this paper.

rupts, possibly forever, the schooling of young girls. Low labor market expectations discourage self-investment, and the lack of a defined work ethic leads to unstable labor market behavior and from there to significant lifetime unemployment rates. Proponents cite these and other possible relationships as examples of how black culture inhibits labor market success. Unfavorable comparisons are made between these behavioral patterns and those of various immigrant groups who were also historically subject to institutionalized discrimination.[2]

The acceptance of culturalogical arguments has been enhanced by two major failures of the discrimination approach: the first, a theoretical failure; the second, a political one. The theoretical failure rests on the fact that neoclassical economic scholars have been unable to produce models that predict that long-term discrimination can be maintained in a market system. According to the Beckerian type model, nondiscriminators, because of their lower costs, should eventually drive discriminators out of the market. The political failure results from policy measures implemented over the past twenty years that have attempted to erase legislatively the accumulated effects of past discrimination. On the one hand, affirmative action policies have failed to erase fundamental economic disparities—primarily because most individuals are not willing to pay for society's past mistakes. On the other hand, because such policies have helped propel some blacks into positions of relative economic power, people are encouraged to believe either that discrimination is no longer a problem in our society or that affirmative action has only helped those who would have made it anyway.

Consider the underlying nature of the culturalogical argument. First, it assumes that observed black behavior is not simply a rational *response* to environmental constraints.[3] If black actions are formulated as rational responses to prejudice, then the whole culturological argument becomes moot. Though the proximate cause of economic differentials is black culture, the underlying sources are still the prejudice in white culture and the ability of whites to translate that prejudice into discriminatory action. Second, to argue that black culture explains race differences in outcomes is like statistically equating black skin with those outcomes: most black adults in the labor market have basic inextricable ties to black culture. Even though some claim that middle-class blacks live in a "white world," and hence have few ties with black culture, this argument is problematic because it infers causality from result. Those blacks who are successful have given up their ties to black culture; therefore, those who have not made it must have failed because they maintain those ties. Besides, many middle-class blacks would disagree that they have cut their ties to black culture; the black experience still colors their world viewpoint and actions.

It is impossible, then, to separate culture and skin color to directly test a cultural hypothesis.[4] An indirect test of another hypothesis may, however, prove useful. Researchers have long had to rely on indirect tests and examination of residuals in discrimination studies. In this chapter I examine the impact of white prejudice in a market where black culture cannot be a factor, and the controlled performance of blacks and other ethnic groups is compared. That market is the adoption market for very young children.

The adoption market provides a unique arena for examining the issues of race and prejudice because, on the supply side, characteristics other than race can be held constant. There is a supply and demand of individual characteristics just as there is in labor markets. Children with particular traits are available in the adoption market, and there are potential adoptive parents who demand those traits by assigning implicit values to them. By considering only very young children, the cultural differences of adoptees can be minimized, if not eliminated. Thus, if there are differences in adoption rates by race, then they cannot be due to the cultural baggage of the children themselves. Is there evidence of racial prejudice in this market? Can its sources be identified? And would we expect behavior in this market to spill over and inform us about other kinds of market behavior? I will argue that prejudice and discrimination do exist in this market *and* that this behavior is indicative of the general thrust of race relations in this country. To do so requires a comprehensive collection of data on children available for adoption, their characteristics, the actual rates of adoption, and the characteristics and behavior of potential adopters. First, a brief digression on data and on the scope of the chapter.

The adoption market has long occupied a shadowy niche in our society. Historically, adoptive parents were those who had failed at procreation, while adoptive children were available because the biological parents had participated in unsanctioned sexual activity or could not provide for their legitimate offspring. Even today, when our social welfare system administers to a much broader clientele, secrecy pervades this market. Thus, we have been sadly negligent about data collection: the standard complaint in the social work literature is that it is easier to find data on dog food production and quality than on children in social services. Available data are often sketchy; national statistics on adoptions are plentiful in some years and nonexistent in others. The last federal report on adoption was based on 1975 data, and until the 1977 survey, *National Study of Social Services to Children and Their Families*, there were no national statistics on the number of children available for adoption.[5] Not enough data exist for any one year to permit discussion of all these dimensions of this market. Nonetheless, secondary data from the past fifteen years can be used to supplement the 1977 survey information. Together they provide ample evidence on adoption markets.[6]

There are further motivations for restricting the scope of the study to young children (where possible). Most social work professionals agree that by the age of 11, children (no matter what their race) have a very low probability of being adopted. Many claim that even 7-year-olds are "over the hill."[7] Older children have already formed personalities; they are more likely to be psychologically damaged by early and bad familial relationships; they are more likely to have assimilated the instability of long-term institutional or foster care. For all these reasons, I have included only children aged 0 to 5 for those data over which I have some control. Also, for obvious reasons, adoptions by relatives are excluded from the study.

The term *market* in itself represents a major departure from the general study of adoption.[8] Referring to adoption institutions and the adoption process in this way would, to many people, appear to depersonalize a very personal decision. But it is important to distinguish between treating children like any other marketable commodity and recognizing that, in the world of adoption, features of a market pertain. There are demanders of adoptive children and suppliers of adoptive children, and the demand and supply are conditioned by economic factors. Prices exist, whether they be the administered prices of public agencies (where all children generally cost the same) or the free-market prices of many independent (arranged by individuals) and intercountry adoptions (which may vary by the characteristics of the child). Furthermore, it is clear that the concept of a market for babies is expanding. The use of sperm banks, in-vitro fertilization, and surrogate mothering—possibilities that only a few years ago seemed bizarre—is growing by the day, and the contractual features of these markets are being tested in our court system.

The decision about whether to adopt (or give up for adoption) is contingent upon price, preferences, and other perceived costs. "Prices" for children vary considerably. Public agency prices are the lowest; they reflect the administrative costs (minus subsidies, in some cases) of the agency. Licensed state agencies are forbidden to buy and sell babies or to earn (pecuniary) profits. Independent and intercountry adoptions are associated with much higher, fluctuating prices. Lawyers who arrange independent adoptions are permitted to exact a fee for services plus payment for the mother's hospital and related childbearing ex-

TABLE 10.1. *Approved Homes and Available Children, by Race and by Agency Auspices (240 Agencies)*

	Approved homes		Children available		Difference between no. homes and children
	Number	Percentage	Number	Percentage	
73 public agencies					
White	4,960	91	4,239	78	721
Nonwhite	511	9	1,162	22	−651
Total	5,471	100	5,401	100	70
167 voluntary agencies					
White	16,456	94	14,153	83	2,303
Nonwhite	1,073	6	2,883	17	−1,810
Total	17,529	100	17,036	100	493
All 240 agencies					
White	21,416	93	18,392	82	3,024
Nonwhite	1,584	7	4,045	18	−2,461
Total	23,000	100	22,437	100	563

Source: Lucille Grow, *A New Look at Supply and Demand in Adoption* (New York: Child Welfare League of America, 1970), p. 8, Table 4.

penses, and since these charges are difficult to police, in practice they often conceal a payment for the baby itself (Posner 1977).

The adoption market has two characteristics that emphasize the role of race and culture. First, most "demanders" in the adoption market are white. Second, black children are disproportionately represented in the welfare system's pool from which adoptable children are supplied: Of the children who were residing in substitute care in fiscal year 1983, 52.7 percent were white and 33.9 percent were black.[9] Only 11 percent of the United States population is black.

In the world where demand and supply equilibrate and race is not a suitable criterion for adoption, one might form the initial hypothesis that all children are adopted and that there is a significant amount of interracial adoption. Table 10.1 shows that, even as early as 1970, this world is certainly feasible. In 1970, 93 percent of homes approved for adoption were white, but white children were a much lower percentage of children who were available. If the excess white demanders went on to adopt nonwhite children (who, in 1970, were almost all black), all children would be adopted and about 61 percent of available nonwhite children would be adopted by whites.

This world, although feasible, does not exist. While interracial adoption was not uncommon during this period (between 1968 and 1973 23 to 35 percent of adopted black children were adopted by whites),[10] only a small proportion of black children available for adoption were actually adopted. In 1969, for example, only 44 percent of available

TABLE 10.2.   *Percentage of Children Free for Adoption for Whom a Home Has Been Found (by Race and Age)*

	Age					
	0	1	2	3	4	5
White (n = 22,827)	92.0	84.0	92.1	81.2	74.4	65.0
Black (n = 6,205)	52.8	58.3	58.7	61.1	70.1	49.5
Difference	+39.2	+25.7	+33.4	+20.1	+4.3	+15.5

Source: Data are weighted and are from *The National Study of Social Services to Children and Their Families*, Department of Health and Human Services (Washington, D.C.: GPO, 1977).
Note: Excludes children for whom the information was not available.

TABLE 10.3.   *Distribution of Finalized Adoptions and Children Awaiting Adoption of All Children in Substitute Care in FY83 and FY82*

% of all children	White	Black	Hispanic	Others[a]	Unknown	Total
Whose adoptions were finalized in FY83	56.4	27.9	7.1	8.0	0.6	100
Awaiting adoption FY83	49.2	41.0	5.5	4.0	0.3	100
Whose adoptions were finalized in FY82	68.5	18.5	4.9	6.4	1.7	100
Awaiting adoption FY82	41.8	45.9	8.0	3.8	0.5	100

Source: *Characteristics of Children in Substitute and Adoptive Care*, The Voluntary Cooperative Information System (VCIS). These data come from state agencies administering public child-welfare programs. Forty-seven states plus the District of Columbia sent data to VCIS in FY82; fifty states plus the District of Columbia sent data to VCIS in FY83. In addition, the FY82 data are revised based on the VCIS statistical bulletin, "Additional Summaries of the FY82 VCIS Adoption Data," published in February 1985.
   [a] Others are predominantly Asians, Pacific Islanders, American Indians, and Alaskan Natives.

black children were adopted, while 92 percent of white children were.[11] At very young ages there is a close-to-100-percent adoption rate for whites—if not excess demand—while black infants and children remain in excess supply. This general result holds for every study since 1969, no matter what its focus.[12] Table 10.2, using national survey data, shows that at each age between 0 and 5 there was an "adoption gap" of from 4 to 40 percent between whites and blacks in 1977. Table 10.3 shows, in a different way, the dissimilarities of race between those actually adopted and those still awaiting adoption in fiscal year 1982 (FY82) and fiscal year 1983 (FY83). In FY83 black children were 27.9

TABLE 10.4. *Percentage of Children Legally Free for Adoption (by Age and Race)*

	Age					
	0	1	2	3	4	5
White (n = 64,378)	44.7	35.3	33.8	18.4	22.1	33.2
Black (n = 33,828)	24.0	9.5	14.5	36.9	12.8	8.0
Difference	+20.7	+25.8	+19.3	−18.5	+9.3	+25.2

Soure: Data are weighted and from *The National Study of Social Services to Children and Their Families,* Department of Health and Human Services (Washington, D.C.: GPO, 1977).
   Note: Includes *only* those children for whom the court or the welfare agency has custody.

percent of those in substitute care whose adoptions were finalized but 41.0 percent of children still awaiting adoption.[13]

Most people believe that these figures are underestimates of the racial adoption gap. Black children are considered to be hard to place, and the welfare agencies have at least three coping mechanisms for this. Subsidized adoption for hard-to-place children has been a growing practice since the 1970s. Adoption subsidies may be available through the child's adolescence, reducing both the fixed and variable cost of rearing an adoptive child. Second, agencies can discourage black mothers from placing their children with an adoptive agency by suggesting other possibilities. The following are typical responses from agency supervisors when they were asked if they mentioned to black natural mothers that the agency may have difficulty placing the child:

Yes. Black mothers are told placement might not be a possibility, and sometimes they say they want the child back if it isn't adopted.

Yes. I think women know before they come in. We mention difficulty in placing to black women just as we do to women who are mothers of children who are hard to place for other reasons.

(Day 1979, 6–7)

Agencies also can choose *when* many children in their care are freed for adoption. Many will not release black children for adoption when there is such a large pool of children already available. Because of this, black children may remain in long-term foster or institutional care. Looking only at those children for whom the court or the welfare agency has custody, Table 10.4 shows that the freeing-up rate is also lower for blacks.

Given this evidence, the next question must be, "Why aren't black children being adopted?" Obviously, both demand and supply factors influence the market outcome. First, however, assume there are no supply constraints and consider the components of demand. What criteria do people use when they demand children?

When economists discuss the demand for children we generally envision a Beckerian type model where couples reproduce to gain utility and among the choice variables are the quantity and quality of children. The quality aspects of children are often proxied by the outputs of parental care that are perceived to lead to labor market success. The child's genetic features remain random variables beyond the choice of the parents (outside of their marriage market behavior). When children are adopted, however, the child commodity to be demanded embodies more explicit choices. Quality can be viewed as having *ex ante* and *ex post* components. That is, parents can *choose, ex ante*, the "quality" of the characteristics of the (already existing) children they are willing to adopt. Several criteria stand out as potential qualitative arguments of the utility function: Youth (the younger, the better) has already been discussed as a positive attribute for adoptive kids. The sex of the child also may be important to many parents, although in the aggregate there should be no dominant sex preference. Normalcy, both physical and mental, lowers the cost and may increase the satisfaction of child rearing. Even genetic similarity is a criterion for selecting an adoptive child; parents may get a "genetic kick" from having a child who looks like them in as many ways as possible. Race itself should *not* be an argument of the utility function—outside of the "genetic kick" possibility—unless parents believe that there are inherent quality differences between races.

This provides two potential explanations for the racial adoption gap. First, it is possible that available black children have fewer desirable characteristics outside of race. For example, they may have higher than expected handicap rates if black families have fewer resources for financing the extra care that handicapped children require. Second, if genetic similarity is a criterion, then whites will prefer to adopt whites over all other children. Those whites who are not able to adopt white children (because of excess demand at administered prices) will either drop out of the adoption market or will have equal preferences for children of other races. There is no reason to expect white parents to get more of a "genetic kick" from staring down at an Asian baby's face than at a black baby's face.

The evidence supports neither of these hypotheses, telling instead quite a different story: exclusive of other characteristics, the color dichotomy is not white over all others but all races except black over black. This conclusion stems from examining (1) agency adoption data, (2) the phenomenal rise in independent and intercountry adoptions, and (3) the attitudes of potential and actual adoptive parents.

TABLE 10.5. *Coefficients from Probit Estimates on the Probability of Being Adopted for Children Aged 0–5*

Variable[a]	Coefficient	T-ratio	Mean of variable in sample
BLACK	−.715	−3.887	.252
OTHER	.190	.758	.170
CHDPROB	−.624	−.819	.009
HANDICAP	−1.065	−3.454	.060
AGE	−.063	−1.076	2.566
GIRL	.176	1.063	.459
CONSTANT	1.106	5.391	—

Source: Data are from *The National Study of Social Services to Children and Their Families*, Department of Health and Human Services (Washington, D.C.: GPO, 1977).

Note: Excludes children for whom the information was not available.

[a] BLACK, OTHER, CHDPROB, HANDICAP, and GIRL are all dummy variables. OTHER implies race other than black or white. CHDPROB indicates where the child was originally seen in social services because of a behavioral problem (like drug addiction or delinquency) specific to itself. The omitted dummies represent a healthy white boy with no behavioral problems.

In the public adoption market the cost of adopting a child is fixed and (outside of subsidies) is more or less equal for all children. Probit estimates on the probability of being adopted from public agencies show dramatically the specific influence that being black has in the adoption market. Being black significantly lessens a child's probability of adoption. Being of a race other than black and white, however, makes no discernible difference in adoption rates.[14] Table 10.5 presents these estimates for the 1977 data on children age 0 to 5. For comparison, the same estimates for all children (age 0–18) are included (see note 14). The dummies omitted from the equation represent a healthy white boy with no behavioral problems. Of the children's characteristics, only *black* and *handicap* negatively influence the probability of adoption. The coefficients are large and highly significant. Age and behavioral problems, which we'd expect to have a negative influence on adoption, have the expected sign but are insignificant for these very young ages. They are significant when all ages are included.

Prices in "black" and "grey" markets for infants and young children substantiate what the agency data suggest. Two emerging markets show that even with a surplus of black children in the United States, parents are willing to pay substantial sums of money, endure many problems, and even adhere to quasi-legal practices to acquire white or foreign-born children. Profit can be the motivating factor in these markets where supply and demand interact to determine price. Repeated testimony before the House of Representatives confirms this view-point. For example:

He [the middleman] seeks a finders fee, which is actually a purchase price for the infant. Once the baby has been reduced to a commodity in this manner, the basic law of supply and demand takes over. But in the baby-selling racket, the fee is not based on reasonable costs. It is based on the laws of supply and demand—and right now the demand is very high and the supply is very low. (U.S. Congress, House 1979, 3, 9)

The past fifteen years have seen a dramatic rise in independent adoptions—adoptions that take place outside of public and private agencies. In 1984 they accounted for 33 percent of all unrelated adoptions. While many are legitimate, a significant proportion of these adoptions were black-market purchases.[15] Currently, independent adoptions are legal in only thirty-eight states, but, as of 1977, there was still no federal law prohibiting the sale of children across state lines.[16] This market operates almost exclusively to procure white babies for white parents. William Meezan (Meezan et al. 1978), who has done the most detailed study of this phenomenon, reports that 98 percent of the independent adoptive families surveyed were white and 94 percent of the biological mothers were white. Sixty-seven percent of those parents who had previously visited public agencies cited a shortage of healthy white infants as their reason for turning to independent adoption.[17] One Miami-based adoption attorney who was averaging $50,000 a year in adoption fees in the mid-seventies says that he rejects women pregnant by nonwhite fathers because (in this market) there are no homes for biracial infants (Baker 1978,76). Costs vary widely: in Meezan's 1976 survey (where there were significant incentives to underreport) the median cost was $2,223, but 18 percent paid more than $4,000.[18] About $12,000 was widely considered to be a standard cost in the mid-seventies, with $50,000 representing a very high figure. *The Adoption Fact Book* (1985), published by the National Committee for Adoption, suggests that $15,000 was the average fee in 1985. Prices also vary by race. One prominent New York–based lawyer was quoted as saying, "It can run as little as twenty-five hundred dollars if you want a Korean child, to a lot more. For a white Caucasian child at birth . . . it doesn't run much beyond thirteen thousand dollars."[19] *There is no independent market for black babies.*

A similar international market has emerged involving the intercountry adoption of nonwhite children by white parents. Since 1970 there have been more than 5,000 children annually adopted from other countries. In 1984 there were 8,327 international adoptions that accounted for approximately 11.3 percent of all nonrelative adoptions.

The trend is toward Asians and Hispanics. In 1984 Asian-born children (mostly from the Philippines, Korea, and India) and Central and South American children (mostly from Colombia, Mexico, and Brazil) accounted for 92.3 percent of foreign adoptions in the United States. American adoptions of black children from Africa are extremely isolated occurrences: only eight children were adopted from Africa in 1984 (National Committee for Adoption 1985, 14–15).

These prospective parents choose to adopt from abroad rather than adopt American blacks. International adoptions are very costly in terms of both time and money. Adoptive parents must deal with U.S. and foreign agencies and lawyers and the Immigration and Naturalization Service, and they must support (outside of other costs) high transportation costs for themselves and/or the child. Nonetheless, they persevere. Why? In William Feigelman and Arnold Silverman's survey (1983), 87 percent of the parents who adopted Colombian-born children reportedly did so because there was no "suitable" American child available for adoption. In the same study a majority of the parents who adopted Korean children cited "social and humanitarian reasons" as most important. Similar results are reported in several other studies (Feigelman and Silverman 1983; 127, 151). In 1971 when the number of parents applying to agencies for Vietnamese children increased dramatically, many agencies felt compelled to respond with, "If you want a child of another race, why go all the way to Vietnam to find one?" (Benet 1976, 140).

Finally, several studies also collected informative attitudinal data. The parents in Meezan et al.'s study of those independently adopting white babies were asked about their feelings regarding adopting nine specific types of children.[20] The final column of Table 10.6, "Could not adopt," shows the attitudinal barriers against adopting black children. Seventy-four percent of the sample said they could not adopt a normal black infant—one who was like the child they *did* adopt in every way except race. Only white children with a noncorrectable handicap and older children of another ethnic group have rejection rates anywhere near those for black children.

These parents represent one extreme of the taste spectrum, however. They have already shown their willingness to pay large sums of money for white children. What about the attitudes of other parents? Tables 10.7 and 10.8 reveal the extent of the bias away from black children even among parents who, presumably, would be most willing to adopt them. Table 10.7 shows the attitudes of one hundred white couples who adopted American Indian children. Mothers and fathers were separately asked whether they would consider adopting a black child. Nearly 58 percent of the mothers and 46 percent of the fathers *could*

TABLE 10.6. *Adoptive Parents' Feelings about Adopting Children Other than White/Healthy Infants*

Would couple adopt:	Easily	Minor reservations	Major reservations	Could not adopt
Normal white child over 2	37%	28%	14%	22%
Normal white child over 6	8	16	28	48
White child with correctable handicap	38	34	12	17
White child with noncorrectable handicap	5	5	29	61
White child with mental illness in background	21	28	23	29
Normal black infant	8	5	13	74
Older black child	2	2	12	85
Infant of another ethnic group (Oriental, Chicano, American Indian)	38	18	16	27
Older child of other ethnic group	8	12	14	66

Source: William Meezan, Sanford Katz, and Eva Manoff Russo, *Adoptions Without Agencies: A Study of Independent Adoptions* (New York: Child Welfare League of America, Inc. 1978).

TABLE 10.7. *Types of Children Parents Could Consider Adopting (by Skin Shade)*

Description	Response categories	Mothers' response	Fathers' response
A child of mixed Negro–white parentage (obviously Negro in features and skin color)	Could not consider	57.9%	45.5%
	Major reservations	20.0	27.8
	Minor reservations	6.3	16.7
	Adopt easily	15.8	10.0
		100.0%	100.0%
Same as above but not obviously Negro in appearance	Could not consider	47.4%	29.7%
	Major reservations	15.8	24.2
	Minor reservations	14.7	28.6
	Adopt easily	22.1	17.5
		100.0%	100.0%

Source: David Fanshel, *Far from the Reservation* (Metuchen, N.J.: Scarecrow Press, 1972), pp. 128, 179, Table V-8 and Table VI-8.

Note: All parents are white adoptive parents who have already adopted an American Indian child. The subjects were told the following: "As you may know, the agency has many kinds of children to place for adoption. Now, I would like you to think back to the time you first came to the agency to apply for adoption. Suppose children of the following types had been offered to you for consideration. I would like you to tell me whether you might easily have adopted such a child, would have had minor reservations, major reservations, or would not have been able to take such a child under any circumstances."

TABLE 10.8. *Willingness to Adopt Hard-to-Place Children at the Time of the Adoption and Afterward*

Willing to adopt:	Parents of Colombian adoptees		Parents of White U.S. adoptees		Parents of Korean adoptees	
	Before	After	Before	After	Before	After
Asian children	59%	70%	32%	46%	98%	95%
Black children	26	37	29	32	61	64
Older children	50	70	53	68	60	83
Handicapped children	28	37	30	30	34	41

Source: William Feigelman and Arnold R. Silverman, *Chosen Children: New Patterns of Adoptive Relationships* (New York: Praeger Publishers, 1983); Table 5-1, p. 130.

Note: All parents interviewed are white Americans. Figures are percentages willing to adopt.

not consider adopting a black child if he/she looks black. The figures drop to 47 percent and 30 percent if the child is not obviously black. Similarly, parents who adopted Colombian children and white U.S. children are least likely to be willing to adopt black children out of four hard-to-place stereotypes. Adoptive parents of Korean children are relatively more willing to adopt black children, although they are less willing to adopt blacks than Asians.

It is possible that these attitudes represent not the exogenous attitudes of prospective adoptive parents but attitudes fostered by the agencies themselves. Some agencies, for example, may discourage white parents from interracial (specifically, black-child) adoption. One early study (Chambers 1970) attempted to address this issue by interviewing prospective parents at several points of the adoption process. Their sample, which contained non–American Indian, nonblack, non-Hispanic adoptive applicants, were initially interviewed regarding their willingness to adopt hard-to-place children with specific characteristics. Although 52 percent were willing to adopt American Indians and 56 percent were willing to adopt Hispanic children, only 2 percent were willing to adopt black children. Later, when some of these parents were actually presented with a choice, they overwhelmingly followed in practice what they expressed attitudinally.

Potential parents must have underlying reasons for their bias away from black children. For very young children it cannot be that parents are worried about any preceding negative cultural baggage that the child carries around. Certainly prejudice is one factor. Even today there are people who are willing to argue—however indirectly or surreptitiously—that black people are inferior.[21] Race itself may not be the issue, but being of the black race may. Rita Simon and Howard Altstein address this point succinctly in their discussion of the 1975 airlift of Vietnamese children:

TABLE 10.9. *Positive Response to the Adoption of a Child among Family, Friends, and Neighbors*

	Parents of whites	Parents of Colombians	Parents of Koreans	Parents of blacks
Wife's parents				
1975	92%	93%	75%	46%
1981	86	95	73	48
Husband's parents				
1975	79	86	61	44
1981	79	89	63	56
Other relatives				
1975	80	87	66	40
1981	75	79	69	43
Friends				
1975	91	96	92	79
1981	89	95	90	87
Neighbors				
1975	78	78	72	54
1981	85	84	76	54

Source: William Feigelman and Arnold R. Silverman, *Chosen Children: New Patterns of Adoptive Relationships* (New York: Praeger Publishers, 1983), Table 5.2, p. 132.
Note: Figures are percentages having positive response to the adoption.

While Americans can become extremely emotional about the plight of Vietnamese children, we continue to ignore a large pool of native-born black children who appear destined to live their lives in a series of foster homes or in institutions. Why, one continues to wonder, did all the major television evening news broadcasts and magazines display a telephone number where information concerning the adoption of Vietnamese children could be obtained and not allow "equal time" for American orphans needing homes? (Simon and Altstein 1977, 65)

In most of the studies already cited, potential parents did not acknowledge that they were prejudiced but did claim that they were afraid of the prejudices of relatives, friends, neighbors, and white strangers—any of which they saw as disruptive to their family life. Their fears may be rational, if overstated. About 37 percent of the close relatives were still uncomfortable with, or rejected, interracially adopted black children in the Simon and Altstein (1977) study, but only 10 percent of the families had trouble with friends and neighbors. Some families had unpleasant experiences with strangers, ranging from stares to insulting remarks and phone calls to having the city council order them out of town (Simon and Altstein 1977, 96). Table 10.9 views the problem from the other side of the coin. In two different periods adoptive parents were asked how immediate associates reacted to their adoptions. Parents of black children got the least positive support from relatives, friends, and neighbors. Social sanctions have always played an important enforcement role in racist societies—forcing nondiscriminators to abide by the "appropriate" rules of behavior. The implicit threat of such sanctions may be sufficient to deter some parents from considering interracial adoption.

Prospective parents may be thinking of these problems in light of the long-term best interests of the child. These parents believe that they could not protect the child from racial problems during adolescence and adulthood. They argue that a black child who grows up in a white middle-class neighborhood "is less capable of coping with problems involving race than one who has grown up 'with his or her own people' and experienced rejection and discrimination more gradually from childhood onward" (Simon and Altstein 1977, 98). Alternatively, prospective parents may presume that a black adoptive child would have problems dealing with black peers and the black community.[22]

Economics plays less of a role in the demand for children in the United States than in other parts of the world but may, nonetheless, influence the decision to adopt black children. If parents expect support from their children in old age, then they would prefer to acquire those children whose expected lifetime earnings are as high as possible. More altruistically, parents may simply desire that their children be successful—that they do better economically than they themselves have done. If parents believe that labor markets have a discriminatory impact on the earnings potential of black workers or that black workers have a lower earnings capacity, then they would rationally adopt children of other races.

Most of these represent legitimate parental concerns, but note that each springs, not from cultural aspects of the black community, but from a long cultural heritage in the white community. Young black children in substitute care are denied access to permanent and secure homes solely because they are black. Potential adopters, their relatives, friends, and neighbors are also employers, managers, employees, and consumers. It is not such a large step from institutional discrimination in the adoption market to other discriminatory behavior.

Adoption practices through the 1950s were guided by the history of race relations in this country and geared toward the welfare of prospective parents. Matching parents and children was the principle of adoption that emerged: adoptable children and potential parents were matched on as many physical, emotional, and cultural characteristics as possible. The most important of these were thought to be race and religion, and they were encoded in the *Standards for Adoption Services* put out by the Child Welfare League of America.

But by 1964 a major shift had occurred in practice, and interracial adoption had become more commonplace. Physical and cultural characteristics were ruled out as matching criteria, and estimated potentialities, values, and modes of life were promoted in their place. In 1968, the subtitle "Matching" was deleted from *Standards for Adoption Services* and social workers were simply charged with the responsibility for selecting families for children. By 1971, matching was completely demand driven, and interracial adoption was institutionalized.

When adoption has been found desirable for the child, and the couple has met the agency's requirements for adoption, an appraisal must be made of their suitability for each other. In most instances, similarity in background or characteristics need not be a factor. It should be recognized, however, that people vary in their capacity to accept differences. If the couple want a child who is like them in certain ways, this desire should be taken into account.[23]

Two critiques of the system emerged in the early seventies that may have restricted, from the supply side, the volume of interracial adoption. Both centered around adoption agencies as white-dominated institutions. First, many argued that black families were specifically being left out of the adoption process because of institutional constraints (such as the financial requirements for adoptive parents) and because white agencies with white social workers had no effective means of recruitment in the black community. This critique spurred many experiments leveled at black family recruitment and toward the recruitment of more black social workers (a correlation was discovered between the number of black social workers and the number of intraracial black adoptions in an agency).[24]

The second critique came from the National Association of Black Social Workers (NABSW). At their meeting in 1972 the NABSW issued a statement regarding transracial adoption, condemning it as unnatural, cultural genocide, and unnecessary:

Black children in white homes are cut off from the healthy development of themselves as Black people. . . . Only a Black family can transmit the emotional and sensitive subtleties of perception and reaction essential for a Black child to survive in a racist society. . . . Black families can be found when agencies alter their requirements, methods of approach, definition of suitable family and tackle the legal machinery to facilitate interstate placements. (NABSW unpublished position paper 1972)

The response to this statement was quite varied, and by 1978 the NABSW was no longer supporting the notion that black foster homes were better than white adoptive homes. They still contended, however, that white adoptive homes were less suitable than black ones.

Did these critiques have the effect of constraining the supply of black children to white families by forcing agencies to change their practices? The answer remains unknown. No statistics are available because no information is kept on agency decisions on adoptions at the individual level. National surveys of adoption agencies conducted by Opportunity: Division of Boys and Girls Aid Society of Oregon (1968–1975) suggest that there may have been some immediate impact. Their data show that the number of white families adopting black children declined 30 percent from 1972 to 1973, 20 percent from 1973 to 1974, and 11 percent from 1974 to 1975. At the same time, however, the number of black families adopting black children also declined in the first two periods by 20 percent and 7 percent (black adoption rose in the third period by 1 percent) as did the adoption of white children by 15 percent and 6 percent (white adoptions rose in the third period by 8 percent) (Simon and Altstein 1977, 30; Day 1979, 100). Unfortunately, it is impossible to determine the source of the difference in decline. It may represent the impact of NABSW's statement or the racial characteristics of the varying number of agencies reporting in each year or the decline in available children because of the abortion option.

Evidence since 1973 is sketchy at best. The Child Welfare League of America, in its *Standards for Adoption Services*, did reinstate race as a potential adoption criterion in 1978: "The adoptive parents selected for a child should ordinarily be of a similar racial background, but children should not have adoption denied or significantly delayed when adoptive parents of other races are available" (1978, 44–45). Interestingly enough, however, in the next paragraph they specifically reject the notion of nationality, culture, or social factors for adoptive home selection: "National and cultural characteristics are not inherited but must be learned. The adopted child acquires the cultural and social attributes of the adoptive family" (1978, 45).

Interviews with agency representatives over the past ten years suggest that the effective impact may have been small but that more sensitivity to the issue has been acknowledged. Many agencies seem to be in doubt about what would be the most appropriate policy to institute, but the majority agree that the best interests of the child are the only suitable criteria for adoptive placement.[25]

In 1985, there were fifteen states that prohibited matching by race and fifteen states that still had some kind of color or culture matching laws, rules, or policies (six of them in the Southeast). Importantly, nearly every single state uses these rules only as a first preference and promotes interracial adoption if there are delays in finding same-race placements. Yet, excess supplies of black children and the independent white baby market remain.

Adoption institutions play a critical role in our child welfare system by taking care of children who, for one reason or another, fall outside the bounds of traditional family organization. How these institutions deal with heterogeneous children informs us about how society is organized. Racial heterogeneity in general does not appear to be the issue in the adoption market; being black does.

This conclusion is not surprising given the unique specter of black–white relations in our country. The evidence presented in this chapter shows that although all are created equal, the market values children differentially. Prejudice has been shown, and further investigation is needed to determine its contribution to that differential. The adoption market, in fact, may provide the grounds for measuring a taste for discrimination. In the public market, the price ($\bar{P}$) of all children is generally fixed and equal, allowing for administrative fees only. Under the current regime there is excess demand for white children ($P_w^\star > \bar{P}$) and excess supply of black children ($P_b^\star < \bar{P}$). If this comes from differences in demand rather than supply (given the outside market for whites), the distance between the two separate demand curves could be used to measure the implicit value of discriminating taste, implying that potential adopters, at least, attach a value to race.[26]

Adoption markets and labor markets serve different functions, and it is unwise to assume that questions relating to the operation of labor markets can be effectively answered by examining adoption markets. But as markets, the two have many common behaviors. If it is true that people maintain prejudiced beliefs, then we can expect their behavior in all markets to reflect those beliefs. The genesis of affirmative action policies was exactly the recognition that the clash between social principles and realities acted to the detriment of black workers. While we should certainly evaluate the bureaucratic failure of those policies, it is premature, at best, to assert that the reasons for implementing them have disappeared.

The negative aspects of black culture, mentioned in the introduction, undoubtedly undercut the opportunities of black workers. But is this the disease or just its symptom? If we believe that black people are rational social beings, then we must accept the possibility that such counterproductive behavior is a response to decades of social and economic stimuli from the majority population. The heritage of race relations in this country pervades the attitudes and behavior of the white population, and it is white culture—not black—that dominates the labor market. Potential adopters, their relatives, friends, and neighbors are employers, managers, employees, and consumers. In these roles they influence the labor market opportunities of all workers. Their culture needs to be confronted, for all have the opportunity, and often the power, to discriminate.

Notes

1. In this chapter, I discuss the culturalogical arguments as they relate specifically to blacks. The same arguments are often made for other minority groups. The cultural theory, and other theories that flow in and out of favor over time, is prompted in part by both the historical backdrop and political climate. In the late 1800s, the science of craniometry joined racist beliefs to implicate genetics and inherited differences as the root cause of social and economic disparities between whites and blacks. Later, geographic differences, most notably the North–South split, were the predominant explanation; most blacks lived in the South where labor markets were less established, and blacks who migrated to the North consistently did better economically than their southern counterparts. After a time, however, it became clear that even northern blacks were not achieving parity with whites. This recognition propelled theories of economic discrimination: wage, hiring, and promotional discrimination were all examined for their contribution to racial inequality. Finally, and recurring most recently, is the rise of cultural explanations for racial economic differences. A new variant of the "Culture of Poverty" school of the 1960s, this theory blames black culture for the lack of economic progress. For examples of the literature on each of these theories, see P. Broca, "Sur le volume et la forme du cerveau suivant les individus et suivant les races," *Bullétin de la Societé d'Anthropologie de Paris* 2, 1861; James Gwartney, "Changes in the non-white/white income ratio—1939–67," *American Economic Review* (December 1970); Kenneth Arrow, "Some Mathematical Models of Race Discrimination in the Labor Market," in Pascal, ed., *Racial Discrimination in Economic Life*, 1972; Thomas Sowell, *Ethnic America: A History*, 1981; Charles Murray, *Losing Ground: American Social Policy 1950–1980*, 1984; George Gilder, *Wealth and Poverty*, 1981.

2. For example, Thomas Sowell in *Ethnic America* says, "Even when color and racial prejudices confronted them—as in the Chinese and Japanese—this proved to be an impediment but was ultimately unable to stop them. . . . But the Irish and the blacks never set up laundries, or any other businesses, with the frequency of the Chinese or Japanese. . . . What made these humble occupations avenues to affluence was the effort, thrift, dependability, and foresight that built businesses out of 'menial' tasks and turned sweat into capital" (1981, 283).

3. Many scholars believe that the organization of black family and community life represents the best response to institutionalized racism. See, for example, Robert B. Hill, *The Strengths of Black Families*, 1972, and *Informal Adoption Among Black Families*, 1977, or Carol Stack, *All Our Kin: Survival in the Black Community*, 1975.

4. Some sociologists and economists would disagree. Some researchers believe that attitudinal data or indicators of cultural behavior (such as the presence of adult males in the household) can be used as direct explanatory variables in a quantitative analysis.

5. A 1978 law was intended to reactivate the comprehensive collection of national data on adoptions but the Reagan budget cuts prohibited their reactivation. The Children's Bureau of the Department of Health and Human Services, the department charged with such information gathering and research, had its staff cut to one-fourth of its previous size.

6. The National Study of Social Services to Children and Their Families (NSSSCTF) represents a massive data collection effort (in 1977) for the Department of Health and

Human Services. It is a survey of public agencies in the United States generating information on the characteristics of the children, the services, and the agencies. It is especially valuable because it provides the adoption status and other characteristics of children. Usable data were collected on a sample of approximately 10,000 children. There is no information, in this data set, on the characteristics of adopters or potential adopters. For further information on the sampling and methodology, see *Phase 1: Public Use Tape Documentation Manual*, NSSSCTF (May 1979). The data are in the public domain.

7. In fiscal year 1983, the median age of children adopted through public agencies was 5.6 years, while the median age for children awaiting adoption was 9.0. Source: Voluntary Cooperative Information Service. *Characteristics of Children in Substitute and Adoptive Care*, 1985, p. 94.

8. A small literature on adoption markets is developing.

9. There is a minor trend toward the darkening of the substitute care population. The 1977 NSSSCTF study showed that 62.2 percent of children in substitute care were white, while 27.6 percent were black (Shyne and Schroeder 1978, table on p. 116). In 1980, Office of Civil Rights data showed 58.0 percent white and 33.2 percent black. The data for FY82 (fiscal year 1982) are similar to those cited for FY83—52.7 percent white and 34.2 percent black. Both blacks and whites are non-Hispanic. Data for FY82 and FY83 are based on forty reporting states that account for about 81.6 percent of the total substitute care population at the end of FY83. See Voluntary Cooperative Information System, *Characteristics of Children*, 1985, pp. 59–61. Statistics are also available for an earlier period (1960 to 1974) for children in foster care in New York City. The percentage of white (non-Hispanic) children monotonically declined from 51.6 to 20.7 percent, while the number of black (non-Hispanic) children monotonically increased from 38.5 to 54.1 percent (see Bernstein, et al. 1975, p. 4).

10. Rita James Simon and Howard Altstein. *Transracial Adoption*, p. 30. Original data from Opportunity: Division of Boys and Girls Aid Society of Oregon.

11. Data based on a survey of Washington, D.C., and Baltimore agencies. See Dawn Day, *The Adoption of Black Children*, 1979, p. 8.

12. In some years and in some places there have been shortages of new black infants.

13. Note the slight difference in definition between Table 10.2 and Table 10.3. In about one-third of the states reporting to VCIS for Table 10.3, children who were in non-finalized adoptive homes were counted as being in foster homes. Table 10.2 includes, for all children, finalized and nonfinalized adoptive homes.

14. These estimates actually underestimate the negative impact of being black because the availability of adoption subsidies is strongly correlated with race. Coefficients, T-ratios, and the sample means for all children age 0–18 are: BLACK (−0.432, −4.767, 0.320), OTHER (−0.029, −0.222, 0.121), CHDPROB (−0.458, −2.656, 0.071), HANDICAP (−1.090, −5.022, 0.053), AGE (−0.111, −13.367, 9.445), and GIRL (0.039, 0.467, 0.420). The chi-squared statistic at 6 degrees of freedom was 304.30. Unweighted sample size was 1,114.

15. Joseph Reid, executive director of the Child Welfare League of America, testified before Congress in 1975 that in 1971 at least one-third (up to 5,000 children) of the independent adoptions were black-market adoptions—transactions in which money, not the child's welfare, was the paramount factor. That projection was expected to rise as the shortage of adoptable white babies worsened (see Meezan et al. 1978, p. 9). Since adoption fees are set by the state, parents who participate in black-market adoptions may lie about the fees they paid when they seek court approval.

16. Connecticut, Delaware, Michigan, and Rhode Island have totally outlawed independent adoptions. Four other states allow placement only by the parent, and six states restrict independent adoptions but allow private for-profit organizations to be licensed as child placing agencies (see *The Adoption Fact Book* 1985, pp. 76–84). Congress has been trying to address the issue of baby selling since at least 1954. In 1977, Harrison Williams introduced a bill to the Senate and Henry Hyde introduced a bill to the House of Representatives on the sale of children in interstate and foreign commerce. Mr. Hyde's opening statements to the Committee on Criminal Justice

reveal the extent of the problem: "Many couples turn to black markets, and a baby, then, is reduced to a chattel and sold for cash and many times to the highest bidder. . . . The fees $10,000, $15,000, and $25,000 are not uncommon" (House of Representatives, 95th Cong., March 21 and April 25, 1977).

17. Meezan et al. 1978, p. 35. In the multiple response answers, 37 percent (the next highest category) reported that staff shortages caused delay.

18. Figures are for 1976. Meezan et al. 1978, pp. 70–71. Several parents refused to answer this question, and many admitted later that they lied to the courts about the fees they paid (a standard practice in this market). Even though 80 percent of these families had reported income over $15,000 and 50 percent had income over $25,000, 25 percent reported that the fees caused them financial strain.

19. Baker 1978, p. 94. 1975 quotation by Joseph Spencer, who is sometimes called the "Dean of Independent Adoption." He has been in the adoption business for over twenty-five years.

20. Specifically, parents who had approached agencies about possible adoptions were asked whether they discussed the possibility of adopting a child other than a normal white infant. They were asked to indicate their feelings about adopting nine specific types of children who might be available for adoption through agencies. All individuals in the sample had adopted independently a normal white child under the age of 2 (95 percent were adopted before the age of 3 months).

21. Some people do still believe that culture is genetically determined. White adoptive parents' rejection of black children could be seen, then, as a rejection of black culture rather than of the purely ascriptive characteristics of the child. They may believe that their efforts at socialization are predestined to be futile. Others may believe that black children genetically have lower I.Q.s, on average, than other children. These views, of course, highlight the insidiousness of racist beliefs.

22. Several studies have examined the difficulties arising from socializing a black child in a white community. Most (Grow and Shapiro 1974; Simon and Altstein 1977; Silverman and Feigelman 1981) concluded that black or interracial children had high rates of social adjustment and racial identity. Ruth McRoy and Louis Zurcher, Jr. (1983) studied black and interracial teenage adoptees in both black and white homes. They concluded that teenagers in both kinds of homes had similar scores on self-esteem measures but varied in their racial self-perception. The key determinant of racial perception for teenagers in white homes was how the parents handled the racial identity issue (some chose to ignore or de-emphasize race) and whether the family attempted to integrate into the black community. This author is not placing a value judgment on the desirability of white parents adopting black children.

23. Child Welfare League of America's *Guidelines for Adoption Service*, 1971, p. 13. Cited in Simon and Altstein 1977, p. 17.

24. See Simon and Altstein 1977, pp. 30–35 for discussion. Several studies at the time (see Simon and Altstein 1977, p. 53:fns 18–20) suggested that middle-class blacks were less apt to adopt because they viewed their middle-class status as tenuous. If true, this would lessen the blame on the agencies. Others argued that, with the use of nontraditional types of adoption, blacks adopted at a higher rate than whites (see Simon and Altstein 1977, p. 53:fn 21, and Robert B. Hill, *Informal Adoption Among Black Families*, 1977).

25. In Michigan, where there is a large middle-class black population, social agencies have erected substantial barriers to minimize the possibility of interracial adoption.

26. This brings to mind Posner's (1977) proposal to eliminate the disequilibrium in the adoption market by allowing a free and legal market for the sale of children. This, he claims, would eliminate two major problems of the current adoption situation: the shortage of babies and the high price of babies that is a result of the inefficiencies of the black market for children. Judge Posner's proposal may, in fact, reduce the inefficiencies of the black market for white babies and could potentially return that segment of the market to equilibrium by shifting out the white baby supply curve. Its impact on the racial "adoption gap," however, is potentially devastating. If black and white children are substitutes, then reducing the average price of white relative

to black children will increase that gap substantially. A correcting equilibrium in one segment of the market worsens the disequilibrium in another segment.

References

Baker, Nancy C., 1978. *Baby Selling: The Scandal of Black Market Adoption*. New York: Vanguard Press.

Becker, Gary S., 1981. *A Treatise on the Family*. Cambridge: Harvard University Press.

Benet, Mary Kathleen, 1976. *The Politics of Adoption*. New York: Macmillan Publishing Co.

Bernstein, Blanche, Donald A. Snider, and William Meezan, 1975. *Foster Care Needs and Alternatives to Placement: A Projection for 1975–1985*. New York: New York State Board of Social Welfare, November.

Chambers, Donald E., 1970. "Willingness to Adopt Atypical Children." *Child Welfare* (May): 275–279.

Child Welfare League of America, [1959] 1978. *Standards for Adoption Service*.

Day, Dawn, 1979. *The Adoption of Black Children*. Lexington, Mass.: Lexington Books.

Feigelman, William, and Arnold R. Silverman, 1983. *Chosen Children: New Patterns of Adoptive Relationships*. New York: Praeger Publishers.

Gilder, George, 1981. *Wealth and Poverty*. New York: Basic Books.

Glazer, Nathan, 1983. *Ethnic Dilemmas: 1964–1982*. Cambridge: Harvard University Press.

Grow, Lucille J., and Deborah Shapiro, 1974. *Black Children, White Parents*. New York: Child Welfare League of America.

Hill, Robert B., 1977. *Informal Adoption Among Black Families*. Washington, D.C.: National Urban League.

Landes, Elizabeth M., and Richard A. Posner, 1978. "The Economics of the Baby Shortage." *Journal of Legal Studies* 7: 323–348.

Maximus, Inc., 1983. *Final Report: Child Welfare Indicator Survey*, Vol. 1 and 2. Report prepared for Office of Human Development Services, Office of Program Development and Administration for Children, Youth, and Families, October.

McRoy, Ruth G., and Louis A. Zurcher, Jr., 1983. *Transracial and Inracial Adoptees: The Adolescent Years*. Springfield, Ill.: Charles C. Thomas.

Meezan, William, Sanford Katz, and Eva Manoff Russo, 1978. *Adoptions Without Agencies: A Study of Independent Adoptions*. New York: Child Welfare League of America.

Murray, Charles, 1984. *Losing Ground: American Social Policy 1950–1980*. New York: Basic Books.

National Committee for Adoption, 1985. *The Adoption Fact Book*.

Posner, Richard A., 1977. *Economic Analysis of Law*. Boston: Little, Brown & Co.

Shyne, Anne W., and Anita G. Schroeder, 1978. *National Study of Social Services to Children and Their Families*. Department of Health, Education, and Welfare, Publication No. (OHDS) 78-30150, August.

Simon, Rita James, and Howard Altstein, 1977. *Transracial Adoption*. New York: John Wiley and Sons.

Sowell, Thomas, 1981. *Ethnic America: A History*. New York: Basic Books.

U.S. Congress. House, 1979. Committee on the Judiciary. Subcommittee on Criminal Justice. *Sale of Children in Interstate and Foreign Commerce* (March 21 and April 25, 1977), 95th Cong., Serial No. 82.

Voluntary Cooperative Information System, 1985. *Characteristics of Children in Substitute and Adoptive Care*. Washington, D.C.: The American Public Welfare Association, June.

Chapter 11. The Social Structure, Socialization Processes, and School Competence of Black and White Children

T HE MOST fundamental division in American society has been between black and white Americans. Long-standing barriers to educational and occupational mobility and pervasive segregation in all major institutions and informal relations have persisted throughout the entire period during which this country became an urban, advanced industrial nation.

Opportunities that had long been open to white immigrants generally did not become available to black Americans until the Second World War. Blacks had been confined mostly to the agricultural sector and to menial service jobs that were marginal to the industrial-corporate sector of the labor market. Thus they were largely excluded from work experiences that promote modernization of attitudes and behavior. Moreover, the achievement of a high-school or even a college education, rare as it was, did not open up to blacks the same opportunities afforded other ethnic groups—opportunities to observe and assimilate the cultural innovations taking place in the mainstream culture. The small black middle class was largely separate from the expanding white middle class, occupationally, residentially, and socially.

As a result, there developed two quite distinct stratification systems: one constituted by the white majority, the other by the black minority. The shape of the two systems differed markedly, and so did (and still does) the economic, occupational, and religious composition of the strata within each race.

These marked and persistent differences in socio-economic position, occupational experiences, and access to other resources resulted in differences between the races in family structure and in modes of socializing children. These differences have become considerably more significant because of changes in the structure of opportunities over the past twenty years. The demand for unskilled and semiskilled workers has sharply declined, and occupations requiring higher education have substantially increased. At the same time, discrimination that formerly barred better-educated blacks from higher-level occupations has substantially abated as a result of civil rights legislation during the 1950s and 1960s and affirmative action programs in the 1970s.

Indeed, not until the late sixties and early seventies did the attainment of higher education begin to afford blacks gains in the labor market at all comparable to those it afforded whites. In their important baseline study, Peter Blau and Dudley Duncan provided firm evidence (based on 1962 national data) that, in their words,

The difference in occupational status between Negroes and Whites is twice as great for men who have graduated from high school or gone to college as for those who have completed no more than eight years of schooling. In short the careers of well educated Blacks lag even further behind those of comparable Whites than do the careers of poorly educated Negroes. (Blau and Duncan 1967, 405)

A decade later David Featherman and Robert Hauser (1978) replicated and elaborated the Blau and Duncan analysis on 1973 data and found that among *younger* cohorts of black men, educational attainment had become the strongest predictor of occupational achievement as it had been for white men ten years earlier, and they concluded that

The schools and especially college education gradually have emerged as important channels for black achievement. Differential education plays a continuing role as a basis of allocating minority men to jobs of various socioeconomic standings throughout their career; in recent years it also is the basis upon which minority men at all occupational levels acquire additional earnings. Among the younger black men in the 1973 study, there were signs of possible racial convergence of these returns, and the trend toward educational equality of the races was a major impetus to these declines in differential opportunity. (Featherman and Hauser 1978, 383)

Just as in the case for black and white men, educational attainment had become the strongest determinant of the occupational attainment of employed black and white women by the 1970s. Although Treiman and Terrell (1975) report that black women average substantially lower earnings than white women with comparable characteristics, this pattern of difference is reversed among college graduates. In fact, highly educated black women average higher earnings than their white counterparts. Nevertheless, while women and men are about equal in their ability to convert educational gains into occupational gains, black and white women still average lower earnings than their male counterparts.

The size of the black middle class has increased substantially over the past twenty-five years, and higher educational attainment has increasingly become the major mechanism for effecting upward economic and social mobility. The occupational opportunities for educated blacks have grown at an unprecedented rate over this period, and according to black sociologist William J. Wilson (1978), they are comparable to those open to whites with the same qualifications.

But structural changes in the economy have resulted in vastly different mobility opportunities for different segments of black Americans. In contrast to the expanded opportunities for well-educated black men and women, the job prospects of poorly educated black, Hispanic, and white Americans increasingly are restricted to the shrinking unskilled, low-wage sector of the labor market. The unemployment rates of young, poorly educated black males have risen precipitously, as have those of poorly educated female heads of households. Low educational attainment, not merely sexism or racism, is one major key to the present plight of these groups. And the relative deprivation and alienation of these groups can only be expected to increase. To the extent that their better-educated ethnic and sex peers succeed in raising their occupational attainments, it becomes increasingly difficult to ignore the fact that low educational attainment increasingly places in jeopardy all individuals, regardless of race or sex, not merely during their years of labor force participation but for the entire span of life (Z. Blau et al. 1978; Jackson and Gibson 1985).

Because occupational opportunities have greatly expanded for well-educated black American youths and have become increasingly constricted for the poorly educated over the past twenty years, it becomes more important than ever to gain a more precise understanding of the social sources of disparity between black and white children in school competence *early* in the school career, when patterned *group* differences between the races are first observed. For evidence is accumulating that both early school success and early school failure have cumulative and enduring effects over the elementary and high-school years (Douglas 1964; Gordon 1972; Becker 1977; Maruyama, Finch, and Mortimer 1985).

Scholastic competence in elementary school strengthens children's academic self-concept and learning motivation, whatever their race or social class, and such children are more likely to complete high school and to thereafter pursue higher education. Poor performance on tests in elementary school, in contrast, engenders feelings of inferiority and anxiety, producing a patterned avoidance to tests and learning generally. Without early encouragement and other positive forms of intervention in the home and school, such students are far less likely to complete high school and are at high risk of unemployment.

The fact that many—but by no means all—black children average lower scores than white children on I.Q. and achievement tests seemed to me to beg systematic explanation. For this reason, I undertook twenty years ago to carry out comparative research on black and white mothers, using as dependent variables the I.Q. and achievement test scores of their children.

I chose to focus on the family because there is a very substantial amount of evidence that public schools, at least as they are presently organized and constituted, do not have as much impact on elementary children's school performance as the characteristics of the family in which those children are born and reared (Douglas 1964; Coleman 1968; Mayeske and Beaton 1975).

My data consist of extensive home interviews with 579 black and 523 white mothers (carried out by black and white interviewers) and the I.Q. and achievement test scores of their fifth- and sixth-grade children, which were obtained from selected public elementary schools in three communities in the Chicago metropolitan area in 1968. Intelligence tests were administered at the end of the second grade, and achievement tests were administered at the end of the fourth and fifth grades. The full details of my analysis are reported in my book (Blau 1981). The present chapter is largely confined to a summary discussion of my findings with respect to the social determinants of black and white children's I.Q. scores, since the black–white I.Q. gap is what educational psychologist Arthur Jensen (1969), prematurely and mistakenly, attributed to genetic differences.

The social structural contexts in which black and white mothers rear children differ in several important ways. These differences influence maternal values and strategies of socialization that, in turn, make for differences in the early cognitive development of children. When these differences are statistically controlled for, the remaining difference in mean I.Q. scores between black and white children becomes less than the observed difference between white boys and white girls and in two subgroups the racial difference in scores altogether disappears.

White middle-class children average the highest I.Q. score (109), black middle-class and white working-class children average identical scores (100), and black working-class children average the lowest score (94) in my sample. A similar pattern of differences is observed with respect to achievement test scores. The mean I.Q. score of white girls in my sample (109) is significantly higher than that of white boys

(105), whereas that of black girls (97) is only one point higher than that of black boys (96).

A comparison of three components of parents' current socio-economic status (occupational status of higher-ranking parent, parents' educational attainment, and a measure of mother's social milieu) revealed that on each measure, black families who are seemingly similarly located relative to white families, in fact, possess fewer resources than those white families. Thus, on each measure the mean scores of white middle-class families is highest, that of black middle-class families is lower, that of white working-class families is still lower, and that of black working-class families is lowest.

The social milieu measure, based on four variables (number of close neighbors in white-collar occupations, number of college-educated neighbors, number of neighbors with a child in college, and the average education of mother's three closest friends) is an important dimension of social status that has not previously been taken into account in comparative research on the two races. It proves to be considerably less strongly associated with the educational and occupational attainment of black parents than of white, an indication that such gains among white families are more readily translated into access to middle-class influences and role models than is usually the case for black families.

In an earlier study dealing with the social processes by which information about modern child-rearing theories become disseminated, I discovered that the social class *origins* of mothers, independently of their *current* socio-economic status, influence the extent of exposure to child-rearing experts and the readiness to adopt their recommendations (Blau 1964). Upwardly mobile mothers in the white middle class exhibited markedly greater exposure to contemporary child-rearing literature and a greater disposition toward change (relative to their mothers' more traditional child-rearing patterns) than upwardly mobile mothers in the black middle class, except among the very small proportion who resided in racially integrated neighborhoods (Blau 1965). These findings suggested the more general proposition that the diffusion of modern theories and practices pertaining to the socialization of children is likely to occur more slowly in a largely *new* middle class, such as the black middle class, than in one containing a more substantial proportion of parents who grew up in and were socialized in middle-class families, as is the case in the white middle class. The study presently under discussion, based on a much larger sample and more extensive data, served to confirm the significance of this structural difference between the two middle classes not only for maternal attitudes and practices but also for children's I.Q. test performance. A very large majority of black middle-class mothers in my sample (82 percent) have working-class origins as compared with only 32 percent in the white middle-class sample.[1] Indeed, the socio-economic origins of black *middle* class parents closely resemble those of white *working* class parents in my sample—not those of white middle-class parents, who average the highest socio-economic origins and grew up with the fewest siblings in larger communities, typically in the North. Black working-class parents have the lowest socio-economic origins, averaged the largest number of siblings, and grew up in the smallest communities, typically in the South.

In summary, although *black middle-class* parents have attained higher educational and occupational levels than those in the *white working* class, the level of their social class origins is much the same, just as are the mean I.Q. and achievement test scores of their children.

Despite the considerable political, educational, and occupational gains that black Americans have made since the end of the Second World War and the significant increase in the size of the black middle class, barriers still persist to free and unfettered association between blacks and whites, even between members of the two races with similar educational and occupational attainment. Informal social relations in school, work, religious worship, residence, and voluntary associations even today typically remain largely separate, so that, structurally, the black and white middle classes for the most part remain quite separate entities.

For black mothers, whatever their social class position, the opportunities for egalitarian exposure to whites—to white friends while growing up or currently and to white coworkers—constitutes a variable of considerable importance.

To propose that, all other things being equal, black mothers (and probably also fathers) who have white friends and/or coworkers become exposed sooner to child-bearing and child-rearing patterns that have come to prevail in mainstream white contemporary society and incorporate them sooner than do their race peers who are isolated from such influences is not at all to arrogate to whites any innate superiority. It merely draws attention to important *social processes* operating in white society that barriers of social segregation deny to black Americans who remain isolated from more or less egalitarian relationships with whites, the majority and more-advantaged race.

Multivariate regression analyses to determine the independent contribution that six components of parents' current and origin socio-economic status made to the prediction of children's I.Q. scores in each race revealed that the predictors of black and white scores were different. For white children parents' education exerts the strongest independent and positive effect, followed by parents' demographic origins (i.e., children of parents who grew up in northern, larger communities scored higher). Occupational status enters the equation but adds less than 1 percent to the variance explained in white children's I.Q. scores. Together these three measures explain 12 percent of the variation in white children's scores.

An additional 2 percent of the variation in black children's I.Q. scores (14 percent) is accounted for by four variables, three of which are *different* from the predictors of white scores: mothers' social milieu exerts the strongest independent effect (and carries exactly the same weight that education exerts on white children's scores), followed by parents' origin social class and extent of mothers' exposure to white friends and coworkers. In short, the more exposure to middle-class influences and role models, the higher parents' origin social class, and the greater exposure to white friends and coworkers, the higher is the mean I.Q. score of black children. Parents' education enters the equation but does not significantly increase the amount of variation explained in black children's scores.

By combining black and white children's I.Q. scores and entering race as a variable in the regression equation, an estimate is derived of how much the observed I.Q. difference between black and white children is attributable to the aforementioned components of socio-economic status (with the white-exposure measure omitted). Five variables account for 23 percent of the variation in I.Q. scores among the whole sample. Race remains the strongest predictor, followed by mothers' social milieu and parents' educational attainment. Occupational status exerts a weak positive effect, and number of siblings in parents' origin families a weak negative effect, but neither variable alone significantly increases the variation explained in I.Q. scores. Controlling for this limited number of variables serves to reduce the observed I.Q. advantage of white relative to black children from 10 to 5.9 points.

Differences in the religious and denominational composition of the black and white social classes prove to be further sources of the disparity in I.Q. scores of black and white children. In both races, among Protestants, Baptists and other fundamentalist mothers average the lowest scores on socio-economic and demographic measures, Methodists/Lutherans rank higher, and High Protestants rank highest.[2] Black Catholic mothers closely resemble black Methodists, whereas white Catholics in my sample are similar to white Baptists. In both races, nondenominational and nonreligious mothers average the highest scores on socio-economic measures, and white Jewish mothers average scores only slightly lower than white nondenominational mothers. In all these religious groups, with the exception of Catholics in my sample, black mothers average lower socio-economic status scores than their white coreligionists.[3]

The pattern of differences in I.Q. and achievement scores of black and white children corresponds almost exactly to the pattern of differences in socio-economic rank observed with respect to mothers' religious and denominational membership. In both races, children of Baptist and other fundamentalist mothers average the lowest and children of nondenominational mothers the highest scores.[4] But a Baptist or other fundamentalist affiliation is more prevalent among black working-class mothers (80 percent) and middle-class mothers (44 percent) than among white mothers, working class (38 percent) or middle class (5 percent).

In both races Baptist and other fundamentalist mothers register higher religiosity scores than other mothers, and black Baptists are the most religious of all.

The addition of religious measures—mothers' religious/denominational affiliation and religiosity—to the other structural variables increases the variation explained in black scores from 14 to 16 percent. Mother's social milieu remains the strongest positive predictor of black children's I.Q. scores; children of Baptist and other fundamentalist mothers average significantly lower scores than children from other religious backgrounds; children of parents with higher socio-economic origins, those of nondenominational mothers, and those of mothers with higher white-exposure scores average higher scores than other black children. The last variable no longer adds significantly to the variance explained once mothers' religious affiliation is taken into account, which confirms other evidence that black Baptist and other fundamentalist mothers have the least opportunities for egalitarian association with whites.

In the case of whites, addition of religious measures to the equation does *not* increase the variation explained in children's I.Q. scores, an indication that differences in the socio-economic composition of religious groups largely account for the observed differences in I.Q. scores of children from different religious backgrounds. With religious variables adjusted for, white children's I.Q. advantage relative to that of black children declines further from 5.9 to 3.9 points.

Extension of the social structural model to include five additional measures—number of children in the family, father presence, sex of the study child, years of mothers' gainful employment over her child's lifetime, and number of mothers' organizational memberships—increases the variation explained in black children's scores to 18 percent and to 15 percent in white scores.

Socio-economic status (the composite measure) remains the strongest predictor of black and white children's I.Q. test performance.[5] And, in each race, children in large families (five or more children) average lower scores than other children. Indeed, in the case of black children, family size exerts nearly as strong an independent effect as socio-economic status does on I.Q. scores, but, of course, in the opposite direction. Black children of fundamentalist and of very religious mothers average lower I.Q. scores, while those of nondenominational mothers average higher scores than other black children; children of mothers with more extended labor force tenure average higher scores than other black children.

Among white children, those with northern-born parents from larger communities average higher scores, and girls outperform boys. Children of nondenominational parents average higher scores than other children, as do also those whose mothers have not held jobs since their child's birth. Children in father-present homes tend to score slightly higher (but not significantly) than those in father-absent homes.[6]

The variation explained in children's I.Q. scores by the full structural model with the races combined rises to 25 percent, and the remaining race difference in test scores declines to 3.5 I.Q. points.

That the presence of a race-by-sex-of-child interaction on I.Q. scores has the effect of increasing the I.Q. gap between the races becomes apparent when girls' and boys' I.Q. scores are analyzed separately. The observed mean difference of 12 points between black and white girls is reduced to 2.7 points, and the observed mean difference of 9 points between black and white boys is reduced to 2.9 points. Thus, social structural variables account for more of the race disparity in girls' than in boys' scores and account for more variation in girls' scores (29 percent) than in boys' scores (22 percent). Finally, with the sexes analyzed separately, it is apparent that *within* each sex the structural model reduces the race difference more than the difference that remains between I.Q. scores of white boys and girls, which amounts to 3.3 points compared to the observed difference of 4 points. Thus, results support the hypothesis that no single measure of social structure is sufficiently comprehensive to encompass the range of differences in the situations of blacks and whites produced by pervasive discrimination *and* segregation historically and currently. Environments are *cumulative*; the advantages afforded whites and the deficits imposed upon blacks separately and together account for the observed disparity in mean I.Q. test performance of black and white elementary-school-age children.

A host of findings from my study provide evidence that children's school competence, measured by I.Q. and achievement test performance, can fruitfully be conceived of as a return arising from an ongoing process of *social exchange* between mother and child. Mothers who have higher educational and occupational aspirations for their children's future as a rule make more demands on their children in the realm of school performance.[7] Such mothers also are likely to invest more time and effort in positive forms of interaction with their children from birth onward to help promote the growth of their children's cognitive and verbal abilities and their sense of self-efficacy.[8] Thus, they become an important source of gratification and support to their children, who are put under obligation to reciprocate that investment, while at the same time their capacity to do so is being progressively enhanced as they move from the home to the school. In short, mothers who place a high value on education and who *implement* their ambitions by a high investment of nonmaterial and material resources at their disposal will, all other things being equal, receive a higher return (measured by children's test scores) on their investment than those who invest less.

But the return on a mother's positive forms of investment is also influenced by the extent to which she believes in and uses punitive forms of discipline.[9] The more she resorts to the latter, the less the return she commands from the child, at least in terms of school test performance and probably also in other activities she values. Thus, a mother who espouses high educational and occupational aspirations for her child and invests in correspondingly more positive transactions with her child but also subjects it frequently to punitive and disparaging forms of control engages in a counterproductive strategy, one that reduces rather than maximizes the return on her investment.

The most counterproductive strategy for the early cognitive development of children is one that combines low investment and high punitive control. Children of such mothers average the lowest I.Q. and achievement scores in both races. This strategy is more prevalent among black than among white mothers. Even black mothers who are high investors rely more often on punitive discipline than white high investors, which reduces the return on their investment (measured by children's test scores) relative to white children.

The addition of the three socialization measures—mothers' valuation of education, investment in child, and belief in and use of punitive discipline—to the structural model serves to explain an identical amount of variation in I.Q. scores of black and white children (22 percent). However, the increment of variation explained in black scores is only 4 percent more with the full model than with the structural model, compared to an increment of 7 percent in white scores. Further evidence of the greater significance of social structural factors as sources of variation among black children's scores relative to those of white children is provided by a comparison of the predictors of I.Q. in the two groups.

Mothers' valuation of education followed by extent of investment in children prove to be the strongest independent predictors of children's I.Q. scores in each race, but each socialization dimension exerts a stronger, positive effect on white than on black children's scores.

It is noteworthy that with socialization variables taken into account, neither socio-economic status nor religious variables even enter the white equation. Only three structural variables persist as significant predictors of white children's scores. Girls outscore boys; children of northern-born urban parents and those whose mothers had not been in the labor force since their child's birth averaged higher scores.

But several social structural variables persist as significant predictors of black children's I.Q. scores. Children in large families, of fundamentalist and very religious mothers average lower scores, whereas children of mothers with more extended labor force participation, those of nondenominational mothers, and those in higher socio-economic families average higher test scores than other black children.

With the races combined, mothers' valuation of education and investment in child also exert the strongest positive effects on children's I.Q. scores, just as they do within each race. Socio-economic status exerts a significant positive effect, stronger than its effect on black scores alone; the negative effects of a fundamentalist background, mother's religiosity, and family size remain significant. Girls tend to outscore boys, nondenominational children tend to score higher than children from other religious backgrounds, and children in father-present families tend to score higher than those in father-absent homes, but none of the latter three variables alone significantly increases the variation explained.

Inclusion of the socialization variables in the equation increases the variation explained in the combined sample from 25 percent to 30 percent. However, it also slightly increases the remaining mean race difference from 3.5 to 3.9 points. I attribute this increase to complex interaction effects between race, religion, social structural, and socialization variables.

The plausibility of the above interpretation is strengthened when I.Q. scores of children in both races within *each religious group* were regressed on the full model. It becomes evident that the mean difference in scores between black and white children of the same religious background is not uniform but highly variable. Indeed, among two groups—High Protestants and nondenominational/nonreligious children—the race difference in I.Q. scores *disappears* altogether (that is, the race measure no longer enters the equation). These two groups are the most advantaged on every social structural measure in my black sample and also employ a more enlightened socialization strategy. But together High Protestant and nondenominational mothers constitute only 18 percent of the black middle class and 4 percent of the black working class.

Among the other religious groups, the largest remaining race difference in I.Q. scores occurs among Baptists and other fundamentalists (6.7 points). Among Catholics, white children's mean score is 5.2 points higher than that of black children, and among Methodists the difference is 4.9 points. Clearly, the primary locus of the *cumulative* structural deficits of black Americans is among Baptist and other fundamentalist blacks who constitute 80 percent of the working class in my black sample. And it is among these mothers—who average the lowest socio-economic status, have the highest number of children, are most religious, and are most isolated from modern mainstream secular cultural and social influences—that a counterproductive socialization strategy of low investment and a high measure of punitive discipline is more prevalent, although by no means universal.

To assess the extent to which observed differences in socialization strategies between the races results from differences in structural contexts in which black and white mothers rear their children, each socialization dimension was regressed on the battery of social structural variables.

Parents' socio-economic status (the composite measure) exerts the strongest independent effect of all structural variables on each of the three dimensions of socialization in both races. That is to say, the value mothers place on school performance and on the future educational and occupational attainments of their child and the extent of positive forms of investment in the child rise, while the belief in and use of punitive discipline decrease, with rising socio-economic status in both races.

Religious affiliation exerts an independent effect only on white mothers' valuations of education. White Jewish and nondenominational mothers have higher ambitions for their children's educational and occupational attainment than other mothers—white and black. The religious factor, however, *is* an independent source variation in the maternal behavior in *both* races. Among blacks, Baptist and other fundamentalist mothers invest less time and other resources in children, and Catholics tend to invest more than black women of other religious backgrounds. Among whites, Catholic mothers invest *less*, while Jewish and nondenominational mothers invest *more*, in their children than mothers of other religious groups. Nondenominational

mothers (both races) and Jewish mothers also average higher investment scores when the races are combined.

Religion is also an independent predictor of extent of belief in and
use of punitive discipline in both races. Among blacks, mothers in
three religious groups—High Protestant, Catholic, and nondenominational—rely *less* on punitive *discipline* than other black mothers,
while among whites, Baptist and other fundamentalist mothers, Catholic mothers, and very religious mothers use *more* discipline than other
white mothers. When the races are combined, religious effects are
strengthened: High Protestant, Jewish, and nondenominational mothers use less aversive discipline than women from other religious groups,
and, regardless of religious affiliation, highly religious mothers tend
to rely more on punitive controls than less religious ones.

Family structure variables exert stronger effects on black than on
white mothers' valuations of education. Family size, in particular, is
a stronger negative predictor of maternal aspirations among black than
among white mothers. Presence of a father in the home is a weak
positive predictor of black mothers' aspirations, but it exerts no independent effect on those of white mothers. White exposure is a weak
positive predictor of black mothers' aspirations. Mothers' years of employment since their child's birth appears to be a weak negative predictor of white mothers' aspirations.

The extent of mothers' investment in child is more strongly depressed by increasing family size among black than among white
mothers. With the races combined, the negative effect of family size
is second only to the positive effect of socio-economic status as a predictor of maternal investment. The beneficial effect of mothers' organizational participation on investment in child is considerably stronger
in the case of black than of white mothers. Association with white
friends and coworkers also promotes maternal investment in their
children among black mothers when other structural variables are
controlled.[10] Both the latter findings serve to emphasize the considerably greater significance that isolation from modern mainstream cultural influences has for delaying the diffusion among blacks compared
to whites of socialization strategies that promote children's early cognitive development.

Current family size does not exert any independent effects on the
use of punitive controls among black mothers, but those who grew up
with many siblings rely more on punitive discipline, and this effect is
strengthened when the races are combined. White mothers in father-
absent homes use more punitive discipline than those in homes with
a father present.

Sex of the child is an independent predictor of maternal values in both races. In general, black mothers espouse higher ambitions for daughters than for sons, whereas white mothers espouse higher ambitions for sons. Sex of the child also conditions maternal strategies of socialization, and the *direction* of the effect is the same in both races: mothers invest more time and other resources in daughters than in sons and use more punitive discipline in relation to sons than to daughters. The sex effect, net of other structural variables, is of about the same magnitude with respect to investment in children in the two races. But black mothers use considerably more punitive discipline in rearing sons than in rearing daughters. Indeed, next to socio-economic status, sex of child is the strongest single predictor of how extensively black mothers rely on punitive forms of control.[11]

With structural variables controlled, the direction of the effect of race is reversed on two of the socialization dimensions: black mothers, all other things being equal, exhibit a higher valuation of education than white mothers, and they invest more time and other resources in their children than their white counterparts. But the inclination of black mothers to rely more on punitive forms of control, particularly in rearing sons, persists and can be taken as evidence that the experience of slavery followed by a repressive system of caste supported by the threat of violence has left its bitter mark on black culture, particularly with respect to the socialization of males. Heavy reliance on punitive forms of control in socializing children may well have been necessary for survival under conditions of subjugation but is dysfunctional for preparing children for the performance of tasks that require the exercise of intellectual flexibility and self-direction.[12]

In summary, the findings of my study provide solid empirical evidence that the mean difference in I.Q. test performance between black and white children results *not* from genetic differences but (1) from identifiable differences in economic and social resources and (2) from differences in the social environments in which black and white parents were reared and in which they rear their children.

As a result of the pervasive discrimination *and* segregation to which all black Americans had been subjected for more than a century after the abolition of slavery, important structural differences have developed (and, although considerably attenuated, still persist) in the two stratification systems that have produced differences in social processes as they affect family structure and the early socialization of children.

In both races mothers' aspirations and socialization strategies are the strongest *direct* determinants of their children's I.Q. test scores. High aspirations combined with a strategy of high investment of time and other resources and low reliance on punitive discipline and disparagement proves to be the most effective strategy for promoting children's early cognitive development as measured by their I.Q. test scores early in their school career. Effective socialization strategies proved to be most prevalent in the white middle class, less prevalent in the black middle class and white working class, and least prevalent in the black working class in 1968.

The effect of significant gains in parents' educational and occupational attainment on children's test scores is optimized in structural contexts that offer parents numerous opportunities to associate with others of more educationally advantaged backgrounds (such as the white middle class) who serve as purveyors of knowledge and behavior patterns (e.g., enlightened socialization strategies) not previously encountered by the new middle-class recruit. The more limited such opportunities are, particularly in a rapidly changing mainstream secular culture, the less pressure there is to relinquish traditional ways and to adopt modern cultural innovations (such as family planning and enlightened socialization strategies) that are largely created and become diffused first among the more highly educated segments of the white urban middle class in American society, spreading later through informal processes of association—coworkers, neighbors, friends, organizational memberships, etc.—among less-educated upwardly mobile members and to working-class parents who have middle-class aspirations for their children.

The black middle class in 1968 was largely a new middle class whose socio-economic *origins* closely resemble those of the white working class but whose average educational and occupational attainments and social milieu approached parity to the white middle class only in two identifiable groups (nondenominational and High Protestant mothers). Among these two groups enlightened socialization strategies were most prevalent, which served to produce parity in their children's I.Q. scores relative to comparable white children. But these groups constituted a small minority of their stratum in 1968 relative to the white middle class (which, in addition, contains a substantial proportion of Jewish parents, disproportionately higher than their representation in the general population).

Overall, the proportion of college-educated parents in higher occupational positions with middle-class origins constitutes a very much smaller segment of the black than of the white middle class. Thus, the *supply* of well-educated influences and role models to which upwardly mobile blacks have access is proportionately smaller and so, therefore, is their *span* of influence relative to their white counterparts. Consequently, the *rate* of diffusion of patterns of small families and enlightened socialization strategies that promote early cognitive development of children has been slower among upwardly mobile blacks than among their white counterparts. Therefore, the articulation is less close between black mothers' aspirations and their children's actual performance on school tests than it is between white mothers and offspring.

To the extent that black parents' educational and occupational gains are coupled with increasing opportunities for informal association with well-educated blacks *and* whites, the pace of diffusion of modern patterns of childbearing and child rearing will continue to quicken and will serve to further close the gap in test performance and educational attainment between middle-class and stable working-class black and white children.

But the gap between poor blacks and other blacks and white Americans has substantially increased. For poor blacks in the inner-city ghettos, the situation has markedly worsened relative to the situation two decades ago. With the exodus of the black middle class and stable working class, a vacuum of middle-class influences, role models, and community leadership resulted; residents of the inner-city ghettos have become more homogeneously poor and increasingly isolated from mainstream black and white middle-class culture and patterns of behavior.

The profile of family characteristics that put the black children in my study at highest risk of school failure in 1968 closely matches the profile of families that are concentrated and preponderant in the black inner-city ghettos today. Poor black ghetto children—children in father-absent families; with many closely spaced siblings; reared by poorly educated mothers without work experience, organizational ties, or exposure to middle-class influences and role models—are most at risk of entering school with severe cognitive deficits. In both races, sons of mothers not in the labor force in father-absent homes average the lowest I.Q. scores, but the relative incidence of families with this *combination* of characteristics was considerably higher among blacks than among whites in 1968. By now this family type has become endemic in the ghettos, and it is these enclaves that contain the highest birth rates and highest number of school dropouts, the highest rates of unemployment and of long-term welfare dependency, and the highest crime and imprisonment rates.

The absence of *any* wage earner, rather than father absence per se, deprives children in poor female-headed families of opportunities to acquire the most rudimentary formal and experiential knowledge about the world of gainful employment. Mothers and children in such families are most removed from the modernizing social and cultural influences that exist in the mainstream society.

During the same era in which there was a population explosion among minority youth, a structural transformation was taking place in the economy—from the manufacture of goods to the provision of higher-order services that produced profound changes in the central-city labor market, particularly in northern cities. Job losses were greatest in industries with lower educational requirements, and job growth has become concentrated in industries that require higher education (Wilson 1985, 39).

Over approximately the same period of time, average earnings of 30-year-old high-school dropouts declined 41 percent, and those of high-school graduates declined 30 percent. Only the average earnings of college graduates increased.

During the last ten years, the number of young people between the ages of 16 and 24 who are ready to enter the labor market in the United States has declined by a little over a million, and that number is expected to fall another million. However, the number of less well educated youth, who are least prepared for the kind of jobs in which there is a growing demand, has increased. And the number of high-school dropouts and teenage mothers is expected to increase by over a million each year at the same time that their chances of finding employment are markedly lower than those of their classmates who graduated from high school. School dropouts' chances of engaging in criminal activities resulting in imprisonment are much greater than are those of high-school graduates. Sixty percent of all prison inmates in the United States are high-school dropouts. In Texas this figure is even higher—85 percent. And prison inmates are disproportionately black and Hispanic (Bonfield 1987).

Poor minority children with cognitive deficits early in their school career more often than not continue to lose ground as they ascend the grade ladder. As the curriculum content becomes more complex, their frustration and alienation mount, and they are the likeliest to drop out of high school.

This chain of events can be forestalled on a large scale only if a quality preschool education program for three- and four-year-old children is put in place nationally especially, but *not* exclusively, in poor black and Hispanic neighborhoods. There is good evidence that early cognitively oriented schooling, with classes small enough so that teachers can identify and deal with problems exhibited by individual children, and which communicates with parents, has positive results over the short run and also over the long run. Longitudinal studies of black children from poor families who participated in a preschool program at ages three and four showed that these children went on to exhibit higher school performance, higher educational attainment, lower high-school dropout rates, lower rates of teenage births, and lower imprisonment rates compared to control groups of nonparticipant children (Weikart et al. 1978).

Investment of resources in well-designed programs to *prevent* school failure will be costly, but the benefits will surely outweigh the costs. For example, a black educator recently estimated that a three-year preschool program would cost about $7,500 per child, which compares very favorably to the $90,000 it costs to house one prisoner in the state of Texas (Sawyer 1988). Can this country afford *not* to act on this issue?

Notes

1. The composition of class origins of black mothers in my sample is virtually identical to that of the wives of black men in a national sample of 20,000 men (Blau and Duncan 1967). There is an underrepresentation in my white sample of upwardly mobile white women, compared to the national sample, but since parents' social class origins are taken into account in the analysis, this disparity does not pose the problems it might otherwise.
2. The High Protestants category is composed of Episcopalians, Presbyterians, and Congregationalists. The nondenominational category is composed of Unitarians, ethical culture members, and mothers without any religious affiliation.
3. Because my sample was drawn solely from public schools, white middle-class Catholics may be underrepresented.
4. Black nondenominational children's average I.Q. score was virtually identical (109) to that of Jewish children (110); that of white nondenominational children was only slightly higher (112).
5. A composite measure was formed of socio-economic status (SES). It is a weighted score based on parents' origin social class, parents' education, occupational status, and mothers' social milieu.
6. Mothers' years of work *appears* to be a negative predictor of white children's I.Q. scores, specifically of white boys, but analysis of variance revealed an interaction effect only among white boys between mothers' marital status and work status. Boys of married, nonworking mothers averaged a slightly higher score (2 points) than those of working mothers in father-absent families. The specific locus of this interaction was among sons of High Protestant mothers. In both races boys of nonworking mothers in father-absent homes averaged the lowest scores.
7. Mothers' valuation of education is based on three measures: their level of aspirations with respect to (1) scholastic performance and (2) future educational and (3) occupational attainments of their child.
8. The investment-in-children dimension is based on four components derived by principal components analyses: (1) frequency of positive forms of interaction with the child during infancy and early childhood (6 variables); (2) extent of mothers' exposure to child-rearing literature (e.g., Spock, etc.); (3) a measure of extent of simple verbal and numerical skills achieved by child before or after school entry; and (4) extent of provision of cultural enrichment experiences before or after school entry (e.g., nursery school, musical instruction).
9. The belief in and use of the punitive discipline dimension is based on five component scales: (1) maternal fatalism, (2) maternal authoritarianism, (3) suppression of autonomy, (4) extent of coercive discipline (physical punishment) employed by mothers

during toilet training and in early and later childhood, and (5) extent of nonphysical forms of control (e.g., disparagement).

10. Black mothers with higher scores on the white-exposure measure also average fewer children in the family than those with lower scores.

11. Social structural variables account for an identical amount of variance in the investment dimension in the two races (37 percent), for somewhat more variance in white than in black mothers' valuation of education (37 vs. 32 percent), and for considerably less variance in the aversive discipline dimension among black than among white mothers (22 vs. 34 percent).

12. Net of I.Q. and SES, extent of mothers' belief in and use of punitive discipline is the strongest negative predictor of black boys' achievement test scores. Indeed, it carries nearly as much weight (but in the opposite direction) as does socio-economic status.

References

Becker, W. C., 1977. "Teaching Reading and Language to the Disadvantaged—What Have We Learned from Field Research?" *Harvard Educational Review* 47:518–543.

Blau, P., and O. D. Duncan, 1967. *The American Occupational Structure.* New York: John Wiley and Sons.

Blau, Z. S., 1981. *Black Children/White Children: Competence, Socialization, and Social Structure.* New York: Free Press.

———, 1965. "Class Structure, Mobility and Change in Child Rearing." *Sociometry* 28:210–219.

———, 1964. "Exposure to Child Rearing Experts: A Structural Interpretation of Class-Color Differences." *American Journal of Sociology* 64:597–608.

Blau, Z. S., P. P. Rogers, G. T. Oser, and R. C. Stephens, 1978. "School Bells and Work Whistles: Sounds that Echo a Better Life for Women in Later Years." In *Women in Midlife—Security and Fulfillment* (Part 1), 61–85. A Compendium of Papers Submitted to the Select Committee on Aging and the Subcommittee on Retirement Income and Employment, U.S. House of Representatives. Washington, D.C.

Bonfield, G., 1987. "When Jobs Beg for Workers." *Houston Chronicle,* November 16.

Coleman, James S., 1968. "The Evaluation of Equality of Educational Opportunity." Santa Monica, CA.: The RAND Corporation.

Douglas, J. W. B., 1964. *The Home and the School: A Study of Ability and Attainment in the Primary School.* London: McGibbon and Kee.

Featherman, D. L., and R. M. Hauser, 1978. *Opportunity and Change.* New York: Academic Press.

Gordon, M. T., 1972. "Mobility and Child-rearing: A Study of the Achievement of Black and White Metropolitan Children." Ph.D. diss., Northwestern University, Evanston, Ill.

Jackson, J. S., and R. C. Gibson, 1985. "Work and Retirement Among the Black Elderly." In *Current Perspectives on Aging and the Life Cycle,* vol. 1 *(Work, Retirement and Social Policy),* ed. Z. S. Blau, 193–222. Greenwich, Conn.: JAI Press.

Jensen, A. R., 1969. "How Much Can We Boost I.Q. and Scholastic Achievement?" *Harvard Educational Review* 39:1–123.

Maruyama, G., M. D. Finch, and J. T. Mortimer, 1985. "Processes of Achievement in the Transition to Adulthood." In *Current Perspectives on Aging and the Life Cycle,* vol. 1. *(Work, Retirement and Social Policy),* ed. Z. S. Blau, 61–88. Greenwich, Conn.: JAI Press.

Mayeske, G. W., and A. E. Beaton, Jr., 1975. *Special Studies of Our Nation's Students.* Washington, D.C.: Government Printing Office.

Sawyer, J., 1988. "Will It Be $7,500 for School or $90,000 for Prison?" *Houston Chronicle*, April 17.

Treiman, D. J., and K. Terrell, 1975. "Sex and the Process of Status Attainment: A Comparison of Women and Men." *American Sociological Review* 40:174–200.

Weikart, D. P., A. Epstein, L. Schweinhart, and J. T. Bond, 1978. "The Ypsilanti Preschool Demonstration Project: Preschool Years and Longitudinal Results." Monograph No. 4. Ypsilanti, Mich.: Ypsilanti High/Scope Educational Research Foundation.

Wilson, W. J., 1987. *The Truly Disadvantaged: The Inner City, the Underclass, and Public Policy.* Chicago: University of Chicago Press.

———, 1978. *The Declining Significance of Race.* Chicago: University of Chicago Press.

WILLIAM DARITY, JR.

Chapter 12. What's Left of the Economic Theory of Discrimination?

Economists who have become intrigued by the phenomenon of black–white inequality in the United States have undertaken a largely empiricist project devoted to the statistical analysis of earnings differentials. Infrequent attention has been devoted to the far greater differences in wealth between the races, perhaps because data limitations preclude meticulous empiricism and perhaps because wealth differentials are less amenable to the choice-theoretic structure most economists prefer to employ as a theoretical rationalization for their statistical endeavors.[1]

Typically, statistical inquiry has meant estimation of regression equations where wages or earnings have been treated as the left-hand variable and various indicator variables capturing human capital or individual productivity characteristics have been used as the right-hand variables. The consistent finding with U.S. data has been the following: for a given bundle of human capital indicators, blacks on average earn less than whites. A significant differential always remains that cannot be explained by the included variables—a so-called unexplained residual (see Williams 1984a and 1987 and Shulman 1984 for detailed discussions).

This type of finding is by no means unique to the U.S. experience. Shirley Dex has summarized the results of human capital–centered studies comparing the determinants of earnings of white and "colored" workers in Britain. Again, despite attempts to control for "schooling, experience, differences in weeks worked, marital status, and urban/ rural residence" these studies "still concluded [with the finding] that residual or unexplained earnings differentials existed. . . ." (Dex 1986, 163). Similarly, Smooha and Kraus (1985) have briefly surveyed econ-

I am grateful to participants at seminars at Wake Forest University, Carnegie-Mellon University, Howard University, the University of Pittsburgh, and the University of North Carolina at Chapel Hill for criticism and helpful suggestions. Two anonymous referees provided detailed, careful, and exceptionally helpful guidance for revisions.

omists' research on earnings differentials in Israel between the Oriental-Sephardic and Ashkenazic ethnic groups. They also find that the Israeli studies conclude "that ethnic origin still has certain weight in determining income after controlling relevant factors" (1985, 155).[2] Banerjee and Knight (1985) have applied the same technique in India, finding an "unexplained" residual for the income disadvantage experienced by members of the scheduled castes. Alejandro Portes now complains that this procedure for decomposing the sources of ethnic or racial differences in income is leading to a mindless proliferation of inquiries of this sort:

This style of analysis seems to assume that a study of the labor market condition of any group consists in adding the appropriate dummy variable or column of regression coefficients to a set of results. Today Hispanics, tomorrow Asians. "Have model, will travel" is the prevailing motto. Although technically elegant, these analyses are intellectually unsatisfying because they fail to come to grips with the ultimately important questions, such as (a) why should the economic outcomes for minorities deviate so much from those in the mainstream, after individual-level characteristics are controlled for; and (b) why should they be so different among minority groups themselves? (Portes 1986, 730–731)

Hopefully, more thoughtfulness about the conventional style of empirical inquiry will lead researchers to confront Portes's "ultimately important questions" head-on; a major purpose of this chapter is to steer inquiry in the potentially more fruitful directions indicated by Portes. The puzzle of interpreting the residuals in earnings equations strongly suggests that status quo economic research on race and ethnicity is inadequate.

For a true believer in human capital theory as *the* theory of income distribution, one who is convinced the regression equations have been specified correctly, the residual should represent purely random or nonsystematic effects. But such an interpretation is difficult to maintain with cross-section data sets, since the residual differences correlate strongly with the race or ethnicity of the individuals in the sample.

For those not convinced that human capital differences are the sole explanation of the gap in labor market performance between blacks and whites, the residual often has been taken to represent discrimination. Specifically, labor market discrimination was identified as the factor that has assigned blacks lower wages or to occupations offering lower pay, even when blacks demonstrably have comparable human capital endowments as whites.

However, this latter reconciliation of statistical evidence with explanation has remained troublesome to certain economists for two reasons: first, this latter group of economists advances an a priori complaint—the theoretical proposition that competition and persistent labor market discrimination are incompatible; second, they advance an empirical complaint—the observation that some immigrant groups, to the United States in particular, faced discrimination in the past but have done quite well economically despite such barriers to their success. The star cases frequently offered are the immigrant experiences of Asian Americans, Jewish Americans, and West Indian black Americans.

These economists doubt that it is legitimate to interpret the residuals in racial earnings regressions as capturing the effects of discrimination. Instead they argue that the residual is capturing cultural differences that generate the remaining differences in earnings between members of various groups who might otherwise appear to possess the same human capital endowments. If culture is viewed as a component of human capital—for example, as Thomas Sowell (1981a) does—then previous regression equations have been misspecified and the residuals are picking up the specification error. Cultural differences, it is now alleged, lead to systematic differences in labor market achievement. The "unexplained" residual in the human capital regression equation now finds an origin in ethnic/racial gaps.

The objective of this chapter is to examine in depth the culturalogical explanation for variations in ethnic/racial group patterns of economic achievement by first presenting an analysis of the reasons why economists increasingly are reluctant to interpret the residuals as evidence of labor market discrimination against the group for whom a given level of individual productivity indicators translate into relatively lower earnings. Next we explore how culture has come to supplant discrimination in interpretations of the residual and discuss how such a transition leads into a logical inconsistency with respect to the concept of competition. This is followed by a demonstration of the fact that ethnic/racial cultural characteristics do not explain well the experiences of specific immigrant groups in the United States, contrary to the claims of economists who are promoting the notion that cultural heritage, in a broadly nationalist sense, is destiny. I then argue that discrimination matters and that the theoretical basis for the operation of discrimination in labor markets is sound when alternative concepts of competition are considered. Last, I advance a historical theory of ethnic/racial inequality that preserves a central role for discrimination, utilizing conclusions from the preceding discussion, followed by some final observations.

How did certain economists reach a point where, on theoretical grounds, they find themselves unable to believe that discrimination can persist in real-world labor markets? Because they carried the implications of contemporary economic theory's use of the notion of competition to its fullest limitations. They were driven by a somewhat admirable and unwavering theoretical consistency to conclude that discrimination cannot be indefinitely an important factor influencing black and white earnings differentials.

Contemporary (neoclassical) economic theory sets as its benchmark the idea of perfect competition—no individual actor ("agent") in a market economy has the ability to influence price via his or her own decisions. This translates into the familiar notion that a condition of universal perfect competition dictates that all market participants are price takers, rather than price makers. For example, the perfectly competitive firm faces a horizontal demand curve for its product. There is a distinct absence of conflict or rivalry, as a placid sameness settles over each of the n-industries that comprise the economy.

Perfect competition also is a static concept of competition because it lacks a process of adjustment. To compensate for this limitation, entry and exit are appended as sources of dynamism. A distinction then is made between short-run and long-run equilibrium. In the short run the number of participants in a market or industry is fixed, even in the face of above-normal or subnormal profits. In the long run the full effects of entry and exit have worked themselves through—as a response to the profit opportunities that become evident in the short run. The number of participants in a market or industry is fixed again, not merely by short-period assumption, but because there is no further *incentive* for entry or exit.

The adjustment process centers on movement into and away from particular industries. Ironically, adoption of such a story about adjustment to long-run industry equilibrium subtly gives way to a different view of competition, a view consistent with the premises of Austrian economics.[3] The Austrian school posits an explicit process view of competition, rather than a state of affairs view of competition. Entry, or the possibility of entry, takes on paramount importance.

Postulating the existence of a latent reservoir of alert entrepreneurs ready to seize any profit opportunities that might arise, Austrian competition deems it largely irrelevant whether individual participants in the market are price takers or not. The key is the capability of human beings, motivated by pecuniary desires, to pursue all conceivable opportunities to reap economic gain.

The Austrian vision of entrepreneurship also gives great weight to human ingenuity, for it is human ingenuity that makes no barrier to entry immutable. Competition will prevail even if attempts are made to curb its essence—that is, freedom of entry—since ingenious entrepreneurs will discover ways to circumvent artificial, or even natural, entry barriers. If the barriers are imposed by state action, entrepreneurial creativity still will find ways to extract profit opportunities, eroding the effectiveness of state action over time. Entrepreneurial ingenuity, it is argued, customarily produces regulation-induced innovations that *de facto* render the regulations empty.

It is really the Austrian process view of competition, rather than the static neoclassical view of perfect competition, that lies at the heart of the demise of discrimination as a viable theoretical phenomenon in modern economics. Consider the following argument: there are two groups who are ascriptively different but who, on average, have the same ability to perform tasks sought by employers. Employers, however, have a preference for members of one group over the other solely on the basis of ascriptive difference. Consequently, a wage differential arises between the two groups, since employers are willing to pay a premium for workers from the preferred, albeit no more capable, group.

In the absence of a process view of competition, the story might end there. But the Austrian process view of competition immediately provides a different conclusion. Alert entrepreneurs, some lacking the prejudices of employers already in the marketplace, would seize the profit opportunities generated by the discriminatory wage gap, enter the market, hire the equally able members of the disdained group at lower pay, drive discriminating employers from the market, and erode the wage differentials. Therefore, labor market discrimination and its effects could only be temporary.[4]

Three types of approaches subsequently have been employed to reconcile competition with market discrimination on the terrain of orthodox economics. These include (1) development of models of discrimination under neoclassical imperfect competition (Swinton 1978), (2) development of models of statistical discrimination due to conditions of risk (Aigner and Cain 1977), and (3) development of models of perceptual inequality (Arrow 1973). But none of these avenues preclude possibilities for erosion of discrimination inherent in the Austrian "entrepreneurial capacity to smell profits" (Kirzner 1973, 229).

In the first case, the entrepreneur eventually will, as suggested, find a way to circumvent the barriers that were the sources of the imperfection. In the second case, the entrepreneur will recognize that profits are to be had by designing new instruments that will improve employers' capacity to evaluate job applicants regardless of the group from which they originate. In the third case, if employers perceive ability differences between members of the two groups that do not really exist, some entrepreneurs will experiment by employing members of the allegedly inferior group. They should, on average, be pleasantly surprised to learn that they get workers of a similar quality at lower cost. Eventually the perceptual veil should be pierced.

Entrepreneurial energy will tear down any obstacles to the pursuit of profit (cf. the implications of Coase's work [1960] on externalities). If discriminatory wage gaps signal profit opportunities, entrepreneurial energy will seek, exploit, and ultimately destroy purely ascriptively based pay differentials. Any differentials that remain, then, must be due to authentic differences in ability between members of the two groups in question.

The application of the Austrian process view of competition to racial earnings differentials effectively obliterates labor market discrimination. On the surface, it propels human capital theory into ascendance. But, as noted previously, statistical inquiry consistently has led to the annoying finding of significant unexplained differences in earnings after controlling for human capital characteristics (e.g., experience, education, etc.). Increasingly residuals are explained as indicative of cultural differences that lead to ethnic and racial differences in economic achievement. The explanation is given added force by the observation that certain ethnic immigrant groups have managed to succeed in America despite discrimination against them. Their cultural endowment not only allows them to translate a given quantity and quality of human capital into above-average earnings among all those with similar endowments, but, in the past, presumably it has permitted members of their group to leapfrog discriminatory obstacles. As a group the immigrants display the tenacity of Austrian entrepreneurs who leapfrog all obstacles. The analogy, while not altogether forced, will prove to be paradoxical.

Thomas Sowell and Barry Chiswick have been at the forefront of those proposing cultural explanations of racial and ethnic success or failure in the marketplace. Both are understandably vague about what culture is, but both argue that it matters. Chiswick (1983b, 334), for example, conjectures that the higher rate of return to education enjoyed by second-generation Jewish immigrants to the United States "may arise from cultural characteristics that enable Jews to acquire more units of human capital per dollar of investment . . . or it may be that there are cultural characteristics that enable Jews to be more productive in the labor market with the human capital embodied in them."[5]

Culture determines patterns of labor market outcomes for ethnic and racial groups. Groups with cultures that dress them for success will reveal this in higher earnings, and groups with cultures that do not will reveal their predestination in lower earnings. But once economists like Sowell and Chiswick pass from the argument that competition drives out discrimination to the argument that cultural differences are a major explanation of racial or ethnic earnings differentials, they seem to have passed simultaneously over into another world. Again, on the surface, it appears that the source of inequality in the latter case is a condition that lies outside of markets. The acquisition of a culture, after all, seems to be an extramarket phenomenon.

An older vintage of human capital argument attributed black–white earnings inequality to educational differences stemming from the dual system of public education in the South prior to the 1960s. The human capital differences themselves were due to discrimination, but it was an extramarket or political discrimination. But in this argument, somehow, the Austrian entrepreneurs were not brought onto the scene to ingeniously offer superior, low-cost educational opportunities for blacks in the private sector.[6] Similarly, it is odd that they do not appear in Sowell's and Chiswick's visions of American immigrant history. For, although culture can be treated as an extramarket condition, it is alleged to manifest its effects in, at least, the market for labor. Therefore, cultural differences implicitly carry with them a market valuation. The ingenious entrepreneurs should smell the profits inherent in creating new markets to facilitate the transfer of cultural attributes from the groups with the advantageous culture to the groups with the disadvantageous culture. Norms of socialization of children, standards of behavior, attitudinal changes, and rituals and traditions that influence labor market achievement presumably can be transferred—at a fee that is an implicit charge against the inferior group's future higher earnings. And the magical portal marked entry should mean, given the profitability of this new venture, that the fees would be driven down over time as more entrepreneurs enter this line of work.

In short, the Austrian process view of competition suggests that market-valued cultural differences should not persist either—no more than labor market discrimination! Even if the group with the disadvantageous culture is hesitant to change its ways because it finds great worth in the nonpecuniary aspects of its culture (ethnic solidarity, collective spirit, etc.), this should not impede the efforts of sufficiently ingenious Austrian entrepreneurs. It simply means that the transactions costs of adopting another cultural pattern are perceived as too high by the group in question. Inventive entrepreneurs, performing the middleman function of cultural transfer, presumably will develop ways to reduce the transactions costs. This would allow the group to acquire aspects of the alien culture that raise their earnings while still retaining the desired features of their native culture.

The key to this line of argument is the underlying assumption that no transactions costs are irreducible over time. If the proponents of the new cultural determinism seek to argue that the price of cultural transfers involves excessive *and* irreducible transactions costs, they must also show that the price of overcoming labor market discrimination does not. The thrust of the Austrian theory is to suggest that *no* transactions costs possess characteristics that lead to irreducibility in the face of human ingenuity.

Barring such a tightrope walk, economists must be led to conclude that either their concept of competition is wrong or their cultural theory of racial economic inequality is wrong. As Rhonda Williams and I suggested elsewhere, "Either Austrian entrepreneurs can undercut both market discrimination and cultural differentiation, or they can do neither" (Darity and Williams 1985, 251).

Of course, a group with an advantageous culture might seek to withhold its "trade secrets" from the marketplace. Then the theorist would have to explain how the group effectively manages to enforce against cartel cheating perpetually. Again, what prevents the alert entrepreneur from penetrating the cartel's gates when there is money to be made from doing so?

If cultural differences are significant or decisive determinants of ethnic and racial economic inequality, then one can ask why such differences persist. Such persistence is intractably difficult to maintain if the economist embraces Austrian competition. Sowell (1981b), for one, seems to have in mind exactly such a view of competition. Chiswick, unfortunately, is silent on this topic. The arguments of both are vulnerable to the charge that markets could be opened up for the transfer of cultural attributes by clever entrepreneurs.[7]

Neither Sowell nor Chiswick make use of the concept of social class in their analysis of variations in ethnic and racial group economic performance.[8] Cultural traits are given an ethnic basis rather than a basis in class status.[9] Again from the vantage point of Austrian competition, this matters little. The individualism of Austrian theory also neglects the class concept. Even if it did not, one can suppose that the Austrian theory would consider transitory all class differences attributable to reasons other than *individual* differences in tastes, desires, ambition, and the like.

If differences in culture are linked to social class and culture is destiny, it might still be argued that the heroic entrepreneurs would find a way to transfer those traits at a low cost to members of the disadvantaged class. The upshot is that economic inequality becomes no more than a matter of individual differences in initiative and ability. There would be no reason in an Austrian world to observe systematic and persistent income variations across ascriptively different groups. The Austrian view of competition implies a tendency toward homogenization with respect to cultural characteristics that are linked to individual productivity. Gaps that might be due to ethnically distinct distributions of tastes in such areas as self-investment, work, and leisure should close if the taste differences are culturally generated.

Ultimately, the Austrian theory necessarily steers analysis away from economic inequality as a group phenomenon and toward economic inequality as a strictly individual phenomenon. To observe systematic and persistent income variations between, for example, blacks and whites in the United States is to suggest that something is inadequate—or wrong—with Austrian economics and its concept of competition. But it is the same concept of competition that was used to discount the importance of discrimination. The Austrian approach indifferently predicts development of markets in cultural or class characteristics relevant to an individual's economic performance. Those all-powerful markets ostensibly will eliminate an uneven distribution of those characteristics by race or class.

But what about the empirical refutation of the significance of labor market discrimination? What about the various immigrant groups who climbed up from poverty while facing discrimination? Doesn't this show that the persistent relative poverty of blacks must be due to something other than discrimination? And might that other something be culture?

Chiswick (1983a, 212) suggests precisely this line of reasoning in a study of the economic achievements of Asian-Americans: "[My] findings for the Chinese and Japanese suggest also that it is incorrect to assume that racial minority status in the United States and discrimination *per se* result in lower observed levels of earnings, schooling, employment, and rates of return to schooling." Chiswick's claim is that some racially or ethnically identifiable groups have managed to display substantial upward mobility in the United States, despite discriminatory practices directed toward them both within and outside the marketplace. His remarks suggest three further lines of inquiry: (1) Were the patterns of discrimination faced by the successful immigrant groups, in fact, much the same as those faced by unsuccessful groups; (2) more generally, were the conditions faced by all the groups similar at the time of entry; (3) were the resources the successful immigrant groups brought with them upon entry into the United States similar to those possessed by unsuccessful groups? In short, is it legitimate to draw inferences about the impact of discrimination by comparing the outcomes for various ethnic immigrant groups?

The answer that follows will be largely negative for three major reasons. First, the nature of the discriminatory experiences of various ethnic immigrant groups was not the same. Second, the timing of immigration was not the same, nor was it associated with the same circumstances in the receiving society. Third, the successful groups, once their prior class position is taken into account, broadly have displayed *lateral* rather than *upward* mobility in their movement from abroad to the United States.[10] In what follows, the large omission from the case being made for culture as destiny will be shown to be the role of social class.

On the latter point, consider first Jewish immigrants to the United States in the late nineteenth and early twentieth centuries. The impression of a dramatic upward shift in class position has been fostered by knowledge of the extreme poverty of Eastern-European Jews upon entry. But a more careful look at the status of Eastern-European Jews prior to immigration yields a different picture. Essentially a middle-class population in Russia, and throughout Eastern Europe generally, Jews were pushed out of their long-standing occupational positions with the growth of anti-Semitism in the region.

Nathan Glazer contends that what is surprising is not the pattern of Jewish accomplishment after entry into the United States but the speed and depth with which Jews had been displaced from their previous social status in Eastern Europe:

What is really exceptional, in terms of the long perspective of Jewish history, is not the rapid rise of Jews in America, but the extent to which they had been forced out of their age-old pursuits and proletarianized. This process was to a certain extent a response to the industrial revolution: everywhere peasants and artisans and small traders were forced to become workers. But in the Czarist empire, where the bulk of Eastern European Jews lived, artificial measures were taken to drive them out of their traditional occupations—Jewish taverns were closed, Jewish students were artificially limited in the schools, Jews were not permitted to live in the expanding capital cities. (Glazer 1955, 32)

The combination of "governmental anti-Semitism and the industrial revolution" led Eastern-European Jews to enter the United States, in Glazer's words, "either as workers or *luftmenschen*—businessmen and traders with neither stock nor capital" (1955, 32). Therefore, they were quite different from other members of the burgeoning American immigrant working class:

[T]hey were not like the other workers who immigrated with them, the sons and grandsons of peasants, bearing the traditionally limited horizons of those classes. The Jewish workers were the sons—or the grandsons—of merchants and scholars, even though the merchants had only their wits for capital, and the scholars' wits were devoted to feats of memory. This background meant that the Jewish workers could almost immediately . . . turn their minds to ways and means of improving themselves that were quite beyond the *imagination* of their fellow workers. Business and education were, for the Jews, not a remote and almost foreign possibility, but a near and familiar one. (Glazer 1955, 32, emphasis added)[11]

The Eastern-European Jewish immigrants were not working class in any sense but a strictly pecuniary one. Having a significant percentage of their population who had already experienced being merchants and scholars meant that Jews were able to guide their offspring into parallel professions in the United States with greater ease, even if the parents or grandparents were not able to obtain such occupations themselves upon arrival. A social-class heritage was available to Jewish youths that was unavailable to the largely Southern European immigrants who arrived in the United States at about the same time.

It would be an error to conflate the initially low incomes of the Jewish immigrants with peasant or working-class origins prior to migration. This is not a straightforward matter—as Chiswick and Sowell would have it—of human capital differences being attributable to differential patterns of individual self-investment that are due, in turn, to differences in work attitudes, education, and aspirations that find their roots exclusively in ethnicity. The roots must be found in a collective inheritance ("memory") of a prior class status in Eastern Europe. As Goldscheider and Zuckerman indicate, it was not those immigrants' Jewishness per se that accounted for their economic success; rather it was the fact that the Jewish immigrants already had been a part of the Eastern-European (urban) middle classes:

Those who have argued for the centrality of Jewish values as the explanation of rapid Jewish integration in America minimize the importance of social class and residential differences between Jewish and non-Jewish immigrants. The superficial similarity of mass immigration from diverse countries and the initial depths of urban poverty common to all immigrants obscure critical differences in the occupational and urban background of Jews and others. (1984, 158)

Goldscheider and Zuckerman report that "[t]he proportion of Jews who declared upon entry to the United States that they were laborers, farmers, or servants averaged less than 25 percent in 1900–1902 compared to 80–90 percent of the other immigrant groups" (1984, 166). They add, "In 1910 and 1914, for example, about 90 percent of the Croatians, Slovenians, Finns, Greeks, Hungarians, Poles, Russians, and Italians compared to 20 percent of the Jews were laborers, farmers, or servants . . ." (1984, 166).

Similarly, Stephen Steinberg has documented the unusual array of skills that Eastern-European Jews brought with them, which, he argues, "gave them a decisive advantage over other immigrants who were entering industrial labor markets for the first time" (1981, 101). Again, one can contrast their experience, for example, with the Slavic immigrants, who were predominantly of peasant-class origin (Balch 1910, 43–45). Jewish immigrant literacy also was greater than that of most other immigrant groups (Steinberg 1981, 101).

Both Steinberg and Goldscheider and Zuckerman indicate that the timing of immigration also was particularly beneficial for the Jewish arrivals. Steinberg observes that "in large measure Jewish success in America was a matter of historical timing . . . a fortuitous match between the experience and skills of Jewish immigrants, on the one hand, and the manpower needs and opportunity structures, on the other" (1981, 103). He argues, in a manner similar to Glazer, that Jewish youth could set higher goals because such goals were conceivable and accessible, particularly within the terrain of the class history of their families and companions. Steinberg concludes tellingly:

[T]here was much in the everyday experiences of Jewish immigrants to activate and sustain their highest aspirations. Without this reinforcement, their values would have been scaled down accordingly, and more successful outsiders would today be speculating about how much further Jews might have gone if only they had aimed higher. (1981, 103)

In the same vein, Goldscheider and Zuckerman observe:

The overwhelming concentration of Jewish immigrants in skilled labor represents a significant difference from Jews in Russia in 1897 and in Austria in 1900. . . . The selectivity of Jewish immigration fit into the particular labor demands and occupational opportunities in America and provided Jews an enormous structural advantage over other immigrants in the pursuit of occupational and social mobility. . . .

Jews did not simply enter schools because they valued education. Their social and economic background, residence, and family characteristics allowed them to take advantage of the expanding educational opportunities [in the United States]. (1984, 167)

Awareness of the prior class position of the Jewish immigrants is the critical piece of information that illuminates Jewish success in the United States. In short, the Eastern-European Jews retrieved the relative class position they had possessed in their countries of origin before they were "forced out of their age-old pursuits and proletarianized," as Glazer puts it. A move into a different social structure, where middle-class status and professionalization was coming to bear far greater significance, further obscured the lateral nature of the move.

The move was facilitated by three additional considerations. First, discrimination and anti-Semitism were indeed present in the United States, but by no means comparable to the degree experienced by Jews in Eastern Europe (see Goldscheider and Zuckerman 1984, 237–238). For example, when efforts were made in the United States to inaugurate quotas to limit Jewish students' access to America's prestige institutions of higher learning, Jewish students already had entered those institutions in proportions that far exceeded their representation in the population as a whole (see Steinberg 1981, 227–252).[12] Quotas could indeed slow Jewish advancement, but they could not reverse the effects of access that already had been achieved prior to their inauguration. Goldscheider and Zuckerman indicate that it was not "anti-Semitism per se" but competition for the limited number of places at prestige schools that led to the restrictive quotas. Anti-Semitism surfaced as a consequence of competition rather than playing a significant role beforehand.[13]

Second, the Eastern-European Jewish immigrants' entry into the United States was an entry into a country that already possessed a Sephardic Jewish elite and a German Jewish immigrant middle class that had been well established in the United States since the colonial era (see Birmingham 1971, Silberman 1985, 42–43). There were tensions, especially between the Eastern-European immigrants and their aristocratic-minded Sephardic predecessors, but nevertheless the latter could provide financial support and assistance to the newcomers—a pattern that was replicated in some form, as we shall see, with other immigrant success stories. Third, the dimensions of ethnic solidarity among Eastern-European Jews that could contribute to collective efforts to achieve in the United States were multifaceted. There was a common religion, a common heritage of oppression that dictated unity for survival, and a common backdrop of institutions entirely under the control of members of the group.[14]

The experience of post–World War II black immigrants to the United States from the British West Indies frequently has been invoked by Sowell to minimize the importance of the racial factor as an explanation for the relative lack of native black American material advancement. Despite sharing the same racial characteristics as native blacks, West Indian immigrants generally appear to have prospered in the United States. The West Indian experience seems to repudiate the notion that blackness alone is sufficient to produce insuperable barriers to economic accomplishment. A closer look, however, is indicative of a pattern of accomplishment that finds its roots in conditions quite similar to those of Eastern-European Jewish immigrants. Although sharing a common national heritage and identity, the same cultural background has not produced comparable patterns of accomplishment for West Indians in Britain and those at home in the poverty-stricken Caribbean countries.

Indeed, Chiswick acknowledges that ethnic culture does not produce the same economic performance everywhere. In a pointed criticism of Sowell's use of the concept of culture, Chiswick (1984, 1159) asks the following rhetorical question, "If culture is the key, why were the overseas Chinese, Asian Indians, Jamaicans, and Lebanese, among others, highly successful, while their countries of origin did not develop?" Finding inadequate Sowell's claim that the explanation lies in "inappropriate government intervention in the countries of origin," Chiswick (1984, 1159) is led to place the entire weight on the self-selectivity of migrant populations, suggesting that there may well be a universal "international migrant 'culture,'" distinct from the culture of their fellows who stay in the country of origin. This would make it easy to explain the differential performance of forced migrant groups, like black Americans, or indigenous people whose lands were expropriated, like Native Americans. But it leaves Chiswick unable to explain the relative lack of economic success of West Indian immigrants to Britain (see Foner 1978), or, for that matter, the Oriental-Sephardic Jewish immigrants to Israel from surrounding Arab states in the postwar period (see Rijwan 1983 and Smooha and Kraus 1985).

Of course, again it should be noted that Chiswick neglects examination of the prior class position of immigrant populations in their countries of origin. Nancy Foner (1978, 1979) has found that the West Indian immigrants to the United States possessed a higher socio-economic background than the immigrants who went to London in the 1950s and 1960s, the difference due to respective U.S. and British immigration policies.[15] Prior class position in the countries of origin again seems to be decisive. The experience of West Indian immigrants to the United States also constitutes an instance of lateral mobility.

The West Indian experience also points toward the key distinction between ethnic (or national) culture and class heritage. Sowell and Chiswick concern themselves exclusively with the former, when it is the latter that counts. It is not West Indian or Jewish heritage per se that is important. What counts is a middle-class heritage that facilitates the ability of an immigrant group to replicate its relative class position as it moves from one society to another. This is not to argue that individuals from an ethnic group can never alter their class position. It is to say that such true Horatio Alger stories are exceptional and are characterized by a high degree of randomness.[16]

Faye Arnold (1984) also suggests that despite a common racial identity, West Indians and native blacks did not face similar patterns of discrimination. The West Indians were viewed as "exceptional" among blacks by the larger white population, as veritable "black Englishmen." Arnold says, "[T]here is evidence the black immigrants' English ethnocentrism, speech patterns, cultural mannerisms, religious preference (Anglican or Protestant Episcopal), dress and general lifestyle 'whitened' (that is, garnered advantages and opportunities typically denied blacks) as they had in the Caribbean . . ." (1984, 56). Official British institutions in the United States treated them as black Englishmen as well; Arnold reports that the West Indian immigrants could appeal to New York's British Consulate, "an agency which regularly mediated various grievances the black immigrants raised in response to blatant illegal acts of discrimination in New York . . ." (1984, 56). Arnold contrasts this experience with that of the West Indians who went to London, who found that "[d]espite the intensity of their Anglophilia and regard for 'the mother country,' they are not perceived as 'black Englishmen' by most whites . . ." (1984, 57).[17]

Furthermore, both Arnold (1984, 61) and Foner (1979, 291–292) emphasize the importance of the West Indian immigrants to the United States coming into predominantly black communities. Maintaining insularity through resistance to intermarriage and to assimilation into the larger black community, and despite elements of tension between the immigrants and the native blacks, entry into black communities mitigated much of the hostility and many of the problems faced by immigrants to London. The substance of discrimination faced by West Indian blacks and native blacks in the United States was not the same, since native blacks constituted a buffer group for the newcomers, as they seem to have served for others (see, e.g., note 13).

As for the Japanese-American experience, Kiyoshi Ikeda's critical observations on a book by William Petersen are revealing. Petersen compared the experience of mainland and Hawaiian Japanese cohorts and concluded that the greater economic achievements of the former were due to the greater strengths of their ethnic culture. But Ikeda observes that the immigrants from mainland Japan came from less-impoverished districts, had higher class standing and literacy levels, and a lower probability of coming from "peasant-agriculturalist households" (1973, 498). These differences in the two groups of immigrants were supported by "[g]overnmental agreements about selective migration . . ." (Ikeda 1973, 498).

The "major denigrations" of the Second World War notwithstanding, inclusive of the infamous internment of Japanese-Americans, Ikeda (1973, 498) contends that there is no basis for concluding that the Japanese-Americans experienced a pattern of discrimination comparable to that of black Americans in the United States. Ikeda notes that, aside from the glaring exception of the Second World War period:

From the inception of immigration, the Japanese in America always had the support of firm, cross-national agreements and legal protections to insure that they could develop and maintain their institutions in a hostile environment. The nationalist government of Japan made every effort to aid its citizens overseas. The African immigrants and their children have never had such cross-governmental supports at any time to recreate parallel tribal communities and cultures. Except in rare instances, deliberate policy and practice prevented such developments. (1973, 498)

Finally, brief consideration is given to the Chinese immigrant experience. The Chinese case does not fit as neatly into the package of ethnic immigrant success stories, since there is a significant incidence of poverty in the Chinese-American population. But to the extent that Chinese-Americans seem to "do better" on average than most Americans (M. Wong 1980, 511–512), their case crops up in the success pot time and again. Steinberg (1981, 130–132) argues persuasively that the differential patterns of accomplishment among the ethnic Chinese themselves can be best understood by the social class factors, once again. Moreover, for a population that had reached only 435,000 by 1970 (L. Wong 1976, 33), the influx of twenty thousand immigrants from China's professional classes in the aftermath of the 1949 ascendance of the Communists in China (M. Wong 1980, 521) would have a marked effect on the mean profile of the Chinese-American population.[18]

Are there ethnic groups that have in fact significantly changed their class status after immigration to the United States? Two examples customarily given are Irish-Americans and Cuban-Americans. The case made for the Irish is especially ironic from the standpoint of Sowell's thesis, since he portrays the Irish as relatively less successful. While acknowledging that ". . . it is clear that the Irish have risen from their initial poverty to reach (or surpass) American standards of income or education" (Sowell 1981, 42), he also describes them as "the slowest rising of the European ethnic groups" (1981, 36). For Sowell patterns of "ethnic ecological succession" were not uniform, and the Irish fall short particularly in comparison with the Jews: "The Jews . . . arrived in the United States with even less money than the Irish; initially earned less than their Irish contemporaries; but then overtook and outdistanced the Irish in income, occupation, and education" (1981, 37). Sowell indicts the Irish inheritance of an "ancient Celtic culture" as a major element that slowed Irish advance (1981, 37). Celtic culture is alleged to be antiliteracy in outlook; Ireland is described as the only major Western nation that did not build a university in the Middle Ages; and the Irish are characterized as being devoid of a significant intellectual tradition (Sowell 1981, 37–38). To compound matters, the Irish-Americans mistakenly, according to Sowell (1981, 17–18, 37), relied excessively on municipal politics as the route to economic advancement rather than on business or scholarship, and the payoffs never matched the investment of resources.[19]

Andrew Greeley contends that Sowell is mistaken in his assessment of Irish-American economic performance. Sowell's mistake, according to Greeley (1981, 6, 112), is due to the former's reliance on census data that mixes Irish Catholics with Irish Protestants in the United States. Greeley says that Irish Protestants are a bit more numerous and generally less successful than Irish Catholics. Greeley describes ". . . the Irish [Catholics] as a group [that has] moved far beyond the average white American in income, education, and occupation" (1981, 4). He reports further, based largely upon data from the late 1970s, "Among Americans under forty, Irish Catholics earn three thousand dollars a year more than the average, have almost two years more of education, and are several grades higher on measures of occupational prestige" (1981, 4). They are, in Greeley's words, "the most affluent gentile ethnic group in America" (1981, 4).

Utilizing data collected in 1977 and 1978 from the National Opinion Research Center's General Social Survey, Greeley (1981, 11) points out that 26 percent of all U.S. families reported an annual income in excess of $20,000, while 30 percent of those families describing themselves as British Protestants reported incomes above $20,000. In contrast, 46 percent of Jewish families and 47 percent of Irish-Catholic families said that they had incomes greater than $20,000. Irish Catholics also rate well above the national mean on occupational prestige scales, years of schooling, and percentage with professional and managerial positions. Contrary to Sowell's dismissal of Irish-American scholarly activity, Greeley finds that Irish Catholics made a low-key, post-1960 surge into U.S. academic circles:

In the years after the Second World War, about one-fourth of the higher academy (top state universities and private universities) suddenly became dramatically and obviously Jewish. In the years after 1960, another fourth of the academy became more gradually, more quietly and more surreptitiously Catholic. So quietly, in fact, that neither the Church nor the academy had noted the change. . . . (1981, 108)

Somewhat flamboyantly, Greeley adds, "The Irish have come to the Ph.D. world, they have come to stay, and they are going to stay as Catholics" (1981, 109).[20]

The largest wave of Irish immigrants came to the United States between 1870 and 1900. Greeley (1981, 114) says, "By 1910, the Irish were going to college and choosing managerial and professional careers at a higher rate than that of typical white Americans. . . ." The Irish

Catholics had reached educational parity with the rest of the nation by the 1930s and already exceeded the national average prior to the Second World War (Greeley 1981, 6). Apparently an ancient Celtic culture did not prevent the Irish Catholics from "[pushing] their way solidly into the affluent middle and upper classes . . ." just as rapidly as the Jewish immigrants (Greeley 1981, 114).

If indeed the Irish immigrants were of peasant origins, their "ethnic history" appears to provide a clear instance of a group that achieved upward mobility in a social class sense. Even Greeley (1981, 115) raises questions about how impoverished and illiterate the Irish immigrants really were, both those who came prior to the mid nineteenth century and those who came after 1870. But if we accept that Irish Catholics, in particular, came from "peasant stock," we are faced with the intriguing problem of Irish-Catholic exceptionalism in the face of mounting evidence that immigrants to the United States typically displayed lateral social mobility.

Again, contrary to Sowell, if the Irish Catholics climbed an urban escalator, it seems they did so by capturing municipal governments as a resource base. Sowell appears to be correct in his assertion that the Irish generally did not build an empire in private industry. Peter Eisenger, utilizing as his main example the case of Boston, stresses that public-sector jobs—in the police force, sanitation departments, and white-collar clerical positions—provided "job security for a small but significant portion of [the Irish] work force and the creation of a small middle-class core group that had found the avenues of opportunity in the private sector closed" (1980, 195). Eisenger concedes that it is hard to detect "a strong link between aggregate economic achievement and Irish political power *in the early decades of Irish urban ascendancy,* [but] it is nevertheless worth noting that the Irish [Catholics] rank today as the most successful white, gentile ethnic group in America in terms of income and education" (1980, 195; emphasis added). Concludes Eisenger, ". . . it would seem unwarranted to argue that the conjuncture . . . between the political power of the Irish over history and their current level of achievement . . . is purely coincidental" (1980, 195).

It may be the case that an ethnic group with a predominantly lower-class prior background must resort directly to politics to alter their class position in part by acquiring an extensive network of ethnic niches in public-sector employment. This may not always prove to be a successful strategy, but it may be the only strategy available to a group that does not already possess a history of middle-class attributes.

Finally, very brief attention is devoted to the Cuban-American immigrants, the high economic achievers among Hispanics in the

United States. Here it seems obvious that the immigrants who entered the United States immediately after the 1959 overthrow of Batista were self-selected members of the Cuban elite. They plainly feared the loss of their privileged status in Cuba after the revolution and were part of a "golden exile" to the United States. Their ability to place funds in Florida and New York banks, as well as their long-standing familiarity with Miami, probably facilitated adjustment for the new Cuban-Americans.

Lisandro Perez (1986, 6) recently has observed that the "golden exile" had dissipated by the late 1960s and early 1970s: "New arrivals were not so likely as the earlier immigrants to be selected from Cuba's displaced elite classes. Increasingly, the migration flow from Cuba was approximating the socio-demographic profile of the island's population." He describes "the Mariel boatlift of 1980"—or the so-called Castro flotilla—as "a culmination of that trend." Nevertheless, Perez finds that ". . . despite the progressive increases in the proportion of Cuban immigrants that did not possess the same characteristics that purportedly gave the earlier exiles an advantage in economic adjustment, the U.S. Cuban population . . . has nevertheless apparently maintained its economic edge in relation to the remainder of the Hispanic population" (1986, 6).

Why is this the case? Perez proposes that the economic transition is eased for the most-recent immigrants by the existence of the community-level organizational structure constituting "the Florida enclave" (1986, 6–8). The prior immigrants who have established a significant economic foothold can integrate later arrivals—even those not from elite backgrounds—into an economic system designed by the earlier (elite) arrivals. But Perez builds his empirical case on the basis of 1980 U.S. Census of Population data that does not reflect the full impact of the Mariel boat lift immigrants. Absorption of a trickle of immigrants from the nonelite strata of Cuban society would not be expected to alter the aggregate picture for Cuban-Americans. It remains to be seen what the 1990 census data indicate when the effects of the large 1980 influx of Cuban immigrants will be present in census results.

In the end, it is really the native black American experience that comes to look exceptional against the backdrop of these immigrant success stories.[21] At this stage, it is not difficult to explain black exceptionalism. Black American exceptionalism vis-à-vis these ethnic success stories originally derives from slavery times. Transplanted Africans, stripped of tribe and clan, were denied knowledge of a coherent class history. Africans from various ethnic and class backgrounds were brought to these shores as a largely undifferentiated pool of slave laborers. New patterns of class differentiation emerged within the incubator of the slave system, along the dimensions of color lines ("mulattoism") and freedman status. The mass of blacks were relegated historically to the lowest strata of U.S. society. When blacks migrated from the South to the North, their class origins were predominantly those of a rural peasantry. Institutions and organizations among blacks, as Ikeda (1973) suggests, were continuously subject to external authority and supervision. Nor was there any cross-governmental support or a preestablished welcoming support group for this population of forced immigrants to America comparable to that experienced by Eastern-European Jews in the late nineteenth century, West Indians after the Second World War, the Japanese in the nineteenth century, the Chinese in the twentieth century, the Irish after 1870, and the Cubans after the 1960s.

Eisenger, while recognizing the importance of control over municipal government to Irish-Catholic economic gains, asserts that increased political control over city governments is likely to have similar long-term effects for blacks (1980, 195–196). Eisenger anticipates that blacks will emulate the Irish pattern of climbing the American urban escalator. But the analogy again appears to be forced. Warren Kalbach in a review of Eisenger's *Politics of Displacement* has observed:

The limitations of black political dominance of the central city are made readily apparent. Central city blacks still depend on the white elites of the larger metropolitan community who have greater access to business and financial resources; lacking an adequate tax base, the blacks need metropolitan reform in order to provide basic services. Their political ascendancy is illusory or at best only partial because, unlike Boston at the turn of the century, the modern central city encompasses much less of the total functional community and enjoys much less autonomy. The author's analysis of the process of political displacement of whites by blacks and its consequences is weakened considerably by his failure to emphasize the significance of the larger metropolitan community as a context within which the city is only a part. (1983, 1069)

A second critic, Seymour Leventman, is even more blunt:

Urban political power as a goal for ethnic groups is much less relevant than in former times. Paraphrasing John Nance Garner's characterization of the vice-presidency, one might say, "Mayoralties today ain't worth a bucket of warm spit." With declining revenues, near bankruptcy conditions, massive unemployment of blacks, conditions of private splendor and public squalor, and increasing urban dependency upon external emergency financing plans, one could almost view with suspicion anyone desiring to become a big city mayor. (1982, 336)

The timing of black ascendancy in American urban politics is more likely a case of too little, too late.

Where ethnicity and class status overlap, a major conclusion can be drawn. Historically, the relative position of ethnic groups disproportionately represented in particular class positions remains remarkably stable as they migrate from one country or region to a new one. The ethnic success stories in the United States merely confirm this generalization. Irish-Catholic exceptionalism can be attributed, in large measure, to the timing of their capture and mobilization of municipal political bases. Although a small percentage of individuals from various ethnic groups may display upward mobility, in general, ethnic groups that have been typically middle class are likely to become middle class again; ethnic groups that have not been are unlikely to become so. Those "cultural" attributes that appear to be associated with economic success are linked primarily to social class rather than ethnicity.[22] Endowments of ethnic culture do not dictate the economic performance of the members of a particular group, but endowments generated from a group's shared experiences in middle-class status certainly enhance group members' achievement. A commonly shared class heritage means the group "knows" in a collective sense how to carve out a preferred niche and what are the requirements—largely of a political power nature—to maintain their position. This is far from being a matter of teaching the young sobriety and proper work habits; it is one of exercising ethnic group control over a tier or set of tiers of a society's occupational-cum-hierarchical structure.

Differences in ethnic culture fail as explanations for differences in patterns of ethnic achievement on theoretical grounds because of what might be termed "the Austrian problem." They fail on empirical grounds because the evidence of ethnic immigrant success stories omits considerations of social class. But a major reason why economists have wandered into the domain of cultural determinism is because of their inability to reconcile market discrimination (or even extramarket discrimination) with competitive conditions. However, there are two alternative conceptions of competition that can be reconciled with market discrimination—classical and Marxist.

Classical competition (see Sraffa 1960) posits a tendency toward uniformity of the rate of profit in all activities. It leaves in abeyance the question of the formation of the general rate of profit toward which all rates gravitate.[23] Be that as it may, rigidities, imperfections, barriers to entry by firms, and the like are irrelevant to the existence of competitive conditions, so long as it is possible for rates of return to equalize everywhere. The *process* of adjustment toward uniformity typically is not fully specified but appears to have something to do with capital mobility where capital has financial form. In Veblen's formulation (1904) equalization takes place indirectly via stock valuation and arbitrage in securities markets. Such factors as monopoly positions, product differentiation, and Veblen's "goodwill" need not be treated as competitive imperfections—since competition inheres in the tendency toward uniformity of the rate of return earned by equity holders for all firms.[24]

In a dual economy—an economy with one sector with high wages and high productivity and one with low wages and low productivity—whites could be overrepresented in the former sector and blacks crowded into the latter sector. Earnings differentials arise between blacks and whites, even if they are equally able, because productivity is determined by differences in sectoral techniques. These differences can persist because the stability condition in classical political economy is uniformity of profit rates. Uniformity of profit rates is feasible if wage differentials offset the sectoral productivity differentials. Employers seek the general rate of profit, and if it can be obtained without transferring equally able black workers to the high-productivity sector, there is no reason for employers to do so.

In short, classical competition reconciles market discrimination and competition by allowing, by definition, rigidities that cannot exist or persist under neoclassical and Austrian conceptions of competition. Like neoclassical competition, the classical version deemphasizes process in favor of identifying competition with the (equilibrium) state of affairs that has a terminal point. For the neoclassicists the terminal point is ongoing price-taking behavior with all enterprises earning "normal" profit. For the classicists the terminal point—the "long-period" position—is the establishment of a uniform profit rate. In contrast both Austrian and Marxist competition emphasize process but differ as to the nature and outcome of the process.

Marxist competition subsumes the classical notion, accepting the view that competition involves a tendency toward equalization of all rates of profit. Competition between capitalists leads not only in the direction of a single rate of profit but also toward formation of the general rate of profit (Marx 1981, 254–301). Monopolies may occasionally deflect the speed with which profit rates equalize, but here monopoly positions are not the antithesis of competition (see Weeks 1981, 164–165). On the contrary, ferocious conflict among capitalists leads them to seek monopoly positions, whether by artificial or natural means. It also leads them toward aggrandizement of the scale of their operations, to centralize and concentrate (Marx 1977, 775–781), which may even facilitate both mobility of capital and equalization of the profit rate. Monopoly positions, cartels, and differentiated products all are indicators of competition *as rivalry* in Marxist theory, rather than indicators of noncompetitiveness, as in neoclassical theory.

Monopoly positions may be long lasting; their duration is indefinite. This is quite unlike Austrian competition's winning entrepreneurs who inevitably will be driven from monopoly positions by the ingenuity of other entrepreneurs who will fashion either a direct or indirect method of entry (Kirzner 1973, 131, 205). The "winners" under Marxist competition can bar, indefinitely, entry of potential rivals. Moreover, the tendency toward centralization and concentration of capital is an immanent law of capitalist development.

Marxist competition can be extended to rivalries among owners of labor powers. Workers also can centralize and concentrate, particularly along ethnic and racial lines. In a hierarchical structure of occupations, workers may struggle for turf by forming allegiances with others of similar ethnic backgrounds. Workers themselves become the primary agents of discrimination although their motives are dictated by the preexisting unequal social structure. The putative line of demarcation between market and extramarket discrimination becomes meaningless. Via control or influence over training, networks (see Holzer 1987), evaluation, information (see Shelton 1987), and the definition of jobs, groups of workers can secure preferred positions for themselves while excluding others. They can try to protect themselves from incursions from rival groups, seek to obtain niches in newly emerging occupational categories, or strive to dislodge groups higher on the scale of stratification.[25] The favored opportunity, of course, is that afforded by entirely new occupations that promise high status and pay and that are not yet occupied by any rival group.[26]

Bonacich's (1979) development of what she terms "the split labor market hypothesis," based in part upon the pioneering research of Oliver Cox (1970) on ethnic antagonisms among workers, provides a foundation for a general theory of ethnic-racial inequality. It is a theory that can be applied to black and white economic differences in the United States as a specific instance of a more general class of phenomena. It also is a consistently Marxist theory of racial economic inequality, where rivalry is recognized not only between capital and labor, or between capitalists, but also between cliques of laborers.

The preliminary observation that has to be made is that modern differences in economic performance between the races, indeed, did arise with the development of capitalism. Racism and ethnic-racial exclusion can be seen as arising largely out of the self-interested actions of workers from the affected groups. The creation of Bonacich's split labor markets was an outcome of competition between labor powers under capitalism. Those groups of workers with greater power could exert sufficient strength to carve out protected terrain in the capitalist labor process.

Competition between workers under capitalism has not been characterized primarily by atomistic wage-cutting by individual owners of labor power but instead by a movement toward concentration and centralization. At first glance, these consolidations may appear to center exclusively on common class status as proletarians in institutions like trade unions, but in fact ethnicity and race play a central role. Competition between labor powers under capitalism is rivalry between ascriptively differentiated workers. Here is where culture has played its important part—*not* in preconditioning the marketplace, but in determining group identification in an ethnically divided labor market.

Since the evolution of capitalism has meant the continual reproduction of a relative surplus population, someone must be cast into the most fragile and desperate strata of the working class. Successful combatants in the competition between labor powers are best protected from falling into the reserve of labor. Conversely, unsuccessful competitors are cast into the reserve with greater frequency. The burden of being part of the relative surplus population will fall unevenly on various racial-ethnic groups to the extent that victory and defeat fall unevenly across them as well. The hierarchical nature of capitalist society has dictated ethnic-racial protectionism.[27]

Who "wins" and who "loses" is not a matter of intrinsic ethnic or racial superiority or inferiority. It is a matter of timing, access to, and familiarity with open terrain. Once in a preferred position, the ethnic-racial group in place will defend its turf against all comers. Displacement of the ensconced group will be desired by capital if the newer entrants are cheaper, but the outcome of the ensuing struggle is not automatic. Displacement may give way to accommodation of new entrants in less-preferred slots once held by earlier entrants who may have moved on to still more preferred terrain. Displacement, arguably, is least likely in the public sector, where employers lack the profit motive to seek out cheaper pools of laborers.[28]

Split labor market theory, in examining the struggle not merely between capital and labor but between high-priced labor powers and lower-priced labor powers, points directly to the struggle over wage determination under capitalism. There are four routes that capital has historically pursued in dealing with wages: (1) at a given wage, capital may seek to lengthen the working day; (2) capital may seek to get labor to accept lower money wages; (3) capital may erode real wages by inflating the prices of wage-goods more rapidly than money wages increase; and (4) capital may seek to introduce new pools of labor that will accept lower money wages. The fourth strategy might converge with the second if capital can get the new labor group to precipitate a bidding war with the workers already in place. It is the fourth strategy that lies at the heart of split labor market theory.

Note that the lowering of the wage in Marx's terms is an effort to raise the rate of surplus value in absolute form. If that possibility does not present itself because of the strength of the working class, capital will move to raise the rate of surplus value in relative form, via the introduction of increasing proportions of machinery. But this leads into the widely misunderstood dilemma that Marx posed—the tendency of the rate of profit to fall. Laborers in place have been able to take a consistent position in resisting attempts to raise the rate of surplus value in absolute form, via the lowering of wages; labor has been more uncertain about what position to take vis-à-vis the introduction of machinery. There is no ambiguity in the analysis here because the introduction of new groups of (cheaper) workers fits squarely into efforts to raise the rate of surplus value in absolute form—which workers already in place will resist.

The very character of the struggle between capital and labor in a society where ascriptive differentiation exists across groups of workers will lead to the reinforcement of racism. These divisions are not exogenous, nor are they solely the product of propaganda directed toward labor by capital. Certainly capital can benefit from divisions between workers, but capital also benefits if it is able to raise the rate of absolute surplus value by introducing cheaper labor or getting labor already in place to weaken its wage demands. So it is valuable to refocus the nature of labor market discrimination from the perspective of labor itself, as the split labor market theory attempts to do.

New groups of workers are not introduced primarily because they will inflame racial tensions—for this can disrupt the order of the workplace. These new groups are introduced expressly *because they can be paid less for the same amount of labor time.* This establishes the importance of Marx's notion of the reserve army of the unemployed that potentially can be activated to become variable capital. The emergence of different groups from the reserve of labor at different points in time is all-important, for those that emerge earliest are more likely to have the ability to protect their position. This is the "inner truth" that lies behind notions of the "urban escalator."

New groups of workers can emerge from the reserve army only to find their path blocked—blocked by workers already in place who perceive the new group as a threat. Indeed, if the new group comes in for less pay in significant numbers, they *are* a threat. For the new group to successfully enter, the established group must be weak enough to be unable to bar their way.[29]

If the established group is strong enough to preserve its own position, then one of three things will happen: (1) the members of the new group will be absorbed into reclassified jobs—at lower pay—that do not threaten the position of the established group; (2) the new group will be absorbed into altogether new spheres of work where an established group does not exist; or (3) the new group simply will be cast back into the reserve of unemployed. If there are certain types of skills required that can be obtained through on-the-job training, the established group can deny access to the new group members by refusing to assist in their training. The established group is strengthened if there are educational credentials and skills specific to the occupation (what Chicagoans see as *specific* human capital) that the new group will have difficulty obtaining. In some fields (e.g., academia) the established groups can set and alter the criteria for entry. To the extent that the new group is ethnically or racially different, the ideology of racism is self-serving to the established group in promoting its struggle against the "outsiders."

The established group, if it is strong, will accept the new group as long as its own pay or status is not reduced and its own numbers are not reduced. This fact explains the successful entry of blacks into particular sectors of the labor market when capital is on a wave of expansion and is the true source of the claim that minorities do better in periods of growth. There will be less of a threat to established work groups during such periods because entirely *new positions* are more likely to be created.

The existence of differences between people that place them in groups identifiably independent from their occupational position reduces the standard analysis of this question to an anthropological problem (see Nielsen 1985). The ultimate claim would be that there are workplace "tribalisms." But the claim being made here is quite different—such tribalist attitudes intensify from the efforts of established groups of workers to resist the raising of the rate of absolute surplus value when capital's strategy is to bring in new sources of labor.

Furthermore, even in a *postcapitalist* era, competition between labor powers, in this style, need not diminish. As unskilled positions with negligible credentialing requirements vanish in the new age of science and technology, the most depressed members of capitalism's labor market will face the near impossible task of entering the labor markets of tomorrow. Those ethnic-racial groups who have staked out their terrain in the aristocratic occupations in the postcapitalist era will not be eager to relinquish their turf to new entrants, and exclusion will appear all the more justified on grounds of merit and qualification. The competing groups will not meet the standards for entry; they will not have had the chance to meet them. As long as postcapitalist (or what I prefer to call *managerial*) society is hierarchical, it will be racist.[30]

Barbara Bergmann (1971) has asked whether racial discrimination can be eliminated under capitalism; the answer from this analysis patently is no. The answer should have been evident from Oliver Cox's (1970, 398) analysis of race, class, and inequality. But as the trajectory of history moves beyond capitalism, the answer still appears to be no. Once racial discrimination is in the air, it becomes a useful means for preserving status by ethnic-racial groups in class-divided societies, whether capitalist or noncapitalist. The greater security of ethnic-racial groups in public-sector occupations signals the potential for still greater ethnic-racial rigidity in postcapitalist society. If Bonacich errs, it is in conceiving the new trajectory that drives unskilled labor out of the marketplace altogether as a manifestation of so-called advanced capitalism, rather than the rise of managerial society.[31]

There is an astonishing volume of evidence to support the implications of this analysis. It is not only fruitful as a basis for understanding the variations that now exist in occupational and wage achievements in the United States. Native black Americans largely have been excluded from elite positions by the mechanism depicted in the split labor market hypothesis and crowded into the reserve of labor by similar mechanisms. The same mechanisms operate on a global scale.

The French Communist party, for example, has sought to protect French workers from incursions by non-French immigrants. The "White Australia" policy of the late nineteenth century provides more grist for the split labor market theory. Crawford and James observe that there was fear that "Chinese poverty and frugal standards of living might threaten Australian living standards" (1947, 59). Even Thomas Sowell offers an instance of white American and Japanese immigrant antagonism that conforms to the thesis of ethnic warfare in labor markets:

The very virtues of the Japanese eventually turned others against them. While Japanese migrants made excellent employees, that made them rivals feared and hated by American workers and American labor unions. AFL President Samuel Gompers denounced Asian workers and refused to allow them into unions, even in segregated locals. The thrift, diligence and ambitions of the Japanese meant that increasing numbers of them began to move up from the ranks of labor to become small farmers or small businessmen. With that, the American farmers and businessmen who had welcomed the Japanese as employees turned bitterly against them as rivals. Moreover, the occupational and geographical concentration of the Japanese in a relatively few specialties in a few communities in California made them far more visible targets than otherwise. As the Japanese in California moved up from the ranks of agricultural laborers to tenant farmers or (more rarely) landowners, the hostility against them as competitors rose from the white agricultural laborers to the white farmers. The additional hostility—now including a more influential class— was enough to launch a wave of anti-Japanese legislation and practices that continued for decades in California. Chief among these was the Alien Land Law of 1913, which forbade the owning of California land by aliens ineligible for citizenship—that is, Asians in general and Japanese, in particular. At the national level, California led the political drive to stop Japanese immigrants from being admitted to the United States. (1981, 162–163)

It is notable that current Japanese-American successes are not in agriculture or landownership, but in professional-level occupations that *expanded* in the postwar era—open, once again, to those who had acquired credentials for entry.

The occupational crowding of the Maori in New Zealand (Brosnan 1987) is indicative of the same phenomenon. The experience of the Jews in Eastern Europe—their displacement through political and coercive measures from their previous pursuits—prior to their migration to the United States (Goldscheider and Zuckerman 1984, 237– 238) is an additional instance. Brown and Philips (1986) have provided a detailed case study of the operation of split labor market conditions in California from the 1860s to the 1880s as employers sought to introduce Chinese laborers in manufacturing.

Of course, Bonacich (1979) also provides many examples to support the split labor market theory, such as the material basis for the historic Afro–Indo antagonism in Guyana. While the country was still a British colony, the local Guyanese labor force, mostly African ex-slaves, called a series of strikes between 1842 and 1847 against planter attempts to lower wages. Planters used public funds to import more than fifty thousand East Indian indentured workers to break the strike. Chinese workers were brought to Mississippi for the same purpose—to undermine free black laborers after the Civil War. Black Americans themselves were employed as strikebreakers against white trade unions in the northern United States early in the twentieth century.

But perhaps Bonacich's most remarkable example of all comes from South Africa's labor history, where white labor's racism blatantly served to promote its struggle with capital:

The displacement reality and threat led to the usual reactions by white labor . . . [w]hite labor's efforts to control capital's access to African cheap labour were seen by themselves as progressive, i.e., part of the class struggle against capital. The Labour Party in the 1930s simultaneously proposed socialism for

South Africa, and promoted the removal of Africans (who were seen as a tool of capital to undermine the class struggle) to separate territories. The Rand Revolt of 1922 was a major uprising by white labor against capital over the displacement issue, which brought the country to the brink of socialist revolution. One of the slogans of the Rand Revolt captures the link between the class struggle and racism: "Workers of the world unite and fight for a white South Africa". . . .

Thus we find the ironic situation that capital was, in a sense, promoting African labor and the breakdown of color bars (in order to increase competition between all workers and undermine the high price of white labor), while white workers were ostensibly fighting against African advance. White labor's anti-capitalism was closely linked with racist policies. (1979, 44)

The caste riots in Gujarat in India (Bose 1981) also fit the bill, since they were precipitated by conflicts arising over affirmative action ("compensatory discrimination") measures, policies ostensibly intended to benefit members of the lower castes. The Indian experience is instructive on another point. The mechanisms of the split labor market generally can circumvent legal remedies introduced on behalf of the excluded group as long as the structural conditions of stratification are unchanged. Thus, as Bose (1981, 713) observes, affirmative-action-style policies in India on behalf of the lower castes have been appropriated by the upper castes on their own behalf.

The same process is evident in the United States with the increasingly diffuse application of affirmative action toward "minorities" in general, rather than native blacks exclusively. Those blacks who have benefited from affirmative action also have been drawn disproportionately from the small middle-class segment of the black population (see Wilson 1981). Reforms of this type usually are advocated and designed by the dominant ethnic-racial groups in the labor market on behalf of the excluded, but either these policies will be gutted if they become viable threats to the preferred positions of the dominant groups or they will be utilized most intensively by the best-placed members of groups with relatively less preferred positions. Affirmative action will not produce parity between races in a fiercely hierarchical civilization.

The phenomenon of ethnic-racial conflict over occupational turf is nearly universal and plainly visible in hierarchical societies, whether capitalist or postcapitalist. In its Marxist competitive foundations, it obviates the puzzles that bedevil orthodox economists who seek to comprehend the persistence of discrimination. It addresses head-on the question of the processes that determine the ethnic-racial composition of the surplus population. Those processes disproportionately locate native black Americans within the surplus population in the

United States.[32] That is the core explanation for racial economic in-equality.

Note, finally, that my argument also differs from certain "neo-Marxian" explanations for racial inequality (e.g., Reich 1981, 267) that depict capitalists as engaged in divide-and-rule tactics with respect to the work force. Certainly capitalists sought to take advantage of racial antagonisms when it served their ends (see Cox 1970), but here white working-class racism need not be due to capitalists' machinations. Instead, it is a consequence of white workers' (or any ethnic group's) own realization that there are preferred positions in the system of occupational stratification to be captured and held. In contrast, the "neo-Marxian" explanation à la Reich, as Bonacich points out, re-quires one to believe that either "the white working class has . . . been duped or bribed" (1979, 40).

In summary, class structure and social hierarchy thus dictate group self-interest in engaging in ethnic warfare to achieve overrepresenta-tion in the comparatively aristocratic occupations of modern society, or at least those that offer secure and stable income.[33] This phenom-enon need not be specific to capitalism. It is specific to any stratified society where certain slots hold more perquisites than others, which suggests that racial or ethnic discrimination need not end with the demise of capitalism. If capitalism is replaced by a hierarchical society of a different type, racial discrimination still will be evident. Public policy initiatives that leave hierarchy in place while seeking an ethnic or racial redistribution of positions do not eliminate the motivations for ethnic warfare. Groups with greater power simply will undermine initiatives, like affirmative action, that appear aimed at uplifting an outcast group.

Ethnic culture thus serves as an instrument whereby blocs of work-ers can consolidate to engage in struggle over turf. The focus shifts toward competition among workers on a monopoly basis, rather than between capital and labor or between capitalists. Exactly how high up the ladder a particular ethnic group can locate itself depends largely on the social-class history its members have shared and the political ammunition they can mobilize. Their recent social-class history, if it involves extensive middle-class experience, gives them an advantage in a struggle with ethnic groups that do not share a similar recent history. An occupational hierarchy potentially can be partitioned so that different clusters of occupations are associated with different class positions (see Wright 1979). Ethnic and racial heritage generally dictate which groups of workers coalesce; class heritage generally dictates where in the scheme of social stratification those workers can lodge themselves.

Culture has a role, but it is a vastly different one from that assigned it by the new cultural determinists. It is a weapon in an environment of trench combat between rival groups in America's workplace. Culture, instead of functioning as a substitute for discrimination in explaining racial inequality, becomes, instead, an instrument that mobilizes discriminatory action. Culture is eminently part and parcel of competition between labor powers; it "is the magnet that provides the basis for concentration of labor powers" (Darity and Williams 1985, 260).

So what's left of the economic theory of discrimination? Quite a lot. But economists need to be considerably more circumspect about what is left of their conventional concepts of competition as well as culture-based human capital explanations for racial inequality.

Notes

1. A rare exception is the 1985 investigation of the racial wealth gap undertaken by Francine Blau and John Graham using data from the 1976 National Longitudinal Survey (NLS) of Young Men and the 1978 NLS of Young Women.
2. Smooha and Kraus (1985, 155) note that the economists who have studied Israeli ethnic income differentials also are divided over the interpretation of the residuals: "Some researchers in this area interpret the residual effects of ethnicity as direct ethnic discrimination, while most hold that the unexplained variance simply stems from unmeasured variables." The latter might include "talent, adaptability and motivation" according to the second group of researchers. That, of course, still leaves open the question, by implication, of why the incidence of "talent, adaptability and motivation" is less among Oriental-Sephardic Jews than it is among Ashkenazic Jews in Israel.
3. Austrian economics is an uncompromising blend of individualism, laissez faire, and faith in entrepreneurial creativity. The contemporary Austrian school has its main intellectual centers in the United States at UCLA, New York University, Auburn University, and George Mason University. In Britain in the 1930s, the London School of Economics fell under the sway of Austrian influences when Lionel Robbins and Friedrich Hayek were there simultaneously. Prominent figures in the modern Austrian tradition have included Hayek, Ronald Coase, Ludwig Lachmann, W. D. Hutt, Armen Alchian, William Allen, and Israel Kirzner. Neoclassicists often dismiss the Austrians as anarcholibertarian extremists and devote little attention to the *theoretical* and *methodological* differences between neoclassical and Austrian economics. Therefore, neoclassicists sometimes unconsciously adopt Austrian modes of thought and, being insensitive to the contrast in approaches, may themselves walk down unintended paths. Members of the Chicago school, in particular, straddle an awkward landscape between neoclassical and Austrian economics. The Chicago synthesis is especially idiosyncratic and requires obscuring essential differences. After all, as early as 1914 the British economist Philip Wicksteed (1914) pushed the radical subjectivist aspects of Austrian economics to such limits that he argued that the supply and demand scissors approach is superfluous. At the core of Chicago economics is the use of supply and demand analysis.
4. Donald Cymrot (1985) claims to have provided empirical proof of the proposition that competitive conditions erode discrimination. He compares relative salaries of black

and white athletes in major league baseball in the United States before and after the December 1975 modification of the reserve clause, which had given team owners, in his words (p. 606), "virtually monopsonistic power." Cymrot finds that elimination of the reserve clause for players with six years or more major league experience led "to the partial elimination of discrimination against nonwhites in Major League Baseball." However, the change in the reserve clause was not triggered by entrepreneurial owners. Rather it was triggered by judicial decisions produced by litigation undertaken by the players. Moreover, Cymrot does not address the selection bias problem associated with the post-1975 environment. Do black athletes with the same evidence of potential as whites get entry into the major leagues, access to the same positions, and access to careers in baseball after their playing days have ended? Cymrot also finds it hard to determine whether the relative improvement in black athletes' earnings was due to the modification of the reserve clause or other social forces affecting the white public's "taste and preferences" for watching black athletes perform.

5. If Chiswick were to resort to the standard interpretation of the residuals prior to the rise of the new cultural determinism, he would be led to conclude that there is discrimination in favor of Jews in today's labor market. Plainly, Chiswick (1983b, 334) is reluctant to draw such a conclusion: "Why do American Jews appear to have higher rates of return on human capital? It seems reasonable to assume that labor market discrimination in favor of Jews is not the explanation." In his review of a book by Sowell, Chiswick emphatically observes in a similar vein: "Group differences in outcomes, holding constant a set of variables are assumed to measure discrimination. While the 'sign' may be right for some situations (e.g., comparing blacks and Hispanics with whites), the successes of various minorities in other countries raise a problem. Surely these successful minorities have not been the beneficiaries of favorable discrimination nor could discrimination by them explain their achievements! Some other factor (or factors) must be responsible for the achievements of the successful groups" (1984, 1159).

6. The distinction between premarket versus inmarket discrimination is popular among economists who acknowledge the existence of racial disadvantage but who believe (or want to) that the labor market processes all entrants in a color-blind fashion. But the distinction is difficult to draw with any degree of sharpness. As Paul Ryan has observed, "A bias toward the exoneration of the market can be detected even in economists whose approach to labour issues is otherwise distinctly heterodox. Thus Phelps Brown . . . in his discussion of discrimination, classifies discrimination in occupational access upon entry into the market as part of pre- rather than (more plausibly) in-market discrimination. The effect is a lightening of the case against the market as a source of inequality" (1981, 19, n. 2). Persistent inmarket discrimination is the trouble spot for orthodoxy, which must see it as something of secondary or tertiary importance or as nonexistent (see Ryan, 1981, 5–6). From the standpoint of the Austrian theory, though, the same forces that allegedly will purify the economy of "inmarket" discrimination—"the failure of the labour market to treat its participants even-handedly, in that it accords significantly different opportunities and rewards to otherwise comparable people" (Ryan, 1981, 4)—also should root out "premarket" discrimination, particularly since "premarket" discrimination also has pecuniary consequences. The distinction is especially forced from an Austrian perspective since entrepreneurs can make markets come into being for items that may not have been previously bought and sold, under the stimulus of profit-making opportunities.

7. If cultural differences are given a genetic origin it may be argued that they are not transferable across groups. In a paper of my own (Darity 1983a, 54), I suggested that Sowell's argument could be interpreted by some—if not by Sowell himself—as attributing genetic inferiority to blacks. He responded, "Anyone who thinks that I actually said what Darity claims I said on page 54 of his article—including 'genetic inferiority' explanations of economic differences—can read any of my writings until he gets eye strain without finding such a thing" (Sowell 1983, 127).

Perhaps Daniel Vining now has a severe case of eyestrain, but he seems to have found that Sowell's analysis is open to just such a reading: "In accounting for these differences [in the economic status of various ethnic and racial groups], which are persistent and widespread, Sowell does not reject the hypothesis that genetic differences are involved. And he goes on to say that even if the differences are all cultural and environmental in origin, then these cultural and environmental differences are of such a character and run so deep as to mimic genetic differences" (1985, 140).

Indeed, what exactly is one to make of the following passage from Sowell's *Civil Rights: Rhetoric or Reality?* "[T]he reality of group patterns that transcend any given society cannot be denied. Jewish peddlers followed in the wake of the Roman legions and sold goods in the conquered territories. How surprising is it to find Jewish peddlers in the American frontier or on the sidewalks of New York 2,000 years later—or in many places in between? No one needs to believe that Jews are *genetically* peddlers. But it does suggest that cultural patterns do not readily disappear, either with the passage of time or with social engineering" (1984, 29; italics in original). Or, the following from *Ethnic America:* "The eastern European immigrants were small and described by contemporaries as 'physical wrecks' and 'as the most stunted of Europeans.' Part of this may have been the result of their poverty and of traditional Jewish de-emphasis on the physical in favor of the mental" (Sowell 1981, 85).

But even if variations in ethnic or racial group performance are given a genetic grounding, Austrian competition still provides a theoretical antidote. Entrepreneurs now would have to go back a step and develop the market for transmission of genetic traits rather than cultural traits. Given economic motives for marriage and procreation, the rise of surrogate motherhood, and the existence of sperm banks, one might argue that such a market is already extant. Austrian economists have not pursued their own logic to these lengths so there is much ambiguity about where they really stand on biological determinism.

8. As Rhonda Williams has noted in an excellent review of Sowell's *Economics and Politics of Race*, "Although his analysis reveals some awareness of the importance of class as a mediating factor in the transmission and reproduction of values, Sowell all but completely disregards the effects of class structure on ethnic and social relations" (1984b, 202).

9. The concept of ethnicity possesses its own ambiguities. A useful explication of various nuances of the concept can be found in Glazer (1977). The following quotations from his essay "Ethnicity: A World Phenomenon" are valuable in illuminating the sense in which the term is employed throughout my chapter:

> *Race* tends to refer to the biological aspect of group difference, *ethnic* to a combination of the cultural aspect plus a putative biological element because of the assumption of common descent. It is possible for a race to be an ethnic group . . . (1977, 198–199; emphasis in original)
>
> There are two important social forms that are *not* ethnic groups. One of them is the political community: the state and its members. The other major exception is one's social class. (1977, 201; emphasis in original)
>
> "Ethnic group", in my usage, refers basically to the vertical divisions of society in contrast to the horizontal divisions. The horizontal divisions refer to *class*; the vertical divisions to *ethnicity*. Sometimes they coincide, as in the case of the Negroes in the American South. (1977, 293; emphasis in original)

Thus, in principle, one can dichotomize cultural patterns that are linked to ethnicity, hence bridging class distinctions among people of "common descent" and "national" background, versus cultural patterns that are linked to class, hence bridging ethnic distinctions among persons sharing a common socio-economic status in a community's given hierarchical structure.

10. By "prior" class position, I mean the relative social standing of the majority of the members of an ethnic group in their country of origin. I do not mean all class positions held over the course of the "long" history of an ethnic group. Immigration may have been precipitated by a coercive loss of such social standing, but what is relevant to the analysis is the *highest* social status attained by the adult generation that constitutes the bulk of the migrants in their country of origin. Typically, the Irish and

Cuban cases are advanced as exceptions to my thesis that immigrant "success" stories in the United States are instances of lateral rather than upward mobility from country of origin to receiving country.

11. Prior class status can be masked by the current occupations held by migrants in the receiving country. But the prior class status can be retrieved rapidly by the younger generation whose parents can "endow" their children with the original social background. Consider the following striking example described in an article in *Time* magazine on Asian-American students: "Daniel Pak, an 18-year-old from Dallas entering Harvard, shines in everything he does, from math to violin. His brother Tony, 20, is studying physics at M.I.T. Their parents had such colleges in mind when they moved to the U.S. in 1970. The boys' father gave up his career as a professor of German literature in South Korea. Unable to get an academic position in the U.S., he eventually found work as a house painter." (Hull et al. 1987, 44).

12. Before Columbia inaugurated restrictive quotas, 40 percent were Jewish. (Goldscheider and Zuckerman 1984, 168). This pattern was commonplace (see Steinberg 1981), and even after restrictive quotas were introduced, percentages of Jewish students at prestigious American universities never fell low enough to approach the Jewish percentage of the U.S. population.

13. Goldscheider and Zuckerman (1984, 137) also comment that in general in the United States throughout the twentieth century, "An expanding economy and a relatively small national Jewish population have made political anti-Semitism insignificant." One can add that the presence of a sizable black minority also has served as a more visible and consistent target for ethnic/racial chauvinism in the United States, thus providing a buffer of sorts for Jews that did not exist in Eastern Europe.

14. Goldscheider and Zuckerman (1984, 170) document the extensive and intricate internal institutional development of organizations within the American Jewish community. For a brief related discussion see Andrew Greeley's (1986) review of their book and for a more detailed discussion see Glazer (1981).

15. Foner (1979) reports that there was selectivity in both countries' immigration policies. U.S. immigration policies simply were more selective. Foner writes: "Various surveys . . . show that while a high percentage of West Indian migrants to Britain in the 1950s and early 1960s were skilled workers . . . , only about 10 percent of West Indian workers emigrating to Britain could be classified as white collar. By contrast, of the approximately 91,000 West Indian legal emigrants to the United States between 1962 and 1971 who were listed as workers, about 15 percent were classified as professional, technical and kindred workers and about 12 percent as clerical and kindred workers" (1979, 290). Steinberg (1981, 104, n. 48) also points out that Sowell's own evidence indicates that West Indian immigrants to the United States possess, on average, superior educational credentials to native blacks. When incomes are compared between West Indians and urban native blacks, controlling for education, the differences all but disappear. This implies that West Indians also possess an "unexplained" statistical residual when compared with whites with comparable human capital characteristics, albeit a slightly smaller residual than the one possessed by native blacks.

Further complicating matters, Bikhu Parikh (1983, 119) has noted that the West Indian performance itself is not homogeneous regardless of the specific island of origin; he points out that Barbadian youths perform better in British schools than Jamaican youths. He does not attribute this to the relative superiority of "Barbadian culture," but instructs us to consider the socio-economic conditions of the family (1983, 117–118). Parikh (1983, 118–119) adds, however, that poor children can do fine in school when stretched or encouraged by teachers. Hence, the provision of inferior schools to lower income children coupled with class-cum-racially motivated reduced teacher expectations condemns most West Indian children in Britain to negative educational experiences.

16. Note the importance Christopher Jencks (1972) and his coauthors have placed on "luck" in dictating interclass mobility. That conclusion is *not* overturned in their

more recent work (1979). Again the alleged instances of en masse upward mobility—the Irish and the Cubans—will be addressed.

17. Arnold adds, "Sooner or later, discovering that white English ethnocentrism recognized few cultures and cultural adjustment, if any, to be equal to its stringent standards, West Indian immigrants were devastated. Their colonial masters in the Caribbean had failed to tell them many Britons believe culturally 'genuine Englishmen' must have the proper heredity" (1984, 57).

18. Again the *Time* magazine study of Asian-American students is informative. The article (1987, 44) inquires about the academic successes of Asian-American youths "whose refugee parents [are] less well educated" and contemplates genetic and cultural explanations, the latter linked to Confucianism. But this inquiry immediately follows a passage (1987, 44) that reports, "Many Asian-Americans come from an educated elite in their native countries. Their children seem to do especially well." *Time* describes a study by psychologist Julian Stanley of 292 preteens who scored high on the math portion of the Standard Aptitude Test. One-fourth of them were Asian-Americans. Seventy-one percent of their fathers and 21 percent of their mothers had doctorates or medical degrees, in contrast with 39 percent of the fathers and 10 percent of the mothers of non-Asians. The same article (1987, 42) reports that a 1965 immigration law eliminated U.S. exclusionary quotas and "[t]hat brought a surge of largely middle-class Asian professionals—doctors, engineers and academics from Hong Kong, Taiwan, South Korea, India, and the Philippines—seeking economic opportunity." These families and their children generally have done well economically and educationally in the United States. But *Time* (1987, 42, 49) also reports that the post-1978 predominantly lower-class immigrants from Indochina remain mired in poverty and their children frequently are school dropouts in the U.S.

19. This latter argument is representative of Sowell's general inclination to attack the efficacy of politics as a route toward ethnic group economic advancement (see also Sowell 1984, 117).

20. Greeley (1981, 108) notes that one-quarter of the U.S. population is Catholic and one-quarter of all U.S. Catholics are of Irish descent, but one-half of all Catholic Ph.D.'s are Irish.

21. Native black Americans are not uniquely "exceptional." There are, of course, other ethnic groups that have experienced less economic success than native black Americans, e.g., Mexican-Americans, Puerto Rican Americans, and Native Americans.

22. In reaction to the "culture of poverty" controversy in the 1960s, Eleanor Burke Leacock made the following comment:

> subcultural variations along class lines . . . come closest to what culture-of-poverty theory is supposedly documenting. However . . . sociocentric methods of data collection and analysis, plus a nonhistorical theory of culture and its relations to personality, have contributed to stereotypical and distorted views of the class-linked cultural variations. (1971, 34)

Leacock's comment applies with full force to the "new" cultural explanation economists like Chiswick offer for the residuals in earnings equations by race and ethnicity.

23. But see Dumenil and Levy (1987) for a formal explication of processes that engender uniformity of profit rates.

24. Paul Ryan (1981, 18) has argued that labor market segmentation exists but is limited by "capital mobility," in a more physical sense of the term capital, or what he terms "indirect competition": "The fact that competition is, in the labour markets of developed economies, rarely direct—in the sense that [if] X is willing to do Y's job for a lower wage the employer will get rid of Y and hire X—certainly allows segmentation to flourish. Segmentation is, however, subject to bounds itself and these bounds may in turn be the product of indirect competition—as when the employer closes the plant in which Y works and moves production to a region where labour can be obtained at X's price, or lower. The increasing mobility of capital and production across national frontiers has augmented considerably the constraints placed upon segmentation by labour market competition, however indirect."

25. Herbert Hill's (1984) paper reveals that racial animosity toward blacks played a key role in Americanization and in unionization among ethnic immigrant groups. Their unions first displaced black workers from skilled industrial employments and then sought to exclude blacks permanently. The theory advanced here can be viewed as offering a unifying explanation for the events Hill describes in his paper.

26. The opening up and growth of entirely new lines of occupations was especially important for second-generation Eastern-European Jewish immigrants' advancement into professional occupations. Even when excluded from non-Jewish legal or medical practices, there was sufficient business for Jewish lawyers and doctors to start their own firms. The creation of new administrative positions with the expansion of government occupations associated with the Great Society programs in the 1960s provided a springboard for economic advancement for the black middle class (see Brown and Erie (1981). Since they were entirely new positions there was not the same degree of conflict over access as there might have been if blacks had had to displace members of other groups already in place.

27. Frank Wilkinson (1981, xi–xii) comments: "The working-class has resisted capital by social and industrial organisation, which had maintained the family . . . , created trade unions, and influenced the state to legislate on conditions in factories, legalise trade unions, protect groups vulnerable in the labour market, and introduce and extend social welfare provision. Worker organisation has never been complete, and there is little doubt that the organisation of certain sections of the labour force has created privileged enclaves and left other sectors more exposed."

28. There are parallels with Julie Matthaei's (1982, 287–332) argument concerning job ladders in managerial positions in the late nineteenth and twentieth centuries. She contends that sex-typed jobs (also see Shelton 1987) evolved during this period when increased worker homogenization took place in the capitalist labor process and male workers successfully reduced prospects for wage competition with women. The notion that capitalists sought to "homogenize" the labor process at the turn of the century is a major theme of Gordon, Edwards, and Reich (1982). In a fascinating review article on the latter's book *Segmented Work, Divided Workers*, Nolan and Edwards (1984, 205–207) challenge the universality of the tendency toward homogenization. Regardless, the homogenization thesis is peripheral to my argument. Workers still may seek to coalesce to exclude others when capitalists are not pursuing such a strategy. As long as there are different benefits associated with access to different jobs—an even more likely phenomenon when homogenization is *not* underway—groups of workers will have an incentive to protect their turf. What is at stake is the spread between high-quality and low-quality jobs or joblessness, and the finiteness of high-quality jobs. Nor does my argument rest on a particular periodization of the history of capitalism. At *all* stages of capitalist development, after primitive accumulation has occurred, there are "reasons" for workers with preferred occupations to guard their positions, and as I argue below these reasons can extend beyond capitalism. I also suspect that gender-based inequality, at the most general level, requires a somewhat different analysis from ethnic/racial inequality; however, I do not address the former in this paper.

29. Here is a material basis for the race relations phenomenon Kevin Brown (1986) describes as "keeping distance."

30. In the interest of space I do not develop my full argument about the emergence of a policymaking, administrative and cultural elite—a managerial class—that is displacing capital for social dominance worldwide. I refer the reader instead to two of my other papers (Darity 1983b, 1986). For a related analysis of the emergence of the managerial class within orthodox Marxism see Rattansi (1985, 652–660 in particular).

31. Taylor, et al. (1986) demonstrate, again using the "vaunted" residual technique, that as more native blacks shift into public-sector employment in the United States, there is evidence of significant discrimination there as well. To the extent that advanced academic credentials are used as access flags for many of those positions, the percentage of blacks who are eligible for such positions remains relatively low. This

contrasts sharply, for example, with prospects for American Jews, whose youth are heavily enrolled in the most prestigious universities in America. Among Ivy League schools, Jewish undergraduates typically comprise one-quarter of the students, ranging from a low of 12 percent at Dartmouth to highs of 30 percent at Yale and Columbia and 36 percent at the University of Pennsylvania. Typically, the U.S. Jewish population is estimated to be a mere 2–3 percent of the national total (see Bell 1987, 16–17).

32. Platzky and Walker's observations on South Africa are especially striking on this point: "It is clear that the changing nature of capitalist development in South Africa has resulted in an increased demand for skilled workers. As a result of increased capitalisation of industry, agriculture and mining, relatively fewer unskilled workers are demanded by the economy. The ruling class is attempting to consolidate an urban black population with a stake in the system. The government is determined to rid white South Africa of the unproductive, the unemployed, the disabled and those too young to work. From surveys and fieldwork it became clear that there are thousands of people who will never gain access to employment in urban areas. Unless they are prepared to work for R [one rand] a day on rural white-owned farms where there may still be some work, *they have been made redundant permanently. These surplus people will never enter the wage labour market under the present system*" (1985, xxii, emphasis added).

33. This approach is antithetical to the premises of so-called neoclassical political economy or the rent-seeking literature that sees interest groups springing up *de novo* out of individual interests without regard for a preexisting historical structure of social classes.

References

Aigner, Dennis, and Glen Cain, 1977. "Statistical Theories of Discrimination in Labor Markets." *Industrial and Labor Relations Review* 30 (January): 175–187.

Arnold, Faye, 1984. "West Indians and London's Hierarchy of Discrimination." *Ethnic Groups* 6: 47–64.

Arrow, Kenneth, 1973. "The Theory of Discrimination." In *Discrimination in Labor Markets*, eds. O. Ashenfelter and A. Rees. Princeton: Princeton University Press, 3–33.

Balch, Emily Green, 1910. *Our Slavic Fellow Citizens.* New York: Charities Publication Committee.

Banerjee, Biswajit, and J. B. Knight, 1985. "Caste Discrimination in the Indian Labour Market." *Journal of Development Economics* 17 (April): 277–307.

Bell, June, 1987. "Kosher Kitchens of the Ivy League." *Washington Jewish Week*, July 2, 16.

Bergmann, Barbara, 1971. "Can Discrimination Be Ended Under Capitalism?" Project on the Economics of Discrimination Discussion Papers, University of Maryland at College Park, January.

Birmingham, Stephen, 1971. *The Grandees: The Story of America's Sephardic Elite.* New York: Harper & Row.

Blau, Francine, and John W. Graham, 1985. "Black/White Differences in Wealth and Asset Composition." Mimeo, University of Illinois at Urbana-Champaign, December.

Bonacich, Edna, 1979. "The Past, Present, and Future of Split Labor Market Theory." In *Race and Ethnic Relations*, eds. Cora Marrett and Cheryl Leggon. Vol. 1: 17–64.

Bose, Pradip Kumar, 1981. "Social Mobility and Caste Violence: A Study of the Gujarat Riots." *Economic and Political Weekly* 16 (April): 713–716.

Brosnan, Peter, 1987. "Maori Occupational Segregation." *Australian and New Zealand Journal of Sociology* 23 (March): 89–103.

Brown, Kevin M., 1986. "Keeping Their Distance: The Cultural Production and Reproduction of Racist Non-Racism." *Australian and New Zealand Journal of Sociology* 22 (November): 387–399.

Brown, Martin, and Peter Philips, 1986. "Competition, Racism, and Hiring Practices Among California Manufacturers, 1860–1882." *Industrial and Labor Relations Review* 40 (October): 61–74.

Brown, Michael K., and Stephen P. Erie, 1981. "Blacks and the Legacy of the Great Society: The Economic and Political Impact of Federal Social Policy." *Public Policy* 29 (Summer): 299–330.

Chiswick, Barry R., 1984. "Review of Sowell's *Economics and Politics of Race.*" *Journal of Economic Literature* 22 (September): 1158–1160.

———, 1983a. "An Analysis of the Earnings and Employment of Asian-American Men." *Journal of Labor Economics* 2 (April): 197–214.

———, 1983b. "The Earnings and Human Capital of American Jews." *Journal of Human Resources* 18 (Summer): 313–336.

Coase, Ronald, 1960. "The Problem of Social Cost." *The Journal of Law and Economics* 3 (October): 1–44.

Cox, Oliver C., 1970. *Caste, Class and Race.* New York: Monthly Reader.

Crawford, R. M., and G. F. James, 1947. "The Gold Rushes and the Aftermath, 1851–1901." In *Australia,* ed. C. Hartley Grattan. Berkeley and Los Angeles: University of California Press.

Cymrot, D. J., 1985. "Does Competition Lessen Discrimination: Some Evidence." *Journal of Human Resources* 20 (4): 605–612.

Darity, William, Jr., 1986. "The Managerial Class and Industrial Policy." *Industrial Relations* 25 (Spring): 212–227.

———, 1983a. "The Goal of Racial Economic Equality: A Critique." *Journal of Ethnic Studies* 10 (Winter): 51–70.

———, 1983b. "The Managerial Class and Surplus Population." *Society* 21 (November/December): 54–62.

Darity, William, Jr., and Rhonda Williams, 1985. "Peddlers Forever? Culture, Competition, and Discrimination." *American Economic Review* 75(May): 256–261.

Dex, Shirley, 1986. "Earnings Differentials of Second Generation West Indian and White School Leavers in Britain." *Manchester School* 2 (June): 62–79.

Dumenil, G., and D. Levy, 1987. "The Dynamics of Competition: A Restoration of the Classical Analysis." *Cambridge Journal of Economics* 2 (June): 133–164.

Eisenger, Peter K., 1980. *The Politics of Displacement: Racial and Ethnic Transition in Three American Cities.* New York: Academic Press.

Foner, Nancy, 1979. "West Indians in New York City and London: A Comparative Analysis." *International Migration Review* 13 (Summer): 284–297.

———, 1978. *Jamaica Farewell: Jamaican Immigrants in London.* Berkeley: University of California Press.

Glazer, Nathan, 1981. "Jewish Loyalities." *The Wilson Quarterly* (Autumn): 134–145.

———, 1977. "Ethnicity: A World Phenomenon." *South Africa International* 7, 4 (April): 197–212.

———, 1955. "Social Characteristics of American Jews, 1654–1954." In *American Jewish Yearbook,* ed. Morris Fine, Vol. 56: 3–35.

Goldscheider, Calvin, and Alvin S. Zuckerman, 1984. *The Transformation of the Jews.* Chicago: University of Chicago Press.

Gordon, David, Richard Edwards, and Michael Reich, 1982. *Segmented Work, Divided Workers: The Historical Transformation of Labor in the United States.* Cambridge, England: Cambridge University Press.

Greeley, Andrew M., 1986. "Review of Goldscheider and Zuckerman's *Transformation of the Jews.*" *Contemporary Sociology* 15 (September): 769–770.

———, 1981. *The Irish Americans: The Rise to Money and Power.* New York: Harper & Row.

Hill, Herbert, 1984. "Race and Ethnicity in Organized Labor: The Historical Source of Resistance to Affirmative Action." *Journal of Intergroup Relations* 12 (Winter): 5–49.

Holzer, Harry J., 1987. "Informal Job Search and Black Youth Unemployment." *American Economic Review* 77 (June): 446–452.

Hull, Jennifer, Jeannie Park, and James Willwerth, 1987. "The New Whiz Kids." *Time* 130 (August 31): 42–51.

Ikeda, Kiyoshi, 1973. "A Different 'Dilemma.' " *Social Forces* 51 (June): 497–500.

Jencks, Christopher, et al., 1979. *Who Gets Ahead?: The Determinants of Economic Success in America.* New York: Basic Books.

———, 1972. *Inequality.* New York: Basic Books.

Kalbach, Warren E., 1983. "Review of Eisenger's *Politics of Displacement.*" *American Journal of Sociology* 88 (March): 1067–1069.

Kirzner, Israel H., 1973. *Competition and Entrepreneurship.* Chicago: University of Chicago Press.

Leacock, Eleanor Burke, 1971. "Introduction." In *The Culture of Poverty: A Critique,* ed. E. B. Leacock. New York: Simon and Schuster.

Leventman, Seymour, 1982. "Review of Eisenger's *Politics of Displacement.*" *Contemporary Sociology* 11 (May): 335–337.

Marx, Karl, 1981. *Capital, Vol. 3.* New York: Vintage Books.

———, 1977. *Capital, Vol. 1.* New York: Vintage Books.

Matthaei, Julie A., 1982. *An Economic History of Women in America: Women's Work, the Sexual Division of Labor, and the Development of Capitalism.* New York: Schocken Books.

Nielsen, François, 1985. "Toward a Theory of Ethnic Solidarity in Modern Societies." *American Sociological Review* 50 (April): 133–149.

Nolan, Peter, and P. K. Edwards, 1984. "Homogenise, Divide and Rule: An Essay on *Segmented Work, Divided Workers.*" *Cambridge Journal of Economics* 8 (2): 197–215.

Parikh, Bikhu, 1983. "Educational Opportunity in Multi-Ethnic Britain." In *Ethnic Pluralism and Public Policy,* eds. Nathan Glazer and Ken Young. Lexington, Mass.: D.C. Heath, 108–124.

Perez, Lisandro, 1986. "Immigrant Economic Adjustment and Family Organization: The Cuban Success Story Reexamined." *International Migration Review* 20 (Spring): 4–20.

Petersen, William, 1971. *Japanese Americans.* New York: Random House.

Platzky, Laurine, and Cherryl Walker, 1985. *The Surplus People: Forced Removals in South Africa.* Johannesburg: Raven Press.

Portes, Alejandro, 1986. "Review of *Hispanics in the U.S. Economy* edited by Borjas and Tienda." *Contemporary Sociology* 15 (September): 730–731.

Rattansi, Ali, 1985. "End of an Orthodoxy? The Critique of Sociology's View of Marx on Class." *The Sociological Review* 33 (November): 641–670.

Reich, Michael, 1981. *Racial Inequality.* Princeton: Princeton University Press.

Rijwan, Nissam, 1983. "Israel's Ethno-Political Cleavage." *Midstream,* June/July.

Ryan, Paul, 1981. "Segmentation, Duality and the Internal Labour Market." In *The Dynamics of Labour Market Segmentation,* ed. Frank Wilkinson. London: Academic Press.

Shelton, Beth Anne, 1987. "Racial Discrimination at Initial Labor Market Access." *National Journal of Sociology* 1 (Spring): 101–117.

Shulman, Steve, 1984. "The Measurement and Interpretation of Black Wage and Occupational Gains: A Reevaluation." *Review of Black Political Economy* 12 (Spring): 59–69.

Silberman, Charles, 1985. *Certain People: American Jews and Their Lives Today.* New York: Summit Books.

Smooha, Sammy, and Vered Kraus, 1985. "Ethnicity as a Factor in Status Attainment in Israel." In *Research in Social Stratification and Mobility,* ed. Robert Robinson. 4: 151–175.

Sowell, Thomas, 1984. *Civil Rights: Rhetoric or Reality?* New York: William Morrow and Company.

———, 1983a. *The Economics and Politics of Race: An International Perspective.* New York: William Morrow and Company.

———, 1983b. "Remarks on Racial Economic Equality: Comment." *Journal of Ethnic Studies* 11 (Fall): 127.

———, 1981a. *Ethnic America.* New York: Basic Books.

———, 1981b. *Knowledge and Decisions.* New York: Basic Books.

———, 1978. *American Ethnic Groups.* Washington, D.C.: The Urban Institute.

Sraffa, Piero, 1960. *The Production of Commodities By Means of Commodities.* Cambridge, England: Cambridge University Press.

Steinberg, Stephen, 1981. *The Ethnic Myth: Race, Ethnicity, and Class in America.* Boston: Beacon Press.

Swinton, David, 1978. "A Labor Force Competition Model of Racial Discrimination in the Labor Market." *Review of Black Political Economy* 9 (Fall): 5–42.

Taylor, Patricia A., Patricia A. Gwartney-Gibbs, and Reynolds Farley, 1986. "Changes in the Structure of Earnings Inequality by Race, Sex, and Industrial Sector, 1960–1980." In *Research in Social Stratification and Mobility,* ed. Robert V. Robinson. 5: 105–132.

Veblen, Thorstein, 1904. *The Theory of Business Enterprise.* New York: Charles Scribner's Sons.

Vining, Daniel, 1985. "Review of Sowell's *Economics and Politics of Race.*" *Population and Development Review* 11 (March): 139–145.

Weeks, John, 1981. *Capital and Exploitation.* Princeton: Princeton University Press.

Wicksteed, Philip, 1914. "The Scope and Method of Political Economy in the Light of the 'Marginal' Theory of Value and Distribution." *The Economic Journal* 24 (March): 1–23.

Wilkinson, Frank, 1981. "Preface." In *The Dynamics of Labour Market Segmentation,* ed. Frank Wilkinson. London: Academic Press.

Williams, Rhonda, 1987. "Culture as Human Capital: Methodological and Policy Implications." *Praxis International* 7 (July): 152–163.

———, 1984a. "The Methodology and Practice of Modern Labor Economics." In *Labor Economics: Modern Views,* ed. William Darity, Jr. Boston: Kluwer-Nijhoff.

———, 1984b. "Review of Sowell's *Economics and Politics of Race.*" *Review of Black Political Economy* 18 (Summer–Fall): 201–205.

Wilson, William Julius, 1981. *The Declining Significance of Race.* Chicago: University of Chicago Press, 2nd edition.

Wong, Legan, 1976. "The Chinese Experience: From Yellow Peril to Model Minority." *Civil Rights Digest* 9 (Fall): 33–35.

Wong, Morrison, 1980. "Changes in Socioeconomic Status of the Chinese Male Population in the United States from 1960 to 1970." *International Migration Review* 14 (Winter): 511–523.

Wright, Erik, 1979. *Class Structure and Income Determination.* New York: Academic Press.

Index

The Editors

STEVEN SHULMAN, *Assistant Professor of Economics, Colorado State University*

WILLIAM DARITY, JR., *Professor of Economics, University of North Carolina at Chapel Hill*

The Other Contributors

ROBERT HIGGS, *William E. Simon Professor of Political Economy, Lafayette College*

JOHN BOUND, *Assistant Professor of Economics, University of Michigan, and Research Fellow, National Bureau of Economic Research*

RICHARD B. FREEMAN, *Professor of Economics, Harvard University, and Program Director for Labor Studies, National Bureau of Economic Research*

JAMES J. HECKMAN, *Henry Schultz Professor of Economics, University of Chicago*

SAMUEL L. MYERS, JR., *Professor of Economics and Director of the Afro-American Studies Program, University of Maryland*

JAMES P. SMITH, *Director of the Labor and Population Studies Program, RAND Corporation*

FINIS WELCH, *Professor of Economics, University of California at Los Angeles*

HERBERT HILL, *Professor of Afro-American Studies and Industrial Relations, University of Wisconsin at Madison*

GLENN C. LOURY, *Professor of Political Economy, John F. Kennedy School of Government, Harvard University*

SHERRIE A. KOSSOUDJI, *Research Fellow, Assistant Professor of Economics and Social Work, University of Michigan*

ZENA SMITH BLAU, *Professor of Sociology, University of Houston*

About the Book

The Question of Discrimination was composed on the Mergenthaler 202 in Trump Mediaeval, a contemporary typeface based on classical prototypes. Trump Mediaeval was designed by the German graphic artist and type designer Georg Trump (1895–1986). It was initially issued in 1954, by C. E. Weber Typefoundry of Stuttgart, in the form of foundry type and linecasting matrices. This book was composed by Monotype Composition Company of Baltimore. It was designed and produced by Kachergis Book Design of Pittsboro, North Carolina.

Wesleyan University Press, 1989